Praise for Richard Eyre and *Spiritual Serendipity*

"Two common 'self-help answers' are 'Positive Mental Attitude' and 'Time Management.' Neither possesses the spiritual dimension of Richard Eyre's thoughtful alternative found in 'Serendipity.'"
—Gregory J. Newell, United States Ambassador to Sweden

"Business is filled with people who have become efficient planners, schedulers, and time managers. Much more rare is an individual who has developed the awareness and flexibility to notice unexpected opportunities. . . . Richard Eyre has written about this rare skill (and how to get it). . . ."
—J. Willard Marriot, Chairman and President, Marriot Corporation

"Ninety-five percent of Americans believe in some form of supreme being or higher power, and more than ever before we are feeling the need to reach beyond *self*-help to find *spiritual* help. My longtime friend Richard Eyre has written a book that not only helps us to discover the best *within* us but also teaches us to find guidance from *without*.
—George Gallup

Other books by Richard and/or Linda Eyre*

Lifebalance
Teaching Your Children Values
Three Steps to a Strong Family
I Didn't Plan to Be a Witch
The Awakening (a novel)
What Manner of Man
Teaching Your Children Responsibility
Teaching Your Children Sensitivity
Teaching Your Children Joy
Don't Just Do Something, Sit There
The Wrappings and the Gifts
Children's Stories to Teach Joy
How to Talk to Your Child About Sex
Alexander's Amazing Adventures: Values for Children
Stewardship of the Heart

*If you have difficulty locating any title, call (801) 581-0112 to order direct

spiritual Serendipity

Cultivating and Celebrating
the Art of the Unexpected

RICHARD EYRE

A FIRESIDE BOOK
Published by Simon & Schuster

FIRESIDE
Rockefeller Center
1230 Avenue of the Americas
New York, NY 10020

Copyright © 1997 by Richard Eyre and Linda Eyre
All rights reserved, including the right of
reproduction in whole or in part in any form.

First Fireside Edition 1999

FIRESIDE and colophon are registered trademarks of
Simon & Schuster Inc.

Designed by Bonni Leon-Berman

Manufactured in the United States of America

1   3   5   7   9   10   8   6   4   2

The Library of Congress has cataloged the Simon &
Schuster edition as follows:
Eyre, Richard M.
Spiritual serendipity : cultivating and celebrating the art
of the unexpected / Richard Eyre.
p.   cm.
Includes bibliographical references and index.
1. Spiritual life.   2. Serendipity.   I. Title.
BL624.E97   1997
291.4'4—dc21   96-40114
CIP
ISBN 0-684-80786-6
ISBN 0-684-83860-5 (Pbk)

"serendipity"

Popular definition:	A happy accident.
Webster definition:	The making of pleasant discoveries by accident, the knack of doing this.
Original definition:	The quality or faculty, through awareness and good fortune, of being able to find something good while seeking something else.
Spiritual serendipity:	The same quality, but with the added input and direction of spiritual receptivity and divine guidance.

contents

Foreword 11
The Land of Serendip 11
A Word from Linda Eyre 15

OVERTURE
18

Living in a World Being Spiritually Reborn 18
A New Paradigm for Living 20
Serendipity 23

PART 1:
The Plight, the Problem,
and the Promise
Serendip, at the transition into the twenty-first century
29

The Plight (of Those Who Live
in Our World) 31
The Problem (of Our Time, Our Place,
and Our Culture) 35
The Promise (of a More Peaceful,
More Productive Paradigm) 39

PART 2:
Walpole: His Nature,
His World, and His Word
London, midway through the eighteenth century
45

PART 3:
The Three Princes of Serendip:
A Fable
Persia, early in the fifth century
53

Prologue	55
The Three Princes of Serendip: A Fable	57
Epilogue	93

PART 4:
Mental Serendipity
Serendip, beginning the twenty-first century
95

Serendipity Today	97
Definition of Terms (the Words That Define the Word)	97
Application of the Attitude	109
The Source (You)	115
The Process (of Gaining the Quality)	117
Summary	127

INTERMISSION
129

PART 5:
Spiritual Serendipity
Our world, at a time of spiritual transition
133

Serendipity of the Spirit   135
Definition of Terms (Higher Words
for a Higher Quality)   135
The Higher Realm (of Soul and Spirit)   152
The Source (the Spirit)   163
The Process (of Seeking the Gift)   164
Praying for Guidance (Four Suggestions
for Developing the Art)   168
Watching for Guidance (Four
Suggestions for Developing the Art)   185
A Truer Overview from the Truest Book   199

CURTAIN CALL
202

Afterword   206
Applications and Promises   206
Assistance   215
Index   217

The Land of Serendip

As I write, I'm sitting on the veranda of my room in Sri Lanka, looking out through the jungle toward the beach, watching a man lead his elephant into the sea for a bath. Perhaps it is a rather extreme approach, but I've come here, halfway around the world, to a teardrop-shaped island in the Indian Ocean, to explore the origins and the deeper meanings of my favorite word, *serendipity*, and to write a book I hope will share the power of these meanings with others.

Serendipity, a word coined by an eighteenth-century British writer named Horace Walpole, suggests an attitude of mind and heart that can give people the means to move from where they are to where they want to be, and perhaps even from where they are to where God wants them to be.

I came to Sri Lanka, which was once called Serendip, because I thought the book ought to carry part of the mystery of this ancient land and of the legend that spawned the word. I will begin, after this brief foreword, by telling you how and why Walpole created the word and about an old Persian fable called "The Three Princes of Serendip" that inspired him. I found the fable, one of the few copies of it left in the world, in the British Museum in London, and retranslated it into modern English. But before we get into that, let me make a comment, based in part on the perspective I feel as I look at *our* world from this faraway place.

Americans, as the world starts not only a new century but a new millennium, live in a unique society and culture that is more challenging, more complex, and more competitive than any other. Compared to people of other places and other times, our lives are bountiful as well as busy, but they are almost always demanding and almost never predictable. No matter what course we choose, life is filled with surprises and unexpected turns in the road

The stress and frustration that most of us feel traces back both to the demands and to the unpredictability. Over and over, it seems, just as we begin to get an idea of where we're going or what we're doing, something comes along— a crisis, a challenge, a circumstance—and suddenly we're in uncharted waters (and over our heads).

The problems we face are too diverse to have

a single answer—unless that answer is an *attitude:* an attitude that can give guidance to life, an attitude that can turn adversity into advantage, impatience into insight, competition into charity, boredom into beauty—an attitude or a paradigm called *spiritual serendipity.*

In a way this trip to Serendip symbolizes the core idea of this book. I came here because I felt guided to or prompted to. It wasn't a particularly logical decision, or a financially justifiable one. And it's not a very planned trip because I don't know the options or what to expect. It is so much easier (and perceived as more desirable) to do things for more practical reasons—and to be in control, in charge, to plan and manage and even manipulate. We like to say, "act, don't react" or "have plans and contingency plans" or "leave nothing to chance" or "never be surprised."

But the fact is that we know so little and control so little. Surprises happen every day. And there are so many big things and so many small things over which we have no control.

The fact is that, on our own, we don't know enough about the future, or about those around us, or even about ourselves to choose very consistently what is best for ourselves and best for others.

But there is a higher intelligence which can prompt and guide our minds and spirits with small, sometimes hard-to-notice feelings and insights that we call nudges or impressions or intuitions or inspirations. *Spiritual Serendipity* is an attitude that increases our receptivity to this purer intelligence. With it, we can discard the futile goal of a totally self-managed life and adopt the goal of a *guided* life. May I find more of it (and share more of it with you) while I am here.

Richard Eyre
Sri Lanka (formerly Ceylon and before that Serendip)
Off the south coast of India

A Word from Linda Eyre

My husband, Richard, you need to understand, is intrigued by somewhat weird, rather obscure *words*. I told him that "serendipity" sounded more like a band or a singing group than a book—and "spiritual serendipity" sounded like a tongue twister or maybe a gospel singing group.

I told him he ought to call the book *Receptivity to Intuition or Inspiration* because that's really what it is about. Or, if he insists on alliteration, how about *Gaining Guidance* or *Discovering and Discerning Deep or Divine Direction*.

Actually, Richard's fascination with serendipity began before and during our courtship and was so intense by the time we had our first baby that he wanted to call her Serendipity. I dissuaded him with my observation that kids might call her Dipity. Still, the best I could get was a compromise and we named her Saren. Except that everyone calls her Sara or Sharon, I guess that has worked out fine (though it is a little embarrassing when people say, "What does that name mean?" and we have to say, "A happy accident"). Someone sent a baby gift that was an embroidered blanket labeled Saren Wrap. I'm just glad our first child wasn't a boy, or Richard would have wanted to name him after the English author who invented the word serendipity: *Horace* Walpole.

Seriously, though, bear with Richard and his strange terminology. I've come to appreciate the word almost as much as he does. It means, at least in this book, a lot of powerful things and it stands for a truly revolutionary new way of living (and a new way of thinking) that increases our *joy* as well as our effectiveness.

I think what Richard has done here is to use the "sandwich" format for this book. The beginning and ending of the book are the two slices of bread—they motivate us by making some remarkable promises about what spiritual serendipity can do for those who obtain it. The "meat" in the middle consists of explorations of the serendipity concept and solid suggestions about *how* people can gain the quality, and through it become more receptive, more aware, and much, much happier.

Let me mention Richard's writing style. Sometimes he writes poetry and sometimes he writes prose. And sometimes, as in this book, he writes some of each and mostly something that is a combination of the two. At other times, he tells a story, usually about a personal experience. It's a little different, but rather appropriate in this book, where Richard is *suggesting* ideas and feelings that we have all had before. He is drawing out of our minds things

that we already know but have not yet connected . . . so that we will read a page or two
and say, "Ah ha."

I've enjoyed working with my husband in
writing this book. I recommend it to you, but
then I can't be objective, can I? So read it and
see what you think, or, better put, see if the
book gives you some exciting new *ways* of
thinking for yourself.

Linda J. Eyre
Serendip, Sri Lanka
(You didn't think he
came here without
me, did you?)

Living in a World Being Spiritually Reborn

What's happening?

I go to New York and the number one play and the number one books are about *angels*.

I walk into a bookstore and the best-selling fiction is on quests for meaning and supernatural insights. The best-selling nonfiction is about values, virtues, the spirit and the soul.

I read the national opinion polls, which tell me that more than 60 percent of Americans feel the need to experience spiritual growth.

I go to my publishers who used to urge me to modify or delete any "spirit" or "soul" terminology in my "mainstream" books, and they now tell me to use more of "those words."

I show them a deeply spiritual book that I wrote for family and friends and not for publication, and they say the general market is ready for it.

Here is what I think is happening: We are living in a world that is being spiritually reborn. We want deeper answers, deeper meaning, deeper feelings. We're more interested in finding divine help than in proving we don't need it. We feel less and less external security on our streets and in our society, so we look for internal security in our souls. We haven't found the answers or the peace we want in the material or the "outer," so we're seeking them in the spiritual or the "inner."

What if I told you that, at some point, self-help becomes an oxymoron . . . that ultimately we all need help from a higher source . . . that relying totally on self is more a folly than a virtue . . . that "there is nothing you can't do" is a fallacy, that the truth is, there's nothing we can do—of real worth— without spiritual help?

Would you feel challenged, combative, prone to argue with me? Or would you feel that I was a kindred spirit, that you and I have something in common? Would you hope that perhaps the book you hold in your hands, though you may have found it in the self-help section, may reveal a new level, a new dimension of help?

A New Paradigm
for Living

Spiritual Serendipity is the first book in the "paradigm trilogy."* It deals with a new paradigm, a different, more spiritual way of viewing and perceiving the events and people in our everyday lives. It is, after all, how we see things that determines both what and how we *feel* . . . and *do*. It is written from the perspective and conviction that we are spiritual beings and can communicate (both "sending" and "receiving") with a greater spiritual being.

This, of course, is a mainstream perspective. More than 95 percent of Americans profess belief in God or a supreme being and over 90 percent of us believe there is a spirit within ourselves that separates from our bodies at death.

---

*The second book, *Spiritual Stewardship*, probes the error and the inaccuracy of ownership and blames most of the world's prejudice, intolerance, insecurity, and guilt on it. It then calls for a paradigm shift to the more tolerant, more fulfilling, and more accurate notion of stewardship. The final book, *Spiritual Synergy*, suggests that the total can be greater than the sum of its parts in three separable and powerful relationships: body and spirit, husband and wife, and man with God.

Together, the three books of the trilogy take issue with what may be the three most frantic pursuits of our day—the pursuits of control, of ownership, and of independence—suggesting in their place the more spiritual pursuits of serendipity, stewardship, and synergy.

Nevertheless, this book is not directly or definitively about God or the spirit. It is about a paradigm—about perspectives or attitudes that can change (enhance and improve) how we see ourselves, our relationships, and our world. It is about viewing things in an eternal rather than an earthly perspective. And since God and the spirit are *reality*, it is about seeing things more *realistically* and more *accurately*. It is about avoiding the deception and pain of viewing things materialistically, coincidentally, or as though man were in charge.

Judging by much of our current literature and entertainment, spiritual perspectives are popular right now, even trendy. But trying to understand things spiritually (rather than just sensually or scientifically) is far more than a recent trend. For most of mankind's recorded history people looked principally to the spiritual or the mystical for answers and explanations. Only during the relatively brief period of the past few hundred years did society look more to the secular than to the spiritual for understanding. (The corruption of many church and religious institutions in the late Middle Ages and the emergence of early versions of natural science caused people to turn from one to the other for answers and explanations.) And it is the *inadequacy* of secular answers that is now turning us back to more spiritual paradigms. We want knowledge and insight beyond what we can learn through our five senses. We want personal answers to questions that science doesn't even attempt to deal with. We want to understand more than academics or philosophy can tell us, and we want our lives and our destinies to be guided by something wiser and more insightful than ourselves.

The basic premise of this book, and the essence of the paradigm it suggests, is that we simply cannot gain enough data through our senses to consistently make the best decisions for ourselves and those around us—that thinking we can do anything and control everything in our personal life is the highest form of self-deceit. The premise here is that most things, even personal things, are beyond our real control, that relaxing and thinking things through often brings more results than thrashing and forcing, and that there exists a source of far higher intelligence and power that we can tap into. In light of that greater source, the goal of a *guided* life is better than the goal of a self-determined life. The most important claim of this book is that people can *develop an attitude and a state of mind* that makes guidance and spiritual serendipity more likely, more frequent, and far more consequential.

Serendipity

Serendipity is commonly defined as "a happy accident" and takes its name from the island of Sri Lanka, which used to be called Ceylon and, before that, Serendip.

The notion of serendipity—of valuable discoveries made while seeking something else entirely—can be illustrated by experience in almost every field.

In medicine, Sir Alexander Fleming left a window open and the wind blew contaminants onto his staphylococcus culture. Before long, as the contaminating mold grew on his petri dish, Fleming noticed that, near the mold, the colonies of staphylococcus were undergoing dissolution. Fleming (who once said "chance favors the trained mind") observed the phenomenon, isolated the mold in pure culture, and discovered penicillin.

In physics, Wilhelm Roentgen, who was experimenting with electricity and vacuum tubes, noticed the fluorescence of a barium phatinocyanide screen that happened to be lying near. He found that this radiation could pass through substances opaque to ordinary light and affect a photographic plate. The X ray was born.

In chemistry, Charles Goodyear, who had tried for years to take the stickiness out of rubber, one night by chance left a piece of rubber smeared with sulphur near a hot stove and the next morning it was vulcanized.

A music teacher named Robert Fouks, walking home through a dense fog, heard his daughter playing the piano, but only one note came through. He used that one bass note to invent the foghorn.

Robert Watson observed that overhead aircraft gave reflected signals from radio waves and thus he discovered radar.

Phoenician sailors used lumps of saltpeter for their cooking kettles. When they melted and ran over the sand they produced glass.

As valuable as serendipity has been through the ages and in the macro developments of so many fields, it can be *most* valuable now, in the micro developments of our everyday lives.

At the birth of a new millennium we have all kinds of new pressures, new complexities, new challenges. We play the faster game of life by new and sometimes blurred rules. Options, opportunities, and obstacles exist in incredible variety! The old tools of time management and the old approaches of positive mental attitude don't work as well as they used to. Trying to control or manipulate or plan everything just sets us up for frustration. There's too much going on, and unexpected changes come too fast.

We miss too much if all we see is our list. We kid ourselves if we think we know enough to plan everything. To enjoy and succeed in this new world we need right-brain receptiveness as well as left-brain logic. For what's here now, and for what's coming, we need new attitudes, new approaches, and new answers. But the answers we need are not really new. They are as old as time—and scripture:

Go to now, ye that say, Today or tomorrow we will go into such a city, and continue there a year, and buy and sell and get gain:

Whereas ye know not what shall be on the morrow . . .

For what ye ought *to say, If the Lord will, we shall live, and do this, or that.*

James 4:13–15

As we try to shift from attitudes of control, manipulation, and self-determination to attitudes of awareness and guidance, it helps to have a *name* for our new approach. Horace Walpole gave us a name, or part of one, more than two centuries ago. He read an ancient Persian fable called "The Three Princes of Serendip," which told the story of three brothers whose alertness and sagacity allowed them to consistently *discover things that were far better than what they had been seeking.* Walpole coined the word "serendipity" and defined it as the gift or faculty for finding something good while seeking something else.

Serendipity can be *developed*, as an attitude of the mind and as a quality of the spirit. It can energize and excite our lives and give us balance between structure and spontaneity, between flat, fixed firmness and free, fun flexibility. It can allow us to get there *and* to enjoy the journey at the same time. It can enable us to tap into a higher, clearer kind of reality and inject joy into what is no longer routine.

And for those who believe in God, serendipity of the spirit can be an attitude whereby our lives become divinely guided rather than self-structured. Serendipity of the spirit can become the connecting bridge between our goals and God's will.

Spiritual Serendipity might be thought of as a spiritually toned self-help book. It is a radical and contrarian book in that it suggests a nearly opposite approach to the traditional self-help panaceas of "positive mental attitude" and "time management."

For many, positive attitude is essentially a self-con. We tell ourselves we can *control* everything and *do* anything, while in fact most circumstances and most people are beyond our control; and without a higher insight and guidance, we ourselves are extremely limited in doing anything of real significance. Serendipity wants us to see the opportunity and the beauty in things as they really are instead of naively wishing things were different, and to seek and trust God's power rather than our own.

The problem with time management is that time is like tides or currents. It needs to be used and harnessed, not *managed*. It is far better to learn attitudes that help us use time and flow with it than techniques for trying to manage it. (Great rowing techniques don't help when rowing upstream in rapids.) There is a natural (and supernatural) ebb and flow to time. Time has eddies and slow, stretched moments when certain things can happen—things that could not be forced at other times. Serendipity teaches us to respect time rather than manipulate it—to shift directions within its flow and to use its power rather than thrash against it.

On one level, serendipity is the ability to notice what others miss—to observe and appreciate beauty, to sense needs and opportunities, to be receptive to impressions, intuitions, and insights. On a higher level, serendipity of the spirit is receptiveness to inputs beyond our senses—to the deeper nudges and inspirations that come to our hearts and our souls.

Part 1

The Plight, the Problem, and the Promise

Serendip

At the transition into the twenty-first century

The Plight
(of Those Who Live in Our World)

On this emerald-green, high-mountained island
in the indigo-blue Indian Ocean
("Sri Lanka" *means* resplendent isle)
workers are fortunate if they earn
100 rupees per week (just under $4).
With that (and the fish they catch
or the rice they grow)
they feed large families.
Yet, as in many poor parts of the world,
people's faces reflect more joy
than discouragement.
Nowhere have I seen a higher ratio
of smiling, open countenances,
childlike in the positive sense that they
never look away from your glance.
Their own glances
are layered with light.
Faces that look out at you
with no self-consciousness
and invite you to look right back in.
The concerns here are as simple as they are severe:
food to eat, a roof,
and shelter in the monsoon season,

basic health care,
and education for the children.

Sri Lankans are an intelligent, joyful people.
Most returning tourists come back as much
for the people
as for the perfect beaches
and cool, jungle mountains.

Because the pace is slow, and the contrasts
vivid,
(and because my word was born here)
this is a good place to think
about the Three Princes and Horace Walpole.
And it is a clear-perspective place
from which to look back and think about
our world,
yours and mine,
the world of Western civilization as it enters
the twenty-first century. . . .

Our world
is boisterously busy!
(and confusingly complex).
Options, opportunities, and obligations
proliferate and
grow like grass
and most problems stem from surplus
rather than scarcity.

Our windows
(they're still rectangular and made of glass but
now
we turn them on and off with a switch
and change their view with a wireless remote)
show us our competitors and
make us materialistic,
conjuring new wants and then disguising them
as needs.

We find that
trying to do it all and have it all and be it all
won't work.
Because there's no time.
No time for "choose to do's"
because the "have to do's"
and the red-tape and responsibilities
swallow up the tiny time allotment of the
every day.

We try to prepare, to prioritize, and to plan.
We make our lists and try to control the
events
that swirl around us,
but nothing ever goes quite as we planned.
Impediments and interruptions
knock us off course
and turn our planners into
testaments of our failures.

Work and family and personal needs
jerk at each other
like a three-way tug of war.
We look around us
and try for comfort (or at least company)
in the fact
that everyone has the same stress, the same
frustration,
the same unbalance.

Part of the problem is that,
woven in and wound around
the accepted thinking
in our society,
is the dangerously stiff and brittle thread
of *quantity*.
We measure (and are measured)
more by how much we do
than by how well we do it;
more by explicit external exhibit
than by invisible internal insight;
more on our breadth than by our depth;
more on our doing and our getting than on
our being;
more on more . . .
more on quantity than on quality.

Success is outer accumulation and position
rather than inner character,
ownership rather than stewardship,
recognition rather than relationships.

And we sometimes reserve our respect
for those who *win*, who acquire, who run things,
forgetting or undervaluing less visible gifts
like sensitivity, spontaneity, and even charity.

So how do we change this system,
this society?
We don't.
What we change is our susceptibility to it,
our stereotyped subscription to its standard,
our dependence on its approval.
What we change is
ourselves.

And the tool
that turns and times the transition
is something this book calls
spiritual serendipity.

The Problem
*(of Our Time, Our Place,
and Our Culture)*

We are a people free and mightily blessed
with almost limitless variety and diversity.
Compared with our forefathers,

we can choose among so many different
lifestyles,
so many different causes, careers,
concentrations,
and circumstances.

With all these blessings, how can we be
frustrated or confused?
Surprise: It is *because* of all we have
that many are perplexed.
More expectations demand more
performance.
More desires demand more work.
More education demands more money.
More needs seem to demand more time.
e. e. cummings may have said it best:
"more, more, more, more, more
My hell, what are we anyway—morticians?"
More expectations, desires, and needs
lead us inevitably to the perplexing questions
of *How* and *Why*.
How do we find the time?
Why can't we ever feel satisfied?
How can we have "outer success" (job, career)
and "inner success" (family, character)?
Why, with technology and
"labor-saving devices,"
are we busier than ever?
How do we handle life's unpredictability?
Why is it so difficult to set
clear long-range goals?

How can we be disciplined and structured
and yet retain some spontaneity and flexibility?
Why does time seem to pass ever faster?
How do we handle life's surprises?
Why do relationships die
before we know they are wounded?
How do we raise moral children
in an amoral world?
Why do opportunities pass by
before we can see them clearly?
How do we discover our unique niche,
our individual destiny?
Why, when we have more of everything,
do we seem to have less of joy?
How do we conform our lives to God's will?
Why do we spend so much more effort on
things
than on people?
How can we know if we've made the right
choices
and are "climbing the right mountain"?
Why do we live, *why* do we love,
why are we here?

What kind of questions are these?
They are the *root* questions
of life!
On their answers hang our happiness here
and our station in the hereafter.
But too many questions—can the whole list
be compacted into one?

Sometimes the spiritual context both
supersedes
and simplifies . . .
equaling a single question:
*How can we request and receive
the guidance of God?*

If we view an unlimited, personal Heavenly
Father,
loving us, caring,
wanting to guide us, prompt us,
enlighten us . . .
but committed to our agency,
thus not interfering, not taking the initiative
from us . . .
If we view our very limited selves,
operating under a veil, aware of only
a thin slice
of reality, a tiny percentage of variables,
knowing too little to sort out our own destiny
and make key decisions
without divine guidance . . .
If we view things this way,
then life is not so much about our own skills
or our ability
to schedule and scheme and sort out success.
Instead, it is about our *receptivity*
and our own ability to request and quest for
light.
And both growth and joy are

more about being perceptive
than competitive,
more about being guided
than about being gifted.
And we should worry more
about not feeling than about not failing.

The challenge of a more spiritual paradigm is
to rise above
the usual treadmill
of comparing and competing,
the usual pattern
of praying deeply only in crisis,
the usual life of essentially drifting into things,
of letting circumstances or envy
or paths of least resistance
decide our direction
instead of shafts of light from above.
(Or at least insightful glimpses from within.)

The Promise
(of a More Peaceful,
More Productive Paradigm)

There is an attitude that can change
the way we see life
and the way we *live* life.
It is an attitude that involves new awareness,

new approaches,
and a fresh answer
to the deepest and oldest questions
of how personal guidance is obtained.

We ask: How do we avail ourselves of the
insight, impressions, intuitions, inspirations
that belief in God tells us
must be possible?
"Ask for it" goes the short answer.
But to be effectual,
asking must be accompanied by an
awareness . . .
by an approach or an *attitude*
that helps us ask the right questions and then
hear (and see and feel)
the unexpected answers.
The attitude can be easily named,
but will take
this whole book
to explain.
It is *spiritual serendipity*.

Spiritual serendipity is not a program
or a technique or a method
or "six steps" or a "sequence of actions."
It's not about how to do something,
or even about what to do.
In fact,
it doesn't have to do with doing.

It has to do with
being.
The changes it advocates are not *out*,
in our actions,
but *in*, in our spirits.
A new attitude, deeply understood,
does more than change *what we do*.
It becomes a part of us and thus
it changes *who we are*.

Serendipity of the spirit requires shifts
in our paradigm.
It suggests a new way of looking at ourselves,
our world,
and our relationship with the Being
who made both.

The attitude holds forth promises so grand
that their mere mention breeds skepticism.
But they are listed anyway
in the hope that your "keep reading" interest
will grow faster
than your "stop reading" skepticism.
Spiritual serendipity,
besides opening you to greater guidance
and incremental inspiration, can:

☐ Relax you, reduce your frustration and
stress,
☐ Increase life's excitement, remove boredom,

☐ Sensitize you to beauty
and deepen your feelings,
☐ Orient you to ideas
and increase your creativity,
☐ Make you more *people*-oriented
(and less *things*-oriented),
☐ Strengthen your beliefs in the Divine,
☐ Let you see more
of life's amusement and ironies,
☐ Make you more flexible, more spontaneous,
more *fun*,
☐ Make your life longer
(time seems to slow down
for those who are highly observant and
aware . . .
and a calm spirit contributes to longevity),
☐ Give you peace and joy,
☐ Make you a better parent, a better spouse,
a better friend.

Forgive the expression of what spiritual
serendipity *does*
before the explanation of what it *is* . . .
but the latter will take a while.

Best to begin with "mental serendipity,"
which comes of sharpened senses
and agile awareness
and is accessible
to anyone who takes the time
to understand and apply.

Then can be approached
the extended concept
of spiritual serendipity
which can unlock the stronger doors
and which is accessible only to those who seek
the higher power
and gain the gift.
But first,
let's discover the word itself. To do so
we need to go back to the word's birth,
back more than two hundred years to England
and to
Horace Walpole.

Part 2

Walpole: His Nature, His World, and His Word

London

Midway through the eighteenth century

Horace Walpole, in a letter written in 1754 to
Horace Mann (it must have been a popular first
name), commented on his attraction to "The
Three Princes of Serendip," whom he had read
about in an ancient Persian fable:

*They were always making discoveries, by accidents
and by sagacity, of things of value that they were not
in quest of.* *

What kind of a man was this Walpole? Did
his interest in the concept of serendipity and
his intrigue with a fanciful fable spring from
the type of person he was?

Walpole was born in 1717, the son of Sir
Robert Walpole who would later become England's prime minister. He grew up a son of
privilege and leisure, a product of Eton and
Kings College, Cambridge. Leaving the university, he set out on a two-and-a-half-year
tour of France. While he was abroad, his father
had him elected to Parliament. His life was
the epitome of the privileges of noble birth
in eighteenth-century England. But Walpole
seemed to derive productivity and widespread
interests from his ease rather than compla-
cency and laziness. Antiquary, novelist, poli-
tician, poet-master, social charmer, architect,

Brewer's Dictionary of Phrase and Fable, Centenary Edition, 1977.

gardener, and political chronicler all became his appropriate descriptions. Always appreciative of the unique and unpredictable, he designed and built a Gothic castle in which he lived and wrote. His environment inspired mysterious stories of romance and intrigue that made him into what some call "the father of the gothic novel" and influenced the writing of Scott, Byron, Keats, and Coleridge. His insightful and voluminous letters and correspondence give us the clearest picture we have of the social and political life of eighteenth-century England.

Hugh Honour, in his book on *Writers and Their Work*, called Walpole "one of the most delightful characters who ever put pen to paper. He knew everyone worth knowing in his elegant age. He had a substantial passion for antiquities, architecture, printing, letter-writing—everything that could enhance the pleasure of life."

You and I may not have much in common with this man who was born into wealth and position, but he had a freshness that we can all admire, and knowing a little about his nature is helpful in understanding the word he coined.

Some of Walpole's literary peers and contemporaries lend personal insight: Macaulay said that "Walpole rejected, with gay abandon, whatever appeared dull, while retaining only what was in itself amusing or could be made so

by the artifice of his diction." James Boswell
spoke of "Harry's constitutional tranquility or
affection of it." Gilly Williams, who knew him
from boyhood said, "I can figure no being happier than Harry." Thackeray who, like many,
felt that Walpole's correspondence was his
greatest legacy and contribution, said, "Nothing can be more charming than Horace's letters. Fiddles sing all through them: wax lights,
fine dresses, fine jokes, fine plates glitter and
sparkle. There never was such a brilliant, jig-
gling, smirking Vanity Fair as that through
which he leads us.*

What was it about Walpole that gave him his
tranquility, or his happiness, or his gift for seeing life as a graphic, sparkling, exciting adventure? Was it an attitude—an attitude he already
had and for which he found a *name* when he
read the fable of the three princes?

As interesting as the views of friends and literary peers might be, Walpole's own words and
self-description carry even more insight. In a
letter to H. S. Conway, dated June 28, 1760, he
writes:

*I have papers to sort; I have letters and books to
write; I have my prints to paste, my house to build,*

*Hugh Honour, *Writers and Their Work*, F. Mildner &
Sons, London, 1957.

and everything in the world to tell posterity—how am I to find time for all this?

And a few more examples, again from Honour:

I love to communicate my satisfactions. My melancholy I generally shut up in my own breast.

This world is comedy to those that think, a tragedy to those that feel.

In short, the true definition of me is that I am a dancing senator—not that I do dance, or do anything by being a senator; but I go to balls and to the House of Commons—to look on, and you will believe me when I tell you that I really think the former is the more serious occupation of the two: at least the performers are more in earnest.

What should we gain by triumph [over the colonists]? Would America laid waste, deluged with blood, plundered and enslaved, replace America flourishing, rich, and free?

This man, then, who seemed interested in everything, who loved fun and spontaneity, who was open and candid about his own feelings and weaknesses, who was part cynic, part political critic, part romanticist, and who was always trying to discover what was inside himself as well as the world around him—this man coined the word "serendipity." The concept of happy accidents and good things discovered through awareness and sagacity appealed to him because so much interested him and because life held such adventure and intrigue for him.

Perhaps the most revealing of all Walpole's insights was the occasion when he tried to see himself through the eyes of one Reverend Mr. Steward, a fellow guest at the country home of the Earl of Hartford.

Strolling about the house, he saw me first sitting on the pavement of the lumber room with Louis, all over cobwebs and dirt and mortar; then found me in his own room on a ladder writing on a picture; and half an hour afterwards lying on the grass in the court with the dogs and the children, in my slippers and without my hat. He had some doubt whether I was the painter or the workman from the factory or the tutor for the family's children; but you would have died at his surprise when he saw me walk into dinner in formal dress and sit by Lady Hartford.

Lord Lyttelton was there and the conversation turned to literature. Finding me not quite ignorant added to the Reverend's wonder; but when he saw me go to romps and jumping with the two boys, he could stand it no longer and begged to know who and what sort of man I really was, for he had never met with anything of the kind.*

*Honour, op. cit.

It appears that Walpole *cultivated* an attitude of awareness, unpredictability, spontaneity, and joy, and that he relished the unexpected, the happy discoveries and surprises of life. Perhaps he found slight frustration in the fact that there was no word to describe the attitude or quality that he most valued.

Then he came upon an ancient Persian fable called "The Three Princes of Serendip." In the story he found a clear expression of his attitude and in the title he found the root for a new word.

Part 3

The Three Princes of Serendip

Persia

Early in the fifth century

Prologue

I have been searching off and on for a copy of this fable for twenty years, and I now hold it in my hands. The story itself is a fairy tale, set in the fifth century A.D. in the royal days of Anuradhapura on the island of Ceylon, which we now call Sri Lanka but which was then called Serendip. It was the time of the Sassanian empire in Persia and of the famous dynasties of Gupta and Vakatakas in India. The original fable was passed from one generation to the next and acquired several different versions. All were essentially about the gift of finding valuable or agreeable things not sought after.

I am at the British Library in the British Museum in the heart of London. There are eleven million volumes here, some of which line the wall, three stories high, that encircles the round reading room where I sit under the huge gold and blue dome that arches eighty feet above my head. William Wordsworth sat here to write. So did Karl Marx.

This copy was printed in Russell Street, Covent Garden, London. It is an old volume, published in England in 1722 for a man named Will Chetwood. It is as old as the copy that Walpole read. It could conceivably *be* the copy that he read. The cover is old leather, polished by the hands that have held it over the years. It was translated from a French edition that had been published earlier in Amsterdam. The French had been translated from the original Persian.

What follows is my own minimally retranslated version. Read it to yourself; try to read it with the same interest and insight with which Walpole read it, and, if you get a chance, read it to a child.

The Three Princes of Serendip:
a fable

There is a land far off, at the very end of the earth, called Serendip—a resplendent island where tall trees grew on emerald mountains. Long, long ago on Serendip, there lived a great and wise king called Jafer.

King Jafer had three sons. When each was born, a strange and beautiful bird with golden wings and eyes like fire dipped low out of the sky, but was seen only by a handful of children near the ancient Mountain of Great Serenity.

The king wanted to prepare his sons well so that they could someday become good rulers of Serendip. He wanted them to learn three things: virtue, science, and wisdom. Being a wise man himself, he asked even wiser men and women, both of his own country and of other lands, to come and teach his sons.

But few teachers would come from other countries because the ocean that surrounded Serendip was filled with great and fearsome dragons—sea monsters who attacked ships with their sharp claws and slapped holes in the hulls with their long, whipping tales. The teachers who did come from other lands were therefore filled with courage as well as knowledge, and they taught the boys to see and perceive with both their eyes and their hearts.

The three princes were good students. Their teachers taught them much virtue, science, and wisdom . . . as well as grammar, languages, poetry, and music. They also taught the management and handling of elephants, the most important and useful animal in Serendip.

When the three princes were no longer boys but young men, King Jafer decided to interview them (and to test them) one at a time. To the eldest prince he said, "I want you now to be king," holding his own crown over the boy's head. The prince noticed that his father's fingers held the crown very tightly, and he said, "With respect, Father, I decline. I am not yet prepared to rule."

When the middle prince came in, the king got up off his throne and offered the magnificent chair to the son, saying that it was time for a new king. The prince listened carefully and heard how strong and clear the king's voice was and told him that he was still a great and able king and could rule yet for many years.

Then the king sent for the youngest prince and asked him to be king. The young prince observed the sparkle in the king's eyes and knew it was a test. "Oh, no, Great King. I am yet a boy and your eyes are still clear, and your mind strong."

King Jafer was pleased—each of his sons had wisdom and modesty. He decided to complete their education by sending them abroad, for he knew that until they had seen other parts of the earth they would not realize how many good people there are in the world, or how many good ideas, or how many different ways there are of thinking, of living, and of being. He hoped that, in addition to enhanced perspective, they might complete a quest that would free his kingdom of the curse of its dragon-infested waters.

He called them to him and said: "My beloved sons, the ancients have said that the mists of yesteryear were marvelously distilled into a magic formula, written in one hundred lines of verse upon a single scroll. The formula-poem is called *Death to Dragons*. A liquid potion can be made by following it, which, when poured into the oceans, will poison and kill the dragons that surround our island. I send you forth to find *Death to Dragons*. Do not return until you find it or until you have my permission to come home."

The three princes, wearing plain clothing and riding unadorned elephants (for they felt they would learn more if they could not be recognized as princes) set off on their journey. As they started their trek to the sea, they *noticed*, more than ever before, the *beauty* of Serendip. They knew they would miss their home and their father, but they were determined to find *Death to Dragons*.

The journey across the ocean to India was a dangerous one, but the princes found a large and fast boat and made it safely across. During the journey they saw several of the ugly and ferocious sea dragons riding upon the waves.

On the other side, the princes began to ask questions and to search for anyone who knew of the formula in *Death to Dragons*. They were adept at asking questions and they did so in such a polite and fair-spoken way that people were naturally inclined to like them and to try to help them. They were directed to a grizzled old sage who had heard of a mysterious one-hundred-line poem. "There is only one copy in all the world," he told them. "It is in the keeping of an ancient seer with strange, shining eyes. His name is Aphoenicius and he carries the poem in a silver cylinder and guards it always. He has a hundred disguises and is at times invisible. He never stays in one place for more than one night."

"Have you ever seen Aphoenicius?" asked the eldest prince.

"He stayed with me one night," said the sage, "and because you are so courteous and because I believe you seek the poem for a noble purpose, I will tell you what I know. At night Aphoenicius spoke in his sleep and said what I believe to be two lines from the magic verse:

> *Though the treasure saline be,*
> *You will not scoop it from the sea.*

The princes wrote down the lines, thanked the sage, and continued their journey.

ventually they entered the land of Persia, which was ruled by the powerful King Behram, and purchased camels to cross the desert. In mid-journey they passed a caravan and were asked by the caravan master if they had seen a camel that had been lost. The eldest prince said, "No, we have seen no camel except those we ride. But may I ask you, Did your camel have only one eye?"

"Yes," said the master. "Then you have seen him."

"No," said the eldest, "we saw no camel. But did the one you lost have a tooth missing from the front of his mouth?"

"Yes," said the master. "You are joking with me. Show me where my camel is."

"We've not seen it," insisted the first prince. "But did it have a lame hind leg?"

With that, the caravan master, convinced that these young men had stolen his camel, had them arrested and brought to court.

King Behram, hearing of the case and finding it interesting, decided to sit in judgment personally. The three princes were not allowed to speak, but there were many witnesses who had heard the eldest prince describe the camel completely, and thus it appeared that they must be guilty. Regretfully (because the young men were polite and upright) the king sentenced them to die, as the law demanded. But Behram was a good king, inclined toward leniency, and offered to pardon them if they would return the camel. The princes could only repeat that they had never seen the camel.

Just then a great bird with golden wings and shining eyes swooped low in the sky. Only one old woman saw it, but immediately afterward the lost camel's owner burst into the courtroom saying that his neighbor had found the camel and begged forgiveness for his false accusation of the three princes.

King Behram, embarrassed by his improper judgment and impressed with the three brothers (who had never revealed their identity as princes) invited them to his castle and asked them to explain how they knew so much about a camel they had never seen.

The eldest prince graciously did so:

"Where we saw tracks, we observed that the grass was nibbled on only one side of the road, so we knew the camel had lost an eye. Along the road we noticed partly chewed bits of grass and concluded that the camel was dropping them through the gap of a missing tooth. And in the tracks themselves, we saw evidence of a dragging rear leg. We know even more than we told, Great King. We know that the camel carried butter and honey. We noticed ants, which seek after fat on the left of the road, and flies, which seek after sweet on the right."

Delighted and even more impressed, King Behram invited them to stay at his palace for a time. They agreed to do so, and continued to ask everyone they met about the old man with shining eyes who carried the formula in *Death to Dragons*. Because they were so friendly, and because their motive in wanting the formula was unselfish and altruistic (to save their island from fierce sea dragons), everyone wanted to help them, but few had heard of old Aphoenicius and his silver cylinder.

One evening, at a dinner attended by several of King Behram's ministers and viziers, the three princes were sitting together and, as they often did, discussing their feelings and the impressions that sometimes came mysteriously to their minds. The eldest said that he sensed that the wine they were drinking came from a vineyard that grew on a sepulcher or cemetery. The youngest prince said he felt that the mutton they were eating came from a lamb that had been raised and suckled by a dog rather than a ewe sheep. The middle brother said that he wished his own impression was as harmless as these, but alas, it was not. He perceived that one particular vizier, seated there in the dining room, had malicious and seditious thoughts and was perhaps plotting to take the life of King Behram.

The king, sitting across the table, heard his name mentioned and insisted that the three princes tell him their entire conversation. When they had done so, King Behram asked them how they were able to perceive such things, and they told him that it was by what they observed and by what they felt in their hearts and minds. The first prince, for example, told him that he had experienced a peculiar and sad feeling as he tasted the wine and then had glimpsed a vineyard-cemetery in his mind. The third prince explained that the mutton tasted slightly unusual and put him somehow in mind of a dog. The second brother said he had noticed one of the viziers change color as the king had spoken earlier of punishing the guilty, and that the vizier's eyes, full of maliciousness and indignation, had not left the king since.

The next day, King Behram checked the accuracy of the princes' feelings. He summoned the wine master, who confirmed that the wine had come from a vineyard planted over a sepulcher. He summoned the shepherd, who told him a story of how a wolf had killed a ewe sheep leaving a tiny lamb, which had been suckled and raised by the shepherd's dog. And in checking court records, he found that the angry vizier had a son who had been banished from the country as punishment for a crime.

Amazed and impressed, the king went to the three princes to ask their advice on how to discover or escape from the vizier's plot of revenge. The second son said he had observed that the vizier had a lady friend to whom he probably revealed his plans.

King Behram located the lady, befriended her, and flattered her with promises of position and gifts. She told him of the vizier's plot, which involved presenting a jeweled cup to the king at the next state dinner and then proposing a toast to his health. The jeweled cup was to contain poison.

When the night of the dinner came and the
vizier presented the jeweled cup, the king said,
"So much feeling comes with the cup that I
cannot accept it until you drink from it first."
In horror the vizier confessed by saying, "I am
fallen into a misfortune that I had prepared for
others." King Behram, urged by his ministers
to put the traitor to death, insisted on consulting first with the three princes. They advised
him to show compassion and to imagine how
he would feel if he had a son and if his son, like
the vizier's, had been banished. Thus the king
adopted an attitude of empathy and arranged
for the vizier to be banished rather than executed—banished to the same land where his
son had previously been sent.

Before his banishment, the repentant vizier
went to the three princes to voice his gratitude.
In their conversation, the princes asked if he
had any knowledge of the ancient sage with
shining eyes who carried the secret of *Death to
Dragons*. The vizier recalled once spending a
night in an inn with such a man, who in his
sleep had muttered a portion of a verse so curious that the Vizier had committed it to memory:

> *And often from the sight is hidden*
> *Such magic not by self-love bidden.*

For saving his life, King Behram offered the
princes any three wishes that he could grant.

They replied that their only wish was to serve him well and to be his friends.

*S*hortly thereafter, King Behram called the three brothers to his side to ask them a great favor. "When my grandfather was king," he explained, "he possessed the great Mirror of Justice, which had the power to reflect both truth and falsehood. Whenever there was a dispute in the land, the two arguing or opposing parties were made to look into the mirror. The rightful or truthful party was reflected as he was, but the wrong or dishonest person was reflected in the mirror with a face of dark purple. The guilty party could return to his former complexion only if he went down into a deep pit for forty days with only bread and water and then came forth and confessed his error to everyone. Because of the mirror there was justice in the land. People dealt with each other fairly and thus grew prosperous and happy."

The three princes listened attentively and with great fascination. (Indeed, listening was among their greatest skills.) The king explained that his father and uncle had fought over the throne after his grandfather's death. When his father won the battle and became king, the uncle, in bitterness, had stolen the Mirror of

Justice, taken it to the far coast of India and sold it to a young king.

The mirror ceased to reflect justice when it was taken out of Persia, but the Indian king who purchased it found that it did something else, also of great value. In his kingdom, a large and terrible five-fingered *hand* rose from the ocean's horizon each morning and hung ominously in the sky beneath the sun all day. In the evening it suddenly descended, grabbed a man from the city or the shore, and hurled him into the sea. The Indian king discovered that, when the mirror was held up to reflect the hand, it changed its behavior, grabbing instead a pig or a dog or some other animal each day to cast into the sea.

King Behram explained that a young queen now ruled the Indian kingdom—a daughter of the king who had bought the mirror. King Behram said that he had petitioned her to return the mirror, but she had steadfastly refused except on condition that someone succeed in destroying or disposing of the hand. "Now," said King Behram, "with my great confidence in you three brothers, I am asking you to go and conquer the hand and then bring the Mirror of Justice back to me."

Without any plan or foreknowledge of what they would do, but with faith in their own ingenuity and in the power and intuition that seemed to guide them, the three princes accepted the challenge of the king. They also hoped that at the far coast of India they could find further clues in their quest for *Death to Dragons*. After brief preparations, they took their leave.

After seeing them off, King Behram walked back to his palace, noticing with great joy the beauty of the fields and forests around him and the rich color and textures of the baskets and rugs made by the people in the villages he passed. He stopped along the way to pray for the welfare and success of his three young friends and thus found himself following their example and their advice to be *watchful, appreciative, and prayerful.*

A few days after the princes had left, a merchant, knowing of the king's great love for music, came to the palace and exhibited before King Behram some instruments and musical treasures brought from faroff lands. In the merchant's company was a young woman of such appealing grace and beauty that the king could not take his eyes from her. Inquiring, he was told that she was Diliramma, a young woman of unknown origin whom the traders had found as a small girl, abandoned in the forest, dressed in blue silk, and wearing a curious necklace of tiny interlocking silver crowns. The merchant had adopted her as a foster daughter. The king, overwhelmed by her beauty, said to the merchant, "She is not of the number who has need of ornaments to set herself off. Rather, the ornaments have need of her to make them more bright and glittering."

Only then was the king informed that Diliramma was also a singer. She was summoned and sang before the king in a way that filled him with such rapture that he could only say, "You have equally charmed my eyes and my ears."

Unsurprisingly, the king offered to make her the palace musician and give her sumptuous apartments in the palace. The merchant, pleased at his foster daughter's good fortune, quickly agreed.

In the days that followed, King Behram was in bliss, hunting in the royal woods by day and listening each evening to Diliramma's songs. He reflected that the only thing that could add to his happiness would be for the three princes to return with the magic mirror.

One morning he invited Diliramma to go on a hunt with him. She agreed, and off they went with a hundred servants, riding the great royal elephants. Most of those who surrounded the king were fearful and subordinate—quick to agree with him and striving to say to him only what he wanted to hear. But Diliramma was different, joking and laughing and saying exactly what she truly thought and felt.

After observing the hunt for a time, and seeing what an exceptional archer the king was, she gave him a challenge. "I would like," she said, "to see you pierce both the hoof and the ear of a deer with a single arrow."

Great marksman though he was, the king thought the task was impossible . . . until he remembered the attitude of the three princes who always looked for a creative or innovative way to do everything. He thought for a moment, then shot an arrow that grazed and tickled the deer's ear. The deer lifted his hind leg to scratch his ear and as it did, the king let fly another arrow which pierced the deer's ear and its hoof. The courtiers and servants cheered and clapped, not only for the king's skill but for his stratagem. Diliramma was also impressed, but she winked and said, "You have deceived both the deer and me and succeeded only through a trick." In sudden silence, all eyes were turned to Diliramma and to the king, whose face turned red with embarrassment and temper. He was not used to any form of criticism or to anyone joking with him. On impulse and in anger he stripped off her cloak and rode off yelling back at his guards to leave her alone in the deepest part of the forest.

When the king arrived back at the palace, he realized what he had done, and inside of him a great conflict arose between anger and love. Love said, "For an indiscretion, for a *trifle*, you treat so cruelly the most beautiful person in the world? Bring her back!" Anger replied, "No, you cannot resent this indignity too much! If you recall her will you not be thought like the weathercock that turns with every wind?"

Recognizing the truth of the first voice, King Behram sent all of his guards to find and bring back Diliramma. But they returned at nightfall, reporting that she was nowhere to be found. Imagining that she had been eaten by a wild beast, the king was heartbroken and felt the terrible burden of guilt. He became very ill, and as days passed his condition grew steadily worse.

*I*n the meantime, the three princes were experiencing a very challenging journey to the far coasts of India in their quest to find and recover the Mirror of Justice. They reached a wide river, which was the boundary of the coastal kingdom. On their side, on the steep rocky hillside that faced the river, was an ancient monastery. The abbot in charge was impressed with the polite behavior of the three princes but became very concerned when they told him of their quest to vanquish the great hand and recover the magic mirror. He told them of a demon who lived underground in the forest on the opposite bank of the river—a demon who took delight in protecting the great hand and who could look up through the earth and see the intent in men's eyes. "I have observed others who came to fight the hand," said the abbot. "If the under-earth demon sees intent to destroy the hand, he pushes the ground up, causing trees to fall and boulders to roll, knocking the men from their horses and either burying them or swallowing them into deep cracks in the earth."

The third prince, always full of courage, said he would cross alone to test the danger. He hired a boat and crossed the river, but just as he stepped to the shore the ground began to heave. Huge stones tumbled in his direction and tall forest trees fell toward him. He scrambled back into the boat and paddled back out into the river just in time.

The other two princes watched from the opposite bank, frightened and confused by what they saw. They pulled their brother to safety and all three returned to the monastery, where they asked the abbot if there was any way to get past the demon.

The abbot told them of the monastery's great library and said he believed that most every answer could be found in books. For the next several days the abbot and the three princes researched and studied. All they could

find was one ancient passage that reminded the
princes of the verses in *Death to Dragons*. It
said:

> *One feather from a peacock's tail*
> *In wisdom's hand may oft prevail.*

Since it was the best they could find, the
abbot presented each of the three princes with
a beautiful peacock's tail feather and said, "It is
possible to follow even a clouded or dark saying part of the way."

Not feeling that they could wait any longer,
the princes hired a boat and set out to cross the
river, hoping that something in their sagacity
or intuition would help them get past the
under-earth demon. They made the river cross-
ing in silence, each searching his mind for a
strategy. Just as they neared the other bank, the
middle prince noticed that his peacock feather
had dots on it that looked like blue eyes. "Let
me go first," he said. "I have an idea." He
climbed from the boat, holding his feather over
his eyes like a mask. He could see through the
feather's tiny cracks, but the under-earth demon saw only the flat, blue eyes of the peacock
feather and could not see the intent in the
prince's real eyes. The earth remained still and
calm. The other princes followed his example,
and all passed through the forest safely.

On the other side they sought out and found

the young queen of the coastal kingdom, who dazzled them with her beauty and courtesy and quickly agreed that they should have the Mirror of Justice if they could conquer the evil hand.

That evening the queen took them to the seacoast where they saw, low in the eastern sky, the terrifying sight of a huge suspended hand. As the sun set, the hand swooped toward the beach. As it did, one of the queen's guards held up the Mirror of Justice. The hand changed direction, grabbed a milk cow from the nearby field, and hurled it far out into the ocean.

The following morning the three brothers went to the seacoast and observed the great five-fingered hand rising in the sky just beneath the sun and gradually moving across the sky.

The day wore on, and still the princes could develop no plan of action. Just as evening fell, a golden winged bird with shining eyes flew silently overhead. Only the youngest prince noticed. Suddenly, without warning, he stepped out onto the beach and asked the guard to lay the mirror aside. As he did, the sun set and the hand suddenly swept down directly toward the youngest prince. As the huge hand came closer with all five of its fingers extended, the young prince held up his own right hand with two fingers extended and the others curled together. Immediately, the hand veered off its course and plunged into the sea, sinking into the depths like a stone. The other two princes rushed to their brother, who explained that a strong impression had come to him that the hand's message was that five men, perfectly united in an evil cause, could destroy the world. His response was that two people, perfectly united in worthy purpose, could overcome all evil and master the universe.

The young queen, who had watched the drama, rushed forward, congratulating the young prince and exclaiming, "Everywhere, true courage meets with quick respect." He repeated to her the message his two fingers had sent to the hand—that two people, perfectly united, could overcome all evil in the universe.

The queen quickly kept her end of the bargain by giving the three princes the Mirror of Justice. She begged them to stay at her palace for a day or two before returning to King Behram and they consented.

That evening they celebrated the demise of the hand at a great palace party. The princes noticed that the queen, despite her joy in her country's deliverance from the hand, still had a look of sadness that occasionally flickered in her dark and lovely eyes. Later, when the other guests had gone home, the princes asked her to share her hidden sorrow.

She told them she had once had an elder sister called Padmini who had been her best friend. One afternoon long ago, on a day when they were wearing identical blue silk dresses and necklaces of tiny interlocking silver crowns, a fierce nomadic tribe charged them as they frolicked together and stole Padmini away. Guards had pursued the kidnappers and finally caught them three days later. But by then the evil men, hoping to escape the guards, had left Padmini in a dense forest. She had never been found.

Deeply touched, the eldest prince said, "As a vine bowed with the weight of grapes, we are honored to share your grief."

The three princes then told the queen of their quest for *Death to Dragons* and asked if she had ever seen or heard of the old sage called Aphoenicius, the keeper of the silver cylinder.

After a moment's thought, the queen recalled the strange but kind man with shining eyes who had whispered to her a short verse shortly after her sister Padmini had been taken.

> *One may seek but cannot borrow*
> *This mystery lying close to sorrow.*

Recognizing the words as another piece in the puzzle of *Death to Dragons*, the princes wrote them down with the other clues they had collected and, leaving the beautiful young queen their fondest wishes and best regards, departed the next morning to carry the prized Mirror of Justice back to King Behram.

As was their practice, the princes tried to observe everything and to learn all they could during their journey. On their way, they came to a small village and decided to spend the night there. They made friends with several of the villagers and were introduced to the village chief. They noticed the worry and anxiety in his face and asked if there was any help or assistance they could give. The chief told them of a rumor that Drakir, the three-headed serpent, had broken loose from his cage high on top of Prison Mountain. Drakir had been captured and imprisoned many generations before by the people of this very village—by the ancestors of the chief and the other villagers who now told the tale of his escape to the three princes.

"The high Prison Mountain is very far away, and if Drakir truly has escaped, it will take some time for him to come. But we must get word to King Behram, for Drakir will surely go there first to get the Standard of Power." They explained that when the ancients had captured Drakir, their leader had been a blacksmith. His leather apron was thought to possess magic. It was called the Standard of Power and was kept at the king's palace. "If Drakir gets the standard," said the village chief, "he will become even more powerful. He will be unstoppable and will take control of all the land."

The three princes told the chief that they were on the way to the king's palace and would extend the warning and safeguard the standard. "Before we go," said the eldest, "is there any more you can tell us of Drakir?" The chief said that they had been warned of Drakir's escape by a strange, elderly traveler with shining eyes who had stayed only one night and had said that the dragon could be overcome only if his three long necks could be twisted together into a single great cord. This would take away his strength. Once his strength was diminished, the great imperial bird, a bird with feathers the color of sky, grass, and sunset, would carry him back to his mountain prison.

Recognizing that the old traveler must have been Aphoenicius, the three princes asked where he had gone and if he had said anything as he slept. The chief said that no one had been with him during the night or seen him leave, but some children had seen a bird with golden wings and shining eyes fly from the house where the old man had slept.

In gratitude and friendship the princes left their peacock feathers with the chief, instructing him to send one of the feathers by runner to the king's palace if trouble ever came to the village. The princes promised that the moment they received one of the feathers, they would rush to the rescue. After making this promise, they set off at a quick pace to return to King Behram.

When the three princes arrived back at King Behram's palace, they were shocked at how very ill the king had become. He lay on his back, white as ash, and could not even lift his head in greeting. The princes, who had been so anxious to present the king with the recovered Mirror of Justice and to warn him of the dragon Drakir's escape, were suddenly concerned only for the king's life and health.

In a feeble voice King Behram told them of Diliramma, of his deep love for her, and of his terrible and angry mistake in leaving her in the woods to die. His guilt and his grief were too deep, he said, and he felt now that he would die.

Quickly the princes presented him with the great mirror, hoping it would lift the weight and gloom from the king. He was pleased, and a tiny flush of color returned to his cheeks, but still he did not lift his head.

Searching for other ways to brighten the king's spirits, the three princes decided to reveal their true identity, knowing that their father was a friend of King Behram. The king managed a slight smile and said he had known that the princes were of noble birth and had received wise tutoring. "Give my regards to your father," he said, "for unless I can overcome this heavy grief I will soon be gone."

Deeply concerned, the three princes went on a long walk together trying to come up with an idea or create some other plan to restore the king's spirits. The eldest said, "Finding a remedy for an affliction of the heart is not as easy as finding a stray camel or uncovering an ugly plot or facing a fearsome hand."

All night they walked and talked. In the morning they went to the king with an idea: "In the seven most spectacular locations in your kingdom, build seven splendid castles. Into each castle put a beautiful princess—a daughter of a neighboring king. Also bring the seven best storytellers in the land and put one in each castle. Use your great wealth and resources to do all of this quickly. Then for one glorious week go to a separate castle each day, first conversing with and getting to know each princess, then listening to the best story of the storyteller."

The idea amused King Behram and distracted him from his own misery. Though still flat on his back, he called in his ministers and started the projects immediately.

*N*ow able to think of something besides the king, the princes turned their attention to the danger of the three-headed serpent. They had not told the sick king of the danger, but they used the authority he had given them to have the Standard of Power attached to the very top of the high flagpole in the center courtyard of the palace. The pole, made of ebony, was very hard and stout. There at the top of the pole, they reasoned, the Standard of Power would be high out of Drakir's reach and in a place where they could keep an eye on it.

*T*he king's engineers constructed the seven palaces in record time, and the king's ambassadors arranged for the seven most beautiful princesses and the seven most creative storytellers to occupy them. The day was set for the king to start his week of visits.

On the night before the king's journey, the three princes sat together discussing their increasing hopes for the king's recovery and their decreasing hopes that they would ever find *Death to Dragons*. The youngest prince glanced out of the window into the moonlit courtyard and gasped as his eyes fell on a fearsome sight. There was Drakir, smoke coming from his three mouths, all six evil little eyes staring up at the Standard of Power high on the ebony pole. As the princes watched from the window, Drakir first tried to burn the pole with a blast of fire from his three red throats. But the thick, hard ebony pole would not burn and the dragon became impatient. Grasping high up on the pole with one mouth, lower with the second, and biting the bottom of the pole with his third mouth, Drakir used his awesome strength to pull the pole right out of the ground.

At that exact moment the princes noticed a fleeting opportunity to do something they had thought would be impossible. They jumped from the window; the eldest grabbed the great dragon's tail and held fast while the middle and youngest princes each seized one end of the long flagpole and ran around and around in a circle, twisting the three snakelike necks together as the three heads continued to hold fast to the pole in defiant anger.

As the necks twisted into one great cord, the dragon's strength drained away and the princes were able to bind the heads together so that the necks could not come untwisted. When they had done so, just as Aphoenicius had promised, an enormous imperial bird with wings of blue, green, and rose, swept out of the night sky, snatched the weakened dragon in his sharp talons, and flew away with him toward the prison place on the distant high mountain.

The next morning, right on schedule, King Behram was carried (he was still unable to walk) to the first of seven castles, which was nestled in a high mountain meadow. The beauty of the place, and the enchantment of the lovely princess who greeted him, lifted his spirits as the three princes had predicted. And the storyteller's tale, later in the evening, was so exciting and engrossing that the king raised his head from his pillow and began to forget his grief and feel some will to live. By the end of the day the king had regained enough strength to sit up in his bed.

Through the days of the week each castle, each princess, and each storyteller was better than the one before, and by the time he reached the seventh castle, the king was able to stand and walk, and some of the light had returned to his eyes.

The three princes had decided to meet the king at the seventh castle, but as they journeyed toward it, they were overtaken by a messenger bearing a peacock feather. Knowing that this was the distress signal from their friends in the small village, they changed course immediately and made haste toward the village, which was at a distance of a few days' journey.

When they finally arrived, they beheld great disaster. Fire had burned the village to the ground. They found the old chief, who told them that several days earlier the villagers had looked up to see the great imperial bird flying over, carrying Drakir toward Prison Mountain. Drakir's evil eyes had seen the village and even in his weakened condition he was able to belch out enough fire from his nostrils as he passed overhead to touch off fire in the village. Strong winds had fanned the flames and the village had been destroyed.

Seeing the misery and the suffering of their friends and brothers, the three princes wept.

"Was any life lost?" asked the eldest.

"Only two people are missing," said the chief, "and neither was a permanent resident of our village. One was the old man with shining eyes who had come again to stay for a single night. The other was a young woman with a beautiful voice whom some villagers had found wandering lost and dazed in the forest some weeks ago. The girl would answer no questions about her identity, but the village nursed her back to health and she had favored them with her lovely singing."

Distraught in realizing that the two who were lost were the very two people they most wanted to find, the princes, after doing all they could for the village, sorrowfully prepared to depart, intent on returning to check on King Behram.

As they left the village, the princes paused to look again at the desolation. As they thought about the villagers who had lost their homes they wept once again, their tears collecting in a hollow on the large boulder where they stood.

When they began looking up, ready to begin their journey, their eyes fell upon a shocking sight. There, in a fire-blackened field near a river stream, was the charred body of a man, burned beyond recognition except for his right forearm and hand, untouched by fire and tightly clutching a silver cylinder.

"The keeper of the secret formula has been killed," they exclaimed, "and though his death brings deep sadness, the magic formula will now be ours."

The eldest pulled the cylinder from the ancient one's fingers and walked down by the stream with his brothers to open it. But what fell from the cylinder was mostly ashes. Only small fragments of the scroll were unburned. The only readable lines were:

Though the treasure saline be,
You will not scoop it from the sea.

And often from the sight is hidden
Such magic not by self-love bidden.

One feather from a peacock's tail
In wisdom's hand may oft prevail.

One may seek but cannot borrow
This mystery lying close to sorrow.

"After so great a search, we have found only the lines we already know," exclaimed the middle prince. "It was a hundred lines and it is lost forever," said the eldest, casting the cylinder aside.

At that moment they heard a sound up on the bank near where Aphoenicius's burned body lay. Looking up, they saw the ashes stir, and a bird with golden wings and shining eyes rose from the spot. As they watched, the bird swooped down next to them and snatched the silver cylinder from the ground at their feet and carried it in flight to the great boulder where the princes had rested and wept. To their amazement, the bird began scooping up their tears into the silver cylinder. Then it flew off into the east like an eagle.

The princes, perplexed by the bird and saddened that their own quest had failed, continued their journey. After several miles they heard screams coming from a wooded valley beneath the trail. Rushing down they caught a glimpse of a girl racing through the trees, chased by a bear. Their own shouts succeeded in scaring the bear off and they rushed to the frightened girl. Thanking them, she explained that she was a homeless girl who had been kindly cared for by the villagers. After their great loss of homes and food in the fire, however, she felt she would be too much of a burden, so she had left, sneaking away unseen.

The princes asked her if her name was Diliramma and as her eyes widened with apprehension, they assured her that King Behram loved her and had almost died from the grief and guilt of his anger, which he thought had cost her her life.

Overcome with joy she told the princes that she was called Diliramma but that she thought she had had another name . . . so long ago that she could no longer remember it. In gratitude for saving her life, she gave them a gift from around her neck, a small and intricate necklace made from tiny interlocking silver crowns.

With great excitement the princes told her that they now knew her true name: Padmini. As they explained, Padmini could hardly believe her good fortune: she had now discovered her own true name and the whereabouts of her sister, and King Behram loved her and wanted her back.

The journey back to the king was pure joy for Padmini. But the princes had mixed feelings. They were happy to have helped so many, yet sad about the failure of their own quest.

As they approached his palace, King Behram came forward to greet them. The joy he felt when he saw Diliramma (Padmini) with them was so intense that even the birds were silent.

In his joy, King Behram found great compassion. He sent the engineers who built his seven castles to assist in rebuilding the burned village, and he had the food and provisions from the castles removed and taken to the village. He sent word to the young queen of the coastal kingdom that her sister had been found and was to become his wife . . . and invited her and all her entourage to come for the wedding and for a long visit.

To make happy endings even happier, the seven princesses in the seven castles married the seven storytellers, who thus became noblemen and kings.

The three princes were filled with joy for so many, but because their own quest had failed, their hearts felt like plump walnuts bored by hungry worms. But the next day, their spirits were lifted by the arrival of a messenger from their own kingdom informing them that their father now wished them to return.

Joyfully and obediently they said their goodbyes and set out on their journey. King Behram wrote a letter for them to carry to their father. The letter said that the princes brought to his kingdom and to his life "a state of splendor and perfect tranquility."

The princes made great haste until they got to the ocean. They found it so infested with sea dragons that there were no more boatmen and no more boats for hire. Finally they found an abandoned boat and set out on their own. Quickly they were surrounded by sea dragons on all sides and thought their lives would end.

Just then they heard the flutter of great wings. They looked up and saw the golden bird with shining eyes, clutching the silver cylinder in his talons. Down he swooped, letting a spray of liquid spill from the cylinder and into the boiling sea. As the droplets fell on and around the sea dragons they went limp and lifeless and slipped silently down into the depths of the sea.

The princes sailed swiftly across the ocean channel and on the shore of their homeland found elephants to complete the journey to their father's palace. Just as they arrived and embraced their father, messengers also arrived with the news that dead dragons now lined the coast and that no live ones were to be found anywhere in the channel.

After all the dragons were dead, the golden bird sprinkled the rest of the silver cylinder's contents out across the emerald mountains of Serendip. As they fell, the tiny droplets turned into the sapphires, rubies, and opals that still exist in abundance in that land.

As his sons told him of their adventures and travels, the wise old father, King Jafer, laughed with delight as they realized that the princes' tears of compassion for the poor and afflicted were the very potion that brings death to dragons—and the formula described in Aphoenicius's verse.

The princes became wise rulers of Serendip. They governed with their sagacity, with their compassion, and with the insight and inspiration they had learned both to seek and to follow.

Wherever there are people and usually when least expected, the bird with golden wings and shining eyes occasionally dips into sight, but it is seen only by those who are looking up.

Epilogue

As with all good fables, each person who reads the tale finds his own set of meanings and messages. And when he reads it again, he may find more.

Walpole felt that serendipity was a quality that grew within people who, like the three princes, had a cause or mission and pursued it with sagacity, sensitivity, and wisdom. But there are additional lessons—all related to this central theme and to each other. There is the underlying message about the ultimate power of charity and compassion. There are lessons about noticing and listening, about feeling deeply, about wishing only to serve, about how *thinking* can be more powerful than *doing*, about faith and intuition in situations where no preplan can exist, about being watchful and prayerful, about thinking creatively and laterally, about following hunches and intuition, about a being of wisdom and inspiration, sometimes in human form, who is only seen by those who are "looking up," about the answers and wisdom of books, about the importance of justice but also about its incompleteness without mercy, about the power of unity and the value of stories and storytellers, and about how

all we ever really know is what we have learned
for ourselves or been taught by the spirit.

There are all kinds of questions to be pon-
dered, about who and what is represented by
the golden-winged bird and the mysterious
Aphoenicius with the shining eyes.

Each message, each lesson, each meaning, is
tied into the deeper substance of serendipity.
The fable may mean even more when you read
it again—especially *after* this book's discussion
of spiritual serendipity.

Part 4

Mental Serendipity

Serendip
Beginning
the twenty-first century

Serendipity Today

Now that we know a little about serendipity's past, it is time to move to the present. What is serendipity *today?* How does it work *now?* What is its relevance to *you?*

All good explanations involve definitions of terms and stories or experiences to illustrate. So we will begin there, and then move to some practical suggestions on how to gain the quality—and how to use it.

We begin with the kind of serendipity that is both generated and received by the mind, and by the five senses that the mind commands. This first level we will call "mental serendipity."

Definition of Terms
(the Words That Define the Word)

Serendipity, according to *Webster's* is "the making of pleasant discoveries by accident, the knack of doing this." Walpole would not have been completely satisfied with Webster's definition! After reading "The Three Princes" he wanted a word that meant more than "luck" or "accident." He wanted a word that celebrated life's sometimes happy unpredictability, but he also wanted a word that had to do with quality of life, a word that recognized the fact that "luck" comes most frequently to those who are aware, concerned, and wise. He created a word, a noun with an adjective form, that to him represented the universal meaning contained in the experiences of the princes of Serendip. "Serendipity" was defined by Walpole as *a quality of mind which, through awareness, sagacity and good fortune, allows one to frequently discover something good while seeking something else.*

Serendipitous is the adjective form. A serendipitous experience is one of unexpected happy discovery, and a serendipitous person is one who makes such discoveries frequently.

Quality of life refers to the joy and fulfillment level of our everyday living. It does not result from material possessions or external lifestyle. A significant and noticeable increase in quality of life results from the conscious development of a particular temperament of the soul which this book calls serendipity.

The *sensual awareness* that serendipity requires can be defined as alertness and effective *use* of the five senses. Each of our senses can be developed—fine-tuned so they present us with more beauty as well as more information, more opportunities and insight as well as more data. When we concentrate *only* on the task at hand, on the schedule, routine, or plan of the day, we are like the plowhorse with blinders on who sees only the straight furrow ahead of him. But when we focus on what is happening as well as on what we are doing—and on what is around us and in us—we begin to see ourselves as part of a far bigger picture and begin to be as aware of the feelings in our hearts as we are of the plans in our minds.

Mental awareness, another serendipity prerequisite, refers to both our education *and* our insights—our accumulated understanding and perspective as well as our alertness and vigilance, and our ability to be in the world and aware of the world in the most positive sense (which does not require us to be "of the world").

Sagacity, says *Webster's*, is "wisdom in one's understanding and judgment of things; insight springing both from education and from alertness." Sagacity, then, requires us to be both informed and aware; alert, sensitive, and empathetic. Just as it has been said that luck favors the prepared, it could be said that serendipity favors the sagacious and the aware.

Good fortune, says *Webster's*, is "luck; good things that happen without work or effort." Walpole wouldn't have wanted his word too closely associated with luck or lack of effort. He thought that serendipity could be obtained in greater frequency by *developing* both sagacity and good fortune. In his mind, then, good fortune was an *attitude* of faith and optimism—an attitude allowing one to see the bright, opportunistic side of unexpected occurrences—a love and an appreciation for surprises rather than a resentment of them.

Indeed, it is possible to *expect* the unexpected, to admit that life is unpredictable and that we control only a very small number of the variables, and then to *decide* to look for the positive interpretation, or "bright side," of everything that happens. This, in Walpole's mind, would constitute the *attitude* of good fortune.

Goals can be defined as "mental pictures of things as we want them to be." Goals are an essential part of serendipity. The fourth requirement set forth by Walpole, after awareness, sagacity, and good fortune, was to be "seeking something." Serendipity happens when we discover something good *while seeking something else*.

It is when we couple awareness and sagacity with purpose and goals that we create the atmosphere and attitudes within which serendipity can flourish.

While serendipity is helped by goals and direction, it is *hindered* by the heavy, overstructured plans and highly detailed lists and schedules that absorb all of our awareness, sucking us away from the opportunities and surprises of the *present*.

Double Exposure

Two competing images superimposed
atop each other
each partially observed, partially obscured,
so that
neither is vivid nor fulfilling.
Like twice-exposed film
our overprocessed plans split
our mind's capacity
between what we've planned and what is.
The picture of all our artificial schemes and
the tight, time-managed lists of what we think
we want to happen
is double-exposed over
the real-life adventure of what *is* happening.
Thus, so much of the irreplaceable present
is unobserved.
Beauties, ideas, opportunities, needs, humor,
and all kinds of
unplannable *feelings*
float by us in the periphery
of our blinder-shaded eyes.

Bridges

Serendipity is a bridge. The metaphor applies
in many ways. The first application is that
serendipity is a bridge between structure and
spontaneity, between discipline and flexibility,

between the expected and the unexpected, between plans and surprises, between relationships and achievements, and between the forced and the fun. The second broad application applies to spiritual serendipity and will be explained in the second part of this book.

Serendipity can be thought of as a sort of bridge between metaphorical regions that are otherwise hostile to each other—lands that, without the "serendipity bridge," we have to choose between because the gap separating them is so wide.

One is the land of structure and discipline, of goal setting, positive mental attitude, and achievement. It is inhabited mainly by high-powered business executives, aspiring yuppies, left-brain thinkers, and superachievers. The other is the land of spontaneity and flexibility, of sensitivity, observation, and relationships. Here we find many artists and creative thinkers, philosophers and would-be Renaissance men, and people who use the intuitive right hemisphere of their brains.

People in one land travel in jet planes, power yachts, and snowmobiles. In the other land, many prefer hot-air balloons, sailboats, and cross-country skis.

Although there are overlaps, we generally associate people in each land with certain things: In the first land, people read *The Wall Street Journal*, dress for success, and listen to motiva-

tional tapes. In the second land, people read
poetry, dress for comfort, and listen to Stra-
vinsky. In land A politics means power, progress, military strength, and tax loopholes. In
land B politics means environmental conser-
vation, peace marches, and government welfare. In one land people live to work and say
things like, "Act, don't react," and "Don't just
sit there, do something." In the other land,
people work to live and say things like, "Go
with the flow" and "Don't just do something,
sit there."

The problem most of us have is that we like
a lot of things about both lands . . . and we like
lots of the people in both lands. And there are
certain parts of us that we know belong in each
land. We recognize that each of the two places
has its own unique beauty and usefulness. We
also know that we appreciate one all the more
after we have spent time in the other—like
going from the snows of Colorado to a beach
in California.

It is serendipity that allows us to get from
one to the other, to spend time in both places,
even to have a home in each land.

Remember that serendipity requires *sensitivity* and highly tuned observation so that we
don't miss things like unexpected beauty,
needs, opportunities, new ideas, and spontaneous moments. If we have this sensitivity and
if we have clear goals and objectives (because

serendipity only "finds something good" when "seeking something else"), then we have the passport and the visa that allows us to move freely between the two places.

With serendipity we can live comfortably in land A because we are "seeking things"—we have goals; we want to achieve, to grow, to progress. But we can also feel at home in land B because we have sensitivity and sagacity and are, therefore, flexible and spontaneous enough to change our minds and change our course when the right moment or the right need or the right surprise comes into view.

Serendipity is not only a bridge between places, it is a bridge between people—and between the two extremes that are sometimes painfully evident in our world. One extreme leans too far left, one too far right.

To illustrate, ponder two people (we'll call them Robert and Bob) with opposite approaches and attitudes. Robert is clean-cut and scrubbed. He's always in coat and tie. He sets goals with precision and regularity. He plans his weeks and his days. He is extremely conservative politically. His heroes, other than Rush Limbaugh and Pat Robertson, are Milton Friedman, Barry Goldwater, and Ronald Reagan, as well as various corporate CEOs and captains of industry. He is a high achiever. He is meticulous in his use of his huge day-timer. He drives a new car. He is financially well off but wants to be rich. He believes in free enterprise, personal responsibility, and progress. He sees technology as having most of the answers for our physical future and has little patience with conservationists who want to stop progress in order to cling to the past. He believes that uncompromised obedience is the central doctrine of God and dislikes people who want to know the reasons for everything.

Bob feels uncomfortable in ties, wears mostly jeans and soft shoes, likes his hair long. His favorite presidents were Kennedy and F.D.R. He sees himself as a social liberal, gets involved in inner-city projects, and feels a strong obligation to help minorities and equalize society. He prides himself on spontaneity and dislikes a lot of structure and routine in his life. He likes natural things and organic foods, does a lot of hiking and camping, thinks preserving the environment should be a higher priority than building another refinery. He seems unconcerned about money and material things. He believes there is a lot to learn from Eastern thought, particularly meditation and "flowing with the current of life rather than always trying to swim upstream." He believes that tolerance and compassion is the heart of true religion and feels that truth is learned largely through questioning and even sometimes through doubting . . . until it can be sorted out.

If you were to ask Robert to compare himself with Bob, he would do so like this:

Me: Winner, clean, proactive, goal setter and planner, freedom, progress, modern, believing.
Him: Loser, dirty, reactionary, aimless, socialistic, backward, out-of-date, doubting.

On the other hand, if you asked Bob to compare himself to Robert, he would do so like this:

Me: Friendly, compassionate, real, natural, thoughtful, love for earth, comfortable, practical, no class structure, independent thinking.
Him: Pushy, selfish, artificial, arbitrary, exploitive, stuffed shirt, class- and prestige-oriented, close-minded, blind faith.

Because of their extremes, both Robert and Bob seem more wrong than right. Each has disconnected himself from an important half of life. Each needs the bridge.

Not only can people who have built the bridge of serendipity have the best of both worlds, they can *become* the best of both. They can be the good parts of Robert and Bob and avoid the dangerous extremes of each. They can derive joy from giving and from getting. They can find real fulfillment in meeting a goal, in checking off things on their to-do list, in competing, and in winning. But they can also feel the joy of a red sunset, of doing a spur-of-the-moment anonymous good turn, of writing a poem, or of winning a small smile from a small child.

Serendipity is a *bridge* that lets us have our cake and eat it too. We don't have to choose between being structured schedulers or flexible free-lancers. We can have both goals *and* surprises, both plans *and* spontaneity, both discipline *and* flexibility. We can ride in jet planes *and* hot-air balloons. We can get there *and* enjoy the journey.

A Curious, Calm Capacity

Academic, analytical, or anecdotal definitions of "serendipity"
are fine up to a point. But they don't define feeling;
and serendipity is a feeling
that most of us know,
whether we've ever called it by the word
or not.
It is the feeling of those rare days
when everything works,
when, without apparent effort,
things just seem to fall into place. . . .

When we're having one of those days . . .
when we've got it,
we know it!
But we can only partially define or describe it,

this subtle sense, so seldom secured,
so soft, so simple, a subtle slowing of time . . .
so that there is enough for beauty,
for love, for people;
and inner peace enough
to look into people's eyes with interest
instead of self-consciousness.
Time to wait for some things to come to you
rather than going after them;
unpressured, uncompetitive, yet confident.

The curious, calm capacity to enjoy simply,
to think freely, to feel deeply,
to observe others
instead of worrying about their observations
of you.

A soft stillness inside, feeling the ground
through shoe soles and the sky all around.
In this mood, surprises come—
unplanned, unexpected,
even unhoped for things—
better than what we planned,
fuller than what we hoped,
and far more interesting.
Surprise and delight,
the world seems open to us, and filled with
unanticipated beauty.
People cease to be threats, bores, irritations,
or interruptions
and become at least interesting,

at best fascinating . . .
and able to provide, somehow, what we need—
even more in fact
than what we knew we needed.

Application of
the Attitude

Structure or Spontaneity

Imagine a carefully planned trip:

Goal: A working vacation,
specific objectives
for accomplishing things *and*
for having fun.

Plan: Very detailed.
Every minute planned,
guidebooks read, lists of
things to see, time allotted,
where to stay, eat, stop, start,
appointments set,
all on paper, all structured.

Results: Some goals met but a lot of:
☐ Irritation (delays, foul-ups,
"the best laid plans . . .")
☐ Disappointment (most things
not as good as their billings)
☐ Opportunities missed (wasn't
looking for them—not on list)

      ☐ Beauty missed (didn't notice it—unmentioned in guidebook)
      ☐ Relationships missed (no time for people without appointments)
      ☐ Fatigue (it's exhausting when you have to force everything)
      ☐ Offense (*given* by irritation, *taken* through impatience)
      ☐ Unwelcome surprises (unanticipated things always interrupting)
      ☐ Stress (feeling the need to get home and rest)

Resolution: Next time plan better, read better guidebook.

Now imagine the opposite—a trip taken on a whim:

Goal: Relax

Plan: None

Result: Some nice moments but a lot of:
      ☐ Frustrations (reservations needed, people unavailable)
      ☐ Wasted time (places not open, keep getting lost)
      ☐ Restlessness (should really be *accomplishing* something)
      ☐ Boredom (not much happening)
      ☐ Stress (wanting to get home where there is control)

Resolution: Next time stay home . . . it's

easier to relax
in familiar surroundings.

Now picture the combination—the serendipity journey:

Goal: Business and pleasure: "get
            there" and
            "enjoy the journey."

Plan: Priorities and necessities planned
            but much room
            consciously left for flexibility and
            spontaneity
            (an *attitude* adventure).

Results: ☐ Objectives met (sometimes
            upgraded, exceeded)
            ☐ Discoveries (often of things
            better than what was sought)
            ☐ Surprises (of beauty, of inter-
            est, of new ideas)
            ☐ Friends found (new acquain-
            tances—common interests)
            ☐ Needs noticed (chances to
            help, teach, give)

Resolution: Keep traveling!

My Epiphany

As a college student, I developed a "positive
mental attitude," set a dozen or so specific
goals every week, and planned every minute of
every day and most of every night. I set high
goals, made detailed plans, and attempted to

shut out anything that fell outside of my plans. I tried hard to force life to work out the way I wanted it, and to reach my own objectives even if I had to step on a few people to do so. Since I saw only what I wanted to see, I was quite happy . . . until finally someone (it happened to be a girl I was dating) pointed out that I was insensitive, self-centered, rigidly structured, obsessed, and selfish, not to mention unspontaneous and un-fun.

By sheer coincidence (or maybe by undeserved serendipity) our last date (the one on which she unloaded) was to a concert given by the *Serendipity Singers*. I had no idea what the word meant, but the next day, sitting in the library and still reeling from my chastisement, I happened to look the word up in the huge, unabridged library dictionary. The definition fascinated me. "The ability, through sagacity, sensitivity, and spontaneity, to find something good while looking for something else." An *ability*, the dictionary called it. Was this the quality by which one could have the left-brain goals and plans of an achiever *and* the right-brain flexibility and sensitivity of an artist? I began to see the concept as a *bridge* between the objectives, structure, and high achievement pattern (which I'd worked hard on and wasn't about to give up) and the fun, flexibility, and lightheartedness that I had apparently lost.

I made the word my motto.

Serendipity is not a compromise or midpoint between structure and spontaneity. It is an ability, a capacity, and a frame of mind that lets a person have more of *both* than he could have of *either.* Setting goals, with an accompanying determination to stay flexible and to keep *looking* for something better reveals shortcuts to the goals one has set as often as it reveals better destinations.

Origins and Results

Mental serendipity involves intense use of the five senses and yields greater beauty observed, adventure, and more pleasure and joy through what eyes see, ears hear, senses sense. Serendipity trains both of the brain's hemispheres to gather and to value knowledge and results in understanding, joyous openings of truth and insight—and eventually, true wisdom.

The *sources* as well as the *benefits* of serendipity can also be social and emotional.

Social serendipity allows us to see all people as interesting, helps us watch for chance meetings, chances to learn, chances to give, and puts into our hands the joystick of friends everywhere, even in places we've never been.

Emotional serendipity lets us become fascinated with (rather than resentful of) our own moods. We *observe* our depression, our pensiveness, even our fear—and find within them insight and depth.

In all cases, serendipity involves a certain combination of awareness, observation, acceptance, and optimism that lets us find the best in whoever we are with, whatever is going on, wherever we are, wherever we are living, and however we are feeling. In all cases we are *finding and flowing* instead of *forcing and fighting*.

Scientists, explorers, and inventors tell us their key discoveries often come in one of two ways:

1. In solitary periods of private, penetrating, almost painful thought
2. In bursts of insight that come not out of analysis but out of observation or incidental conversation—or simply out of nowhere (from some source beyond)

It is the same with *our* discoveries, about ourselves and about life. They come to us either through deep, free thought or through observation and awareness—all of which are destroyed by trying to control everything, by excessive and exaggerated "positive mental attitude," by forcing the issue, by frantic activity, and by planning every minute.

For many years, our society has recognized the need for *balance* in life—for prioritizing and taking care of things that really matter. While we talk more and more about the *problem* of balance, we keep getting offered the same tired old "cures" of positive mental attitude and time management. So many people carry both to excess. Positive mental attitude starts to mean "ignoring reality and trying to force everything to be as I want it" and time management begins to suggest "making longer and longer lists and trying to do more and more things."

Serendipity is an alternative attitude. It does involve being positive and having goals, but it *also* involves flexibility, spontaneity, sensitivity, and the relish of surprise.

All of this brings us to our first formula, our first equation for serendipity, our first motto. In longhand it would be "Live with acute awareness and steady sagacity and ponder deeply life's goals and destinations." In shorthand, *Watch and think*.

The Source
(You)

An Umbrella and a Lens

Whence cometh serendipity?
From ourselves!
It is a quality and a gift
that can be given only by ourselves

and only to ourselves.
We give it by teaching ourselves to
watch and think,
to look for beauty, ideas, relationships,
to relish the unexpected . . .
to welcome surprises as opportunities,
even if they delay or alter
(and sometimes replace)
the goals we have thoughtfully set and
pursued.

Mental serendipity
is a translucent, rose-colored
umbrella
that overarches
our physical, mental, social, and
emotional lives,
making them dynamic, and allowing each part
of us
to see happily through rain or shine.

And serendipity is an infrared, wide-angle lens
that lets us see more
and see each part clear, and bright, and light,
even in night.

The development of serendipity
is not merely a mental process
(like learning a new memory technique)
or a physical process
(like muscle conditioning).

Rather, it is an attitude
of thoughtfulness and watchfulness
that changes how we see the world
and how we want to live in it.

The Process
(of gaining the quality)

"Exercises"

To go into training for a race, one sets up a regimen of regular exercise and disciplined habits.
To become watchful and thoughtful enough to
summon serendipity we need training exercises
or habits that attract the quality. Nine exercises
follow—but first a story to refocus the *nature*
of serendipity.

While I was living and working in London,
the president of our organization flew in from
the U.S. headquarters. I was asked to meet his
plane and take him to his hotel. The late flight
arrived at the end of a long Heathrow concourse in the still of the night. The president,
an elderly man, was tired and jet-lagged, yet I
saw in his eyes, his words, and his handshake,
an awareness, a concern.

Walking down the concourse with him and
his personal assistant, a man named Arthur, I
noticed that his briefcase had a broken hasp

and sagged open. I walked a half step behind, ready to retrieve anything that might fall out. Then his assistant noticed the problem and took action, dramatically pulling off his belt and fastening it around the briefcase. The president watched, with a twinkle in his eye, and said, "Thank you, Arthur, but are you sure we don't now have a more serious problem?"

As we proceeded toward the airport exit I noticed how aware he was—how interested in the environment and the people that passed. Repeatedly he caught someone's eyes and nodded a greeting.

Finally we emerged to the waiting chauffeur-driven Rolls-Royce, a huge, long limousine I had hired in an attempt to increase his comfort and signify the respect of those of us who ran the British office. I worried now that he would think it pretentious and out of place, but he climbed in without a word. As we drove down the dark motorway toward London, he stirred, stood, walked up to the front seat, and put his hand on the shoulder of the professional chauffeur who came with the car. "Young man," the president said, "it's very late and I'm sorry if we are keeping you away from your family this evening."

This wise leader didn't focus on the majestic car, or on hurrying to his hotel, or on his own fatigue. What he saw were the needs, the

people, the opportunities, and even the humor
of the evening. None of what he said or did was
planned or scheduled; all was an outgrowth of
who he was and what he noticed.

How do we train ourselves to see with that
sensitivity and that serendipity. Here are nine
answers (some may sound strange—until we're
reminded that the aim is to help us *watch* . . .
and *think*):

1 Write
Poetry

You have to see something rather clearly
to write poetry about it.
Further, you have to see with some insight,
or involvement, or irony
and to *feel* something in what you see.
Writing poetry (even attempting) forces one
to notice, and to think, and to feel.
Worrying about the poem's quality or your
ability
is mute,
because the readership is *you*.

2 Slow Down

Consciously walk a little slower, *move* a little
slower.
Hurry tramples watchfulness
and thoughtfulness.
Smell the flowers, feel the sun, pause to
breathe.
Notice the needs of others
and try to feel empathy.
Sometimes relaxing your pace
can lengthen your stride.

3 Welcome Surprises

And anticipate them, look for them,
expect them,
relish them.
Surprises, well received, don't
knock you off course.

They reveal new destinations
and new directions.

4 Enjoy the
Journey—Now

"Are we having fun yet?"
says the popular T-shirt message.
Thinking of the happiness
and fulfillment of life
as a misplaced thing, likely to be found later,
after you "get there,"
is living in a low realm of high folly.
Look for (and find) joy today.
Notice the moments,
Remember that life is not a dress rehearsal.

5 Hold "Sunday
Sessions"

Spend a half hour alone,
on the first day of the week,

looking ahead to the other six, and
thinking about
what matters, about priorities and
opportunities.
Without goals, serendipity won't work.
We need the "else" if we want to
"find something of value while
seeking something else."
Regular Sunday sessions *adjust* and *refine* goals
as new options appear and new capacities grow.

6 Simplify and Set
Your Own Standards

The trading of time for things is usually a
bad deal.
When the *things* are the expensive trappings
of style,
image, and impression,
the trade-off can be a disaster.
Advertising is the fine art
of trying to make us think
we need
what we actually only want.
And trying to impress others with the newest

and costliest
car, fashion, brand name, address, toy, or trend
is the depth of bad-deal trade-offs
and the height of self-deceit.

7 Make Goals Without Plans

While goals are an indispensable part of
serendipity,
tight, over-detailed plans are *not*.
Spend your Sunday Session and other
"thought time"
conceptualizing your goals, visualizing them,
and laying out a general route toward them,
but acknowledge that your actual path
will be some combination of the schedule
and the surprise.

8 Set Up Split-Page Scheduling

If you're a list maker
make your list (or write your schedule)
on the left side of your page.
Draw a line down the center
and leave the right side blank until day's end.
Then, there on the right,
jot down the day's serendipity
(think back, remember
a new acquaintance, a fresh idea,
a child's question,
an unexpected opportunity, a friend's need,
a chance meeting, a beautiful flower).
For fun, at the end of the week,
look back on the lefts and rights of your days
and discover
that what "just happened" on the
unknown right
is often more valuable than
what you made happen on the known left.
If you are already committed
to a particular type
of schedule book or planner,
stay with it, but alter it by putting a vertical
"serendipity line"

down the center of every page.
Keep your structure to the left,
your spontaneity to the right.
If you are free of present commitments
to a particular type of planner,
try the monthly "anti-planner"
mentioned at the end of this book.

9 Have Faith—Believe in Serendipity

"Nothing is coincidence,"
says Redfield in *The Celestine Prophecy*.
Believe it.
There is something cosmic that connects
everything.
When we believe in the connections we begin
to see them.
When you miss a flight, maybe there is
someone you should meet on the next one.
Have faith that things happen for a reason,
that there is opportunity (and beauty)
in everything.
We attract serendipity by believing in it.

"Life as Experience" and "Goals Without Plans"

Too much planning can make the actual experience of living almost anticlimactic. (There may be times for reading the script, but it's never as exciting as ad-libbing.)

Too much *thinking about* something removes us from it—we become observers, analysts, spectators, or critics rather than participants.

If we can approach life more as an *experience* that contains vast variety and infinite potential for surprise, we will find ourselves dealing less with success and failure and more with progress and growth.

If we have to think about every detail of our lives, we ought to sometimes think about them *after* they have been lived (when we can learn from experience), not always *before* (when the very thought may intercept or alter the experience). The best time to be aware of details is not before or after, but *now*. Approaching life as an experience makes us, moment to moment, more aware of what is happening and of what we *are* feeling—and less aware of what we planned to have happen or wish *had* happened. Thus we see the opportunities we could never have planned and realize far more serendipity than we otherwise could.

It is not goals that get in the way of experience or serendipity—it is inflexible plans.

Goals can coexist with real-time experience—they can shine like beacons and allow us to see our experiences more clearly and more in the light of what we could learn from them or make of them. Know well the destination of a goal, but use the serendipity of a compass to get there, not the rigidity of a road map.

Summary

Walpole, whether he knew it or not, told us *how* to get mental serendipity in his definition of the word.

"The ability," he said, "through *sagacity* and *good fortune* to find something good while *looking for* something else."

Three requirements:

1. *Sagacity:* Notice, watch, observe, be aware, learn, refuse to wear the blinders of obsession or self-consciousness.

2. The attitude of *good fortune:* See changes as opportunities, surprises as excitement, disappointments with silver linings.

3. Thoughtful *goals:* Set and list objectives and pursue them until something else (better) is discovered.

And while Walpole did not profess to be a spiritual man or to have coined a spiritual word, serendipity, even as he defined it, is at least partially a quality of the spirit because it is only with the "deeper eyes" of the spirit that we really see and become truly sagacious.

But there is a level of serendipity beyond the concept that Walpole conceived. It is not coincidentally but *purposefully* spiritual. We will get to it after a brief intermission.

i n t e r m i s s i o n

I've taken to putting intermissions
in my books
for the same reason they occur in stage plays:
to give the audience a chance to stretch
and to ponder the plot
before it thickens.
This book has a particular need
for a break and a breather—
because at this point, we change *levels.*
The serendipity we turn to now
is a quality of the soul
rather than of the mind.
Our sources shift from senses to spirit,
and our attitude from flexibility to faith.
Even the underlying question changes from
"What do I want, and how can I find it?"
to
"What does God want for me,
and how can I receive it?"

In the book *Lifebalance* (coauthored with my
wife, Linda), there is a section on balancing
structure and discipline with spontaneity and
flexibility. In it, we introduced serendipity as

the bridge between the two and presented concepts like split-page planning to encourage
readers to cultivate and value unexpected opportunities and spur-of-the-moment impressions or ideas. During the writing of *Lifebalance*
there came many moments when we wished to
say things about serendipity that were inex-
pressible in secular wording. It was during that
time that I realized that my definition now
went far beyond Walpole's and that I had
begun to think of the word as a spiritual term.

I realized that the most profound moments
of serendipity in my own life—the times when
I had truly discovered something of great value
while seeking something else—had resulted
from spiritual promptings. I realized that the
awareness needed to trigger the most valuable
kind of serendipity comes not from any of the
five senses but from the far higher and far
deeper "sixth sense" of the spirit.

If Walpole could invent a word, I decided,
then I could certainly modify it and expand its
meaning. From that moment, "spiritual serendipity" became part of my inner vocabulary
and the quality to which I most aspired.

The problem with writing *this* book is that I
don't know just where readers are as they
read—how far along they are with life and with
thinking about life. It took me decades to get to
here. If I had read this book twenty years ago,
I'm not sure I would have "got it." I was still

into positive attitude, time-management, self-help, getting more done, ownership, accumulation, *control*. "Work and plan" would have meant more to me—much more—than "watch and think."

But times are changing. I'm certain that far more people are ready for serendipity today than were ready twenty years ago. There is a yearning for peace, for harmony, for commitments, for a slower yet more purposeful pace.

If you've come this far into the book and you're feeling like it's a bit too ethereal— if you're waiting for the car chase, the special effects, the three easy ways to get rich quick . . . you might want to set it aside. Come back to it in a few years when you feel the need for a higher source of help and when your heart starts telling you that maybe quality matters more than quantity, peace more than power, character more than control, and family more than fortune.

One other quick intermission comment:

Please keep in mind that this book is about an *attitude*. Forgetting what it is about can lead to misunderstandings.

One friend, very much into New Age and eastern philosophy and religion, read one portion of an early draft of this book and exclaimed, "This sounds like Buddhism—all this business about meditation and slowing down and being aware of what's inside of you."

Another friend, a Christian and equally candid, who read a different portion said, "You're just talking about the Holy Spirit but using some new terminology."

In fact, the book is not about the Holy Spirit or the ideals and gospel of Christ, but it is about an *attitude* of our spirits (actually of our *souls*) that can make us more receptive to both.

And its objective is not the blissful *detachment* of Buddhism, but the deeply *involved* awareness and experience of serendipity.

Incidentally, I'm happy to say that both friends understood much better after reading the entire book.

Sit back down now.
The lights are blinking, and it's time
for the second act,
the second level of serendipity.

Part 5

Spiritual Serendipity

Our world

At a time of spiritual transition

Serendipity of the Spirit

Even though it is best understood after understanding mental serendipity (and best applied by one who has learned to apply mental serendipity), *spiritual* serendipity is something completely different—a separate and higher form—different not only in degree but in kind.

With mental serendipity, our sagacity comes through the awareness of our *senses*, through the light and insight of our own feelings, and from the wisdom of experience and education.

With spiritual serendipity, our sagacity comes through the awareness of our *spirit*, through the light of inspiration, and from the wisdom of God.

Just as the quality itself is higher, so is the method and process of pursuit higher—and harder. But it is worth all the effort we can give, because the rewards of spiritual serendipity are peace as well as power and serenity as well as success.

Definition of Terms
(*Higher Words for a Higher Quality*)

Our spirit: The "hand within the glove." The essence of who we are . . . which continues after the body dies. The part of us that comes from God, that can communicate with God, that can return to God.

The Spirit: The light and power and influence that comes from a higher source—from God. (The name one gives God or the denominational religion, if any, that one follows matters less in the application of spiritual serendipity than the acknowledgment that God's spirit can guide ours and the commitment to both seek and follow that guidance.)

Gift: While mental serendipity is a gift from ourselves, spiritual serendipity is a gift from God. Since it relies on powers and perceptions beyond our own, it can be given only by that higher power. Still, it is *we* who determine whether we obtain the gift, because it is freely given to all who desire it and do what it requires.

Gifts: Each individual is unique—particularly in terms of his inherent talents and aptitudes, or "gifts." Gifts can be of a spiritual as well as a physical or mental nature and can include varied kinds of receptivity to nudges and inspiration.

Sixth sense: Thoughtful individuals recognize that the five senses are not their only source of knowledge or information. We can tune in to promptings, impressions, and insights. Our sixth (and far most valuable) sense consists of the feelings of our spirits.

Nudges or promptings: Impressions that come to our minds via our spirits and from The Spirit.

Tuning in: Like a faint radio signal, nudges can be tuned in and amplified until they become clear and spiritually audible.

Inspiration: A more direct term describing the impressions and guidance that can come from the mind of God to the mind of man.

Ask: We are given (both as a privilege and as an admonition) the opportunity to ask God for personal guidance. Asking, because of the power it connects us to, should be undertaken soberly and cautiously, and with a commitment to acquiescence and submission to God's will and wisdom.

Confirmation: Most believers, regardless of creed or denomination, agree that God's answers usually come not in detailed instruction but in directional promptings or in *feelings* of light or calmness or clarity that *confirm* our own directions or inclinations when they are right. When they have made a wrong decision, those who are receptive and spiritually in tune get the opposite feeling (confusion, murky hesitation). God seems to want us to sort things out the best we can and then bring our answer to him for confirmation—like a wise father who says, "I won't do your homework for you but I'll check and correct it with you after you do the work." Confirmation is the light, warm, calm, sure feeling by which we know our decision is right. Absence of that feeling is the dark stupor of thought that tells us we must work through the decision again.

Spiritual serendipity: That quality or gift which, through sagacity of both senses and spirit, and through the grace of God, allows one to ask for and receive guidance (inspiration and confirmation) relative to his purpose, his family, his service toward others, and his day-to-day activities.

Light and Guidance

As with mental serendipity,
spiritual serendipity cannot be completely
defined
with words
(because, more than a word, it is a feeling).
Words are useful in attempting definition only
if they generate some image or glimpse
of the feeling.
Spiritual serendipity is the soft,
sweet submission
of spirit to
a conscious, welcome dependency on God.

Within spiritual serendipity is the
righteous, rigorous realization of the fact
that when it comes to long-range planning,
life is too complex for our own calculations.

Thus the goal of a guided life—guided
by a higher (indeed, highest) intelligence.

Spiritual serendipity is sunshine
that lights and reveals parts of the
landscape of the future
that would otherwise be dark and unnoticed.
This higher perspective brings calm, peace,
clarity.
It slows time down, enhances beauty,
and makes love, empathy, and sensitivity
more natural.
It is the influence
of a higher, wiser, stronger Spirit on our own.
This Spirit gives life and light to the body,
and transmits to and affects our every part.

*One hundred and fifty years ago, a man named
Parley Pratt spoke of a spiritual force that adapts itself to all our organs or attributes; quickens all the
intellectual faculties; increases, enlarges, expands,
and purifies all the natural passions and affections. . . . It inspires, develops, cultivates, and ma-
tures all the fine-tone sympathies, joys, tastes,
kindred feelings, and affections of our nature. It inspires virtue, kindness, goodness, tenderness, gentle-
ness, and charity. It develops beauty of person, form,
and features. It tends to health, vigor, animation,
and social feeling. It invigorates all the faculties of
the physical and intellectual man. It strengthens
and gives tone to the nerves . . . it is . . . joy to the*

*heart, light to the eyes, music to the ears, and life to
the whole being.* *

Pratt also compared the spirit with electricity,
explaining how it could warm and light
those who, as pure conductors,
let it enter them.

The metaphor of electricity
(dramatic then because electricity was so new)
is perhaps even more accurate
now that electricity is
everywhere present
and always at our disposal.

The spiritual circuitry,
into which we can "plug" ourselves,
is always there, always available, always
complete.
No new line ever has to be jerry-rigged to
answer
our asking
or meet our needs.

We simply must understand how to plug in.
When we do, the world, along with ourselves,
is transformed.

The power of God's spirit, transmittable to
ours,

*Parley P. Pratt, *Key to Theology*, Deseret Book Co., 1965.

is so vast.
And its vastness alone, like a slow, sweeping river
turning a waterwheel generator
makes it peaceful and calm, easy while strong.

We plug in with a three-prong plug
of awareness:
First, a prong of *sensual awareness*
that reveals opportunity, need, and deep reality to us
through our five senses.
Second, a prong of *spiritual awareness*,
a knowing both of our own spiritual selves and of a higher Spirit
together with an in-tuneness that pulls us to prayer.
Third, a prong of *attitudinal awareness*
that allows us to *expect* discoveries of interest and joy,
to savor the surprises of sense and of spirit.

It is this attitude, herein called
spiritual serendipity,
adopted into our souls,
that calms us, opens our vision,
and sweeps us into the currents of light.

We pursue serendipity of the spirit
by developing a deeper kind of awareness
that comes

through the senses,
through the spirit,
and through an attitude that values, cultivates,
and interconnects the two.

Many and varied writers and thinkers
(including M. Scott Peck in the single best-
selling modern book
of the last two decades*)
have concluded that a loving God must want us
to become more like Him.
It could be well argued that the
accumulation of additional awareness
is synonymous with progress
and that the difference between men and God,
vast as it is,
is essentially a difference in awareness.

We may be ready now for a clearer, simpler
definition
of spiritual serendipity.
It is the aware, submissive, and sensitive
condition of our spirits
which makes them susceptible
to the calm, the light, the peace, and the power
of God's spirit.

This higher serendipity
has the excitement and intrigue of a great *game*

*The Road Less Traveled

in which we ask questions and make requests
and then try to summon the sensitivity
necessary
to recognize the answers
that come sometimes in disguise
and often with much stillness and subtlety.

Realizing the Ramifications

There is one last word to complete our "definition of terms." But before we get to it, pause
for a moment to reflect on the overwhelming
ramifications of this higher, more spiritual perspective. It is nothing less than a new way to
view yourself, the people and circumstances
around you, and the whole meaning of living
here on this planet.

Once we have truly acknowledged that there
is a higher intelligence, a higher power, a
higher *being*—that He is interested in us and
that His spirit can communicate with ours—
everything should change, particularly our way
of making choices, setting goals, and living
from day to day.

Mental serendipity enhances our joy and expands our opportunities through better use of
our own sensitivity and our own senses.

Spiritual sensitivity takes joy and opportunity to a different level by accessing parts of
God's total awareness and insights. Like flood-
lights coming on in a stadium; like shifting into

a higher, smoother, faster gear; like suddenly seeing through a window instead of into a mirror . . . we can feel differently, we can see better, we can be more.

Spiritual serendipity means abandoning the limiting oxymoron of self-help and turning to the liberating principle of faith, which is our final term to define. *Faith*, this paradigm-changing principle and spiritual-serendipity prerequisite, means three things:

1. A true, mind-changing *belief.* Substantial majorities profess belief in God. But real faith requires a realization of the powerful, personal implications of that belief. Faith means an acknowledgment of our own extremely limited perspective and potential and of the ultimate perspective and power of God. Faith means a grasping of the reality that He is there, that He is aware, that He cares, that He communicates. Faith means actual acceptance of His love and concern for us and real belief that His spirit can guide ours; that we can *feel* what is right; that there is a sixth sense (of spiritual feelings) that we can trust and rely on; that when our abilities and capacities run out, we can reach up and grab onto an ultimate capacity and power.

Many may have to pause and seriously reflect on this—and pray about it—before the balance of this book can have real effect. "Be still and know," the scripture says. Be still and think about feelings you've had that you know were right, about times when you've known you were more than a temporary mind and body, about times when you've felt (even fleetingly) something awesome, something bigger than yourself. Be still and know.

2. A *commitment* to seek God's guidance, and to strive to confirm our lives to it, even to submit and turn ourselves over to it. Beyond understanding there must be action. Beyond belief there must be commitment. Like anyone, God is more likely to give guidance that will be *followed*.

The whole notion of serendipity is "finding something good while seeking something else." The crux of faith and spiritual serendipity is trusting that what God will guide us to (if we ask, if we seek, if we see) will be better than what we could find for ourselves.

3. The *mental effort* of asking for and receiving guidance, of watching for and finding answers, and of visualizing something the way it could be, mentally seeing what has to happen to bring it to pass and then applying your power and prayer's power to do it.

It has been said, "When we work by faith, we work by mental and spiritual effort rather than by physical force."

The Second Bridge

While mental serendipity can make a bridge between our structured and spontaneous selves, spiritual serendipity can be the span between our goals and God's will, between our limited ability and perspective and His ultimate knowledge and power, between our finite senses and His infinite awareness.

The bridge of spiritual serendipity is essentially the application of faith to rise above ourselves and go beyond what we could be alone. This divine-girded bridge has unlimited span. It can give us the best of yin and yang, it can draw down power that connects and synergizes the otherwise opposites of aggressiveness and sensitivity, ambition and peace, confidence and humility.

Recall Robert and Bob (from page 104), the extremes on the right and left. What if each were asked about their spiritual views—particularly about their impressions of Jesus Christ—and the kind of example and model they thought He was? Robert's logic might go something like this: "Christ was the most *successful* being of all time. He had the objective of changing the world and He did it. He was totally disciplined, totally strong. He overcame the world. He taught people self-reliance and gave them confidence. His goal for us is eternal progress. Right and wrong were absolutes for

Him. He told us the path was straight and narrow and said He could not look on sin with the least degree of allowance. He expects us to stay on that path, and to remember that where much is given, much is expected. He exemplified self-discipline and taught that faith without works is dead."

Bob, on the other hand, would say: "Jesus Christ turned man's selfish and conceited beliefs upside down. He showed that real greatness is measured not by how many serve you but by how many you serve; not by what you get but what you give. The outer trappings of success meant nothing to Him. He was interested in the *inside* of people. Those He condemned were the 'successes,' the people who thought they had achieved. He cared about everyone, He gave to everyone, He wanted happiness for everyone. He taught us that people matter more than things. He taught us humility by letting us know that He was our salvation, that it was by His grace we are saved after all we can do."

Who is right? Robert or Bob?

Both are right.

Christ, particularly for Christians, but actually for anyone who studies His life and attitudes, can be thought of as the embodiment and the perfect example of *all* attributes—even those that we often think of as the antithesis of each other. Christ was not a compromise between good qualities. He was the epitome of all good qualities.

Consider briefly a list of qualities that we normally consider to be opposites, that usually stand opposed or in contrast to each other. Then realize that Christ exemplifies what is best about each side of each pair:

ambition	vs.	interest in "insignificant" persons
self-development	vs.	self-denial
masculine qualities (strength, power)	vs.	feminine qualities (tenderness, gentleness)
confidence	vs.	humility
conviction	vs.	sympathy
stern personal standards	vs.	tolerance
susceptibility to deep grief	vs.	boundless joy
commitment	vs.	patience and freedom from anxiety
calm compassion	vs.	righteous indignation

Lao Tzu, founder of Taoism, six hundred years before Christ, said, "If there ever comes a being who is both the yin and the yang, that being will not be a man, he will be God."

For Christians, Christ is that being. His example expands our perspective and, for those with faith, our potential. But the essence of all great religions generates peace and purpose as it *combines* all truth, and pulls all things together. True spirituality is the best of both worlds. It is the ultimate *balance*. It teaches us to pursue all of Robert's righteous qualities and to overcome all of his self-righteous ones. It teaches us to pursue all of Bob's sensitivities and concerns and to cast aside any of his weakness or lack of direction.

Spiritual serendipity, because it draws on higher powers exemplified by Christ, can become a bridge between *all* good qualities, even those we often see humanly personified as opposites.

The gospel of Christ
(or the true teachings of any great religion)
nourishes our spirituality and
draws us toward the best of both worlds, . . .
and promises,
if we are wise enough to learn and to follow,
that we can ultimately be partakers of
the best of *all* worlds.

A more pointed definition of faith
is "spirit-reliance,"
juxtapositioned against self-reliance.
Yet the two are not opposites.

One is a progression of the other.
We rely on self until we reach our limits,
then we bridge to spirit.

Imagine for a moment that God, our spiritual
father
made this earth
of options, opposites, obstacles
and opportunities
as a learning place for us
(mortality is a school and a test)
so that we could experience, grow,
become more of ourselves
and more like Him.
(The easiest things to imagine are things that
are true.)
Imagine that, like a college student away from
home
we learn self-reliance and independence here.
But access to home—guidance, support—
sustains us and unlimits us.

Faith, the bridge between what we can do
alone
and what God can do with us,
is the core of spiritual serendipity.
Alone, self-reliance wraps us in the small
package
of ourselves.
We burst through and billow beyond
with the spirit-reliance of faith.

With self-reliance alone we see
along the narrow shaft of our own
weak light,
a tunnel of dimness,
focused on a fabricated future,
passing through a present of
magnificent light.
Faith splits open our tunnel of limitation
and floods us with the beauty and possibility
of now.
Faith is about the future,
but it operates in and on the present.
It is an enhancing of the *awareness*
that is the core of serendipity.

"Today, well lived,"
said the Sanskrit poet,
"makes every yesterday a dream of joy
and every tomorrow a vision of hope."
Faith draws nudges, not blueprints.
God shows us the next step
but wants faith exercised again and again
before we see all that is at the top of the
staircase.
Thus He keeps us watching, looking, seeking
(unstagnant, unsatisfied, unasleep).
And He keeps us asking
and thus closer, more in contact
with Him.

The Higher Realm
(of Soul and Spirit)

One of the most fascinating (though perhaps least quoted and least understood) verses in the New Testament was mentioned briefly in the Overture. It comes from the fourth chapter of James, verses 13 and 14.

Go to now, ye that say, Today or tomorrow we will go into such a city, and continue there a year, and buy and sell, and get gain:
Whereas ye know not what shall be on the morrow. For what is your life? It is even a vapor, that appeareth for a little time, and then vanisheth away.

One remarkable thing about these verses is the *current* sound of their terminology. With minor adjustments they seem to translate into blunt criticisms of the self-help, pseudo-positive attitude and goal-setting salesmanship mentality of today. It could almost read:

Go on, you who say, Our plan calls for us to go into such and such a city tomorrow, and over a year's time we will meet the sales and profit quotas and accomplish our business plan:
Don't be so presumptuous. You can't plan or control very much of what will happen in the future. Who do

you think you are? You are not of that much consequence, and you won't even be around for very long.

The scriptural advice that follows in the very next verse of James is also as current and as important today as it was then:

For that ye ought to say, If the Lord will, we shall live, and do this, or that.

The fact is, only God knows enough about the circumstances of our future (or about our abilities and gifts) to be able to tell us what we should do and who we should be.

But is James (held by most scholars to be Jesus' half brother—raised with Him in Mary and Joseph's house) telling us not to set goals or make plans? And is that what Jesus Himself meant when He said, "Take no thought for the morrow"?

Let's defer the question for a moment—long enough to tell a story:

I was sitting in my management consulting office one day late in autumn, writing a memo to a client. The Sunday before, Linda and I, in our traditional "Sunday session," or planning time together, had looked at our long-range goals and reviewed our commitments to certain things we wanted to do professionally over the next five years.

The phone rang in the outer office and my

receptionist buzzed me. "A President Tanner on the phone for you," she said.

"What President Tanner?" I inquired. "President of what?" She said she didn't know, so I pushed the lit-up button on the phone and said, "Hello." (Luckily I didn't say the first thing that came to mind, which was the line from the movie *A Thousand Clowns* where Jason Robards says, "Hello, is this someone with good news or money?")

It was a secretary on the other end of the line who said, "Mr. Eyre, President Tanner would like to speak with you."

"Which President Tanner?" I asked again.

"*The* President Tanner," the voice said icily.

Suddenly I realized that it was Elder Tanner from the presidency of our church, calling from the world headquarters. I didn't know him personally and couldn't imagine why he would call.

After a greeting and some friendly questions about our family, he asked if Linda and I could come and see him the next day. Our church has a lay ministry where people are "called" to serve in various administrative positions—usually for relatively short periods of time but often at some personal and professional sacrifice—so we felt some apprehension when we entered his office the following day.

President Tanner, in his charming, gracious way, engaged us in pleasant small talk for a half hour (we becoming more curious and more *worried* every minute). Finally, amidst questions about family and general well-being, he popped the question: Would we be willing to leave our home and career for three years to go to southern England and supervise the church's affairs there?

In the brief time we spent thinking about it, it became obvious to us that if we really believed—and if we really wanted to put God's will above our own—we had to say yes to such a call. We did, and it was to become one of the greatest opportunities and experiences of our lives.

When we got back to our house after the meeting, we noticed our carefully calculated five-year goals still laying on the desk where we had worked on them the day before. We picked them up and realized that they had been completely superseded by our call. At that moment the verse from James echoed in my mind: "You know not what shall be on the morrow." Our five-year plans had vanished like vapor. I suppose the experience could be called serendipity because it was a happy surprise, and it transcended what we had planned. It was a *macro* level example of what happens all the time on the micro level. Spiritual serendipity is not usually a three-year calling. It's a small need, an unexpected opportunity, a flash of insight or idea,

a little impression to do or say something, or
an unexpected chance to deepen a relationship.

Ask and Answer

Was James discouraging goals and plans?
What did Christ mean when he said,
"Take no thought for the morrow"?
Was He speaking only to His apostles
or to those who receive some majestic calling
from God?
Is it only major events or spiritual epiphanies
that alter our aims, puncture our plans?
Or are there smaller things—little, subtle,
unexpected, impossible-to-anticipate
situations, events, occurrences
(and also feelings, promptings,
and impressions)
that enter our lives almost every day?
Of course there are!
We really *don't* know
what the morrow will hold!
The question is not
whether we can anticipate, predict,
and plan everything.
(We *can't*.)
The question is whether we will try to avoid,
ignore,
or push aside
things not of our making, things which don't
quite fit

with our plans.
We could have said no to the life-changing
three-year call
("No, thanks anyway, it doesn't fit into our
five-year goals."),
but to do so, we would have had to commit
the absurdity
of putting our objectives above God's.
So what about the smaller but similar day-to-
day absurdity
of pushing plans instead of following feelings—
feelings of the spirit which come as soft, silent,
inner suggestions
and which may be subtle, unexpected answers
to questions about what is best for ourselves
and for others . . . keys
to seeing beyond sight,
to the desires of our hearts,
to the questions of our prayers.

So back to the question we left hanging:
Is James telling us we are unwise
to set goals and make plans?
Is life a card game
with results based mainly on
the luck of the draw?
Or a chess game where we are pawns
moved by other's dominance
or by acts of God?
No.
But life might well be thought of

(by a believer in a personal God who cares
about us
and who can guide us)
as a different kind of game, a game of
Ask and answer.
We *ask* for insight and direction to know
His will. We ask in simple prayer
to know what is best for ourselves
and for others . . . to know beyond what we
can see. We ask in our own words.
And He *answers*—always—
but not always in the way or at the time
or the place
we expect.
The answers,
(always in God's language
of inspiration, impressions, feelings, and light)
may come quickly and directly to us as we ask
and analyze,
ponder and plan;
or they may come *later*,
in unexpected forms at unexpected moments.

These answers may be missed by those with
rigid plans
(because they may not acknowledge or even
notice
an answer
that fits outside of those plans).
Answers are also missed by those
without *any* goals

(because without some goals
or hopes or dreams
they cannot ask the right questions
nor have they *thought* enough to be able to
recognize
the answers when they come).

In this game the wise player *connects*
the answers that come
with the goals he has set
and with the questions he has asked.
The game is won by thinking hard
("mental effort")
about the right goals and the right questions
and *finding*
(or recognizing when they faintly appear)
the right answers.

Ask and answer is a difficult game
but an uncommonly rewarding one.
And the winners are the thinkers,
the observers,
the inquirers, and the listeners.
Think of it for a moment in terms of *realms*:
There is a low realm
in which people float, sometimes passive,
sometimes resentful,
letting the world push, mold, shove,
and shape them
as it will,
following the course of least resistance . . .

going nowhere, hurrying.
There is the middle realm
where people do their best to take control
of themselves and their destinies,
shaping events, setting goals,
making things happen,
drawing a blueprint and then building it.
There is a *higher* realm, higher than the low,
and higher than the middle.
It involves first:
Prayerfully, carefully setting goals,
asking, striving to have enough inspiration to
make them
conform to God's will.
(Sometimes God "gives us a light"
even as we pray.)
Second:
Watching for answers, further light and
knowledge,
nudges
that make our destiny, our foreordination, and
God's will
more clear . . . and then accepting them,
acting on them,
from moment to moment,
and changing our goals when necessary
to fit
the clearer view.

Better Than a Light

Sometimes God delays the light in order to allow us to develop faith, not answering at the moment we ask, but later, wanting us to be able to both wait and notice. The beauty of having faith to ask and to follow shines through the well-known verse:

I said to the man who stood at the gate of years
"Give me a light that I might step forth"
and the voice came back to me,
"Step out into the darkness
and put your hand in mine,
for that
is better than a light,
and surer than a known way."

It was suggested earlier that the key to mental serendipity is "Watch and Think." The corresponding methodology for spiritual serendipity is "Watch and Pray."

Watch and Pray

Answers come sometimes as we pray,
sometimes later as we watch.
This higher realm of guidance involves a
whole new
approach to life—
an approach where we prayerfully set

long- and short-range goals,
but continue to watch and pray for the added
insight
and the expanded opportunity that may lift
those goals
to higher and happier and healthier levels.
It is an approach that requires
frequent reevaluation, meditation, prayer,
and faith.

It is an approach exclusively available to those
who believe
in a personal God who can and will give
light,
and in the fact that we ourselves possess
far too little knowledge, far too narrow an
understanding
to adequately guide ourselves.

All who believe in these two things (God's
love and
our own inadequacy)
have the reason for wanting—
and the perspective required for gaining—
spiritual serendipity.

The Source
(the Spirit)

We have defined spiritual serendipity as
a feeling, a quality, an attitude, a condition of
our spirit
(calm, aware, peaceful, still, sure)
that makes us more receptive to *His* spirit.
The answers and insights we are looking for
are often already here—around us and
inside us—
although sometimes subtle, sometimes hidden.
Serendipity of our spirit lets us see them,
find them,
feel them.

God's spirit is the source of the serendipity
of our spirit.
Perhaps there are other *partial* sources:
Deep meditation may bring a certain stillness,
making us prone or susceptible
to unexpected discoveries about self and life.
And a slow, measurable alpha-state
brain wave pattern,
which brightens creativity and sharpens
insight,
can be obtained
through techniques ranging from
breathing discipline to hypnosis.

These things tone us and tune us to what is
already inside
of our spirits
and sometimes attract a flash, a glimpse, a
brief infusion
from the spirit-light that surrounds us.

But the Holy Spirit is the complete source,
the reliable source,
the true source.

When we *ask* for the Holy Spirit
to guide our growth,
to give us wings of thoughtful awareness,
we connect ourselves directly,
we plug into the source-current
of spiritual serendipity.

The Process
(of Seeking the Gift)

Now, the bold revelation:
This book proposes nothing less than
a new way of planning
and a new way of living.
As suggested earlier,
The new way of living is called "watching."

The new way of planning is called "prayer."
Watch and pray.
These two words are the process, the how.
Watch and pray is the simple (and Biblical)
formula
for serendipity of the spirit.

Time now to unravel the simplicity—
to open up the formula's two elements,
discover their makeup—
so both can be reconstituted
inside our souls.

Higher-realm watching is a physical art,
and a skill of *sense and mind*
that can be enhanced and magnified
by the spirit.
Higher-realm prayer is a spiritual art, and a
skill of *soul*
that can be both directed and answered
by the spirit.
Both of these arts/skills/gifts can be learned,
developed, improved.

The admonition to watch
occurs dozens of times in scriptures
and holy books.
In the New Testament,
it is frequently repeated advice
of Christ and His apostles.

Think of two different but complementing
connotations:
watch *for* and anticipate the good . . . and
watch *out* for the bad.

Scriptures admonish us to watch *unto* prayer.
It is as we watch that we learn to recognize
and "see"
just what it is that we should pray for.
Thus, watching leads us to pray.
And prayer, in turn, leads us to watch
because it brings impressions, insights, ideas
about
what to watch for.
We should watch that we might better pray
and we should pray
that we might better watch.

Prayer, when it is watchful, is thoughtful,
insightful,
and directed to the real needs
that our awareness
has revealed to us.

Watching, when it is prayerful, is transparent,
clear,
and free of the self-conscious filters
of pseudo self-reliance.

But enough theory.
Just how do we perfect the art of true watching?

And how do we develop our sagacity and our
ability
to ponder, to magnify light,
and to marshal our own inner sight so that it
mingles
with the higher sight of prayer?

In approaching the *how*, two preface
caveats . . .
First: How to watch and how to pray are
questions which
require individual answers,
not collective ones.
Directional pointers can be given,
but not a full personal explanation
(a compass rather than a road map).
Second: Since watch and pray
are like chicken and egg
(adroit watching enhances our prayer and
adept prayer enhances our watching),
they need not
(perhaps should not) be approached
sequentially.
They can grow together.

But for discussion . . . prayer first . . .
because it is the power that lifts our watching
above the level of mental serendipity, which
we have
already discussed.

Praying for Guidance
(Four Suggestions for Developing the Art)

When we say "praying for guidance" we could also say:

Admitting what we don't know
and asking someone who does,
or
Admitting what we can't do
and asking someone who can,
or
Seeking internal and external answers
through thought and prayer,
or
Creating things spiritually
before we create them physically,
or
Developing a superior alternative to
(or an advanced form of) planning,
or
Setting and regularly adjusting goals
in an attempt to match His will,
or
One-half of the formula for spiritual serendipity.

How to improve your prayer? Four suggestions:

1 Hold Regular Sunday Sessions and Set Goals Without Plans

Expand the Sunday-session suggestion
of mental serendipity
to include the spiritual element.
Set aside an hour of Sunday solitude
to review the directions and goals of your life
through thought and prayer.
Think of yourself as a ship
with internal compass and guidance systems
but also able to get bearings from the heavens.
Project in writing where you want to be
and what you want to have "brought to pass"
(in your family, in your work,
in your personal life)
five years from now.

Then check it through prayer against
God's will.
Adjust your goals (or refine them)
from week to week
during this prayerful Sunday session.
Reflect and ponder on how you will get to
these goals
(from where you are now)
but be content with broad-brush pictures
and conceptual images.

Stop short of the detailed, complex plans
that assume you know more
than you really do
and block the way of both inspiration
and discovery.

When I first made a commitment to the idea
of Sunday sessions, I was very disciplined and
rigorous about the process. I even used an an-
tique hourglass to graphically concentrate my
mind on the future (the sand in the top) and to
impose the use of the *whole* hour. My habit was
to carefully and prayerfully review and think
through my longer-range goals, then to decide
on weekly goals that would move me along toward them. I then planned each of the next six
days, in rather exhaustive detail, often hour by
hour, in an attempt to assure myself of reaching the weekly goals.

The results were not altogether satisfactory.
Unanticipated and irritating things came up
every day, and there was often a certain amount
of frustration at the end of the week when all
the goals were not met. Too much planning!
On the other extreme, whenever I missed
holding my Sunday session, the week seemed
aimless and even more frustrating. Too little
planning!

Then one week I had an experience that gave
me some unexpected insight. I had started my
Sunday session, complete with hourglass, and

had reviewed my long-term goals, thought-fully, prayerfully set some clear objectives for the coming week, and written them in my little pocket diary. Just as I was beginning my detailed time plan (*when* and *where* and *how* to do *what*), I was interrupted by a small family emergency and never did make it back to finish my session. During the week ahead there were no detailed plans and lists to check off, but I did glance frequently at the goals.

When the next Sunday came, I grabbed my trusty hourglass and sat down, determined not to be deterred this time from my full one-hour planning regimen. As usual, I started by reviewing my goals for the past week. To my surprise, I had met them all. I had done so *without* detailed time planning or scheduling—almost subconsciously it seemed.

And as I thought about it, I realized that the week had been more pleasant than usual—more natural and somehow slower, easier. It seemed as if I'd enjoyed myself more, noticed more, perhaps had more fun. I hadn't felt the aimlessness that was usually the penalty for missing a Sunday session; *nor* had I felt the pressure and the irritation of a lot of little detailed plans that kept getting interrupted or went unimplemented.

But wait, I'd always been taught—I'd always *taught*—that goals weren't much good without plans: you have to count the cost, you have to decide the where, when, and how as well as the what!

Then something occurred to me: When we set goals, and pray about them, we receive God's confirmation on *what* we should do. To ask for similar confirmation on the detail of exactly when, where, and how we should do them may be slightly presumptuous and may signify an unwillingness to go some of the distance by faith. We can have some ideas about when, where, and how, but recognizing how little we know, and how much is beyond our control, these ideas should be flexible.

Then something else occurred to me: Having a conceptual picture of how we hope to *use* time to reach worthy goals is one thing, but closely planning and scheduling all of "our" time not only assumes that we know more than we do, it assumes (dangerously) that time really *belongs* to us. Perhaps it is more accurate to think of time as a temporary stewardship that God has given us. Perhaps our objective should be to use it according to His will. We should plan to devote time to goals we have prayerfully set. But we should be committed to *watch* both for unexpected moments and methods to reach these goals and for other, unplanned ways in which He wants us to use His time.

Then a third thing occurred to me: Planning is like aiming. No matter how well you aim, you may (especially if your target is moving) *miss*. But with certain servomechanisms, like heat-seeking guided missiles or sound-seeking torpedoes, you just aim in the general direction of the target and the mechanism automatically makes whatever adjustments are necessary to score a hit. Goals that are well and prayerfully set are "guided." What we need is the *thought* to take careful aim, followed by the *faith* to keep the guidance system working.

God often confirms the *what*
and helps us with our *aim* as we *pray*.
Then, if we are spiritually sagacious,
He refines and adjusts the
where, when, and *how*
(and sometimes even adds to the *what*)
as we *watch*.

2 Develop the Skill and the Habit and the Power of Thoughtful Asking

Ask
is the most repeated admonition in scripture
and is the key that unlocks blessings and guidance
without violation of our agency.

Think about that.
If God has given us mortality
to progress, to develop, to grow into ourselves,
then we must have agency and options.
And if He intervenes without invitation,
agency is undermined.
But when we ask, it is *our* initiative,
and guidance is answers, not interference.

Because of its power, we must be careful
in our asking.
"Beware of what you want," the saying goes,
"for you will get it."
G. K. Chesterton said,
"By asking for pleasure, we lose the
chief pleasure,
for the chief pleasure is surprise."

But when asking is thoughtful,
and when it follows unselfish
thanking,
it polishes us and pleases our Father
and prayer becomes sweet and delicious
and
hard-to-conclude.
Good askers are good listeners
and willing to watch and wait.

Prayer sometimes yields inspiration about
what *we* can do to answer our own question or
meet our own needs. One praying for a solu-

tion or answer might be spiritually prompted to a place, a person, or a passage that contains the form or formula needed. One praying for material needs or deeper fulfillment might be spiritually directed toward a new field or a different kind of work.

Other times prayer is not the source of an answer or the channel by which we are guided to do something ourselves. Rather, it *is* the answer and brings about the change by itself without directing us to do anything!

Sometimes prayer is the source of power.
Sometimes it *is* the power.
More things are wrought by prayer
than any of us dream. . . .
Lincoln said, "Sometimes I am driven to my knees
by the overwhelming conviction
that I have nowhere else to go."
God, just as a wise earthly father might do,
often prompts us, guides us toward our own answers,
helps us solve our own problems.
And when needs and worthy requests
are far beyond us,
He lifts us beyond ourselves
or gives to us beyond our understanding.

There are at least four very different types of prayer in which God's guidance is sought:

Prayer for *light*, where we seek a clear mind, insight, wisdom, true impressions and direction toward correct decisions and God's will— so that we can decide what to do and then do it.

Prayer for *might*, where we ask for the power to be able to do what we ourselves cannot do.

Prayer for *change* wrought by God, where we ask God to bring to pass things far beyond our own capacity or power.

Prayer for *confirmation* after we have made a decision and are requesting God's approval before we implement it.

3 Learn the Fourth
(and Most Forgotten)
Type of Prayer

Think further about prayers for confirmation.
Acknowledging the short limits of
our understanding,
we seek confirmation—the still, sure nod that
says
"yes"
to our own careful conclusions, goals, and
decisions.
At this level, our prayers are true-false
rather than multiple choice or open-ended
and God's promise

is of a yes (a burning or a calm knowing)
or a no (a stupor of thought).

Confirmation, once received,
is confidence,
assurance and support in hard times . . .
and freedom from
the plague of the second guess.

I learned God's pattern for giving prayer-
answer confirmation on our decisions from a
wise old mentor. I had gone to him for advice
when I realized I was in love and needed to
make the biggest decision of my life—about
marriage.

My wise friend listened, amused, to my love-
sick account of exhilaration mixed with trepi-
dation and asked me if I had prayed.

"Nonstop," I said. "I've thought of nothing
else and I've prayed to know what to do."

"You've left out the middle step," he said.
"First you must ponder and analyze your own
heart and mind—praying for clarity but not for
an easy answer. *Then you make your own decision.*
Then you take that decision to God in prayer
and ask for a spiritual confirmation that it is
right.

"Think about it," he said. "Would a wise father just give you important answers, or would
He encourage you to work out your answers as
best you could and then bring them to him to

be checked or approved?" Then he gave me a challenge. "Fast for a day or two to develop humility and clarity," he said. "Then make your decision, take it to the Lord, and ask Him a single simple question: 'Is my decision *right?*' Ask for validation, for approval, and for the ringing affirmation of the spirit that will allow you never to doubt." He went on, "I promise you that one of two things will happen. Either you'll have a clear, calm feeling of sure confirmation, or you'll have a troubled stupor of thought indicating that you should rethink, that you should go back to the drawing board, that for now at least your decision is not right."

I followed his advice. Making my own decision was not difficult. I simply acknowledged that I was deeply in love with Linda and that my heart and mind had decided to ask Linda to be my wife. Then, fasting, I went to the mountains, knelt in the snow, and asked for confirmation.

After a time, it came softly and peacefully, with *deep* reassurance. A similar confirmation, through a similar process, came to Linda. Since then, through all the thick and thin, all the ups and downs of our marriage, we have never doubted, never second-guessed, never looked back.

A confirmation is a pure, sure yes,
a green light to go ahead,

an assurance from one who knows all
that you who know so little nonetheless have
made a decision that is right.
A divine confirmation is a heart-deposit of
peace,
a sure memory
to fall back on when doubts drop in.

Another time, years later, we applied the three-step confirmation process to a very different type of decision. I had been offered a presidential appointment to direct a once-a-decade White House conference. It dealt with a worthy subject (children and parents), it was a clear opportunity, and it would allow us to spend a year at our "other home" in Washington, D.C. It also seemed to open doors to the other contributions we hoped to make. Linda and I analyzed it, talked to the children, and became collectively excited about a tentative decision to go.

But in prayer the confirmation didn't come. We wanted it, we tried for it, we even tried to imagine that we had felt it. But with spiritual confirmations, if you're not sure you've felt them, you haven't.

We discussed it again. We couldn't think of any negatives other than the inconvenience of a move back to Washington and the need to turn parts of our business over to others for a time.

Then we rationalized a little. Maybe it didn't matter that much to God whether we accepted or declined. Maybe this wasn't a stupor of thought we were getting but rather an "Okay, fine, go ahead if you want to." We went ahead. It was one of those interesting decisions that wasn't really wrong, but it wasn't really right either. Only a few weeks after our return to Washington, President Reagan was shot and the difficulty of his recovery, coupled with other factors, led him to de-emphasize the conference and redirect most of its activity to a state level rather than the national level that I was assigned to direct.

With hindsight we realized that there were ways in which we could have had the same experience without giving up as much as we did. I could have chaired the conference rather than being its director, made a part-time rather than full-time commitment, kept the other parts of my profession going. We had made a decision based on limited foresight and realized now that what had come to us in prayer was a stupor of thought, signaling the need to rethink, to take a different approach.

A stupor of thought is a signal
to start over.
Either the wrong fork has been taken, or
something has been left out, a piece is missing
somewhere.

Or perhaps the timing is wrong.
The stupor is the *absence* of sureness
and is both as real and as valuable
as the confirmation, which is
(unless we give up)
yet to come.

4 Develop the Attitude of "Nothingness"

G. K. Chesterton said,
"It is impossible without humility
to enjoy anything—even pride." He also said,
"If a man would make his world large,
he must make himself small."
Indeed, we cannot fully appreciate God's
greatness
or maximize the power and use of faith
until we understand (or at least acknowledge)
our own nothingness.

God wants us to know both how unlimited
our potential is
and *how far* we have to go to reach it—
so that we can feel both the confidence and
familiarity
of closeness
and the humility and awe of distance.

A great speaker once brought those two, humility and confidence, together in my mind. He spoke of the number of stars that astronomy had discovered (it was some unimaginable number—a seven followed by fifteen zeros as I recall). To illustrate how large the number was he asked us to imagine a book with that number of pages. How thick would the book be? One hundred feet thick? A mile? A hundred miles? "No," he said, "a book with that many pages would circle the world a thousand times." Then he said, "That's how many stars or suns we've located. Each of them has planets circling it, and you are a tiny speck on one of those planets orbiting around one of those stars."

I remember feeling myself grow smaller and smaller and disappear into total insignificance.

Then the speaker concluded with one powerful statement that restored the balance of significance and nothingness. "When I look out upon the heavens," he said, "I see the *handwork* of God. But when I look out on your faces, I see God's *offspring*."

As God's children
we have unlimited potential.
But how important to remember,
always remember,
especially in prayer,
how very far we are from that potential . . .

to *exercise* humility for self and awe for God,
to sense the vastness of the distance between.

"Beware of professed Christians"
said C. S. Lewis
"who possess insufficient awe of Christ."
Neal Maxwell said,
"The more we ponder where we stand in
relation to Christ
the more we realize that
we do not stand at all . . .
we only kneel."
The "attitude of awe"
is an essential part of the recipe
for spiritual serendipity.

Besides asking for light, might, change, and confirmation, there are two other ways to feel the calm, aware feelings and the guided promptings of spiritual serendipity through prayer. One is to simply *ask for the feeling*. Once you have felt serendipity of your spirit, recognized it, identified it, desired to have it more, *ask* for it in prayer. Focus your faith (mental effort) on how it feels, on why you want it, and on God's power to give it—and *ask* for it.

Another (less direct but equally effective) way to ask for spiritual serendipity is to ask *for opportunities to give service*, for enhanced sensitivity and awareness of others' needs. *Ask* for promptings of insight or empathy that would allow you to lend a hand, give a compliment, share a burden, ease a pain, be a friend. It is the mirrors of self-awareness and self-preoccupation that close us in—and block out the broader awareness that triggers serendipity. The clear windows of bright perception open when we look for the needs of others and ask for opportunities to serve. With the noticing of needs comes the insight of ideas, the receiving of relationships, and the observation of opportunities of all kinds.

And the feeling of peace, worth, and light that comes from the smallest act of giving or serving is so similar to the feeling of spiritual serendipity that it must *be* spiritual serendipity.

Can we further define and understand serendipity by putting it up against its opposite? The antonym of serendipity is *selfishness*. A preoccupation with *my* needs, *my* goals, *my* problems, and *my* point of view relegates us to the dark tunnel of predictable prejudices and the dungeon of self, shutting out the sky of other possibilities, other people, and the endless space and freedom of serendipity.

Watching for Guidance
(Four Suggestions
for Developing the Art)

When we say, "watching for guidance," we could also say:

Perceiving the answers that are already there,
or
Seeing through windows
instead of into mirrors,
or
Taking off our blinders,
or
Seeing with ears and hearts as well as eyes,
or
Noticing what's going on inside
and outside ourselves,
or
Feeling when to act,
and acting on what you feel,
or
Looking for God's will in all situations,
or
The other half of the formula for
spiritual serendipity.

How to improve your watching? Four suggestions:

1 Add to the Attitude (of Sagacity)

Mental serendipity requires sagacity
and an attitude of calm, interested watching.
Spiritual serendipity requires the addition of a higher
and deeper watching
through a still, observant soul, and
through the inner eye of the spirit.
For this higher realm, we need an open heart
and the kind of wise watching
wherein we not only try to see the little things
but try to see them *as answers*.

Once we have asked we must watch for
unexpected answers
in unexpected forms.
Answers are sometime found in silver linings,
and other times in the clouds themselves.

Taking off on a business flight one evening, we flew west, up into a heavy cloud bank and toward the sunset. The deep gray was haloed by gold and the metaphor of "silver linings" passed through my mind. We entered the cloud and experienced some bouncing and buffeting. Then we burst through it directly in-

to the yellow brilliance of the setting sun—high
enough now that the sun had come back up. It's
interesting, I thought, that the clouds which
often dominate our vision are only vapors—
while the silver lining is the reality of the sun.

The attitude that spurs spiritual serendipity
not only causes us to look for silver linings,
but helps us understand that,
despite appearances,
they are vaster and stronger by far
than the clouds in front of them,
and are provided by the same source
and force.
Ask as though everything depended on God
(because it does).
Watch as though everything depended on
you
(because the answer may be right in front
or right inside of you).
Do not limit your watching or looking
to your solutions, your answers,
your interests.
Look wider. See 360 degrees.
By looking away, we see deeper inside.
And by seeing the needs of others,
we find answers for ourselves.

2 Add Gratitude
to Attitude
(and Also Fasting)

Why would gratitude help us to watch?
Because gratitude is awareness of blessings!
The same perceptive inner sight that reveals
gratitude
for what *has* happened
also reveals answers and guidance
in what *is* happening.

Thankfulness is perfect training for
watchfulness.
One who sees the past's blessings
sees also the present's answers
and the future's opportunities.

Fasting, going without food for a day
to cleanse and purge the body,
also opens and tunes the mind and spirit.
Anciently it was a principle often used
in connection with asking
for blessings,
but it can also assist in giving thanks
for blessings.
When we fast with thanksgiving
and joyful hearts,

"fasting" can become a synonym for
"rejoicing."
It can sharpen our physical senses
and tune in our spiritual senses, making us
highly
susceptible
to spiritual serendipity.

Many years ago, we started a Thanksgiving
tradition in our family of listing our blessings.
Before we sit down to eat the turkey dinner, we
make a list on a long roll of cash register paper
of every blessing we can think of. Everyone in
the family gets involved and we list everything
from "a free country" to "indoor plumbing."

After dinner, we have contests to see who can
read the entire list in the shortest amount of
time.

Each time we practice this tradition, we realize that gratitude is more than something we
owe to God. It is a beautiful *feeling*. It is something we should summon and savor as a gift to
ourselves.

"Gratitude."
A trivialized word, or at least undervalued.
We say "thanks"—or feel a fleeting wave
of appreciation—just a thin skin
covering over our take-for-granted
mantra mentality.

Instead, gratitude can be a joyful awakening to
God's glory,
to our own happily dependent childhood,
our ultimate-potential nothingness,
a powerful spiritual emotion,
thrilling us to our core, tearing our eye,
striking deep-space awe
and humility so pure it hurts.

Without humility we develop a
preposterous paradigm
of world-shrinking, self-bloating arrogance
or imagined self-sufficiency.
Humility has only two approaches:
crisis or gratitude.
And scripture calls "more blessed"
those who are
"humble without being compelled
to be humble" (approach two).

Not some luxury, then, gratitude,
not some diversion to indulge in
occasionally,
not mere etiquette or brief warmth-flashes.
But a way of life, a profound gift/skill
(itself worthy of high thanks)
involving seeing, feeling, sharing, and
abundant love,
Yielding humility, perspective, peace, and
abundant joy.

3 Respond to
(and Remember)
Spiritual Promptings

When a "nudge" or impression touches our spirit
(sometimes just brushing gently across it)
the worst thing we can do is to ignore it.
The second worst thing we can do
is to forget it.
These impressions often reach clarity only for an instant and then
begin to fade, dim and dissipate . . .
unless we seize them and transfer them
into our conscious mind,
where they can be held solid and clear.

So many experiences of failure illustrate this need to tune in. I think of the time when we moved to England for a year. We had three teenagers—all of whom got incredibly home-sick, one in particular.

Just a week after we arrived, and *before* homesickness began, I was running an errand with our fifteen-year-old and felt a clear "nudge" to talk with her about the homesick-ness that would probably set in after the excite-ment wore off. It was clear to me for a moment just how to explain certain things—just what to say to prepare her and soften the blow. Just then we got to where we were going so I decided to wait and discuss it later.

A half hour later, on the way home, I brought up the concept of homesickness, but the clear insight into how to explain it and prepare her for it was gone.

Several days later, when the symptoms had arrived in force, we talked again (I talked, she *sobbed*) and I was able to explain some of what I should have explained earlier. As I did, I realized how much more good it would have done if I had followed the first nudge when it came.

Learn to recognize impressions that come
from the spirit,
and categorize them not with imagination,
superstition,
or chance
but with inspiration and light.

Focus on nudges or impressions or little
flashes of insight
and *remember* them.
If possible, act on them immediately.
(I've decided that the best reason to have a
cellular phone
is that you usually *reach* people
if you call them the minute you feel the
nudge.)

If you can't act immediately on impressions,
capture them by writing them down.
As you write, they will expand and become
more clear.
Writing can be thought of as the "tuning in"
that makes a faint signal
audible and understandable.

4 Use Split-Page Planning with "Nudge Notes"

When a spiritual impression comes,
it may not be something you can act on
immediately but
something you should do at some particular
future time . . .
or it may be someone you should see,
or something you should say.
The best place to make notes on these nudges
is in your planner or date book,
so that you commit yourself to a specific time
on a particular day.

Other impressions may come in the form of
broader, longer-range ideas
that can be implemented over time,
or they may come in the form of new insights

that have no particular
or immediate application
but bear remembering.
These longer-range impressions also need to
be captured
in writing.
When they are not written down, they are
loose
and somehow "soluble" . . . they dissolve and
disappear.

I once experienced a particularly forceful lesson on taking seriously and accepting the reality of spiritual impressions. As a young man I
had taken a little time off from college and was
doing a period of volunteer and humanitarian
service in an inner-city ghetto. Another volunteer and I lived together in a small apartment
in a high-rise building. Our supervisor, an en-
ergetic older gentleman, lived on the next floor
with his wife. We called him Elder.

One night late, there was a knock at our
door. It was Elder in a long nightshirt who
said, "My wife is traveling this week so I'm
alone. Could I join you two for evening
prayer?" We invited him in and he suggested
that we kneel down and that I say the prayer. A
little nervous and anxious to impress him, I
went on and on with quite a long prayer, not
wanting to leave anything out.

At one point in the prayer I paused and, with

my head bowed and my eyes closed, I heard the unmistakable sound of a pencil writing on paper. Not wanting to glance up, my first thought was that my roommate, bored with my long prayer and unaware of the importance of our visitor, was starting his nightly letter to his girlfriend.

When I finally finished and looked up, I was shocked to see that it was Elder who had been writing. He had a yellow pad, which was now covered with his long-hand scrawl. He got up, walked to the door, thanked us for letting him join us, and turned to go.

Then he turned back, a twinkle in his eye, and said, "You're probably wondering what I was writing down during the prayer. Simple, really. My memory isn't what it used to be, and when I pray I often get answers, or at least impressions about things I should do. I find that if I don't take notes I tend to forget some of them." With that, he was gone. I remember lying awake that night, thinking, "Prayer is *real* to him. God is real to him. Elder asks, he listens, he takes notes."

Whether nudges come during prayer or meditation or just as we go along living life, it is important to value them, to take them seriously, to remember them, and to act on them. Both short- and long-range nudges can best be recorded with split-page planning described on page 124. Impressions that dictate action can be committed to by an entry on a particular day ("scheduled" on the left-hand side). Broader ideas and insights from the same source can be captured (and expanded) in the form of notes on the right-hand side. Whatever kind of date book you use can be turned into a split-page "anti-planner"* by the simple addition of a vertical line to divide each day. During Sunday sessions, have a flip-through review of the week just passed. Pay special attention to any "nudge notes" on the right-hand side of each day. Think about how they can be implemented in the future.

Keep Track of Serendipity

As I finish the last pages of this book I am sitting on a Sri Lanka beach watching men bathe their elephants and women wash their clothes in the sea. In my hand is my anti-planner, where I write my goals and record impressions.

My plans and notes are a little different here than they would be back in my normal world of home and office. But the principles are the same. As I flip back through my split-page days, I find some Sunday-session goals on the left-hand side of various pages—things like

---

*So named because, unlike most planners, it helps you become oriented to relationships rather than to achievements and to unplanned serendipity rather than planned schedules. (See the last page of this book for information on how to obtain anti-planners.)

"Finish writing Chapter 4" or "Review materials for scuba diving certification test." Also on the left side I see reminders to myself about appointments: "Meet Mr. Ilias at gem factory," "Call Nihal about taxi," "9:05—Flight 515 Air Lanka." Also on the left side I see where I recorded nudges or impressions that I felt I could act on at specific times: "Call long distance to office—get note off to Boyson," "Visit the Bureau of Child Care and Adoption."

But as I look back through the planner pages, I find (as I always do) that the greater value is on the right-hand (serendipity) side of the pages. Here are names and notes about people I met unexpectedly, ideas and feelings I had on subjects ranging from new books to how to get my thirteen-year-old to clean his room, promptings and impressions about things I ought to do and people I ought to call when I get back, and notes on beautiful moments experienced. Whereas the entries on the left-hand side are in the future tense (goals, appointments, etc.), the things on the right are past tense—serendipitous things recorded after the fact. Things like: "Found Henry and the outrigger at Bentara Lagoon," "Had feeling that I should find original Persian fable on Serendip to start book," "Met Tim and Sue at shipping counter," "Followed huge sea turtle while diving," "Impression to spend more time helping Josh with history homework when we return," "Nudge to call publisher and get book distribution in England," "Found Sri Lankan musical instrument store," "Gorgeous sunset across Indian Ocean."

Each entry on the right-hand side brings back a clear memory of a person, a beautiful moment, or a feeling or impression that rang clear and true and needs to be remembered and acted upon. These impressions become a key input on future Sunday sessions as goals are set and time is scheduled.

The entries during our time in Sri Lanka are different from those of normal days at home in normal pursuits. But they are no less exciting or important, because no matter where you are, serendipity removes ruts from life and *converts* routine into surprise and excitement.

How easy it is to slip into life's ruts,
to let routine and rigidity rush and ruin
our days.
Blind routine is ice,
stiff, unflowing and unfeeling,
sitting on the surface of life,
But warm rays of spiritual serendipity can
melt the ice,
letting it flow into and around life's bumpy
topography,
touching the beauty and the pain,
welling up and surging through both sadness
and joy.

Sometimes serendipity even evaporates the ice,
lifting life toward higher, purer feelings and
letting us glimpse the higher realm.

If we want to transform our life's ice
into geysers of water and steam,
we need to warm it, steady and slow, in the glow
of spiritual serendipity.

A Truer Overview
from the Truest Book

This book has tried, through words and
images,
to suggest the formula or recipe
for calmness,
for watching,
for sagacity, and for peaceful, thoughtful
prayer.
But there is a far better statement
of the necessary ingredients of spiritual
serendipity,
far more beautiful,
far more clear, filled with perfect images and
feelings.

The best way you could finish this book
is to set it aside
and read instead from The Book.

Jesus' Sermon on the Mount, recorded in the book of Matthew, has an almost infinite number of messages and light-giving interpretations. One such message, one way to read and interpret the sermon is as an explanation and set of directions of and for spiritual serendipity. Here, read, and feel some of its paraphrased messages and see how they point us toward the attitudes this book has tried to describe:

1. Build your house on a rock—seek treasures in heaven.
   Build your life
   on strong, righteous goals,
   but once they are set . . .
2. Take less thought for the morrow—don't try to plan
   everything.
   Be more like the lilies
   of the field, the birds of the air—
   spontaneous, sensitive, flexible.
3. The light of the body is the eye—see and watch
   and be filled with light—
   ye are the light of the world!
4. Ask, knock, and answers will open.
   Look for those answers and accept them,
   even if they come in unexpected forms.
5. Do not anger or lust—control the mind
   and think purely and deeply.

6. Turn your other cheek—give your cloak—
   love enemies.

7. Instead of judging, strive to *see*
   and understand.

8. Fast in secret, pray in the closet, let not
   the left hand
   see what the right hand gives—have pure,
   inner motives.

9. Rejoice—even in adversity—
   relish and welcome surprises
   and unexpected turns of all kinds.

10. Don't let salt lose its savor—
    don't let life get boring—
    keep your freshness
    and spontaneity.

11. Be perfect—or at least develop the
    perfect attitude
    of receptivity, acceptance, awareness and
    peace;
    record and remember and implement
    every prompting that the
    Spirit gives.

Perhaps it is through something like spiritual serendipity that the meek inherit the earth, and that the humble in spirit *see* the kingdom of God. Read the greatest Sermon again, directly from its source in Matthew's fifth, sixth, and seventh chapters. Read it as a recipe for spiritual serendipity and rediscover its peaceful wisdom.

Curtain Call

Dusk:
sitting on the front veranda of the 130-year-old
Empire Colonial Galle Face Hotel
in Sri Lanka's capital—Colombo.
Looking north where the grassy expanse
called Galle Green
(filled with kites, brass bands, and watchers)
spreads parallel to the sea.
Our plane leaves late tonight—Air Lanka 515
to London.

This land of Serendipity allows you
to take as much of its name home with you as
you wish,
for free
(the minute it was not free it would not be
serendipity).

I came with the goal of
teaching by writing,
but how often I've paused to
learn by watching.
I've decided
that when we look hard enough

for serendipity
and believe in it,
we get a new sense of what's important
(even a new value system)
as a bonus.

I'll bring this book with me
when I leave Serendip tonight,
finished.
But I know now
that there must be two more books.
A spiritual trilogy.
Because I've realized
(here, even as I wrote)
that there are
three
prevalent, popular, pursued, applauded
desires which
diminish our spirituality,
dilute our joy,
divide our faith:
The desire for *control*,
the desire for *ownership*,
the desire for *independence*—
their prickly, rigid, self-directedness
works against the softer flow of the spirit.
Their walls block the bridges;
their mirrors obscure the windows.

We should seek the guidance of serendipity
rather than the tyranny of control,

the freedom of stewardship
rather than the bondage of ownership,
the linkage of synergy
rather than the isolation of independence.

Do you see the need for book II and book III? We live in an age when it is common and even popular to seek spirituality, yet we cling to three perceptions and paradigms that are spirituality's antidotes. Control is fine as an element of self-discipline; ownership is great as an economic principle; independence is important as a part of personal responsibility.

But as pervasive *attitudes*, each becomes dulling, manipulative, isolating, and drains away the power and energy of connected, interdependent spirituality.

We seek to *control* everything when real spirituality is lodged in letting the spirit control us—in noticing the beauty and opportunity of circumstance, in finding good currents instead of swimming upstream, in seeking and accepting *guidance* from our ideas, our impressions, and our insights—in becoming sagacious enough to find the joy of spontaneity and inspiration, the adventure of the unexpected, the attitude of *spiritual serendipity*.

We seek *ownership* (which, as a paradigm, always brings with it envy and jealousy or conceit and pride) when true spirituality is obtained from understanding that we own nothing and

God owns all, from seeking, instead, treasures of heaven, from adopting the attitude of *spiritual stewardship*.

We seek extreme forms of independence, when real spirituality is logged in dependence on God and on His spirit, in learning from, magnifying, and combining with other people, in operating from the attitude of *spiritual synergy*.

The best alternative attitude to control
is
spiritual serendipity.
The best replacement paradigm for ownership
is
spiritual stewardship.
The best adjusted approach for independence
is
spiritual synergy.

One down, two to go.

a f t e r w o r d

Applications
and Promises

This book wants to end
as it began—with promises.
Hopefully we have made a circle that captures
the ideas necessary
to make the promises look more accessible in
the Afterword
than they did in the Foreword.
Recall the promises back on pages 41–42
and,
based on the pages between there and here,
think for a moment about the *applications*
of spiritual serendipity—
about the benefits that come from being
watchful and prayerful
and using the resulting calm, receptive
serendipity
in each facet of our lives.

1 In Our Work

Spiritual serendipity relaxes us, reduces stress;
helps us find adventure in the day-to-day
possibilities
and opportunity in the small unexpected,
lets us start seeing creative solutions and
cultivating ideas
and lateral-thinking approaches.
Even if your work is, by nature, very routine,
spiritual serendipity will allow you to see and
appreciate
small things about
people and ideas and beauty and situations.
We should realize that serendipity and routine
are mutually exclusive.
Then we should choose serendipity.

I once had a business associate who wrote me
a letter containing his philosophy: "Try never
to be surprised. If you are surprised, it shows
you're not a very good anticipator or planner
and your business life will be unpredictable and
constantly upsetting. Act, don't react, because
we're all judged by what *we* make happen. Learn
to control the people and things around you."

I recently sent him an alternative approach

with parallel wording: "Try to find surprises
every day. If you're never surprised it shows
you're not a very good watcher and your business life will be dull and consistently boring.
Learn to respond as well as to act, because the
very measure of our mortality is how we respond to the things that happen to us. Learn to
control yourself."

It is possible to go to work with two minds:
One is for making the list, the quota, the
deadline, the deal.
The other for noticing the needs,
the opportunities,
the beauty and the humor.
We can write the first, in future tense,
on the left
and write the second, in past tense, on the right.

We can live both sides,
blend them, balance them, be them both.
In addition to our goals and mission statements,
we can learn to rely on nudges, impressions,
and
the spiritual sixth sense
to deal with the ongoing questions of work,
to know what, when, where, and how . . .
to succeed both at getting and at giving.
To our ability to work and plan
we can add our ability to watch and pray.

2 In Our Families

Spiritual serendipity helps us see our spouses
and children
more clearly and more individually
so we can spot their needs and
share their joys.

Children are not lumps of clay and we are not
sculptors.
Children are seedlings and we are gardeners.
Each seedling is unique,
needing a particular kind of
watering, nurturing, cultivating.
Our job is not to change their species
but to make them the best of what each
already is.
We know by watching.
Spiritual serendipity also helps us keep
the essential element and energy of humor
in our families and relationships,
and the excitement of flexibility and fun . . .
and it reminds us that our priorities are our
children,
not our plans.

I recall one evening when the "plan" was an
early dinner to allow time for a family activity

before the younger children's bedtime. But the junior high boy was late getting home because he'd had to start over on his crafts project at school which was due tomorrow. It would have been easy to get mad at him except for his look of excitement and pride. He'd learned to use the band saw. He'd discovered a new interest, a new skill. It had been so exciting to him that he'd cut his piece of wood after making only one quick measurement, ruined his project, and had to start over. On his second try everything worked out fine, except that redoing the project made him two hours late getting home. Our late dinner was spent in a discussion that applied the principle of "measure twice, build once" to many different aspects of life. Then since it was late, we all went for ice cream in our pajamas. Nothing went as planned, yet everything turned out *better*.

In a world where the most common
parenting methods
are manipulation
and where we too often push our kids
to become extensions of our own egos,
it is such a relief to adopt a parenting attitude
that is based more on watching
than on winning,
more on feeling than on fighting,
and more on "consulting" and communicating

than on controlling and coercing.
We can draw on a higher power for the higher challenge
of raising children.
We, their finite parents, can ask for help
from their infinite parent.
And with spouse or partner
the surprise and spontaneity
we once called courtship
can now be called marriage serendipity.

3 In Giving Service in the Community or the Church

Spiritual serendipity makes us more
people-oriented,
more *aware* of feelings, needs, opportunities.
This empathy makes service meaningful
rather than mechanical.
God, who knows the needs of all men,
can reveal some of them to you,
and allow you the joy of being His instrument
in meeting them.

"What do you pray for each day?" I remember the question from a teacher of a particularly memorable Sunday school class. She got some standard answers: for safety, for health, for friends and family.

Then she intrigued us all by saying that there was one thing that we would receive every time we prayed for it . . . and that the answers would give us a new level of interest and joy in life.

She let our anticipation build for a moment and then told us that the "always answered" prayer was for opportunities to help or serve others. "Ask for that," she said, "and then *watch*. God will put opportunities in front of you and in each one you will both give joy to someone and find joy for yourself."

The quality of other-awareness and empathy
is both the precipitator and the result of
serendipity.
Service is an exercise in empathy,
and empathy is another word
for the awareness that opens up
channels of inspiration about who needs what
and provides
a million entry points for serendipity.

4 In Leisure and Play

With spiritual serendipity
there is always something to do
even when there's nothing to do.
We see more possibilities, challenges, options,
feel more interests and emotions,
and live longer in the same amount of time.

I remember one particularly beautiful spring day—sunny, bright, beautiful in every way until I looked at the calendar: April 15—income tax day. But, still, I remember thinking, "If I can finish this tax return during the day we can get out and do something relaxing this evening."

But what a day, what a fresh, steady breeze, and what an idea from the six- and eight-year-olds who see kite flying as the ultimate fun.

Figures can be written and subtracted and added after dark, but kites can't be flown. What a day, what a sight to watch the children's eyes dance like their kites, and what a warm memory to carry me through the dark late hours of figuring income tax. (And how lucky that the post office stays open until midnight.)

When asked why we vacation, play, recreate,
we say, "To release, to unwind, to relax."
The same answers could be used
for the question,
"Why serendipity?"
Serendipity is peaceful awareness
and enlightened insights.
Through it, we can
maximize the pleasure and renewal that
leisure is for.

There are a lot of applications
of spiritual serendipity,
a lot of reasons for wanting the quality,
but the reasons all telescope, umbrella, and
fold down
into one word and one reason:
The word is *joy*
and the reason is *progress*
and serendipity is the discovered path
winding along the unending, ever-climbing
ridge
that leads to both.

a s s i s t a n c e

Some people come to the end
of a book they've come to believe in
and ask
"How?"
They say "Thanks for the textbook
but where is the workbook?"
As it turns out, there is a workbook
for spiritual serendipity
in the form of a larger book and an audio
seminar,
both called *Lifebalance*.

It took me and Linda twenty years of writing
to reach the conclusion that what we really
wanted to say (and what we really wanted
to have) was *balance:* Balance between work,
family, and personal needs; balance between
structure and spontaneity, balance between relationships and achievements. We tried to understand and explain all three kinds of balance
in the book *Lifebalance*, published by Simon &
Schuster.

That book is very much about serendipity,
but very little about spiritual serendipity. This
book can be thought of as the spiritual supple-

ment to that one (or that can be thought of as the secular supplement to this one).

Lifebalance, however, comes with some things that this book doesn't. It has step-by-step *methods* and suggests life-pattern-changing *habits*. And it "fits together" with an eight-session Lifebalance seminar (each session consisting of an audio tape, a workbook, and a set of "anti-planners," which *teach* the steps involved in obtaining balance and developing serendipity).

One final thought: I've tried to make this a spiritual book but not a religious one. I felt this was important because the principles of spiritual serendipity are true (and usable) for people of any religion—or of no religion. Still, there are those who inquire about my own personal religious beliefs. For them I have written a book called *The Wrappings and the Gifts*. It is available by calling either of the numbers below:

- To ask questions about any aspect of serendipity, lifebalance, or the author's broader beliefs . . . or about membership in HOMEBASE, an international organization of over 100,000 parents who work cooperatively to implement the ideas and directions suggested by the Eyres' books, call (801) 581-0112.
- To simply order books, anti-planners, or the eight-part Lifebalance seminar, call (800) 772-4859.

index

achievements, 102–3, 104, 111–12
advertising, 122
alpha-state, 163
anti-planner, 125, 196–98
"Ask and Answer" (poem), 156–60
asking, 164, 173–76, 200, 212
  definition of, 137, 145
  for the feeling, 183
  for opportunities to give service, 183–84
  see also prayer
attitude, 13–14, 22, 131–32, 141–42, 204
  of awe, 182–83
  of good fortune, 100
  of "nothingness," 181–84, 190
  positive mental, 24, 26–27, 100, 102, 111, 114, 115, 131, 152
  of sagacity, 186–87
attitudinal awareness, 141–42
awareness, 100, 114, 141–42, 151
  mental, 99
  self-, 184
  sensual, 98–99, 141
  spiritual, 141
awe, attitude of, 182–83

balance, need for, 114–15, 149, 215
beauty, 42, 98, 101, 103, 116
  missed, 110
belief, 125, 144–45
  in God, 20–21, 26, 38, 40, 105; *see also* spiritual serendipity
blessings, 188–89
boredom, 110
Boswell, James, 49
brain, hemispheres of, 25, 102, 112, 113
brain waves, 163
bridges, 101–13, 129, 146–51, 203
British Museum, 55–56
Buddhism, 131, 132
Byron, George Gordon, Lord, 48

Celestine Prophecy, The (Redfield), 125
cellular phones, 192
change, prayer for, 176
Chesterton, G. K., 174, 181
Chetwood, Will, 55
children, 179, 209–11
Christianity, 132, 147
church, 21
  service to, 211–12

coincidences, 125

Colderidge, Samuel Taylor, 48

commitment, 145

community, service to, 211–12

concern, 98

confidence, 181–82

confirmation, 172
    definition of, 137–38
    prayer for, 176–81
    stupor of thought vs., 138, 177, 178, 179–81

control, 24, 131, 203, 204, 205, 207

Conway, H. S., 49

cummings, e. e., 36

"Curious, Calm Capacity, A" (poem), 107–9

"Curtain Call" (poem), 202–4

disappointment, 109

discipline, 101, 102, 107, 129

discoveries, 111

"Double Exposure" (poem), 101

Elder, 194–95

emotional serendipity, 113–14

empathy, 120, 139, 184, 211–12

England, 55–56, 117–19, 191–92

enjoying the journey now, 111, 121

exercises, 117–25
    enjoy the journey now, 121
    have faith, 125
    hold Sunday sessions, 121–22, 123
    make goals without plans, 123

set up split-page planning, 124

simplify and set standards, 122–23

slow down, 120

welcome surprises, 120–21

write poetry, 119

experience, life as, 126–27

faith, 100, 125, 146, 161, 181, 183
    meanings of, 144–45
    self-reliance vs., 149–51

families, 209–11

fasting, 178, 188–89, 201

fatigue, 110

Fleming, Sir Alexander, 23

flexibility, 42, 101, 102–3, 104, 107, 111, 112, 115, 129, 172, 200

foghorn, 24

Fouks, Robert, 24

Friedman, Milton, 104

frustrations, 24, 41, 110, 170

gifts, 190
    definition of, 136

glass, 24

goals, 102, 103–4, 106, 107, 115, 116, 122, 126–28, 143, 153–60, 196–97, 200
    definition of, 100
    structure vs. spontaneity in, 109–13
    without plans, 123, 126–27, 169–73

God, belief in, 20–21, 26, 38, 40, 105; see also spiritual serendipity

Goldwater, Barry, 104

good fortune, 98, 127
    definition of, 99–100

Goodyear, Charles, 23–24
gothic novel, 48
gratitude, 188–90
guidance, 22, 38, 137, 139,
    145, 150, 168–96, 204;
    see also asking; prayer;
    watching for guidance
Gupta Dynasty, Indian, 55

Hartford, Earl of, 51
Heathrow airport, 117–18
HOMEBASE, 216
homesickness, 191–92
Honour, Hugh, 48–50
humility, 181–84, 190

independence, 203, 204,
    205
India, 55
insight, 98, 114, 136, 155,
    163, 184, 192
inspiration, 136, 174–75
    definition of, 137
inventions, serendipitous,
    23–24
irritation, 109

James, General Epistle of, 25,
    152–53, 155, 156, 157
Jesus Christ, 146–49, 153,
    156, 165, 183
    opposing qualities of, 148
    Sermon on the Mount of,
    200–202

Keats, John, 48
Kennedy, John F., 105

Lao Tzu, 148
leisure, 213–14
Lewis, C. S., 183
life, quality of, 98
life as experience, 126–27

Lifebalance (Eyre and Eyre),
    129–30, 215–16
Lifebalance seminar, 215, 216
lifestyle, 98
light, 161, 200
    prayer for, 176
"Light and Guidance"
    (poem), 138–43
Limbaugh, Rush, 104
Lincoln, Abraham, 175
lists, 100, 101, 124
    of blessings, 189
love, 139, 190, 201
luck, 97, 98, 99

Macaulay, Thomas Babing-
    ton, Baron, 48–49
Mann, Horace, 47
marriage, 211
Marx, Karl, 55
materialism, 33, 98, 122–23
Matthew, Gospel according
    to, 200–202
Maxwell, Neal, 183
meditation, 105, 131, 162, 163
mental awareness, 99
mental effort, 145, 183
mental serendipity, 42,
    97–128, 143
    application of, 109–15
    as bridge, 101–13, 146
    components of, 97–100,
    117–19, 127–28, 186
    development of, 116–25
    exercises for, 117–25
    forms of, 114
    motto of, 115–19, 131, 161
    sources of, 113–17
Middle Ages, 21
might, prayer for, 176
modern world, 31–43
    plight of, 31–35
    problem of, 35–39

mottoes, 113
  "Watch and Pray," 161–62,
    164–67, 173, 206, 208
  "Watch and Think," 115–
    19, 131, 161

"nothingness," attitude of,
  181–84, 190
nudge notes, 193–96
nudges (promptings), spiritual, 136, 137, 151,
  191–96, 201, 208

observation, 102, 103, 114
offense, 110
opportunities, 98, 100, 101,
  103, 116, 141, 155, 184
  to give service, 183–84
  missed, 109
optimism, 100
ownership, 34, 98, 122–23,
  203, 204–5

paradigms, 13–14, 20–22,
  144, 190, 204
Peck, M. Scott, 142
penicillin, 23
Persia, 55–94
Phoenicians, 24
planning, 24–25, 33, 99, 100,
  101, 102, 104, 107, 114,
  138, 152–60, 200
  in families, 209–10
  goals without, 123, 126–27,
    169–73
  split-page, see split-page
    planning
  structure vs. spontaneity in,
    109–13
  at work, 207–8
play, 213–14
poetry, 119
politics, 103, 104, 105

positive mental attitude, 24,
  26–27, 100, 102, 111,
  114, 115, 131, 152
Pratt, Parley, 139–40
prayer, 164–84, 201, 211–12
  attitude of "nothingness"
    in, 181–84
  for change, 176
  for confirmation, 176–81
  for guidance, 168–84
  for light, 176
  for might, 176
  in Sunday sessions, 169–73
  watching and, 161–62,
    164–67, 173, 206, 208
  see also asking
promptings (nudges), spiritual, 136, 137, 151,
  191–96, 201, 208

radar, 24
Reagan, Ronald, 104, 180
Redfield, James, 125
relationships, 34, 102, 110,
  111, 116, 156, 184,
  209–11
restlessness, 110
Robards, Jason, 154
Robertson, Pat, 104
Roentgen, Wilhelm, 23
rubber, vulcanized, 23–24

sagacity, 98, 100, 104, 127,
  135, 167, 204
  definition of, 99
  in watching for guidance,
    186–87
Sassanian Empire, Persian, 55
schedules, 99, 100
  see also planning
science, 21
Scott, Walter, 48
self-awareness, 184

self-consciousness, 108
self-help, 19, 26, 131, 144, 152
selfishness, 184
self-reliance, 149–51
sensitivity, 102, 103–4, 112, 115, 117–19, 139, 200
sensual awareness, 98–99, 141
Serendip, Sri Lanka as, 11–14, 23, 55
  see also "Three Princes of Serendip, The"
serendipity, 15–16, 23–27
  adjective form of, 98
  definitions of, 5, 11, 23, 97–100, 112, 127
  emotional, 113–14
  in inventions, 23–24
  origin of term, 11, 12, 16, 25–26, 51, 52, 97–98, 99–100, 127–28, 130
  social, 113
  see also mental serendipity; spiritual serendipity
Serendipity Singers, 112
Sermon on the Mount, 200–202
service, 183–84
  to community or church, 211–12
silver linings, 186–87
sixth sense, 144, 208
  definition of, 136
slowing down, 120
social serendipity, 113
soul, 129, 141, 165
spirit, 137, 163
  definition of, 135–36
Spirit, 137, 139, 141, 163–64
  definition of, 136
spiritual awareness, 141
spiritual rebirth, 18–19

spiritual serendipity, 35, 102, 128, 129–32, 135–216
  as bridge, 146–51
  components of, 135–51
  definitions of, 5, 138–43
  development of, 164–67
  in families, 209–11
  in giving service to community or church, 211–12
  higher realm of, 152–62
  in leisure and play, 213–14
  as paradigm, 13–14, 20–22, 39–43, 144, 190, 204
  promises of, 39–43, 206
  ramifications of, 143–45
  Sermon on the Mount and, 200–202
  source of, 163–64
  at work, 207–8
  see also prayer; watching for guidance
split-page planning, 124, 130
  anti-planner in, 125, 196–98
  with nudge notes, 193–96
spontaneity, 42, 101, 102–13, 115, 129, 200, 201, 204
Sri Lanka, 31–32, 196, 202
  meaning of name, 31
  as Serendip, 11–14, 23, 55
standards, 122–23
Steward, Reverend Mr., 51
stewardship, 20n, 34, 204, 205
  of time, 172
stress, 41, 110, 207
structure, 101, 102–13, 129
stupor or thought, 138, 177, 178, 179–81
Sunday sessions, 121–22, 123, 153, 196–97
  goals without plans in, 169–73

surprises, 100, 102, 107, 111, 115, 116, 123, 201
  unwelcome, 110
  welcomed, 120–21
  at work, 207–8
synergy, 20n, 146, 204, 205

Tanner, Elder, 154–55
Taoism, 148
Thackeray, William Makepeace, 49
Thanksgiving traditions, 189
Thousand Clowns, A, 154
"Three Princes of Serendip, The," 12, 25, 32, 47, 52, 53–95, 97, 98
  Aphoenicius in, 60–61, 63, 77, 79, 83, 85–87, 91
  British Museum's copy of, 55–56
  Death to Dragons formula-poem in, 59, 60, 61, 63, 66, 69, 74, 77, 82, 86–87, 91
  Diliramma/Padmini in, 69–72, 76–77, 85–86, 88–90
  Drakir, the three-headed serpent in, 78–80, 82, 83–84, 85
  great hand in, 68, 72, 75–76
  great imperial bird in, 57, 62, 75, 79, 83–84, 87–88, 90–91, 92
  King Behram in, 61, 62–72, 78, 80–82, 84–85, 86, 88–90
  King Jafer in, 57–59, 91
  lessons to be learned from, 93–94
  lost camel in, 61–63

  Mirror of Justice in, 67–68, 72–73, 75–76, 78, 80
  monastery in, 72–74
  peacock feathers in, 74, 79–80, 85
  princes tested in, 58–59
  sea dragons in, 57–58, 59, 60, 63, 90–91
  Standard of Power in, 78, 82, 83
  under-earth demon in, 73–74
time, 27, 33, 110
  stewardship of, 172
time management, 24, 26, 27, 115, 131
tuning in, 137, 141, 191, 193

"Umbrella and a Lens, An" (poem), 115–17

vacation trips, structured vs. spontaneous, 109–11
Vakatakas dynasty, Indian, 55

Walpole, Horace, 32, 43, 47–52, 55–56
  accomplishments of, 47–48
  background of, 47
  "serendipity" coined by, 11, 12, 16, 25–26, 51, 52, 97–98, 99–100, 127–28, 130
Walpole, Sir Robert, 47
Washington, D.C., 179–80
"Watch and Pray" (motto), 161–62, 164–67, 173, 206, 208
"Watch and Think" (motto), 115–19, 131, 161
watching for guidance, 185–96
  fasting and, 178, 188–89
  gratitude in, 188–90

sagacity in, 186–87
spiritual promptings in,
    136, 137, 151, 191–96,
    201
split-page planning in,
    193–96
Watson, Robert, 24
White House conference on
    children and parents,
    179–80

Williams, Gilly, 49
wisdom, 98
Wordsworth, William, 55
work, 207–8
Wrappings and the Gifts, The
    (Eyre), 216
Writers and Their Work (Hon-
    our), 48–50, 51

X ray, 23

THE EARLY YEARS OF

the Les Paul Legacy

1915–1963

THE EARLY YEARS OF
the
Les
Paul
Legacy
1915–1963

by Robb Lawrence

Hal Leonard Books • New York
An imprint of Hal Leonard Corporation

ISBN: 978-0-634-04861-6

Published by:
Hal Leonard Corporation
7777 W. Bluemound Road
P.O. Box 13819
Milwaukee, WI 53213

 Library of Congress Cataloging-in-Publication Data

Lawrence, Robb.
 The early years of the Les Paul legacy, 1915-1963 / by Robb Lawrence. -- 1st ed.
   p. cm.
 Includes index.
 ISBN 978-0-634-04861-6
1. Electric guitar--History. 2. Gibson, inc.--History. 3. Paul, Les. I. Title.
 ML1015.G9L39 2008
 787.87092--dc22

                        2008009624

Printed in U.S.A.

First Edition

Visit Hal Leonard Online at **www.halleonard.com**

Contents

vi   FOREWORD

viii   PREFACE

x   ACKNOWLEDGEMENTS

1   CHAPTER 1
Les Paul — The Man, the Musician, and the Wizard

49   CHAPTER 2
Gibson Experiments with the Solid-Body Guitar

65   CHAPTER 3
The "Goldtop" Les Paul '52–'53

89   CHAPTER 4
Improved Goldtop Les Paul Models '53–'57

129   CHAPTER 5
The Les Paul Amplifier

141   CHAPTER 6
The Les Paul Custom Models '54–'61

179   CHAPTER 7
The Les Paul Junior, TV, Special,
Melody Maker, and EB-0

213   CHAPTER 8
The Sunburst Les Paul Standard Models '58–'60

261   CHAPTER 9
Sculptured Les Paul Models
and the SG Guitar '60–'63

280   INTERMISSION

282   INDEX

Foreword

When I was a kid, piano was number one. The guitar was absolutely a rarity, a nice little thing to have sitting in the corner. What held it back was volume. In Waukesha, I was leading two lives: one was electronics and one was music. And I knew from way back that the two had to go together.

As time went on, the guitar—not the piano—became number one. I knew that the electric guitar was going to be a very powerful instrument. This changed the world.

There was a great marriage between Mary Ford's singing and my guitar music. The two combined were both warm and comfortable. The sound of the solid guitar was so different than what the public was used to that it caught on immediately. It was beautiful and had a natural guitar sound, but it was powerful. You could hold it, hug it, and love it. That was the plan.

During the late sixties I grew restless after a self-imposed retirement, eager to share my new ideas with Gibson and the world. Within a few years, thanks to Bud Eastman at *Guitar Player* magazine, Robby Lawrence visited me while he was researching the history of American guitars.

Robb had a lot of enthusiasm, lots of thoughts and dreams. He wanted really to get down to the nitty-gritty—what made this, what made that, why did they do this, why did you do that. He asked a lot of good questions. He loved to take good pictures and write good things. When he came here, it seemed to me that he knew what he wanted, what his dreams were—and he was going to fulfill those dreams. And I think it's great. I think it's a good idea and proved to be right.

His passion piqued my interest, too, and our friendship grew. Over the years, various significant events took place, and we shared loads of adventures. I advised him to hold his material back till the time was right. And now is the time.

CNN once asked me, "How does it feel to have your fingerprints everywhere on the earth?" I responded that it's beyond believing, it's beyond wishing, it's beyond anything you can imagine, that I would be lucky enough to have that. It's something very special to be able to have a number one instrument that is so well-liked.

Les Paul guitars are selling as much in Caribou, Alaska as they are in China or Russia or anywhere you want to go. And when you lay it out, you do this and you do that and finally when the thing unravels, well all of a sudden your dream comes true. I just believe that's what makes you do it. You do it because it makes you happy.

And I insist on happiness. Everyone acquires it in their own way. Mine happens to be that I'm terribly pleased with the way my life has turned out. I love music and I love people. I want to play for people. I want to do it for others.

This book, with my blessings, is a lasting contribution to the world of electric guitars. It tells about things that you wouldn't normally know about. And I think that's important. Here is the real story of my life and the Gibson solid-body guitar that bears my name.

Les Paul

Preface

I would like to share with you the wonderful world of Les Paul, the man who truly changed popular music and the guitar world. This book and its companion, *The Modern Era of the Les Paul Legacy, 1968–2007*, on Les and Gibson's Les Paul solid-body guitar have been quite an undertaking. My odyssey began in the fall of 1967, when I bought my first Les Paul guitar, and continues to this day. I first met and interviewed Les on July 19th, 1972. Through the years, it has been a joy to know the man and treasure the instrument he endorses. We've been through many good times, seeing all the great shows with many amazing guitar players. We've driven across the country together. For a time, I lived with Les, his son Bobby, and Wally Kamin in Mahwah, NJ. All in all, it has been a treasure chest of memorable experiences. Since we met, Les has taken me under his wing and shared so much, I can honestly say he is one of my true mentors. It has been an honor and a privilege to be his dear friend, West Coast guitar tech, and devoted fan.

The author, La Jolla, CA, fall of 1971

From the beginning, my vision of these books has been an epic one: full-color, beautifully illustrated coffee table books that celebrate Les Paul—encompassing the man, the musician and showman, the electronic genius, and the marvelous marriage of his talents—and include an in-depth look at the fine tradition of Gibson's solid-body guitars.

While writing the first byline for *Guitar Player* magazine's "Rarebird" column during the early seventies, I photographed many guitars and interviewed scores of people, honing my skills. While gathering more information on the rich history of American guitars, I eventually began to realize the enormity of these projects. There weren't any full-color books on this popular instrument, yet there were multitudes of guitar players all over the world. I felt it was important to do the subject justice and wait till the time was right. This meant creating in-depth scholarly books that take years to research and bring to publication.

Though others eventually came out in the seventies and eighties, none were produced like a great coffee table book, lavishly designed with full-color photography. Not until a series of large-format British books on myriad popular musical subjects were produced, would marketing these beautiful books become a reality. My future works would be specially geared for our favorite subject, the rich lore of American guitar history. It is one of the most important symbols of Western culture and deserving of such a treatment.

Luckily, I got out there just in time to travel the country and interview virtually all the important people behind these instruments. This included inventors, craftsmen, salesmen, and many musicians who built, sold, and played them—those who created the music and the guitar's mystique we admire. All this naturally goes hand-in-hand with the evolution of both the guitars and the music. Inevitably, many old-timers that I interviewed and photographed have since passed, including the Dopyera family, Mr. Rickenbacher, the Beauchamp family, Paul Barth, Leo Fender, Doc Kauffman, Freddie Tavares, Semie Moseley, Jimmy D'Aquisto, Julius Bellson, Seth Lover, Walt Fuller, Nick Lucas, Roy Smeck, Alvino Rey, Barney Kessel, and some others that I had the great pleasure to get to know and to whom I am deeply indebted.

These books on Les Paul's Legacy are my gift to the world, for all to enjoy and treasure. I hope everyone gets as much out of them as I did in creating them.

Robb Lawrence
2008

Acknowledgements

First of all, I dedicate this book to its namesake, Les Paul, to the legacy and spirit of Orville Gibson, and to all the fans of their tremendous solid-body guitar.

Special thanks and recognition go to many people who have been instrumental in my career as a guitarist, guitar enthusiast, and writer. This book is the result of 35 years of guitar research, photography, and many memorable experiences with Les Paul and our friends. There are many people I thank for their kind permission to photograph their guitar collections and those who shared with me their recollections of how Les Paul and the Gibson solid-body influenced them.

I would like to thank the following people for their guiding light and inspiration: in the beginning, John Dopyera and apprentice Dave Flood, for sparking my interest in American guitar history; guitar heroes Nokie Edwards, Bob Spickard, and Brian Carmen; Les Paul, for sharing so much with me all of these years; my parents, Bob and Sue, for their unending love, support, and understanding to see these guitar history projects come to fruition. I will be forever indebted to: my grandparents, for their spiritual guidance and setting an example of fortitude and dynamic lifestyles; Bill and Rosemary Adams, for encouraging their son Anthony and me to create our masterpieces in life; Bud Eastman and Jim Crockett of *Guitar Player* magazine, for getting me started with my literary career, writing the "Rarebird" column in the early seventies; Merald Kirkman and Barbara, for their gift of transcribing early interviews; Beverly O'Daniels, for guiding me to learn to write and edit properly during the early eighties.

I must express gratitude to my first San Diego guitar buddies who were there when we discovered the forgotten Les Paul guitars during the mid-sixties: Mike Duerr; Paul Cowie; Mike Sterling; Greg Collier; and Peter Webster, for my first Les Paul. I am grateful to my friends Jim and Joyce Peterson and Jonathan Glasier at La Jolla music where I taught guitar when the Les Paul model re-emerged.

Much appreciation goes to the dedicated folks, past and present, at Gibson in Kalamazoo who shared their time and vivid memories of how it was: Julius Bellson; Ted McCarty and family; Seth Lover; Walt Fuller; Kenny Kilman; Tiny Timbrell; John Levy; Aaron Porter; Jim Deurloo; and Chuck Burge.

Deserving of recognition for their invaluable help are all the great folks in Nashville who carry on the fine tradition of Gibson instruments: Henry Juszkiewicz; Walter Carter; Mike McGuire; Rick Gembar; Al Carness; and Jim "Hutch" Hutchinson.

Many thanks go to a true Gibsonite, Mitch Holder, for his gracious input, catalogs, factory photos, and constant inspiration. I must mention the true genius of the late Ted Greene, who was behind me in so many ways spiritually with the guitar and its history. I need to thank: Les Paul's other West Coast protégé, guitarist Del Kacher (Casher) and his wife Eicho, for their invaluable input on Les's career, interviews, and our great studio parties on Les Paul's birthdays; and fellow rental, tech, and guitar enthusiast Andy Brauer.

There are a few photographers and players I want to mention who kindly filled in some spaces with concert/portraits, cover photos, and personal guitar photos: Neil Zlozower; Martin Garrett Miller; Mike Slubowski; and Elliot Michael (Rumble Seat).

The gracious guitar store owners who shared their inventory and private collections include: Norm, Marlene and Jordan Harris (Norm's Rare Guitars); Dan Duehren and David Swartz (Norm's and California Vintage); George Gruhn (GTR and Gruhn's Guitars); Matty Umanov; Prune Music; Paul Herman; Ray Scheer; Larry Thomas; Dave DiMartino; Dave Weiderman; and Drew Berlin and Dave Belzer (Guitar Center L.A.).

For the many photographs done at numerous memorable guitar shows by Texas/4 Amigos, I would like to thank the kind courtesy of Larry Briggs and family; Dave Crocker; and John Brinkmann and family.

The fellow player/collectors who so kindly let me photograph their beloved collections: Steve Soest; Bill Feil; Dave Amato; Rich Stillwell; Albert Molinaro; Lou Gatanas; Mac Yasuda; Barbara Sutherland; Billy Gibbons; Twiggs Lyndon; Barney Roach; Erhard Bochen and family; Alphonse Baumann; Laurence Juber; Warwick Rose; Mike and Jim Tilley; Bernard Ayling; Joe Ganzler; and Jim Gentry. Forgive me if I left any of you out!

For their guitars, constant enthusiasm, and companionship, it is most fitting to acknowledge the following dear friends: Albert and Karen Lee; Michael DeTemple; Bobby Zinner; Richard Fortune; Bruce Gary; Jamie James; Warren Klein; David Petrie; Nite Bob; Perry Margoleff; Peter Huggins; and Kim Shaheen. Also, my neighbors who make my life complete: Steve and Cyndi Weinstock; Billy Green Bush; Leo and Lee LePlante; Steven "A.J." Kamont; Will Olvis; Randy Strom; Jim Wiebe; Cat and Tori Castro; Key Francis and Pilar; Caroline Michaels; and Mark Olla. And, of course, the girlfriends who stood by me through the years: Rachel Masters; Susan Simmonds; Diana Madera; Kim Nguyen; Nilita Escobar; and Carol Creekmore.

Many thanks go to pickup specialists Seymour Duncan, Bill Lawrence, and Lindy Fralin.

Fellow writer friends who should be praised include: Tom Wheeler; Andre Duchossoir; George Gruhn; Walter Carter; Paul Day; and Jay Scott. The Les Paul Forum members also played a part with their dialogue of some obscure facts and valued opinions with vintage and modern Les Paul models.

Sincere appreciation to my friends in England, including: Jeff Beck; Alan Rogan; Lee Dickson; Paula Chandler; and John Catto.

I am deeply indebted to the many talented people at Hal Leonard Corporation who have contributed to making this book a reality: Brad Smith; John Cerullo; Richard Slater; Jackie Muth; Linda Nelson; Jana Ranson; and Mark Baker.

I have many fond memories and appreciation for the friends who passed away over the years who truly loved Les Paul guitars and keep the inspiration instilled in my heart: John Cipollina; Link Wray; Michael Bloomfield; Phil Pierangelo; Leo Mehren; Mike Parker; Peter Gibson; and Ralph Perry.

And finally, I would like to thank Les Paul's inside family for so many years of great times: Rusty Paul; Colleen, husband Gary Weiss, and Bobby Paul; Wally Kamin; Joan and Ralph; Wally and Elenore Jones and Gail Bellows; Zeke, Bea, and Suzie Manners; Bob Summers; Greg Corronna; Chris Lentz, Charles Dzuba; and Michael Braunstein.

Thank you all for making this a reality, a book the world can enjoy for many years to come.

Les Paul — The Man, the Musician, and the Wizard

Les Paul — The Man, the Musician and the Wizard

The person we know today as Les Paul is a most creative musical and electronic genius. He virtually launched the entire popular music world into a new dimension of sound after helping to pioneer electric guitar playing, then made a celebrated collaboration with the Gibson guitar company to create the most elegant solid-body guitar ever built.

It all began when Lester William Polsfuss, the second son of George and Evelyn Stutz Polsfuss, was born on June 9, 1915 in Waukesha, Wisconsin. His Prussian paternal grandfather, August Polsfuss, had emigrated from Germany in 1870 and settled near Milwaukee, and soon after, married Henrietta Degler, a nice local farm gal. August had established his own farm near Pewaukee lake in the heart of Wisconsin's Dairyland. Because of the farm's close proximity to the day's popular health spas (the rejuvenating waters were quickly turning the area into the "Saratoga of the West") August earned a lucrative income. By 1881, the couple had welcomed a baby boy named George William Polsfuss.

Waukesha's Arcadian Mineral Springs was one of the more successful water companies that produced local natural soft drinks.

Great ad with a child reaching for the Arcadian ginger ale, a natural mixture that complemented their popular cherry ale.

Sometimes Lester would walk the six long miles along the rail tracks to the beach, "just to make sure I didn't get lost. When I got older, I would play my music out there too." This is Waukesha Beach Hotel, where the electrified T. M. E. R. & L. line ends.

A scene from the popular Waukesha Beach at Pewaukee Lake circa 1907 where many locals rode a special small train out to swim and go boating. In later years when Lester visited, many would also enjoy the added amusement rides.

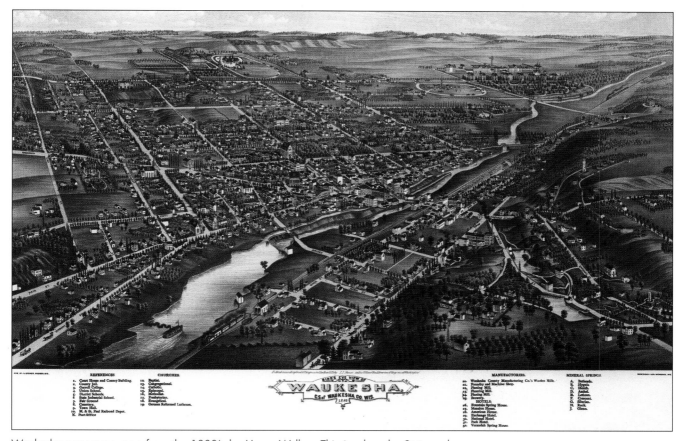

Waukesha panorama map from the 1880's by Henry Wellge. This is when the Stutz and Polsfuss families first arrived to the area. *Courtesy Image Trader and Library of Congress*

Also in 1881, Wendle Stutz arrived from Germany and likewise settled in Pewaukee. Leaving behind the family's livelihood of brewing fine beer, the Stutzes found steady employment in America difficult to find, and barely got by. Wendle's wife, Elizabeth Meyer, tragically died during Evelyn's birth in May of 1888. To help sustain the family, the Stutz offspring had to work, including little "Eva," who as a teen, became a fine seamstress. Fond of the local dances, nineteen-year-old Evelyn met and fell in love with the tall and dashing George Polsfuss in 1907. She was quite attracted to an ambitious fellow like young George, and his whole family. They were married within

"Horeb Spring lends its charm toward making Waukesha the 'Saratoga of the West.' Its waters are free to all and its picturesque pavilion, in a beautiful park devoted to the mineral springs of Wisconsin, is filled with visitors during the summer season." (1906 postcard description)

that same year in Waukesha, the town to which her family had just moved. The newlywed couple had found a nice two-bedroom apartment near her father's home with lots of shiny oak flooring and a big picture window. Soon after, upon Evelyn's persuasion, George agreed to drop the middle "s" in his family name, modifying it to "Polfuss"—although this change was never legally made official.

Life was very good in those days—the Polfusses had plenty of homegrown vegetables from the farm and a natural, healthful lifestyle. In 1908, Ralph—an easygoing baby—was born. Although Evelyn had wanted a little girl, it was Lester who came along in June of 1915. Any second thoughts she'd had about having another boy disappeared when she discovered his creative musical talents. Perhaps due to the German lullabies she sang to him while pregnant, or the many songs she regularly sang while doing house chores, the adorable little red-headed Lester became a singing and dancing prodigy who was performing for Evelyn's friends by the age of three.

Meanwhile, the enterprising George had started a lucrative car repair shop just as the age of automobiles was catching on in America and Europe. George's business savvy was another trait that the young Les picked up on, and which would have a profound impact on his later years. By 1919, George's business expanded to include a cab service, and the Polfusses moved into a beautiful two-story home with a view of the hills and nearby river. Evelyn even got her dream instrument: a player piano with plenty of music rolls of the current tunes. She also helped out with the cab biz and would take little Lester on rides regularly.

One day when Lester was just eight years old, he found himself attentively watching a nearby ditch digger play the harmonica on his lunch break. This thoroughly mystified Lester as he stood in front of the fellow while he played away. When the harmonica player asked Lester what he would like to hear, the shy boy was dumbfounded and speechless. Soon the fellow showed the young boy how to play the harmonica, then actually gave it to him with some important advice. Recalling the incident years later, Les Paul wrote:

"The ditch the men were digging that day held no fascination for me, but I stared in mute admiration at the grizzled laborer playing a battered harmonica during his lunch break. I was in fourth grade then, and I thought: 'If I could only make music like that!' Suddenly the workman offered me the harmonica. 'Go ahead, son, try it.' 'I can't play,' I said. The old man regarded me for a moment. 'Son, you hang onto that mouth organ, and pretty soon you'll have it licked!' Then he added nine words that were the wisest counsel I was ever to have: 'Don't say you can't till you prove you can't.' (*Reader's Digest*, 1957)

When Les brought that harmonica home, Evelyn promptly boiled it clean. As he learned to play it he noticed that the sound of the now water-soaked harp produced a unique bluesy sound. Lester persuaded Evelyn to buy only high-quality harps, to which she complied, since she wanted her son to be the very best. Les practiced constantly (much to his brother and cousin's consternation) and soon won a PTA contest and the admiration of his school chums. He was beginning to get a very good response to his performances for the sidewalk crowds of Waukesha. His audiences thoroughly enjoyed his lively stories and clever tunes, which brought him sizeable tips in those days.

Evelyn's beloved piano was the next thing to assault. He punched extra holes in the player piano scrolls to create new musical parts, which sometimes required that he tape over the bad notes—experiments that would ultimately fuel ideas for future sound recordings. Les even experimented by attempting to run the player piano with

a Hoover vacuum motor, then cleverly put it all back together, to keep the peace.

Although he was initially interested in becoming a piano player, Les was really intrigued after hearing a guitar on his new crystal radio. He then changed his preference for good and became more fascinated with the guitar and banjo. His piano teacher had no idea how talented Les really was, suggesting to the Polfusses that her guitar-distracted student stop his lessons. Lester had other things on his mind!

The Sound Begins

It basically all started in their living room in Waukesha. Young Lester had almost everything he needed to begin his future right at home—a battery-type radio, a wind-up Victrola phonograph, his mom's Kimball player piano, and the telephone. All these fairly recent new technological advancements were right at Les's fingertips. A tinkerer by nature, he would experiment and take almost everything apart to understand its workings. Although his punching holes in the piano rolls didn't go over too well, it proved early on that sound-on-sound wasn't a pipe dream.

Like many of the others who enjoyed radio in those days, Les would spend endless hours scanning the airwaves for distant stations and new music. One of Les's favorite radio stars, and one on whom he patterned his early style, was Deford Bailey, one of the Grand Ole Opry's first black blues harmonica players. Les eventually built his own crude crystal-radio set and proceeded to listen to classic radio shows and the popular barn dance music that filled the radio waves from far and wide.

Les and his buddy Claude Schultz would pal around, getting into mischief as many kids do. One day, Claude loaned Les a large, carved-wood Majestic radio so they could enjoy the great radio broadcasts together—although he figured it wouldn't be long before something radical would happen to it. Les's inquisitive mind led him to take it apart and see how it ticked, too. His electric shop in school wasn't enough to satisfy his budding brilliant mind for electronics. Les always had to build something up and perfect it. He went about acquiring old discarded radio equipment, and spent time at the local radio station learning all he could from their technicians. This soon led to his own pirate basement radio station from which he broadcast locally. Although it could be heard by only a few homes in the neighborhood, still the young announcer spoke through the airwaves as though a seasoned pro. In later years, Les would do the same thing on a bigger scale. Of course, the young budding wizard was

(Above) A young Lester, with his new Sears Troubadour guitar and harmonica rack, all dressed up in the white outfit purchased for him by his mom. He even used a plain Hawaiian G string for bending instead of a taut-wound string.

(Above) Pie Plant Pete (Claud J. Moye) & Bashful Joe (Joseph Troyan) both signed this *Favorite Old Time Songs* book cover when it was new, circa 1945. Artist Claud (also known as Asparagus Joe for his later Champion releases), during the twenties, sang and played old-time country guitar with a harmonica neck brace he called the "two-cylinder cob crusher." He was with the WLS radio station in Chicago starting in 1927 and traveled with their troupe nearby. A few years later Lester would go to see him, which led to his first guitar lessons. The young student even mimicked his sailor attire in the beginning. Claud and Joe had their memorable duo together from 1936 to 1947 with many great performances and radio shows in their day. Note the beautiful prewar 000-28 Martin.

(Right) Supertone recording of "Waiting for the Railroad Train" penned by the yodeling Pie Plant Pete.

(Far right) Sheet music with a teenaged Lester, who originally posed with Rube Tronson's group. This photo was taken much earlier, before the WJJD radio performances.

hearing the popular banjo and guitar players regularly on the radio. Les now wanted to get into the strings! At this point Claude says that he gave Les a crude, broken up guitar without any working parts—or strings—but nothing happened with it.

Meanwhile, Claud J. Moye, a.k.a. "Pie Plant Pete," was a local favorite that Les and Evelyn would go see regularly. Claud did the Chicago-based WLS station's comedic hill-billy routines. The two met, and Claud could instantly tell of Lester's great interest in the guitar. So he handed Les his guitar and wrote out a guitar lesson for him to study. He took Lester under his wing as a young pupil when he saw how earnest and eager Les was.

Soon it was time to add a guitar from the Sears and Roebuck catalog for $3.95, paid for from his paper route. When that cardboard box arrived with Lester's first guitar inside, Evelyn exclaimed, "Your guitar has arrived!" He quickly pulled it out, causing one string to catch the edge of the box, plucking a note. His Mom came running into the living room from the kitchen exclaiming, "Lester! You're playing great already!"

Les began playing local events with Pie Plant Pete and picking up some valuable tips. Since Les, with his freckled face and red hair, was now playing with Pie Plant Pete, Evelyn dubbed him "Red Hot Red," and his musical career had begun! The guitar was truly his calling; within a few years, he was playing country hillbilly music with his guitar and harmonica just like Pie Plant Pete. Les went one step further and fashioned a swing-able harp bracket that he could flip with his chin to get another key. He practiced music all the time and rarely joined his school buddies' activities. Guitar was an all-consuming thing for Lester (just as it was and is for many of us readers!).

5

During this time, Nick Lucas had become the world's first popular guitarist. Also known as the "Crooning Troubadour," who sang beautifully and played snappy flat-picked guitar runs, Nick was, to many, the first guitar "hero," and inspired many young guitarists during the 1920s.

Shortly thereafter, another soaring guitar star was making the airwaves in a big way. The incomparable jazz great Eddie Lang created rich, harmonic chord structures and fantastic solo passages that took the guitar to new heights. Les and many others idolized these popular masters who championed the guitar throughout the country and abroad.

"Red Hot Red" started playing at the Lions Club and drive-in theaters, making up to $35 a week. Many of his gigs were outdoors. In order to be heard, he built his own little public address system and a primitive electric guitar. This consisted of a vertical phonograph pickup stuck into the guitar by the bridge and plugged into his radio for an amplifier.

(Above) The second recording of the original Nick Lucas tune, which is actually one of the very first guitar-solo records ever recorded! "Pickin' the Guitar" and "Teasing the Frets" (2536A/B) on Brunswick Records, circa October of 1923. The first version was recorded for Pathe Actuelle in July of 1922. By May of 1929, Lucas recorded his two-million seller recording of "Tip-Toe Thru' the Tulips" for the first *Gold Diggers of Broadway* film.

(Left) Here's my first portrait (circa 1973) of the late Nick Lucas with his original Gibson Nick Lucas "Special" signature model. He graciously posed in front of the Fortenoy building in Hollywood where he kept his second residence, top-floor apartment for many years. Nick is still "Tip-Toeing Thru' the Universe" in our hearts!

(Below) Nick Lucas in a rare publicity still from the twenties, playing his trusty Gibson.

When I asked Les about those days, he had the following to say:

(Above) Promo picture from *The Big Broadcast* film with crooner Bing Crosby and original jazz great Eddie Lang playing his favorite L-5.

(Below) Eddie Lang's Okeh release of Rachmaninov's "Prelude" and "A Little Love, A Little Kiss."

Robb Lawrence: How did it all start electrically?

LP: *I started playing in 1929. Before long I took the phonograph pickup and jabbed it into the top of the guitar and bought a microphone and I bought a PA system and started singing out at drive-ins around Waukesha, Wisconsin. And that's when they would all honk their horns and leave a tip for me with the waitress, and the guy was paying me five bucks a night and I'd make twenty bucks in tips, see; and it was a real good deal. Now with that PA system, I started to play band concerts, the bandshells, and concerts in the park. And those were $10. For a kid in 1929, it was good money. I had to be heard—just me singing and playing guitar and harmonica. I had the harmonica rack. I was doing Donovan and Dylan long before they were born.*

RL: What style of music were you playing?

LP: Same thing they're doing, same idea—folk music, the folk thing, road songs, popular songs. If you want to, go dig in the hills of Tennessee or Kentucky or Arkansas in the real hillbilly country. I was a real hillbilly! The songs were like songs that became hits, like "The Cat Came Back," for instance. "I Never See Maggie Alone" was another one. And then I go back earlier to the very first things like, "Adam and Eve," "My Lost Rib." It goes back to things like "Barbarell" and "Later, When the Work's All Done This Fall." That was a cowboy song. And "Letter Edged in Black," "The Wreck of the '97," and "Casey Jones."

When I went to hear Donovan at Carnegie Hall, I was amazed to hear him sing the same melodies, playing the kind of harmonica and doing what I did in 1929. If I had any idea that it would someday be that commercial, I might have stayed with it. But I thought it was a downer, a bummer, bad news. The public was interested, but I had an ego trip going where I wanted to be a great guitar player and I wanted to play jazz, so I had only one thing in my mind. I was idolizing people like Eddie Lang and Carl Kress. Later Django Reinhardt.

Sunny Joe Wolverton Enters

Les enjoys telling this great story about when he was just sixteen, his friend Harold Vinger yanked on a string Les kept attached to his toe for emergencies. He was alerting him to an amazing musician named Joe Wolverton. He was playing nearby on that warm, spring night and wanted him to come on down. Les climbed down from the second story and off they went to the nearby club. Since Les was under age, he proceeded to sneak into the dance hall through the bathroom to hear this live cowboy band led by Rube Tronson. He stood up front and was totally amazed to see a guitarist playing above the 3rd fret—at the time, he said he thought the rest of the higher frets were there just for decoration! "Joe was the best guitar player I'd ever come across. I'd never heard anyone like that before. He was really good!"

Les had brought his second guitar along, a resophonic/ampliphonic (Dobro/National) guitar per chance he could learn something. Sunny Joe riveted the young guitarist with some fancy violin pizzicato techniques… new things that Les had never seen or imagined. He invited him onstage to play a few of Lester's numbers with Rube's Cowboys. Turned out, when it came time for his solos, his Dobro was much louder than Joe's guitar. They hit it off instantly that night and became fast friends, even though Joe was considerably older. Les then had Joe on his radio show the next night to perform. Les learned some of Joe's tunes right away and also played some of his hillbilly routines for him. Thus began Les's next major turning point.

In the next year Les began performing in Rube Tronson's group for $10 a gig without Sunny Joe, who had taken a temporary, better paying gig, and thereby left Les with the guitar duties. Les held his own as one of the most proficient musicians in the group. During that year, Les and Joe had formed their own duo, working at a number of radio stations around Racine and Milwaukee. Joe sang and played jazzy fiddle and wild guitar. His quick and flashy style left a lasting impression on young Lester; an influence that gave him the verve,

speed, and inventiveness that would mark his guitar-playing style for decades to follow. Joe was noticing Lester's talent, and put more emphasis on technique in his lessons in order to prepare him for the future.

Around this same time, Les finally got his first serious guitar. Joe took them on a trip to the Gibson Company in nearby Kalamazoo, Michigan to pick out a new guitar. They walked around the factory and watched the craftsmen build beautiful "Master Model" guitars, such as the L-5, which was built as an orchestra guitar to project well. On their tour, they got to see the Gibson men at work doing their magic. "There was no finish on them, and they varnished it afterwards," say Les. "The craftsmen would tap the top of the guitar and listen to the tone of the resonance. He tuned it to a certain pitch, which was very important. So that's the key to those old L-5 guitars." These particular instruments were done with careful hand-staining of the Cremona sunburst colors and then took three months to cure the finish. During their visit, Les received his own beautiful $50 L-50 archtop from Joe and used it in their duo. This was the first of many Gibson instruments that would grace Lester's career.

(Above) Photo of Les and Joe playing away as radio stars of 1933, pictured here in the Gibson *Gazette*.

Featured by
SUNNY JOE & RHUBARB RED
"The Ozark Appleknockers," Over CBS

(Left) Sheet music with a great picture of both Les "Rhubarb Red" Paul and "Sunny" Joe Wolverton (playing his L-5) as the Ozark Appleknockers with CBS.

Gibson L-50 archtop round-hole model with its great reddish shading, which sold for $50. Les received one of these from Sunny Joe when they visited the Gibson factory in 1932. Very similar to the Carson Robison model and Kalamazoo versions. *Courtesy Singing Strings, Encinitas, 1973*

Sheet music of "Me and My Burro," showing Les as "Rhubarb Red" with his very first L-5 (pre-1929 dot-inlayed model) and harmonica rack, playing a G7 chord.

(Right) Joe's trio with Les and Fry performed at the 1934 Chicago World's Fair for a company that made the "Big Yank" work shirts. They performed at the General Exhibits Pavilions shown here near the South Lagoon. Note the famous Sky Ride tower in the background.

Meanwhile, Les was playing guitar after school on radio station WHAD for a local patent-medicine nabob—a gig in which, besides playing guitar and doing announcements, he had to box the medicine, too! In 1932, an opportunity to do the KMOX radio show "Farm Folks Hour" for good money came up. Les actually left school and traveled with his mother all the way to St. Louis to join up with Joe Wolverton and his Scalawags. Evelyn turned right around in the bus station and went straight back home. She knew music was young Lester's calling and was determined to give him the best opportunity to get him started. With his harmonica, guitar, jug, and funny stage antics, Evelyn soon dubbed him "Rhubarb Red," similar to Pie Plant Pete's name—since the red rhubarb plant is a popular pie ingredient. With his hair tinted even more red than usual, Les started pulling off lots of gags and shenanigans. Once Les's chops were up to par, Joe gave him a matching L-5 archtop, just like his. Soon many had a hard time telling them apart, with Les's remarkable playing emerging. Life was quite good on and off the radio.

Joe and Les found themselves playing their popular hill-billy-country, jazz-flavored tunes on various radio shows as the Ozark Appleknockers around St. Louis and Chicago. All along, Les had been leaning towards the electric guitar since his early experiments. They had seen some in a store in 1932, but Joe wasn't quite ready to get one yet. Nothing could compare to their great L-5 tones. At that time, Gibson hadn't released their electrics, and most were either quite primitive Spanish guitars with inadequate electronics, or the Hawaiian steel models just coming on the market.

They finally ended up performing as a trio with Fry Peters for the Reliance Manufacturing Co. at the Chicago World's Fair of 1933 and 1934. Due to popular demand (and near riots), the fair was continued into the next year. This unfortunately was to be their last gig together. After weeks of great performances, Les and Joe had a disagreement and he let Les go his own way—and pursue his fascination with the electric guitar.

Jazz Guitar and the Les Paul Trio

Les really wanted to be a great jazz guitar player. He idolized players like the incomparable Eddie Lang and the jazz guitar duo of Carl Kress and Dick McDonough. Soon he formed his first Les Paul trio consisting of bassist Ernie Newton and rhythm guitarist Jimmy Atkins (Chet's older brother), and the three headed for New York after flipping a coin.

Les told his guys a tall story about knowing the famous bandleader Paul Whiteman, whom he said he could set up an appointment with. They were out of work, so the other guys bugged Les about getting a gig with Whiteman. So Les made the phone call, got turned down, didn't tell his bandmates, and suggested that they go over to Whiteman's office, figuring that once there, he would just wing it. They went up the elevator to Whiteman's office, and Les told the two to wait outside while he waltzed in to meet with him. Whiteman had Les quickly escorted out of his office (rather rudely), but Les proceeded to tell the guys that Paul had said to come back tomorrow. While leaving the office, Les and the guys inadvertently got into the elevator with bandleader Fred Waring, whom they ended up auditioning for—and with whom they got a job! The three soon joined his Pennsylvanians.

Gibson *Gazette* photo of Les with orchestra leader Fred Waring. Les played with them for over five years, and slowly integrated the electric guitar into the large ensemble.

The Waring orchestra posed with Les Paul (on the far right behind the bass player) circa 1940. They did "Chesterfield Pleasure Time" radio broadcasts on Wednesday nights on CBS.

Les is busy here playing a solo on his Gibson ES-150 with the Waring orchestra.

The Electric Guitar Takes Over

During the latter part of 1936 into '37, Les was one of the first guitarists in the orchestras on radio to utilize the electric Spanish guitar. The Fred Waring orchestra would broadcast two different CBS shows on Wednesdays, one with the electric guitar and one with the acoustic guitar.

Les remembers:

"I really believe that the first person to use the electric pickup, to exploit it, was when I was with Fred Waring in the latter part of '36, '37—in there. Between there and 1941 was the real exploitation of the electric Spanish guitar, where they can hear it three or five nights a week, or whatever nights I played a solo with Fred Waring.

"In fact, when I started, we gave the listening audiences a choice. We played one show with the straight guitar and one show with the electric guitar, and the mail poured in—because there was such a controversy over whether to play the straight guitar or the electric guitar. Fred Waring, Jimmy Atkins, Ernie Newton my bass player, and myself finally had a meeting; say, this is 1937 somewhere. We recorded the first show, which was at seven o'clock, for the East Coast, and we did another show at eleven o'clock at night from New York for the West Coast. They didn't have a delay in recording and all this, not as good. So what we did was, we recorded the first show with the straight guitar and the second show with the electric guitar, and did the same thing [opposite the next week].

Then we all went up and sat down and listened in Fred Waring's office to both records and took a vote [flipped a coin], and said this is going to be the final vote. Whatever it is, that's it. And if it's the straight guitar, we'll stay with the straight guitar. That's for the broadcast because the mail was astounding. There was more mail coming in for whether Les Paul played an electric or acoustic box than Fred Waring got for all his whole Pennsylvanians. There was such a controversy over this radical move, and the vote for the electric. So it was unanimous to go electric, and Fred Waring said, 'Well, Les, I'm glad you did it because now at least the people in the audience can hear you and you can express yourself.'"

An acoustic performance on NBC with Les, Ernie Newton, and Jimmy Atkins as the Pennsylvanians back them up.

Other popular guitarists were listening to the radio shows and were copying Les's licks on their shows. "Oscar Moore at that time was listening to me when I was with Fred Waring. If I played a run on Tuesday night, you'd bet you would hear it from Oscar Moore on the next record with Nat King Cole. If it had anything that he liked, he used it. He made no bones about it. And later, I caught myself admiring what Oscar Moore was doing because, as he was becoming more popular, I was hearing him doing things I never thought of doing."

When asked about playing electric guitar with the trio, Les and bassist Wally Kamin had the following to say:

LP: Electric started, as far as I could figure, it's got to be '33, '34, definitely. Because in '34, in that era, is when I went to the Bismarck Hotel, and that went all the way up till '37. I'm playing electric till '37; I was playing electric when I came to New York, and I'll tell you what I got, and I'm sure Jimmy Atkins can verify it.

WK: You were playing electric on the afternoon "Rodeo Radio" show.

LP: Oh, sure! I'm just spot thinking. See, when Jimmy Atkins, Ernie, and myself formed our Les Paul Trio and came to New York in the later part of '36, I went to Lafayette and bought the speaker and their amplifier. And I had some pickup permanently mounted in the guitar that I cut a hole in the top of, the guitar at that time in '36.

Now if I back up, in '34, '35, that era, I can remember because the guys would stand on my cord. And if they stood on my cord and I moved, I would rip the pickup and everything out—the bridge and the whole bit because at that time, the pickup was fastened to the bridge. Two adjustable screws, it slid on and that held the pickup in shape, and the pickup ran all the way from the back to the front of the guitar.

WK: And the cord was part of the guitar. When you unplug, you wrap it around the guitar. If you walk away with it plugged in, you ripped the guitar up.

LP: And then on the steel guitar, you got to go back to that very same time. Alvino Rey was also involved in playing the electric guitar, and he must have been not the first, 'cause Orville Knapp, I believe, I heard.

WK: Alvino told me he had an electric in '29. Al's got a few years on us, too, you know.

LP: Then you see, he can go back even farther that that. As far as my life is concerned, the electric guitar really came into being after I started to get out in the public where I was playing, not so much in the saloons.

(Author's note: Alvino performed with Horace Heidt's Orchestra with an Electro "Frying Pan" Hawaiian guitar by Rickenbacher. Jack Miller is the steel guitarist who performed in Orville Knapp's orchestra with an early Electro "Frying Pan," and wrote a feature article in a 1934 DownBeat Magazine issue about the new electric guitar and its merits on the bandstand.)

The electric guitar was so new at the time that there wasn't a Musicians Union listing for it, and Les felt there should be. "I remember the New York Musicians Union, when I asked them if they would please start categorizing the guitar players separately—the electric guitar from the regular guitar. Because the regular guitar I considered another, different instrument. At that time, there was like, one, let's say at that time—Charlie Christian hadn't come to town yet. There was a guy named Leonard Wehr. You can count them on one hand—Floyd Smith with Andy Kirk; there were probably ten guitar players on the East Coast that were playing electrics."

Around this time, Gibson was supplying Les (noted Rhubarb Red in the log books) with an experimental L-7 electric with the first long-style ES-300 pickup (which he didn't care for) and the twin-pickup electrified L-5 model as shown in his early Gibson ad.

While performing with Waring and living in Queens, New York, Les began "tearing it up" at late night jam sessions. By 1939, Charlie Christian arrived in New York City playing with the Benny Goodman Sextet. Les was one of many who admired his fluid, hornlike lines and great phrasing abilities. The two became acquainted and would go uptown to jam early bebop at Minton's Playhouse in Harlem. Les recalls, "Charlie and I used to ride the subway with our matching Larson Brothers guitars we ordered with 1" thick maple tops. With those maple amps, they were too heavy for us!" Les learned some important ideas from Charlie about playing dynamics.

Les had a small rehearsal room in the basement at Electra Court where numerous local musicians would frequent. He went to a local radio parts store and got a dual-tube transmitter (only one-tube oscillators were allowed by the FCC for amateurs). The "Booger Brothers" radio station was then born along with a cute mascot kitten on board. Great jamming ensued and the signal could be heard halfway across the Brooklyn bridge! One hot day in 1941, they were jamming down below to keep cool. Les recalls, "I stuck my hand into the transmitter when I shouldn't have." He inadvertently reached to adjust something while holding his guitar and was nearly electrocuted. While Les yelled to turn it off, Ernie Newton quickly knocked the guitar away. After being immersed in a tub of ice, Les spent weeks recuperating at a local hos-

pital wrapped like a mummy. Meanwhile, Charlie Christian was unfortunately dying down the hallway of tuberculosis. Christian's short but stellar career with the popular Goodman group had an enormous impact on the electric guitar's influence. (Author's note: In 1975, while driving up the East Side Highway of Manhattan, Les pointed out the hospital across the river where he recovered and Charlie didn't.) By this time, Les was wanting to reach stardom outside of the restraints of the orchestra.

Les Paul looking quite dapper with his Gibson Super 400 with tassel attached. This picture was used (and touched up) by Gibson in the 1939 catalog. He felt the 18" body was too big at the time. Les often signed this promo picture during the thirties for fans as Rhubarb Red. *Courtesy Les Paul*

The Experimenting Begins— With an Epiphone

After his long and successful engagement with Fred Waring, Les intended to set out for California, but got sidetracked in Chicago in 1940. He became the musical director for radio station WJJD, and played as a staff guitarist with Ben Bernie for Wrigley Gum on CBS. It was during this time that he became friends with George Barnes, another great guitarist in the Chicago area. They would do many jam sessions together and pal around. While there, one day Les got a call from a fellow who, because he had caught his hand in a bread-factory wrapping machine, wanted to sell his Epiphone guitar and amp. That electric guitar was the first one Les modified to use as a prototype for experimentation with his different pickup configurations. Les began collecting Epiphone Zephyr models exclusively because they were inexpensive ($150), and had a large, square opening on the back that enabled easy access to the pickup and electronics.

The Epiphone Company has a fine tradition of producing banjos, stand-up basses, and archtop jazz guitars. Originally established in 1873 by Greek lute- and violin-maker Anastasios Stathopoulo, the company began making their House of Stathopoulo banjos. Eventually, the founder changed the company name to the Epiphone Banjo Corporation after his son, Epaminondas, or "Epi," the oldest of three sons (Fritzo and Orthie were also active in the company). Many commercial items were named with "phone" during those years (Vitaphone, Vegaphone, etc.). Their well-respected Recording banjos of the late 1920s were made by master craftsmen and exquisitely done.

During the early 1930s, Epiphone mounted a serious challenge to Gibson's L-5 with their new lineup of high-quality Masterbilt jazz guitars. Gibson soon came out with their newly expanded archtop ƒ-hole series, including the Super 400. Epiphone featured slightly larger sizes and fancier high-end models, such as the popular De Luxe and Emperor Concert guitars (Les still keeps an acoustic blonde De Luxe near his bed). Many radio broadcast musicians and big band orchestra guitarists endorsed Epiphones, including George Van Eps, Tony Mottola, Allen Reuss, Hilton "Nappy" Lamare, Smiley Burnett, and Freddie Green of the Count Basie Orchestra.

In the late 1930s, Epiphone launched their Electar electric instrument series that included Hawaiian steel guitars, amplifiers, and the Zephyr Spanish series. These Spanish models included both a standard Zephyr (c. 1939) with laminated maple construction and natural finish) and a fancy Zephyr De Luxe (c. 1941). Epiphone electrics featured an exclusive "Mastervoicer" tone control, which went from mellow to normal to brilliant voicings. Early versions had horseshoe magnets and then, primitive slug-polepiece pickups, which eventually evolved into an adjustable screw magnet pickup. Dual pickups and a Regent Cutaway Advanced version of the De Luxe and Emperor models were eventually added to the line in the late 1940s.

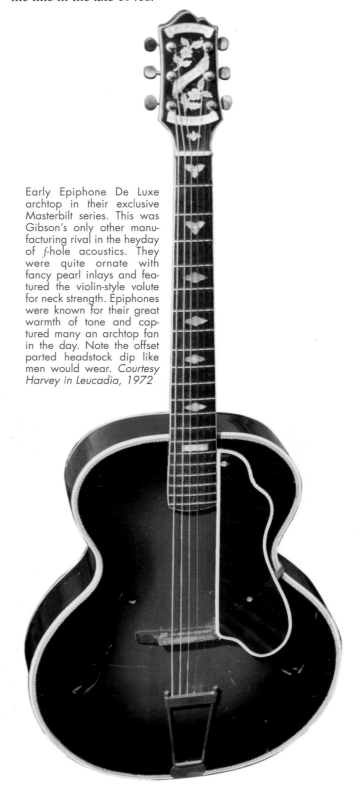

Early Epiphone De Luxe archtop in their exclusive Masterbilt series. This was Gibson's only other manufacturing rival in the heyday of ƒ-hole acoustics. They were quite ornate with fancy pearl inlays and featured the violin-style volute for neck strength. Epiphones were known for their great warmth of tone and captured many an archtop fan in the day. Note the offset parted headstock dip like men would wear. *Courtesy Harvey in Leucadia, 1972*

Les installed a late '30s Gibson fancy bar-magnet-style ES-250 pickup on one Zephyr guitar, and in later years, put a heavyweight brass, Paul Bigsby steel-guitar pickup on one of his experimental steel-plate versions (*See* "How High the Moon" sheet music). Before the dual-pickup guitars were commercially introduced, Les had his own experimental twin-pickup specials, and would often hide the fact in photos with his arms concealing the front rhythm pickup from sight!

One day, Les found a box of Rickenbacher vibrolas in a music store and brought them home to try out. Clayton "Doc" Kauffman invented and patented his "Vibrola" in 1929, and used a motorized version on the novel 1937 Rickenbacher Bakelite Spanish vibrola guitar (a cousin to the solid-body guitar). Doc went on to team up with Leo Fender for their first steel guitars and amplifiers. Les Paul began using these vibrolas exclusively.

Meanwhile, Les regularly visited Epiphone's Manhattan factory (located at 142 West 14th Street) on weekends to tinker around with his constant flow of ideas. He also made up the infamous "Log" with two wings of a discarded Epiphone body and a pine 4" by 4" down the middle (Les's prototype of what basically became the ES-335!). After playing an uneventful evening with the initial Log (without its wings), Les tried it again with the full Epiphone body, and received a much better audience response. Now there are a few authorized replicas of his famous Log guitar that reside in various museums.

Les continued tinkering with more Epiphones and came up with reinforcing the instruments with something more rigid. The metal-plate-enhanced Epiphone guitars were all developed during this furtive period of experimentation. Les elaborates on the steel-plate guitars: "You get a jazz guitar player, he's going to say, 'Well, I want something light that vibrates against me, so and so.' And then I said, I have to make a choice, because I go back many, many years ago—and you can go down and look at any of my guitars, and through the inside of there was a plate of steel, to make them solid. So when I was playing a hollow-body guitar, if you ever looked inside, you would see a big plate of steel in there that my strings were resting on, and not on the top. There were two holes drilled, and the whole unit was resting on steel. So when you pick up one of my acoustical boxes, the *f*-holes have black tape under them so no one could look in. And when you played the guitar, the guitar sounded like a solid body. But I knew that's where it was, way back in the '30s and the early '40s. And that steel, if you go down in the basement, you'll find maybe fifteen of those guitars have steel going through them. I can go way back to the middle '30s or late '30s, and that's what I was doing."

Les was onto something big. Another breakthrough was near as his pickup technology grew with his studio experience. Being the eternal perfectionist, Les continued his personal saga of the artist in search of the perfect electric guitar.

The experimental "Log" guitar 1941 prototype Les put together with a cut-up Epiphone body, a Douglas fir 4 by 4, and an L-12 Gibson neck. Note the Kauffman Vibrola. Evidence of prior drilled holes on the body show it had another setup beforehand. *Courtesy Les Paul*

California, Decca Records, & Uncle Sam

Les finally headed for California in late '41 and began working with Bing Crosby, the Andrews Sisters, Hedda Hopper, and other top artists, quickly establishing quite a reputation as a hot guitarist on the West Coast. He formed various trios and began playing at Club Rounders at Sunset and Vine in Hollywood.

Once when Les and I walked by, he pointed out the building, which is still standing, and mentioned that he eventually took over the club, which he named the "Les Paul Club." Les had a new trio then that consisted of Cal Gooden on rhythm guitar (an L-5), Paul Smith on piano, and Clint Nordquist on bass. They were doing sessions for Decca records and other local studios. Even though the Epiphone guitars were some of his favorites, Les was still endorsing Gibson guitars. While all this was happening, Les was living a few blocks away on Gordon Street. Previously, in 1937, he married Virginia Webb, whom he had met in Chicago. They had two children: Russell (Rusty) and Gene (Les Paul, Jr.).

Les was brought to Decca Records by Jack Kapp of Chicago. This liaison was quite advantageous for getting gigs to backup various artists and staff musicians at NBC Studios. When the Armed Services called Les in 1943, he began doing transcriptions and radio shows for the AFRS (Armed Forces Radio Service). This enabled him to perform and record with other enlisted artists. Les, in his Army olive drab, supported Major Meredith Willson, and went on the road to Army camps backing up Dinah Shore and the Andrew Sisters.

(Above) *Bandleaders* April 1946 article about Les on the move. Picture from Don Ameche's "What's New?" broadcast with Joe Rann, Les, and Bobby Meyer. Interviewer Johnny Frazer met up with multi-talented Les in his studio garage during a rehearsal, and caught him in action.

(Right) This 16" radio transcription (for airplay only) features the Les Paul Trio circa 1946. Les did his Orthotone release and his MacGregor country material for UTS.

(Left) '40s ad for Les playing at Club Rounders in Hollywood, across from Fife & Nichol's music store on Vine Street. Note the plug for "Begin the Beguine" on Decca.

(Left) The Andrews Sisters wartime song folio was quite popular. Les and his trio collaborated with them in July of 1946 on "It's a Pity to Say Goodnight" and "Rumors Are Flying"—the latter of which went up to No. 4 on the charts, even with competition from six other versions. They supported the hit with a long national tour later that year.

(Above) The Andrews Sisters' 1946 hit "Rumors Are Flying" with Vic Schoen's Orchestra featuring Les Paul's expressive fills and solo work. They sold over 90 million records total and also recorded with Bing Crosby, Burl Ives, and Woody Woodpecker!

(Left) "At Ease," a 16" (transcription #612) for the Armed Forces Radio Services, featuring Meredith Willson, vocalist Martha Mears, and "Les Paul on the electric guitar" performing "Geannine I Dream of Lilac Time," "Highland Fling," "Taking a Chance on Love," "Way Down Yonder in New Orleans," "This Is the Army Mr. Jones," "Don't Blame Me," "Wishing," and "Everytime." Willson was Les's commanding officer in the service, and went on to write the Broadway hit *The Music Man*.

(Above) Reverting to using his previous "Rhubarb Red" moniker for more country tunes, Les performs "Billy Sunshine" and "Sad Sam" on this Air Force Radio Service Audiodisc 16" transcription acetate. Note the extra three holes.

(Left) One of Les and his trio's early efforts for old friend Jack Kapp at Decca Records. Hawaiian music was still quite popular, and this series of recordings ensured a success prior to his later Decca releases.

(Above) Decca 78 release of Les Paul and his trio's version of Cole Porter's "Begin the Beguine," backed by "Dark Eyes"—recorded December 12, 1944.

(Above) Bing Crosby with Les and his trio doing the hit tune "It's Been a Long, Long Time," recorded July 12, 1945. Popular with Americans returning from the war overseas, the tune stayed on the charts for sixteen weeks.

(Above) Here is a 1945 *Gibson Spotlights* ad for Les Paul as a Hollywood NBC radio artist with an electrified Dual (bar-magnet) pickup natural L-5.

(Left) A custom-made Recordio Disc by Wilcox-Gay of a live performance of Les Paul. These portable machines could cut a plastic record right on the spot, live or off a radio broadcast.

Decca 33-1/3 release in Australia and New Zealand of *Galloping Guitars* by Les and his trio, under the Festival label. Tracks include "Blue Skies," "Dark Eyes," "Steel Guitar Rag," "Guitar Boogie," "Begin the Beguine," and "Dream Dust." Note the Epiphone guitar, modified with two pickups.

After his short stint with Uncle Sam, Les was honorably discharged and returned to California in 1945. He joined "California Melodies" Mutual Network Air and played with many famous entertainers (including W. C. Fields) on various radio shows and recordings. Les and his trio re-banded to record more transcriptions and the celebrated "Hawaiian Paradise" discs, which featured beautiful melodies. This led to sessions for "Begin the Beguine" by Cole Porter, "Dark Eyes," and "Blue Skies" by Irving Berlin. Meanwhile, Les became friends at NBC with Bing Crosby, who let him perform "Dark Eyes" on the "Kraft Music Hall" show. This eventually led to them collaborating on a new arrangement of "It's Been a Long, Long Time," released in September of 1945, and on which he plays an extended solo. It soon hit No. 1 in the States. Bing was impressed with Les's technical and musical talents, and wanted to back him with a studio—which Les eventually did at home.

Les playing the wacky, aluminum-bodied, headless guitar live with his trio. He and his friends hammered out the body in 1942. It was built with long-shafted tuners that extended up to the top sides. Unfortunately, its metal body kept going out of tune under the hot stage lights.

Meanwhile, recording with the famous Andrews Sisters and Vic Schoen was in the works, with a tour and extended engagement at the New York Paramount Theater. This was the beginning of a string of Decca records, including "Rumors Are Flying" with the Andrews Sisters. They also appeared in the film *Sensations of 1945*, and with George Burns and Gracie Allen on the radio. Les also did the popular "Guitar Boogie," previously recorded by Arthur Smith, and "Steel Guitar Rag" in early 1947. He used the unique headless aluminum guitar for early versions of "Caravan" and "Somebody Loves Me" with the Andrews Sisters. During one of his last sessions in 1947, before he retired to his private home studio, Les recorded the memorable Frank Loesser tune "What Are You Doing New Year's Eve?" with the renowned Dick Haymes. Les's formative days at Decca were quite productive, and certainly laid the foundation for a bright and popular future.

Birth of the "New Sound"

Up to this time Les had never been very satisfied with the sounds of his recorded guitar and other instruments. He and Bing Crosby had recently cut their Decca hit. One day, while driving down Sunset in Hollywood as he returned from a session with Bing, Les was discussing his dissatisfaction with the current studio techniques (like the distant miked recordings), and Bing said, "Why don't you just build your own studio and get the sound you want." Les said, "No, I can't bother to. I'm too busy." And then a few minutes later he said, "Why the hell not! I'll make my own records and get the sound I want."

This was a major turning point—Les decided to really do something about the poor state of recording capabilities. He began to experiment with making his own recordings at home. Soon the famous Les Paul Garage Studio on North Curson Street in Hollywood was born.

Another reason why Les developed his new recording sound was actually inspired from his mother, who accidentally mistook George Barnes for him on a radio show. Les hadn't been on the radio for over a year, so he decided to come up with a unique and personal sound that his mother would always recognize!

This was the beginning of something very special. Everybody came by and recorded at his studio, including Peggy Lee and her husband, bandleader Dave Barbour. Les's first step in achieving a different sound was to have the artist perform close to the microphone, as opposed to the accepted recording practices—a technique that gave the recording a great presence, and which is widely accepted today.

The Curson garage studio was soon in great demand because of Les's secret recording formulae. When people came by, everyone had to climb in the back window to get in! (That particular house, which was originally located on Curson Street, is now located in Pasadena. The woman who currently owns it called in during Les's 1994 interview on Ray Bream's KABC talk show to tell the story about it being moved out there. It's still intact.)

Les's first record cutter was made out of spare parts, i.e., a used Cadillac flywheel as a precision recording lathe to cut his discs on acetate. Like he first did with his mom's player piano, punching holes in the roll, he started experimenting with sound-on-sound recordings. Now Les could play all the parts himself: the rhythm, melody, harmony backgrounds, and bass—even the percussion parts, which he created by tapping the strings on the guitar! No additional arranger, producer, or engineer was used; Les performed all these tasks himself.

"That's how it all started. You record on a disc, and you play the disc back and record on the second machine with what you laid down on the first recording. Play along with it, and you now have the two together on the second record." Les had a very distinctive sound of his own, with slap-back echo and many other kinds of special techniques that he began developing with multiple sound recordings. Thus, the "New Sound" was born.

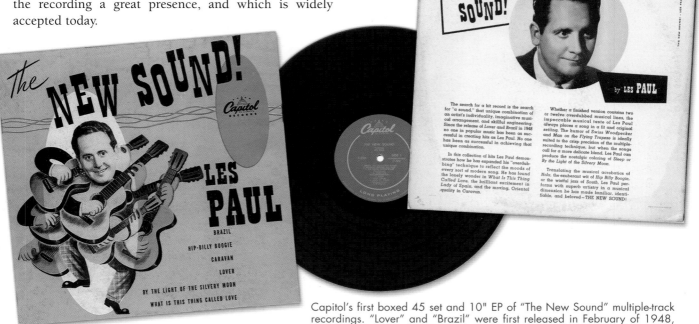

Capitol's first boxed 45 set and 10" EP of "The New Sound" multiple-track recordings. "Lover" and "Brazil" were first released in February of 1948, and went flying up the charts. These fabulous over-dubbed recordings, with speeded up guitars and echo, turned the music world on its head.

LES PAUL
popular favorite

Les is playing wildly on the cover of *Metronome*, April 1951.

GUITAR	
Les Paul	615
Billy Bauer	578
Tal Farlow	538
Chuck Wayne	534
Dave Barbour	145
Laurindo Almeida	143
Oscar Moore	132
Eddie Condon	112
Irving Ashby	101
Barney Kessel	86
Jimmy Raney	75
Ralph Blaze	71
Tony Rizzi	70
Tony Mottola	51
George Van Eps	40
Benny Heller	35
Alvino Rey	30
Django Reinhardt	27
Perry Botkin	20
Johnny Smith	20
Sam Herman	18
John Collins	17
Remo Palmieri	17
George Barnes	15
Freddy Green	15
Nappy Lamare	15
Danny Barker	14
Tiny Grimes	13
Mundell Lowe	12
Floyd Smith	12

Les spoke more to me about the "New Sound":

RL: When was the first sound-on-sound done?

LP: The first sound-on-sound was on a recording lathe. It wasn't on a tape; the first records that came out—"Lover," "Caravan," "What Is This Thing Called Love"—all those early recordings, they were all made on disks. That's how it started. You record, you make a disk, and you play the disk back, and you record on the second machine with what you had laid down on the first recording. Play along with it, and you now have the two together on the second record.

RL: Didn't you also develop the first sound-on-sound recording studio?

LP: I did that too. You're talking about 1945–46. That was in California. That's when that started. I had done sound-on-sound long before that. I have records here that go back to 1936, where I played sound-on-sound. But I didn't do it commercially—but I have it written down that I played the bass part, I played the rhythm guitar part, and I played my own part, all on my guitar. And it will say "Rhubarb Red" three times, "3x," and written in 1936. And the only reason that happened was because I didn't have anyone around to jam with that I wanted to try out runs, so I would make a multiple.

I never realized it had the potential until I ran into the echo that I could produce by feeding back—looping back the original sound off of the disk. I put the playback head behind the cutting head—and this kinda upset the industry a bit—and then changing speed did a pretty good job. And so, between that and the ideas, making "Lover," the sped-up sounds, and the echo, etc. This created a whole new bag.

Les outright won the 1951 *DownBeat* magazine best guitarist poll. Note the numerous Gibson artists on the roster.

Wally Jones was someone very important behind the scene, directly involved with Les's studio equipment and his fabulous sound. The original 10-watt amplifier and microphone mixers were designed and built by Wally. He had a knack for making super clean sounding mixers for multiple tracking (unlike the commercial studios that got more and more 60-cycle hum per pass). These mixers were later analyzed by other electronic engineers. They were at a loss to explain their inherent perfection. His sound system was state-of-the-art for decades. With Wally's help over these years, Les's concept of hi-fi sound (top equipment and microphone technique) was unparalleled.

Many engineers and artists would crowd into his unorthodox studio to marvel at what came off the disk and out of a cheap speaker. Crosby was so knocked out that he had Les furnish a professional Les Paul Sound System in his house. When installed, the doors and frames had to be removed in order to accommodate the large setup!

Here's Wally Jones, Zeke Manners and Del Kacher at Del's Hollywood studio. Del recalls, "Wally and Zeke had paid me a visit at my recording studio back in 1986. We were clowning around that day and took this (straight) picture. Wally had already built my custom pre-amp by that time."

The Wally Jones Mixer
A glimpse into the genius behind the Les Paul sound
by Del (Casher) Kacher and the author

A very important part of Les Paul's sparkling guitar tone was achieved by an advanced mixer built by Wally Jones. Engineers of the day weren't aware anything of this sort existed, nor could they figure out how it worked. Wally's genius lay in his creatively designed circuit with simple components. Everyone marveled how he could engineer such an efficient device with minimal hum, hiss, or noise.

Wally built a few versions to use for live concerts, mobile recordings, and in the famous "Garage Studio" on Curson Street (where the early disc-to-disc multiple recording hits were done). These special pre-amp units (dubbed the "Wally Jones Mixer" by Les and Mary) are also pictured in the Mahwah studio during his Ampex tape "sound-on-sound" recordings era. They were remarkably quiet despite the fact that he was multi-tracking so many generations (overdubs). A normal mixer could not have produced such superb recordings. I was surprised by his response when asked about its design.

Del Kacher: Where did you get the parts to build Les's mixer in those early days?

Wally Jones: *I built the mixer with junk that was laying around the house when we moved to Burbank Boulevard. in 1942. I designed the mixer to have the output at 600 ohms. It had very limited headroom and Les had to be very careful not to hit the strings hard to avoid going into distortion.*

Wally evidently used common elements but with an exotic design. Between 150 to 600 ohms, output is considered low impedance. This was standard for the pro audio industry when going into a disc cutting amplifier and other audio gear. To create an even input signal, Les naturally exhibited excellent control of his right-hand picking technique and dynamics. This exceptional dexterity was akin to a human limiter—even with his impaired arm.

DK: *What are the fundamentals of how it worked?*

WJ: *The mixer had [both] a guitar and tape input. My meter [on the mixer] was a decibel meter and not a VU* meter that had ample headroom and reserve [as] used on professional tape machines. There is more headroom on VU meters than on the decibel meter used on Les's mixer. If you peg [overload] a VU meter into the red, there's no problem with distortion. But the decibel meter that goes over 0 volume level would immediately go into distortion.

Low level guitar output, line-level turntables, and tape machines are mismatched levels. The mixer needed to work (match levels) between these mediums without problems—and Wally's mixer did this superbly. Here, headroom refers to amount of signal the input can receive. In this case, ample (or reserve) meant that the meter could swing higher than it normally would be operated at. It still has to be set at a minimal volume, or it would exceed the voltage and create clipping (or distortion).

The deci-bel measurement is a tenth of a bel (as devised by Alexander Graham Bell). A decibel meter generally measures acoustic sound pressure. In this configuration, it measures the amount of volume and must be maintained close to zero level at all times. Otherwise, if it's below zero, not enough signal is available to make a quiet/clean recording. If it exceeds zero level, the signal will go into distortion. Decibel meters were used for disc cutting and the excursion of the cutting needle had minimum (or little) tolerance. Therefore, the dB meter was a commonly used component during those times.

WJ: *The input stage was very quiet and never overloaded [or] went into distortion. The signal-to-noise ratio had to be [adjusted] on the input. If there's noise on the first stage you'll ruin your signal-to-noise ratio. Also, I powered the mixer with Les's Gibson amplifier because it was there.*

The mixer was an extremely low noise system, therefore the signal exceeded the inherent thermal (ambient) noise floor for best quality. The adjusted hiss and hum level had to be 50 dB below the signal-to-noise ratio. Wally's mixer did not have its own power supply, so the mixer derived the DC voltage power by tapping into the Gibson [EH-150] amp. His tube circuit mixer design was ahead of the technology of the time.

DK: *So how did you develop this technologically advanced mixer?*

WJ: *This is not a new invention, but just plain common sense!*

Les Paul has always shown his gratefulness and gratitude for the brilliant genius of Wally Jones—you can include me on that also.

Del's notes:

During the early fifties, everyone wanted to sound like Les and Mary. I had my own radio show in Hammond, Indiana at sixteen, and the problem I had was noise building up after each [overdub] using Magnecord PT-6s. I drove the transmitter engineer crazy trying to have him figure how to make quiet recordings. He was always glad when I left the transmitter tower! I never knew until years later, it was Wally's mixer that made the difference. One must remember, there was no Radio Shack, Guitar Center, or anywhere then to buy a mixer as today. In the early 1950s, the new trend with Patti Page, Kay Starr, and many others was to double- and triple-track their voices to sound like two or three singers. They couldn't technically [generally] go beyond three overdubs without built-up noise. The recording engineers for the big record labels always wondered how Les Paul could make such noiseless and upfront recordings. Les Paul's original recordings are clear and compare well to many of today's best digital recordings. Wally later built me a guitar tube preamp with the similar circuitry built into Les's mixer, but it included a power supply and EQ at 5K to put a bite into the guitar.

One night we were riding in the car going for pizza and listening to one of his recordings. I marveled how well thought-out, seemingly complex and yet uncomplicated his recordings were—so I asked how he did it. Les said, "If it's complicated, I'd never touch it. I only do things that are simple." The moral is: make it simple.

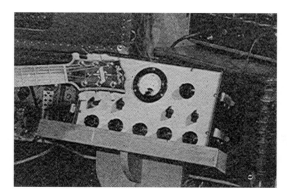

An early version of the famous Wally Jones mixer that originally helped create the Les Paul sound.

And Along Comes Mary...

After Les had moved from Gordon Street, by the Gower Gulch Beachwood Studios, down Sunset Boulevard to Curson Street, he set up his studio again. Les thought it would be a good idea to incorporate a female singer into the act for performances and recording. A friend told him about Colleen Summers, who sang and played guitar with Gene Autry. The talented Iris Colleen "Somerset" Summers had also been singing with Jimmy Wakely and Stuart Hamblen. She came over from her home in Pasadena to Les's makeshift home studio.

Les hadn't been quite prepared for her to arrive. The musicians were already playing in the studio when Colleen showed up, and Les was mowing the lawn in his army fatigue outfit and boots. "I was even picking up beer cans with a flashlight at night!" remembers Les. Here's this pretty singer arriving and Les is all messed up. So, he says, "Oh, everyone is in the garage. Go on in." Meanwhile, he quickly goes into the house afterwards and cleans himself up. Then he goes into the studio garage to properly greet her. This funny intro was the beginning of another important chapter in Les Paul's life and another of his many great musical experiences.

After Les's arduous efforts in the Curson Street garage studio (and over 500 discarded acetate discs), the "New Sound" made its debut with "Lover,"— a tune from the 1932 film *Love Me Tonight*. The song features some descending, riff-laden guitar work and quick hammer-ons with a series of ninth chords that follow. Les's new "bag of tricks" was finally unleashed with all the stops pulled out—echo, reverb and delay, speeded-up guitar with phasing and flanging. Also featured on this inaugural track are the Epiphone Zenith (which he dubbed the "Clunker" in later years) for the high parts, and the 4" by 4" Log for the main parts. His secret experiments in the Hollywood garage studio finally came together with "Lover." After Les perfected it, he slipped it on a turntable at a "smoked out" musician party a few blocks away, and totally surprised everyone—including Mary! He did it on acetate with his balanced

Mary and Les warming up together with the slightly modified Gibson L-12, and very modified Epiphone "Clunker."

Great Bruno photos of Les and Mary. Mary looks absolutely stunning!

Les Paul and Mary Ford

by Hyman Goldberg
Cosmopolitan, January 1955

When he felt that his multiple-recording technique was sufficiently far advanced, Les started looking for a vocalist. (His first "New Sound" releases were "Lover" and "Brazil," made without Mary Ford.) "At first," he says, "I thought I'd ask Bing to come in with me. But then I figured that if he did, it would be his record and not mine, so I decided to get a girl vocalist. Someone told me about a girl who was singing with Gene Autry and playing a guitar, so I called her up for an audition."

"That phone call was the greatest thing that ever happened to me," says Mary, who has been Mrs. Les Paul—or rather, Mrs. Lester Polfuss since December 1949—"because I'd always considered Les Paul to be the best guitarist in the world. And when he started telling me about his new multiple-recording idea, I was fascinated."

Mary Ford is a gentle, sweet-faced girl with blue eyes and brown hair, deeply religious—her father is the pastor of the Church of the Nazarene in San Gabriel, California—who looks considerably younger than her thirty years. Born and brought up in Pasadena, California, Mary comes of a musical family. "My mother and father," she says, "are both musical, and all my sisters and brothers—I've got three of each—and all. I learned to play the guitar and sing hymns and later hillbilly music when we were very small." Mary left her home to join Gene Autry's troupe before her family moved from Pasadena to nearby San Gabriel. Show business, however, has had no effect upon her early upbringing, except possibly to strengthen her faith.

"It's a miracle," she says, "what has happened to Les and me. I'm sure such things don't happen to people unless they have faith."

Les thought he should come up with a catchy name for both of them for their new duo. He renamed her "Mary Ford" because it was a easy name to remember, it flowed with his stage name, and had a commercial ring to it.

Capitol's promo story of Les Paul and Mary Ford states: "Les Paul, whose Capitol records revealed the "New Sound" in music, signed an exclusive Cap contract in 1948, and was featured on "Brazil" and "Lover," which developed into his first disc hit, and established him as an amazing guitar virtuoso. A few years later, Les decided that he would "share billing" in his act with his charming new wife, Mary Ford, an excellent singer and guitarist in her own right. Between the two of them, in their fabulous recording setup in their Hollywood home, they have turned out some of the most unique "sounds" ever made available on disks; and their technique yet remains a mystery to even Capitol's top engineers."

Cadillac flywheel disc-cutting lathe. This is actually one of the few songs recorded with Leo Fender's Dual Professional two 10" (angled-front) tweed combo Super-amp that he'd given to Les.

The chemistry of Les Paul's immense and varied talents with Colleen's remarkable singing and guitar-playing talents complemented each other perfectly, and truly created a musical marriage made in heaven—one that the whole world embraced during their outstanding career together as Les Paul & Mary Ford.

Things were good. Here's a touching picture of Les and Mary, captured smiling.

The Car Crash

On Jan 11, 1948, while driving back to California from a holiday visit in his hometown of Waukesha, Les and Mary's car slid off an icy overpass and into a stream a few hundred feet below. Les was laying down in the back seat resting when Mary lost control. He reached around with his right arm to protect her as they hit a support and headed down to the bottom of the ravine. It was three long hours before anybody knew they had even crashed. The first ambulance took Mary away while Les lay in icy snow for nearly eight hours until the second ambulance arrived for him.

They were first taken to nearby Robertson Hospital in Chandler, then to Oklahoma's Wesley hospital to recover for a few days (my friend's mom actually took care of them). Mary was extremely lucky to only have a broken pelvis and other minor injuries. Les, on the other hand, had broken six ribs, his nose, pelvis, collarbone, and his spleen had been punctured. Worst of all, he had broken his right arm in three places, including his right elbow, which had been seriously crushed. They eventually sent him to California, where the doctors debated as to what to do with his elbow. Many at the hospital thought he would lose his arm, but the medical team knew of his great guitar playing and did their best to save it. The head surgeon, Dr. Robert Knight, performed the miraculous surgery into the late hours. He set Les's arm at a 90-degree angle towards his belly button, complete with seven screws in his upper arm so he could still play guitar. Les remembers, "And then in 1948, I tipped the car over. So for two years, I was out of business. The automobile accident—that's when I was doing all my thinking."

Years later, Les says he wished that they set his arm a little higher so that he'd be able to play more comfortably. It still sometimes aches, and he has occasional dreams about the accident. Les, however, was a real trooper through all this adversity. Thank goodness we didn't lose both of them!

Les's instrumentals, "Brazil" and "Lover," were released February 23, 1948—one month after the accident. NBC Radio personality Dave Garroway enthusiastically promoted Les's "New Sound" Capitol recordings, creating a real buzz in the music world. *Billboard* magazine charted "Lover" at No. 21 and "Brazil" at No. 22 here in the States; and the British releases did well too. Meanwhile, Les was having a slow and hard recovery both in and out of the hospital. Feeling so unwell, the hit records had

little impact on him at the time. But as he felt better, he was determined to get on with his music career. During his recovery, he continued to complete the overdubs on a few more hits—with the guitar placed flat on a table so he could play with his healing arm still in the cast!

The 1949 issue of *Newsweek* ran the headline, "PAUL'S COMEBACK." The story outlined the car accident from the previous year (and everyone's belief that it was the end of his career) and his opening that week at the Blue Note in Chicago with the Les Paul Trio, which was to include Mary on second guitar. In the interview, Les discussed his desire to reach a more popular audience in the future. (Glad he got his desire!)

After miraculously recovering from this whole ordeal, Les was finally back in action. Les soon added Mary to the trio, when they played at his brother's Club 400 tavern in Milwaukee. He knew Mary was quite good on the guitar, and she picked up on what Les was doing instantly. Their dynamic duo was soon to be unleashed. They were booked at the classy Blue Note in Chicago, with the press on hand that first night. But because both Les and Mary showed up dressed in casual attire, they almost lost the gig! Their usual lounge-act shtick of jazzy pop, hillbilly-comedian, corn-ball-ness filled the place with Rhubarb Red fans and jazz listeners. They soon won them over after some great tunes and charming charisma.

Les then decided to bring Wally on board as their new bassist. Les had jammed with Wally years before at a bowling alley nightclub, and was developing a good friendship with the multitalented fellow. The "team" was now formed. Around this same time, Les and Mary finally decided to get married. They had a small private ceremony without much fanfare. They were soon to become one of the newest and most popular romantic musical teams in America. These two alliances were to form a strong bond for many years to come with their popular careers.

Les and Mary live with bassist Wally Kamin (and Mary's sister Carol singing harmony backstage) at the Del Mar Fair Grandstands, circa 1951. Les was blowing some hot licks that afternoon with an orchestra near San Diego. *Courtesy J.T. Kane*

Les & Mary Radio Show

Hollywood's Radio City, May into June of 1950

The show begins with beautiful echo-laden cascading guitar lines of "Dry My Tears" composed by Les.

"It's 'The Les Paul Show.'

The Les Paul Trio and one recording machine are teamed up in a quarter hour of music that could only happen on a transcription. And if you think you're hearing double, it's only because of the electronic trickery of…… Les Paul!"

Les: Hello again. This is Les Paul speaking. And with me are the other members of the trio, Mary Ford and Eddie Stapleton. Eddie plays all the rhythm instruments at one time. And Mary is also quite busy singing all the vocal parts.

Mary: Hello. Les, I'm sure many of the listeners would be interested in knowing you play all the guitars on this show.

Les: Yeah, that is interesting (they laugh). Well it sure gets busy around here. And while we're in a busy mood, let's get busy with "Brazil."

Music starts the lively instrumental Spanish favorite with Les's inimitable guitar magic.

Eddie: … Les and Mary wrote this little tune. Mary's going to sing all three of the vocal parts and Les is going to play a whole mess of guitars.

Les: It's really nothing. Here is the tune, "Cryin'."

Mary's multiple voices layer the tune beautifully. A classic hillbilly song, "There's No Place Like Home," continues showing their true country roots. Then they break into a version "'Deed I Do."

Les: And that was Mary singing "'Deed I Do." And believe me Mary, I just think that's great… Anyway, we're going to close the show today with a condensed version of "Lover."

Mary: Oooh, this is what I've been waiting for!

Les: Well, I'll do it just for you!

They break into the rollicking "Lover." The next show picks up with a version of the melodic "Nola" also featuring the novel sped-up high-pitched guitar sounds.

Mary: Les… I think you ought to tell them about that little guitar you just played with the weird sound.

Les: Well, that guitar is about 18 inches long and it's tuned about an octave higher than the big standard guitar. And that's how we get that different sound. Now back to more music. This time we all get a workout with "The World Is Waiting for the Sunrise."

The high-pitched guitar sounds were actually played on an electrified mandolin. It was a very effective technique where he used only four strings and sped it up, creating a most unique sound layer.

Les: It might be a good idea to explain to the listeners just what happens on this show.

Mary: Les plays not one guitar, but as many as seven or eight of them, which he does with his electrical gadgets.

Les: I do? Oh, I might add the same idea is used in the vocals. So don't be surprised when you hear Mary singing as many as four parts at once. Maybe I'd better do something with just four guitars. Here's a thing called "Hip Billy Boogie." Stand back and give me room!

Les and Mary's Radio Show

Here's Les and Mary with Wally Kamin, all smiling right by the famous horse racing track where the "turf meets the surf."

Ezekiel Mannes, known as "Zeke" Manners, was also a close friend for many years. He was a talented writer and pianist recording numerous tunes including the famous "Pennsylvania Polka" covered by the Andrews Sisters. While living in Hollywood, he started the original (and highly sensational) radio Beverly Hill Billies group, and wrote popular square-dancing books. Zeke later became a disc jockey in NYC, and then in Los Angeles on KFWB. He was actually with Les and Mary in Jackson Heights when they recorded "How High the Moon." Zeke spent many quality years with Les and Mary.

The following is my interview with Zeke Manners and Del Kacher in 1997;

Les with Beatrice and Zeke Manners.

ZM: Out came "Lover" and "Brazil!" Kind of knocked me on my ass! It was brought to me by Capitol Records and I was mixed up. All these trios—Les Paul, Page Cavanaugh, Bobby Troup, even Nat King Cole had a trio. They were all different trios. I heard about Les. Didn't say anything about a trio and I raved about it. I very soon took it home and figured out what the heck he was doing with the speed-ups. You could tell. I knew it right away, 'cause he could still play—you know what I mean? So I doped that out—all out. But I was amazed at the whole damn thing. The arrangements were there. Those things had to be planned out!

DK: I think that on his arrangements, he's kind of underrated as an arranger because they all really were by-products of him learning from Fred Waring.

ZM: That's right!

DK: And Fred Waring had a lot to do with Les's concept of how to do an orchestration.

ZM: Les says, "You block them out," you know. A little bit of the vaudeville training. I have an idea that it could be instilled in him through everybody including Paul Whiteman.

DK: He was a very unique musician who—as a guitarist—always listened to the orchestra as an entire entity, which gave him the ability to learn the art of orchestrations and apply it to the guitar, rather than just listen to them as a guitar player, or as a drummer, or as a saxophone player. And that's where I think he conceptualized the guitar as an orchestral thing.

Another thing I think that had a lot to do with his orchestration abilities was, the trio always had a structure with the piano player, whether it be Paul Smith or Milt Raskin or any of those great pianists. And if you listen to any of his trio arrangements, they are very, very complicated. And the guitar is like, one voice of four-part harmony with the piano playing the other four parts. And Les really captivated all those concepts from the pianists that he used. And he always managed to use pianists that were always exceptional.

ZM: See, I used to have long talks with Les. He says, "What kind of player am I?" I said, "You're a lyric player. You play the words." Which is what he was doing. Play the damn lyrics. Don't play anything else. Let me hear that sound. You know if you hear (sings). It is harder to write "You Are My Sunshine" than it is to write a complicated, complex piece of music. You see, musicians don't write hit songs. They write a lot of songs.

RL: How did you meet Les?

ZM: I came on the air and heard he was in this accident… and I practically cried with the people. I said (as I played the record), "You know the fellow who did 'Lover' and 'Brazil' was in a terrible accident and his elbow was knocked off." I found out the hospital got five thousand pieces of mail. So I heard he was 4 or 5 blocks from where I lived and I called. He said, "Come on over." And he's sitting there with his arm in a cast.

After he got well, I used to get transcriptions and dump them in my Cadillac and drive over to Les's place. Could be the "Lone Ranger," could be all the ABC shows. And then he would record on the back of the records. We had a lot of them—and a bottle of booze. I got them for nothing. They were throwing them out. I just had all those so I donated them.

RL: *What else do you remember about Les Paul's studio?*

ZM: *He had a garage studio and I know how he built the disc cutter. I'm sure you know about the disc cutter… the flywheel and where he got the idea for the dentist cord and the pickup arm on this side, so you get the tic-a-tic-a, you know. I said, "How is it your records stand out?" He says, "I use a 50-watt recording amplifier." Well, I don't see how the hell you could use 50 watts but that's what he was using.*

DK: *Sure. The more wattage you use, the better headroom you have for your cutter. He was a good brain picker.*

ZM: *He was the best brain picker in the world. He would call them sharp. Sharp meant he could use you. He knew what kind of guys to be around. And I introduced him, strangely enough, to some pretty damn sharp guys.*

RL: *What happened with Les and Mary when they recorded "How High the Moon" at Jackson Heights?*

ZM: *They didn't have any money to go first class. I got a call from Les on a Sunday morning, "You and Bea, you gotta come over. We got it!" I was living on Riverside Drive (across the river in Manhattan) and we're going up Northern Blvd., about 86th Street, in there. It's down in the basement and the temperature is about 102 degrees. He's got the Ampex with the one extra head, and the Wally Jones mixer—and it's hot as hell! Now he says, "They don't like music upstairs." So we had to put on earphones—my wife, me, Les, and Mary. We got to be thinking "How High the Moon" and he started out with his first track. Then he would do another track. Every time he'd do a track, he went in the back and changed something. I thought he unscrewed the erase head. And I could never understand. He was disconnecting something in back… Anyway, Mary went in there and sang her heart out. And they did seven takes. And the last was always with the thumb bass. He heard something and then he says, "Mary, we're going to do it again because you're going to cringe." Son of a bitch! He made her do it over from the very beginning. They finished that "How High the Moon" and it was just—well, we blew our minds!*

Susie Manners, Zeke's daughter, recalls being with Les, Mary, and her family in the studio in 1953: "I was about five. My father was on WINS radio and he had his own live Zeke Manners TV show in New York. Bea, Zeke, and my brother, we all went to their home recording studio in New Jersey. Not only was it a lot of fun, it was very lively and happy with a lot of wonderful music. I remember the harmony even as a little girl… and the wonderful sound of Les's guitar. Mary's voice was absolutely the greatest. I listened to them live—and I listened to them record. I remember hearing 'How High the Moon.' They were playing it and singing it. They also used to joke around a lot. And my father would play the piano, Les would play the guitar, and Mary would sing. And they would all put it down on a recording. There would be takes sometimes that were really funny. They were always friendly because they were the best of pals. Everybody was happy. It was like going to a family but there were two families. And then, of course, meeting the baby Colleen. I remember Mary bringing in the baby and how happy Les was. These were just really happy days filled with music, joy, and laughter. It was fantastic."

ONE-MAN SHOW—"Zeke" Manners—that irresistible one-man show—popular RCA Victor recording artist greets ABC listeners Monday through Friday at 7:45 a.m. PST over the Pacific Coast network with vocals, records, accordion music, piano "doodlings," and a line of extemporaneous chatter.

Zeke Manners doing his popular morning radio show in 1946 from the RCA Victor Radio News.

The Hit Parade Begins

When Les and Mary first broke with "How High the Moon" in March of 1951, it went to No. 1 and sold 1.5 million records, prompting a Capitol Records executive to comment, "It hit like a gangbuster!" Their next hit, "Mockin' Bird Hill," saw the No. 2 spot. This unprecedented double succession of hits by two relative unknowns took the musical world by surprise. Their catchy, melodic tunes, like "I'm Sitting on Top of the World," just stuck in your head. That first year alone netted them over 500K, and it was just the beginning—a big change from 1950 and before. Even "Nola" was a top seller in Japan and Yugoslavia. Playing the London Palladium for $11,000 a week, and Chicago's Theatre for $18,000 for a week's performance was a handsome fee for the new duo.

Millions were playing Les and Mary's records at home and hearing them on the radio. By 1952, with the next few hits, their record sales went over ten million. They were truly on their big Hit Parade with "Tennessee Waltz," "Mockin' Bird Hill," "Tiger Rag," "In the Good Old Summertime," "Meet Mister Callaghan," "I'm Sitting on Top of the World," "Bye, Bye Blues," and their No. 1, "Vaya Con Dios (May God be With You)," in 1953.

Besides their great musical talents, it was the "Sound" that also captured the public's ears. The driving feel of "How High the Moon" was something new, with its up-front, smooth vocals from Mary and Les's gang of galloping, cooking guitars that drove the music at breakneck speed. Snappy and smart, flashy and slick, they had it all—uptempo and wonderful slow tunes, like "Just One More Chance" and the soulful "Vaya Con Dios," that sold over 2-million records. Then they followed these with a beautiful ballad, "I Really Don't Want to Know." And their instrumental songs, like "Whispering," showcased so many guitar sounds. Les also incorporated muted chicken-picking to the clean bass runs, the sped-up racing guitars of "Tiger Rag" and "I'm Sitting on Top of the World," and tasteful, echoed guitars in "Meet Mister Callaghan."

New York—Tops on the hit parade and thus bait for *Toast of the Town*, Les Paul and Mary Ford were guests on that program recently. Here Ed Sullivan explains the technical problems of the TV camera to Les and Mary. The popularity boost their Capitol record of *Mockin' Bird Hill* gave the pair was just a prelude to the success of their *How High the Moon*.

Here's Les and Mary getting ready for their debut on the original "Toast of the Town" TV variety show that soon became "The Ed Sullivan Show."

(Above) At the suggestion of Mary's sister Carol, "How High the Moon," by Morgan Lewis, was cut in their Jackson Heights basement studio, and went straight to the top of charts in 1951.

(Left) Les and Mary's biggest hit, "Vaya Con Dios (May God be With You)," released in the spring of 1953, sold over three million copies. It was their all-time best seller, even though the flip side, "Johnny (Is the Boy for Me)," was a borrowed Russian melody.

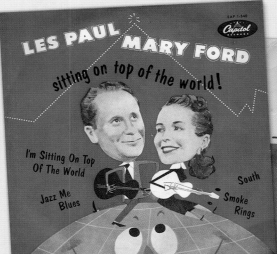

MOCKIN' BIRD HILL
(TRA-LA LA TWITTLE DEE DEE DEE)
Words and Music by VAUGHN HORTON

Sincerely
LES PAUL
and
MARY FORD

SOUTHERN MUSIC PUB. CO., INC.
1619 BROADWAY, NEW YORK 19, N.Y.

(Above) British Capitol 45 extended-play release of "Sitting on Top of the World," with a knockout triangular centerpiece for playing on either record-player spindles or large center. When a chauffeur mentioned the title while driving Les along Riverside Drive in East Manhattan, Les came up with the song, which was recorded in the spring of 1953, and featured Mary singing "I'm sittin' on top of the world, just rollin' along, rollin' along."

(Right) "Mockin' Bird Hill" was another smash hit (that Mary didn't particularly care for). Patty Page had had the original hit on Mercury, but Les and Mary's "tweedle-dee-dees" version was tops. Record stores often pushed Capitol's version when customers asked for the hit.

(Below) "Meet Mr. Callaghan" was a short and well-recorded single with a great melody line. It had a sparkly sound with high octaves above the fundamental melody line. A muted melody verse followed with a tremolo-picked bridge section that Les says reminded him of the snake-rattles sound he once heard in Mexico. It was suggested (to the duo) by Lou Levy, the Andrews Sisters' manager.

As Recorded by LES PAUL on Capitol Record #2193

MEET MISTER CALLAGHAN
By ERIC SPEAR

PIANO SOLO
40¢

LEEDS MUSIC CORPORATION • NEW YORK • CHICAGO • HOLLYWOOD • LONDON

1951's recording successes were dominated by newcomers. In the old days, big-name tunesmiths and singers made the new hits. Now it's the reverse: hit records make new name performers and songwriters.

This year's top record, "Tennessee Waltz," brought singer Patti Page out of relative obscurity. "How High the Moon" did the same for Les Paul and Mary Ford. Another 1951 best-selling record, "Come On-a My House," changed Rosemary Clooney from a $150-a-week performer to a $3,500-a-week star. "Be My Love" made opera-style singer Mario Lanza an RCA-Victor recording star. The current top record is "Because of You," by newcomer Tony Bennett. (*Quicknews*, 1951)

(Above) "Jazz Me Blues" was a well-known Dixieland tune by Tom Delaney, which, as the flip side of "Just One More Chance" did well, too. This happy photograph of them shows the modified Epi that was used on the recording.

(Below) Colorful artwork for "Bye Bye Blues" showing Les and Mary with small portions of their new Gibsons visible. A whitewashed, mahogany frame adorned their last big-time album. Recorded in 1953 in Stroudsburg, Pennsylvania with the Les Paul Gibson guitars.

(Above) "The World Is Waiting for the Sunrise" was co-written by June Lockhart's father Gene. Benny Goodman did a popular version in 1948. The descending triplets lick is one that Les perfected over the few years before it was recorded here. Many takes were recorded, and the final version featured an intro from his later "Down in Jungle Town." It was recorded with the Epi pictured here.

(Left) Les and Mary's second song folio of later tunes, sold through Leo Feist. It included "Goofus," "Tiger Rag," and "Josephine," among others.

(Below) Early "Hit Makers" compilation. Their first hit songs were released in various formats.

(Above) Les and Mary's Christmas EP short album with sweet and nice versions of popular seasonal tunes.

(Above) The "Jungle Bells" spoof is based upon a silly version of "Jingle Bells," published by his Deerhaven Music Corporation.

(Below) A rather formally dressed Les and Mary for their *Time to Dream* LP set over a bay city at dusk. Les is playing his fancy Custom model (with hidden front pickup). For the period it was released, it was elegantly done, while every pop record was showing rockers in funky attire!

(Left) An original "Les and Mary's Christmas" yuletide season's greeting card.

(Above) Capitol's Star Line reissue of Les and Mary's hits.

(Right) A great promo for the "Tiger Rag" hit in 1952 *Music News*. It was a 1912 Dixieland tune he first submitted to NBC as a sped-up demo without a vocal, and was not released commercially. Les really polished it up quite well to orchestrate it. The final version featured the muted guitar sounds and sped-up parts in unison… and included Mary Ford's great voice, of course. The caption reads, "Les Paul and Mary Ford launched 1952 with their version of 'Tiger Rag.' Pictured with the famous movie tiger Satan, it was made at Mabel Stark's Jungle Compound near Los Angeles. "If it is necessary," Les says, "to make these tie-up publicity pictures, my next records will be 'When the Swallows Come Back to Capistrano,' and 'Hot Canary'."

music news

MARCH 1952 • VOL. 10 • NO. 3

10¢

(Above) A very entertaining "Patti Page Show" still where Mary and Patti are both playing Gibson guitars with Les looking over them. Patti would sing songs like "How Much Is the Doggie in the Window." They were doing some multiple-track recording tricks on the show.

(Above) Great formal picture of Les and Mary with an early Gibson LP model by Maurice Seymour. He was *the* photographer for Chicago and the most expensive. This photo shows his superlative lighting and refined compositional skills. *Courtesy Les Paul*

(Left) Here's a nice shot from the same photo session, with a little more light on the duo.

(Right) Les and Mary (with her stunning white dress) are performing in the Cocoanut Grove Ballroom at the famous Ambassador Hotel (home of the Golden Globe Awards) in Los Angeles. *Courtesy Rumble Seat Music and Capitol Records*

LES PAUL MARY FORD

Vaya Con Dios
How High The Moon
Lover
Tennessee Waltz

MA1-1585
Capitol RECORDS
COMPACT DOUBLE 33

© CAPITOL RECORDS, INC.

(Left) This is another nice portrait done by master photographer Seymour. It was made into a signed flyer for their concerts.

(Above) Small 33 rpm EP Capitol release used by DJ Chuck Thompson.

(Left) December 1954 issue of *Recordland* with Rosemary Clooney and our now-famous duo in color!

(Below) Article reviews Les's studio efforts and courting Mary. Pics of an interview, outdoor concert, and adoring fans surrounding them (wearing crowns) for autographs.

Recordland
DECEMBER · 25 CENTS
YOUR RECORD STARS MAGAZINE

AUGUST, 1955

GENUINE-LOVE

By Les Paul

Mary and I just recorded a song called "Genuine Love" for the Capitol Record people, and I can honestly say that I haven't enjoyed making a record as much as this one in a long time. First of all, the song has a natural rhythm to it, and secondly (and most important), the words to this tune started me a-thinkin' just how wonderfully genuine my love for Mary is.

There are times when I get awfully moody and a bit jumpy, especially when a recording session is coming up, but my honey just smooths things out. There are just so many things that Mary has done for me that I couldn't possibly put it all down on paper, for I'd have to write a book to do so. She is my guiding light, my inspiration, a perfect mother and wife, and she is the most unselfish woman in the whole wide world. Our little son Rusty also feels the way I do about Mom! He won't go to sleep unless Mary kisses him goodnight, and strictly off the record — neither will I. My love for Mary is a genuine love, and it'll last forever.

I want to thank HIT PARADER for giving me this opportunity to voice my sentiments. I also hope that you readers will derive enjoyment from reading this story and listening to our song.

By Mary Ford

I credit my success in the music business directly to my husband; for without his patience and faith in my ability, there would never have been a musical team called Les Paul and Mary Ford. Les is a master guitarist, as well as a fine composer, and everything he knew he taught to me.

On the other hand, whether or not I was music conscious, I still would've married Les. I fell in love with "my guy" the very first time I met him a number of years ago. My life with Les is just wonderful; for he is always sweet, sincere and loving. My son and I love him with all our heart and soul. He is an ideal father and the perfect husband.

Les and I recently cut a new record for Capitol about him. The tune "Genuine Love" is a pretty rhythm number with a real fine lyric. When I first glanced at the title I immediately thought, "that's the way I love Les — genuinely," and that's the way I shall always love him!

For some personal reasons (as you know now), I hope this tune catches on because I label it "my song for Les."

(Editor's note: Neither Les nor Mary knew that the other was writing this column. These feelings were voiced separately by the two — and their "Genuine Love" for one another expressed itself spontaneously.)

(Above) Great little Hit Parader "Genuine Love" vignette about Les and Mary's affection for one another. Neither had read the other's response prior to the interview.

(Right) This great article is on the spacious Paul home in Mahwah, New Jersey, showing the various rooms and even Rusty playing a Goldtop guitar.

Mr. & Mrs. Music...

les paul & mary ford

AT HOME WITH LES PAUL AND MARY FORD

By BERNIE PERRY

35

HAPPINESS AND HITS
LES PAUL & MARY FORD

(Below) 1953 *Metronome* Success of the Year article on Les and Mary.

Here Les and Mary sing up another one of their hits, accompanying themselves on electric guitar, at club.

SWINGING AND SWAYING — Les Paul and Mary Ford, spending an evening with Sammy Kaye and his band.

(Above) An older pic of the duo and a shot of them with bandleader Sammy Kaye.

les paul mary ford

SUCCESS OF THE YEAR

Tin Pan Alley is buzzing! That's not so strange; it usually is—but this time it's buzzing about something pretty special. All the talk around the music world concerns a new addition to the Les Pauls, and it's not a new million-seller record. No, it's something more important—a brand new baby, which will mean another big hit for Les and Mary, who are noted for a long succession of happiness and hits.

Show business is made up of lots of wonderful people, but there are none nicer than Les Paul and Mary Ford. They have come up to the top after a long hard struggle, but they have lost none of the "stuff" that has endeared them to millions of music lovers who buy up every disk that Capitol puts out by the pair. When they appear in person, they are gracious and so wonderful to their fans that it seems impossible that they sign as many autographs as they do. In short, these two haven't forgotten who put them on top — their fans.

Les and Mary avoid the spotlight as much as possible. They have moved to a beautiful home in the hills of New Jersey, and Les has fixed up an electronic studio where he and Mary, with their oldest son Rusty, can spend many happy hours experimenting with the new sounds that have brought fame and fortune for the pair. They are content to let other people be seen in nightclubs and on the screen, while they find contentment with their family and their music. The entertainment world owes a lot

to the Pauls of New Jersey. Les was instrumental in originating a new phase of the music business. His multiple recordings and echo chamber have written one of the most successful chapters into the history of popular music. Les and Mary have turned out hit record after hit record, and today they stand head and shoulders over all other recording artists in the amount of records sold in the United States. From "Brazil," one of their first, to "Whither Thou Goest," their latest record, "Mr. and Mrs. Guitar" have set the pace. Not long ago Capitol announced that Les and Mary's record of "Vaya Con Dios" had become one of the biggest money winners in Cap's history—and that is only one honor among hundreds that have come to the fabulous twosome.

When we talked to Les a while back, he told us that he was working on some new gimmicks that would be ready for the music world in a very short time. What they were Les wouldn't tell us, so we will have to wait and see. He did let us know about the new member of the family, which as we write this, is forecast for the first week of December. Les and Mary would like a little sister for Rusty, so they both have their fingers crossed.

SONG HITS is proud and happy to salute two great assets to the entertainment world—Les Paul and Mary Ford. Music is their business, but happiness and hits are the results of the efforts of the greatest twosome in the game today.

NOBODY ever connected with jazz has ever made any greater a splash in the waters of the moon than Les Paul has in the last sixteen or seventeen months. For "waters of the moon" read "cash register." And understood that when it is written that Les Paul was "connected with jazz," an understatement has been perpetrated. More often than not today one hears everything but jazz in a Les Paul record. But there are exceptions, and those sides remind one that this boy was once one of the best, that he used to display his fretful facility in the frame of jazz more often than not, and that he's still capable of the kind of beat and musicianship that made his V-Disc version of *Dark Eyes* so entrancing and with it his *All of Me*, which was all of Les.

All of Les—that means a Wisconsin origin (Waukesha, 1916), an early harmonica wizardry (at 14, in Milwaukee), the National Barn Dance program (playing the character of "Rhubarb Red"), Fred Waring (for five years), Bing Crosby (on records), the army, the backyard garage (where Les perfected his multiple-tape recording technique). All of Les—that means plenty of comedy, low and high, and gimmicks to catch the laughs. The tricks which Les first displayed publicly in his recordings of *Lover* and *Brazil* were as much as Les can intend anything. Then they were meant to amuse. Then of Les and his wife, Mary Ford, a deadpan hill-billy which was one of the

(Above) Tin Pan Alley is buzzing! Spotlights on Les and Mary with their top-seller "Vaya Con Dios" plus a hint of Les's new "gimmicks" for the guitar, and a sister for Rusty?

Les Paul and Mary Ford show their pet pooch the inside of an old-time recording machine that still works. Les and Mary would sou...

(Left) April '54 pic showing Les and Mary with their dog by the old Victrola, doing the "His Master's Voice" pose.

Music VIEWS
MAY • 1954

les & mary

36

(Left) May of '54 *Music Views* cover with a great pic of them playing the Gibsons.

(Right) 1954 *Music Views* page showing life at in Ramapo Valley. Both Wally and Carol Kamin are shown living there. Les and Wally tried to resurrect the old aluminum guitar. *Photos courtesy Ed Bergeles*

LES 'N' MARY

A secluded white cottage in the Ramapo Valley, N.J., is the home and recording studio of "Mr. and Mrs. Sound," Les Paul and Mary Ford. Here they cut "Vaya Con Dios," their big hit of 1953.

Les and Mary take time out for relaxation and a bite to eat before putting the finishing touches to their latest disk, "Jungle Bells" and "White Christmas."

Mary rehearses while sister Carol Kamin prepares lunch.

The famous duo at work. Beautiful new studio and control room cost $60,000.

Carol's husband, Wally, is technician, plays bass and acts as secretary. He and Carol live with the Pauls.

Les and Wally repair one of Les's many guitars. They constantly try to produce new effects and improve the techniques that keep their disks on top.

PHOTOS: ED WERGELES—NEWSWEEK

WHEN THEY FIRST STARTED OUT. Les Paul and Mary Ford—real names Mr. ... recording in basements and bathrooms to get the eerie sounds that made them famous. Now ... work in their own sound studio rigged with the latest recording gadgets. Here they rel...

112

(Left) Fantastic article in the January 1955 issue of *Cosmopolitan*. Mary holding their Chihuahua and Les outdoors with their collie.

UNTIL THEY MADE *"How High the Moon,"* Les and Mary were just a good guitarist and a little-known singer. Then fans latched on to their New Sound, and "Moon" sales soared.

(Right) The bathrobe guitar kiss!

Les Paul and Mary Ford (continued)

WITH THIRTEEN-YEAR-OLD RUSTY, one of Les's two sons by a former marriage, Les and Mary go fishing. Kept bus... in the past by night-club dates, recordings, and stage and TV shows, the Pauls had no home and no free time. Now the... work at home and enjoy their nine acres. Mary's sister Carol and her husband, Wally Kamin, live and work with them

(Above) Rusty, Les, and Mary in the front yard taking off to go fishing with the collie in tow.

Les Paul and Mary Ford

...usical sleight of hand, they make a guitar and voice sound like ... and vocal chorus. The result is sometimes weird, but it has meant ... and a big batch of hit records for this husband-and-wife team

...OLDBERG

...enerally un-...en an irregu-... a steady flow ...ency amount-... of a million ...can be veri-...mone bracket. ... remarkably ... years—with ...d his pretty, ...ile, who goes ...is convinced ...made the bar-...unintention-...ngs deeply. ...ywood at the ...curity. Well-...les is an ex-... though not ...al not send ob-...was gratifying ...ch as to impel ...ent to play the

guitar accompaniment for some of his recordings. And then Les's mother, back home in Waukesha, Wisconsin, wrote him a crushing letter.

"I heard you playing on the Bob Hope radio show last week," wrote Mrs. Evelyn Polfus, "and I liked you fine."

Case of Mistaken

This would have made ... for the fact that he hadn... Bob Hope show for seve... Sitting in the sun on th... $125,000 home—which al... cording and television a... Ramapo Mountains of Ne... a tall, full glass in his han... rueful smile on his broad ... recalled this juncture in ... very depressing," he said... mother thinks you sound lik... guitar player—no differen... what's the use, I thought...

knocking myself out to be better than any other guitar player, and my own mother didn't know me. It was enough to make me want to quit."

Les did not quit. With his amazing technique—his playing was first called the New S...

LES ADJUSTS DIALS as Mary sings behind a glass panel in making one of their famed multiple recordings. Les plays rhythm, melody, harmony, and background on his guitar, imitates saxophone and other instruments.

...D MANTEL are some of Les Paul's 150 electric guitars. A ...teen, Les turned to song writing while recuperating from a ...cident in 1948, and wrote "Cryin'" and "Counterfeit Love."

(Above) Les with his rack of modified Goldtops. Note the one he's holding and the far-right guitar—both have factory Tune-O-Matic bridges, two controls, and outputs on top! The second guitar is one of the first two sent over and has the ES-175 tailpiece with a bar bridge.

UNABLE TO READ A NOTE OF MUSIC. Les is also self-taught as a sound engineer. Yet on his own, he has developed sound techniques many experts are unable to duplicate. Here he and Mary adjust some equipment.

115

(Above) In the studio with Les and Mary. Les adjusts the console, below.

Les Paul Mary Ford

DEERHAVEN ROAD
OAKLAND, NEW JERSEY

January 27, 1956

Chuck Thompson
Station W A L A
Mobile, Alabama

Dear Chuck:

Hope you haven't sold our space on your tie rack -- really this is the first chance we've had to write. We've been filming a TV series and between the filming and recording the music for the shows we've been up to our ears lately, but anyway we're here now.

Please let us know if there is anything else we can do for you, and until next time Mary and I send our very best.

Yours,

(Left) Personal letter to Alabama DJ Chuck Thompson who promoted Les and Mary on his radio shows for years. *Courtesy Chuck Thompson, 2004*

Live Performances

During 1951, Les and Mary performed at the famous Paramount Theater on 42nd Street in New York City. It was a lengthy engagement—they played four shows daily for fourteen days. They performed between movies, starting at noon and running through 9 P.M. Elaine Vaughan, who had also worked the shows said, "We had twelve people who worked in the six ticket booths. The shows were so popular, the lines would go all the way around the back of the building by the backstage entrance." Les and Mary were originally the opening act for Frankie Laine; they were so sensational that they soon became the headline act.

Les and Mary took off from New York for England on September 3, 1952 for a series of concerts.

They traveled first-class aboard the famous Cunard Line's *Queen Elizabeth* steamship, staying on deck B, stateroom 79. Carol and Wally stayed in a cozy berth one floor down, enjoying their romantic vacation onboard. The troupe landed in a drizzly Southampton harbor a few days later amidst a lively group of fans. Savvy magazine reporters somehow gained early access onboard in order to get an exclusive interview with and photos of the couple before they disembarked. Meanwhile, Wally, who had fallen ill from food poisoning, was being pushed in a wheelchair while all the baggage and musical instruments were heading for customs. Les and Mary were whisked past the excited horde of fans and media and onto the train to London. Luckily, the gear got through, but unfortunately, the band charts were lost. The group went straight to the famous Palladium theatre for the beginning of a two-week stint. The talented orchestra leader quickly wrote up new charts and truly saved the day.

This sticker was affixed to their guitar cases as they left for Southampton, England on the *Queen Elizabeth* in September of 1952.

The *Queen Elizabeth* passing the *Queen Mary*. At the time, they were the largest superliners in the world.

Being in close proximity to Paris with a few days to kill, Les and Mary jumped over to France in search of guitar great Django Reinhardt. After bribing some cab drivers and meeting Reinhardt's other relatives, Les finally got to meet his hero—which became a momentous occasion for both guitarists.

In August of 1953, Les and Mary performed at the Chicago Theater for two weeks. They did four shows, between movies, that included both matinee and evening performances at noon, 2 P.M., 4:30 P.M., and 8:30 P.M. (At the time, film was replacing vaudeville, so the shows were vaudevillian in nature.) The Chicago Theater was the Mecca for Midwest live acts. Some ticket-buyers would actually sit through two movie showings just to see Les and Mary perform. At the time, Wally Kamin played a gold-painted upright bass that had a raised gold Gibson logo on it. Carol Summers Kamin, Mary's sister, was once again offstage singing her harmony parts.

"The whole show with the orchestra was quite amazing," according to Del Kacher. "It was incredible, with Les playing his Goldtop Gibson. He was absolutely stunning. The sound he got out of the guitar filled the entire theater with a clear bell-like tone. I never heard a sound like that before. Because he didn't have the multiple recording to back him up, he had the orchestra play the other sped-up guitar parts on trumpets. It sounded fantastic playing his

arrangements with him on lead guitar. It absolutely sparkled with the spontaneity of a live orchestra. When he finished playing 'Lover,' there were beads of sweat on his forehead—meanwhile, Mary was nonchalantly relaxed and lovely. They made a fabulous team. That live performance really did it for me! He made it really work." All this excitement is through the wide eyes of Del Kacher, a fifteen-year-old Hammond, Indiana boy. Mary had the new Polaroid camera and graciously snapped a picture of Les and Del together, which Les signed. This was quite an experience for a young guitarist of the '50s.

(Above) The cool and collected guitar-slinger Les Paul at the Chicago Theater, talking to a young Del Kacher (who's enthralled while playing the master's Goldtop). *Photo by Mary Ford. Courtesy Del "Casher" Kacher*

Film and TV Takes

Abbot and Costello Presents

An episode of this comedy show features Les and Mary starting off with a lip-synced version of "I Really Don't Want to Know." This slow ballad has them using the modified gold guitars. Les's guitar has the Kauffman vibrola and pointer knobs, while Mary is playing the original unbound fingerboard gold model with a DeArmond and a mystery lead pickup. They do two syncopated duet guitar parts together beautifully. Then they go live, and Les talks about a piano player's hit parade in Texas, and starts his tuning shtick and harmonic shenanigans. Mary imitates Les's zipping slides as they go into "No Place Like Home," and she slides the last note even better than Les. Les tries to further stump Mary, first with odd stops and timing, then lyrics, but can't outfox her. He says, "Name is Les," and starts singing rounds, then does his hammer-ons and pull-offs. Knowing Mary has one up on him, Les finally reaches over to stop Mary's strings once she really gets going—and he actually broke a finger in the process! Meanwhile, Mary—being a real country pro—harmonizes perfectly with the hillbilly tune. Then they break into a short lip-synced version of "Tiger Rag." Mary sings, "Here kitty, kitty, kitty. Here puss, puss, puss," and Les does his pull-offs on the "meow" parts of "Hold that tiger!" Mary clearly shows in that live clip that she can really hold her own playing hot guitar licks and keeping up with Les's odd time. Much of this shtick was worked up with Joe Wolverton many years before.

(Below) Here Les is trying to stump Mary to no avail. Her quick wits and sharp guitar playing are quite evident during this live portion of the show.

A few times a day starting in 1953, the "Les and Mary at Home" show would showcase them on television with a 4 ½ minute song with an interesting little story line.

Listerine Presents

The episode titled "Les Paul and Mary Ford at Home" opens with the "Vaya Con Dios My Love" theme playing in the background. The scene features Les playing his black Custom Gibson while standing near the barbeque and wearing his folded-over chef's hat, while Mary is lounging nearby. They go into "I Can't Give You Anything But Love," and the camera zooms in on Les's black Custom guitar with the hidden front pickup. During the solo, Mary does the "oohs." (At the end, it breaks into a Listerine commercial with Betsy and Bob Martin's halitosis, or bad breath, problem and her sour face! Later they kiss after taking the mouthwash.) Les then breaks into a ditty with some high-octave parts and says, "So long folks."

The next segment is set in a kitchen with Les fixing the cord on an iron as Mary unpacks groceries, and "I'm Sitting on Top of the World" starts. There's a close-up of the Custom Les Paul guitar during a short solo, and Mary's smooth vocals continue as she puts a cookie in Les's mouth. It breaks to commercial and returns with Mary saying, "The refrigerator isn't working." Les says, "Maybe I can serenade it back to life with 'This Can't Be Love,'" and then he plays both parts as he nudges the fridge. Mary is then seen on the phone, and soon discovers Les had the iron plugged in instead and is defrosting the freezer with it!

At the end, the titles say, "Les & Mary at Home, brought to you by Listerine Antiseptic, a film by Dumont Electronicam (an Instructo-Corp TV-Film System)." It was written by Eileen and Robert Mason Pollock and directed by Herbert Hirschman. The *TV Guide* blurb on the short, five-minute "Les & Mary at Home" shows said, "It's hard to pinpoint when the shows air, and they're way too short."

(Right) Robert Saudek's innovative "Omnibus" television show with Alistair Cooke interviewing Les and Mary about their remarkable sound-on-sound capabilities.

Omnibus

To many 1953 circles, television had not yet earned the respect of intellectuals and journalists. The Ford Foundation suggested to ABC that they do a progressive series on forward and provocative subjects, and "Omnibus" became a reality. It took the risk of featuring not-ordinarily viewed scenes on national TV. Robert Saudek, then the vice president of ABC, produced this innovative show, which showcased the most imaginative and articulate American people, including scientists, artists, dancers, architects, and musicians. Alistair Cooke was the show's well-spoken host. One of its most popular segments featured a special musical act with a technical angle—namely Les and Mary. The following is an excerpt of the episode's interview segment, which also featured narrator Hume Cronyn:

Alistair Cooke: Now, if the sales figures are on the level, I think there's no question that two out of three of you at least know that this is the music of Les Paul and Mary Ford—and here they are! (Les and Mary enter with their hit record playing in the background.)

Hume Cronyn: Saudek's creativity was on full display in a segment featuring Les Paul and Mary Ford. The famous duo was invited not just to perform, but to demonstrate their pioneering recording techniques. (Les starts off with his two Ampex machines and early modified Goldtop with a miked Pro amp turned up in the corner).

LP: You turn the tape machines on (he switches on one machine). They're just standard, regular Ampex tape machines. We play the first part on the guitar— this is the rhythm part (he plays the basic track). You play the second part to this (he reaches over to the machine). Yeah, they're both on... all right (he plays a higher fill part).

AC: You play all this to Mary, is that right? Or does she do it separately?

LES PAUL & MARY FORD 1953

Here we see Les preparing the Ampex recorders and playing his modified Goldtop.

May of 1953 *Audio Engineering* Magazine special on Les's "World of Sound" Mary sings away while Les picks in the control room.

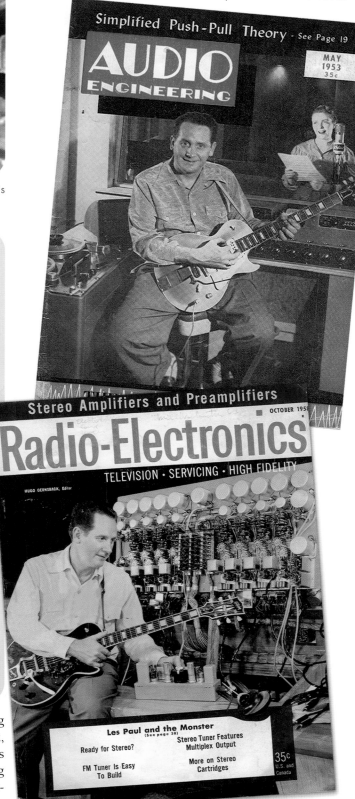

LP: *Well, Mary will hear the part that's already made, and she sings onto it.*

AC: *I see.*

Mary Ford: *I'll play the first part first.*

LP: *Okay. All set Mary?*

MF: *Yes. Give me a G chord.* (Les starts the machines and she begins singing, holding just one headphone on.)

MF (singing): *"Somewhere there's music, how faint the tune. Somewhere there's heaven, how high the moon."* (She ends with her wonderful vibrato.)

AC: *Now, how many tracks… what's the most tracks you've ever made?*

LP: *Well, the most that we've put out on the market is twelve guitars and twelve of Mary singing.*

AC: *Does that mean… twenty-four tracks?*

LP: *Very good!* (Mary and the audience all laugh together.)

AC: *Well* (calms his throat), *could you play that back to us and maybe put in a twenty-fifth?*

LP: *Sure! It will actually be twenty-six because Mary will sing one and I'll play one.*

AC: *Twenty-six tracks… of "How High the Moon?" Twenty-six parts… recordings!*

LP: *Well… parts. All set?*

Then they break into their famous hit recording, playing right along at breakneck speed. Les whips some quick, flashy stuff out while those beautiful Ampex machines reel away. Les's echoed parts and Mary's glorious backing voices were already included. With the previously prepared segments, it actually sounds remarkably like the original recording! This great television segment was just a glimpse of the things to come for Les and Mary.

October 1958 issue of *Radio-Electronics* featuring Les Paul and the Monster! Here's an underside view of the recording console, round white step-pots, US Navy headphones, and his grey mic preamp.

(Above left page) Eric Leslie takes us on a tour of Les's home studio and discusses the techniques of getting the exciting "New Sound." Lower left shows the console room with Ampex recorders, the mixing board, and the stacked eight-track "Octopus" (dubbed by W.C. Fields).

(Above right page) Left picture shows the eight-track heads, while the right has the cutting lathe to cut grooves into an acetate lacquer disc for final EQ mixes.

(Left) 1957 shot of the Ampex stacked eight-track "Octopus" recording machines.

(Right) 1955 *Hi-Fi Music at Home* issue with article on Mr. And Mrs. "Sound." Great cover with Customs and multiple guitars.

(Right) Inside pictures from the Les Paul *Now* LP with early shot of Les in his lab showing his portable Ampex machines and old bottle-covered microphones. Included are pictures of the control room and console.

(Below) Les's early Telefunken carbon microphone from his personal collection.

This is where it all started

Master control panel overlooking the NEW studio

METRONOME
MUSIC USA

May, 1957   35¢

LES PAUL AND MARY FORD IN HI-FI

SPECIAL HI-FIDELITY ISSUE

(Above) May of 1957 *Metronome* issue
with Mary Ford doing vocals.

(Left) Les with his Navy headphones and the Custom with hidden pickup.

(Below) Great Ampex ad from 1958 showing their professional lineup.

LES PAUL: "I want sound as it really is."

(Above) "I want sound as it is!"
article showing Les recording with his
Custom and Mary singing nearby.

(Right) The magic sound factory!
Here are some pictures of studio
gear including Wally Jones' mixers
and underside of the "Monster."

43

The Gibson Liaison

The main subject of this book is the legendary Les Paul Gibson guitar. Les had been playing Gibson instruments for many years, and had wanted the company to make a solid-body guitar before they were actually ready to. Finally, a deal was made with Mr. Berlin of CMI and the company president Ted McCarty in 1951. This topic is covered in-depth in chapter 2.

Both Ted's and Les's families would socialize through the years while the guitar was being produced. The following interview is with Ted McCarty's daughter Susan, who was an impressionable young lady during Gibson's wonderful heyday years that produced their first solid-body guitar.

RL: *Please tell me about this great picture of all of you together?*

Susan McCarty: *It was 1952. We were in a hotel room. They were performing, I believe. I think we had gone up to the room before their performance. We were visiting and having a drink, and we went downstairs and they performed. But I can't tell you where it was because I forgot. It's written on the back of the photo.*

RL: *So you are all together.*

SM: *Yes, we are all together. It was normal. And you know, I didn't realized at the moment how special it was. It's just something you did. And then they would perform and we watched. Sometimes they would be playing somewhere, and we'd sit in the front and then, when they were done, Mary… she was such a pretty lady. She just came and sat down and gave me a butterfly hairpin. Here I am, a little girl, sitting there, and she gave that to me. She was very nice to me. They were just nice people.*

RL: *And they used to come visit?*

SM: *Um-hmm. And my father could tell you stories about that, because they would come, even to our home in Kalamazoo after… in the late fifties and early sixties, they would come. If they were around, they would drink beer by the… At the time, Les Paul was a real big beer drinker. And my dad would talk about how you would have to go out and get the whole trunk of the car filled with beer and bring it in because Les Paul was coming to drink beer (laughs).*

RL: *So how old were you when your father started at Gibson?*

SM: *Eight.*

RL: *Do remember how that happened? Where you were living?*

SM: *We were living in Winnetka, Illinois. He'd been working for Wurlitzer. And, as a child we knew he had quit Wurlitzer, and he was looking for a job. And he would go on interviews and he'd, you know, do it. And as a child, I wasn't paying a whole lot of attention. And he came home one day and said we were going to move to Kalamazoo, Michigan… and we all laughed. Because we all thought he was kidding. What do you mean Kalamazoo? Who ever heard of that? And so we moved to Kalamazoo. And there was a period of time… he must have started in the spring of '48 because he went back and forth to Kalamazoo, and we were still in Winnetka until the school year was over. He bought the house. He painted and did whatever inside. And then we moved that summer.*

RL: *And what street was that on?*

SM: *Glenwood Drive. That's the old Glenwood Drive house. 2311 Glenwood Drive. And then we moved to 2412 Bronson Boulevard. We built a house and we moved down there, 1955 maybe.*

RL: *Did you ever go to the factory with Ted?*

SM: *Oh sure. Oh yes.*

RL: *What do you remember?*

SM: *It was just always so interesting.*

This is Ted McCarty with his wife and daughter along with Les and Mary. Susan's caption reads, "Left to right: Ted, Susan, Les Paul - front row, Back row - Elinor and Mary 1952."
Courtesy Susan Davis

Shades of a great past prophesy a greater future for *Gibson*

George Barnes, Les Paul, Nick Lucas, Paul Martin—such artists keep alive the fame of Gibson guitars these war years; for they depend upon them to make the most of their talent. ● Gibson performance speaks for itself in their hands with top bands like those of Dorsey, Scott, Rey, Krupa, Goodman. ● Shades of a great past indeed, forecasting postwar Gibsons that are the finest yet.

Gibson INC. KALAMAZOO, MICHIGAN

1940 Gibson catalog with Les Paul, Nick Lucas, George Barnes, and other popular Gibson endorsees who promise great music and products for the upcoming post-war years.

From Capitol to Columbia Records

Les Paul really knew how to produce some fine records. He had a motive for every song. He was a frontrunner as far as being one of the first producer/artists. Then things started to slack off for Les and Mary's catalog during the mid '50s. Capitol's Tommy Morgan was basically pushing his records and things weren't selling too well. Record promo staffers would go out to the record stations and say hello in order to promote the new records. As good as they were, they still weren't selling. Les tried many ways to get with it and nothing worked. The recordings were actually quite pristine and clinically clean with the new eight-track Ampex machines. Some say Les was almost manufacturing the feeling, which seemed to cause the recordings to lose their heart and soul—which people picked up on. They turned instead towards the new wave of rock 'n' roll. Plus, times had changed; rock 'n' roll had arrived, and musical tastes were shifting.

Mitch Miller, of "Sing Along with Mitch" fame, signed them up with Columbia Records in 1958, and released "Swingin' South," "Lovers' Luau," "Warm and Wonderful," and a country effort called "Bouquet of Roses." Early Columbia hit tracks, like "Jura (I Swear I Love You)" and "The Poor People of Paris," had some verve comparable to Les and Mary's hot Capitol releases. The duo's recordings were finely recorded and very well executed—but almost too predictable at times. Going from having big hits to not having any causes a freefall for anyone accustomed to a hit parade. Playing songs that people didn't necessarily want to buy was no longer an option. It seemed that the harder Les and Mary tried, the more they were out of step. They even did a version of Hank Williams's "Your Cheatin' Heart," which had a rock 'n' roll flavor and featured a harmonica part and even a fuzz guitar! Their stint at Columbia from 1958–63 just didn't get the ball rolling again. Les's fine guitar work and Mary's vocals, which ranged in execution from melancholy to cheerful, were inspiring, clever, original, and harmonically daring. Clearly they were left behind with the musical times, as many

More Hawaiian-flavored tunes, this time with Mary's sweet vocals. The actual photo was staged in New Jersey!

Columbia release of country tunes. They called a nearby music store to get the Les Paul SG model for the photo session.

were during those years. Les did a brilliant job of creating new records, but a lack of hit material limited their success. The new public was interested in other trends—which soon shook the world.

Things unfortunately were slowly deteriorating on the home front. Mary was used to relaxing at home and enjoying the easy-going lifestyle, while Les kept up his busy pace, going full-tilt and staying up late working long hours. Mary became exhausted from their active schedule and the raising of their two kids. (After trying to conceive a child for a while, in 1953, Les and Mary finally adopted a little girl they named Colleen. And then to their surprise, little Bobby came along in 1957.) After six years of raising the kids, Mary and Les unfortunately separated in 1963, and a divorce ensued. As their relationship ended, the Gibson guitar deal fizzled, and their record sales ebbed. It was time for a break, so Les retired… temporarily.

Another early '60s release of standards like "After You've Gone" and "Come Back to Me." These tunes became "novel experiences when dusted off and polished to a high shine by Les Paul and Mary Ford."

Gibson Experiments with the Solid-Body Guitar

True origins of what became the Les Paul guitar go back to 1950, when they developed their first prototypes of their Spanish solid-body guitars. Gibson had previously made electric Hawaiian guitars during the 1930s that featured 5/16"-thick tops that stopped feedback successfully, and also true solid-body steel guitars like their Ultratone model in the late 1940s. After becoming aware of Fender's new "Esquire" solid-body at the 1950 summer NAMM (National American Musical Merchandisers) convention, Gibson's new president Ted McCarty felt they, too, could easily build one—and add to it their traditional Gibson flavor.

"We wanted to keep an eye on it," says Ted, "and see what they were going to do with it… you know. Nobody was making one in those days except Paul Bigsby, and that's where he [Leo] got his sample—from one of the fellows—and put it on the market. Which is all right; that's his business.

"Because, when Leo was making his, he used ash wood, and it was all flat. And I said, 'Well, if we're going to make one, we're going to put our regular archtop on, same as we had on all of our other guitars.' And we did. We spent a year making… we made lots of guitars, seeking what we thought was going to be the best. And that's what finally became the Les Paul guitar."

(Above) The famous 1917 Gibson factory sporting a new red color photographed here in 1975.

(Right, above) Special large body 1937 EH-150 7-string steel guitar in natural figured maple. One of three built measuring 14 1/2" wide and 4" deep with 5/8" 5-ply laminated sides and customary 5/16" book-matched top and back. This guitar's body construction gives it great acoustic and electric volume without feedback.

(Right) 1949 Gibson catalog cover, "Favorite of the Stars." Note Les wearing glasses. He's in good company with Dave Barbour, George Barnes, and Oscar Moore.

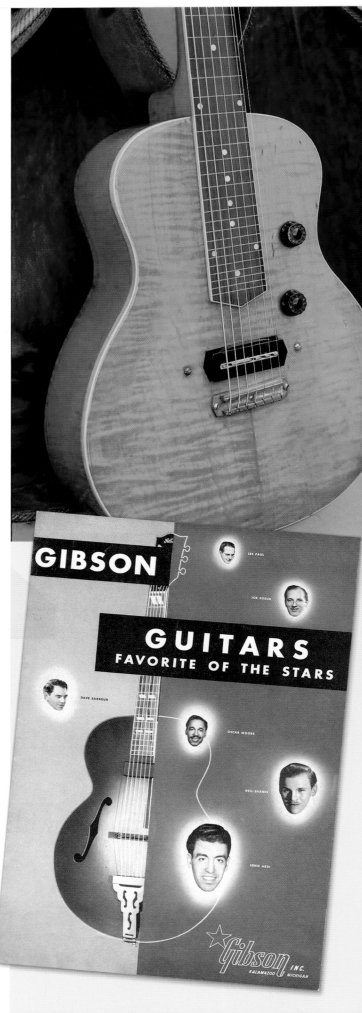

(Left) Paul Bigsby single-cutaway solid-body guitar #2. Merle Travis had him build the first one to his specs in 1947. Bigsby used birds-eye maple with contrasting walnut pieces on many of his instruments. *Courtesy Richard Allen*

(Above) The post-war Gibson EH-125 Steel guitar shows the earliest known solid-body construction prior to the BR and Ultratone series.

(Left) Gibson's solid-body maple Ultratone steel guitar is depicted here available in white with striking coral pink and gold-highlighted plastic covers. Its high volume (without feedback) capabilities were quite apparent.

THE GIBSON ULTRATONE ELECTRIC HAWAIIAN GUITAR

Gibson is justly proud of its newest Electric Hawaiian Guitar, whose streamlined beautiful design is matched by its perfection of performance.

Of maple, the Ultratone is enamelled sparkling white and is trimmed in coral, gold and silver. A custom-built white and silver plastic peg-head cover serves to protect the player's left arm and clothing from sharp edges, and to cover the machine-head string posts.

The coral unit cover is decorated by a gold and silver design and has a twofold purpose in acting as a hand rest for easier playing and in protecting the player's right sleeve.

The modernistic plastic fingerboard is of silver with position dots of varied colors. A specially engineered pick-up has six powerful magnets which insure clear and sustained tones in all registers, and the three instrument controls provide any desired volume in a wide range of tone colors from deep mellow bass to clear resonant treble.

The Ultratone is now available with either six or seven strings.

The Experiments Begin

From the actual, first-hand interviews between myself and Les Paul, Gibson president Ted McCarty, Julius Bellson, Walt Fuller, CMI salesman John Levy, Gibson rep/player "Tiny" Timbrell, and Hollywood veteran repairman and Gibson consultant Milt Owens, I have tried to accurately piece together the evolution of Gibson's solid-body electric Spanish guitars.

Master musician and engineer Lloyd Loar had left the Gibson ranks over a dispute concerning electrics, and did his unusual Vivi-Tone electrics during the 1930s. Based on a vibrating bridge design, they didn't catch on.

Other electrics like Rickenbacher's Electro A-25 and Gibson's ES-150 then set the stage. Slingerland's late-'30s, 401 solid-electric Spanish was small and impractical. In the early '40s, a gentleman from Iowa by the name of O.W. Appleton approached Gibson with his visionary custom, single-cutaway, solid-body with a Gibson neck. The world still wasn't very interested at that point. With his winged "Log" Epiphone, Les Paul had also been trying to convince Gibson to make a solid-body guitar during the '40s. The company, in effect, politely declined, even though Les had been endorsing Gibson!

By 1950, the early Spanish solid-bodies of Paul Bigsby and Leo Fender had become a reality, and were creating some excitement on the West Coast. The introduction of the Fender Esquire electric Spanish guitar at the 1950 NAMM trade show caused some eyebrows to rise and prompted a lot of jokes; but the Western Swing players and many other adventurous musicians quickly adopted the new Fender's ringing highs and inherent sustaining qualities.

This also caught the attention of Ted McCarty and Maurice Berlin of Chicago Musical Instruments, Gibson's parent company. They soon discussed these California "upstarts," and decided to do something about it. They had been building the EH-125, Ultratone, Century, and BR series of solid-body Hawaiian guitars for a few years; it wasn't that far of a stretch to make a Spanish model, too. Mr. Berlin then had Ted McCarty and the Gibson engineers start their initial experiments.

(Above) Leo Fender gave this to Les Paul back in 1951. This early guitar (#1751) is the transition "1951 Fender" solid-body built between the Broadcaster and Telecaster models (February to August). Les received this instrument, along with a tweed linen-covered Dual Professional (pre-Super-amp) 2-10" angled front combo amplifier, while living in Hollywood, CA.

(Below) 1930s Vivi-Tone electric instrument catalog showing Lloyd Loar's guitar years after his Gibson days. *Courtesy Julius Bellson*

True Prototypes

Gibson's first experimental solid-body Spanish guitars were virtually solid versions of their basic ES-125 model, in different sizes. They were test-bed prototype instruments designed for hearing the tonality and practicality of purely solid-construction models. Gibson luthiers actually built them with a simple non-cutaway, flat top and back, sunburst-finished, unbound mahogany bodies, and a single P-90 pickup placed in the center.

(Above) Chicago Musical Instruments corporate office on N. Cicero Ave in nearby Chicago, Illinois.

(Right) Catalog depiction of Gibson's popular ES-125 electric guitar. The earliest solid-body experiment by Gibson in 1950 had this basic (although slightly smaller) shape, color, and electronics.

(Below) Maurice Berlin was founder and president of CMI and became Secretary-Treasurer of Gibson in 1944. His happy demeanor was apparent from this close-up photograph.

Julius Bellson recalls, "Well, we make quite a few proto-types. But sometimes they're never completed. And they never come out on the market, or they come out several years later. We made a completely solid-body instrument, which wasn't any good. It was so dang heavy because, you know, it was a full-sized instrument almost." This instrument—the first large, Spanish solid Julius described—must have sounded terrific, but was highly impractical as a production instrument. The next prototype was a similar, non-cutaway Gibson design that was made smaller for obvious weight reasons—around 12 3/4", like the new three-quarter-sized ES-140 model.

The smaller, experimental solid guitar was officially named the "Ranger." This very guitar was sent with Gibson's top salesman, Clarence Havenga, to Los Angeles in late 1950. CMI's salesman John Levy feels Clarence's fieldwork and overall enthusiasm was also quite instrumental in helping Gibson develop the guitar. "I think at that time, the man who would be most responsible for the Les Paul guitar would be Clarence Havanga, sales manager for Gibson," says John. "Clarence was known as 'Mr. Gibson,' and was quite a character."

Tiny Timbrell, the L.A. Gibson rep saw the actual proto-type in Toluca Lake, and discussed with Clarence the merits and drawbacks of the guitar. His personal eyewitness account distinctly recalls that the name "Ranger" was imprinted on the pickguard with a similar logo style as the later Gibson amp. Aptly named from early rock-etry and American pioneering nomenclature, the Ranger was clearly breaking new ground and scouting the way of the future.

Gibson endorsement portrait featuring guitarist/salesman "Tiny" Timbrell. Tiny was a popular Gibson rep in California for many years after performing with the Harry James orchestra.

Tiny stated that the guitar resembled a non-cutaway sunburst Les Paul Junior model flat-top with a pickup placed in the center of the body (as on their current electric Spanish models). He said the neck was a simple, unbound rosewood fingerboard with dot inlays. Scale-wise, the earlier, large version possibly had the 25 1/2" scale length, like found on the current 1950 ES-150 guitar. A medium, 25" scale may well have been used on the Ranger, instead of the production 24 3/4". Details on the bridges and tail-pieces weren't specifically discussed. I imagine they were much like other Gibson models, with a freely attached, compensated bridge and small ES-125-style trapeze tailpiece (with a high-set neck).

Clarence also showed the Ranger to Milt Owens, the longtime Hollywood repairman for many Gibson artists in the Los Angeles area. Milt told me of Clarence Havenga's visit with the new solid-body Gibson, and similarly described the Ranger guitar to me.

As basic as this early effort was, it was certainly a big step for Gibson. Forging ahead with solid-body guitar technology would create a wonderful new world of guitar playing, and would soon generate a new musical genre to the world. The Ranger was the first jumping board to the next step in the evolution of Gibson's solid-body future.

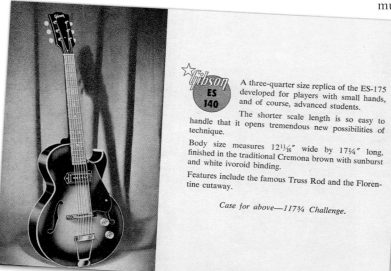

Gibson advertisement for the new ES-140 3/4: a three-quarter-sized jazz guitar that set the stage for the basic Les Paul guitar shape and size.

A three-quarter size replica of the ES-175 developed for players with small hands, and of course, advanced students.

The shorter scale length is so easy to handle that it opens tremendous new possibilities of technique.

Body size measures 12 11/16" wide by 17 1/4" long, finished in the traditional Cremona brown with sunburst and white ivoroid binding.

Features include the famous Truss Rod and the Florentine cutaway.

Case for above—117 3/4 Challenge.

Maple

After their initial field-testing of the Ranger guitar and its sonic feasibility, Gibson felt it was necessary to add the cutaway for optimal upper-fingerboard access; plus the mahogany prototype didn't have quite enough sustain. They decided also to utilize hard rock maple to further enhance its acoustical tone. McCarty's engineers knew they had to keep the weight reasonable with a solid-body instrument. Continuing the small body of the Ranger and utilizing the cutaway of the new ES-140 3/4 jazz guitar was a natural starting point. Its sharp Florentine cutaway design was then incorporated on those early guitars.

I asked Ted McCarty to tell me more about these early guitars:

TM: *During that year, when we were building the guitar that later became the Les Paul guitar, we tried all sorts of things. We probably made, I don't know, a half dozen. We try this; try that. We make them and listen to them. We even used a piece of railroad rail and put the strings on it and the bridge and a pickup so we could listen to it and see. Because at that time we were trying to see how long of a sustain could you get. And we found out that when you have a very stiff, hard thing like that, it rings and rings and rings and rings and rings… and no guitar player would like that. So it was an experiment we tried.*

RL: Then you decided to make an arched-top design?

TM: *Absolutely! Because Leo Fender had a flat deal and we didn't believe in that. Paul Bigsby made his flat, and so Leo copied one of his guitars and that's why it was flat. Now, our Orville Gibson was the original developer of the carved-top guitar. Why? Because he was a violin-maker. He made violins and his violins all had the typical violin archtop… so we put it in the guitars. And when we did it, I said, "Look, if we are going to make a guitar, we are going to make one that will be different than anything that Leo was making." Because that was going to be the competition; and it was and is.*

RL: Why was maple chosen?

TM: *Because it was hard. It gave you the sustain and it gave you strength. And mahogany because it was a fine wood—Honduras mahogany. Not the cheap African stuff. We used nothing but Honduras, and all of our necks were cut on a bias out of a… we bought our Honduras mahogany that was usually about 36" wide, 5/4" thick, and 30' long, and we bought it by the [train] car load.*

As Ted said, approximately half a dozen or more prototypes were built with presumably different variations. From 1950 into 1951, Gibson continually experimented with solid maple bodies, different combinations of laminations of mahogany and maple, and tried various grain directions to study the acoustical tone. They even sought some outside engineering advice. Numerous ways to attach the neck were tried. The arching of the top evolved with the experiments in neck angles. One-piece maple tops were built, but deemed impractical for mass production due to long-term warping factors. After all the combinations, they eventually settled on the two-piece, carved maple top with the mahogany body and neck.

These instruments were finished in both their standard Cremona sunburst and some in natural lacquer. Says Ted of the prototype finishes: "Our original prototype ones were sunburst because that's what we made. All our guitars were sunburst. We did it on all of our guitars—L-5, Super 400. They were all sunbursts, so that was the way we finished the guitar."

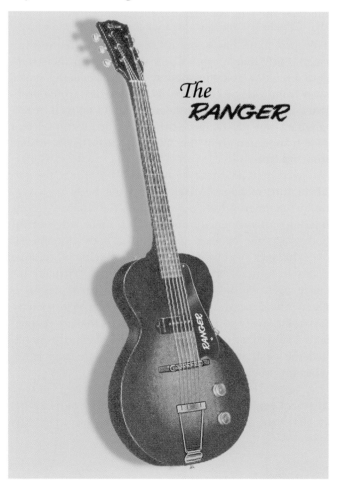

This is a conceptual representation of the 1950 Gibson Ranger solid-body from vintage catalog artwork. It depicts the basic attributes (non-cutaway single pickup and flat construction) according to Tiny Timbrell and Milt Owens, who examined the guitar. Creative graphics are courtesy of Mitchell Costa.

1951 Gibson Prototype Solid-Body

Only one surviving carved maple-top prototype of the Gibson solid Spanish guitar has surfaced thus far. A past Gibson plant foreman/designer Larry Allers, made it a point to save this very important guitar. Dale Wills showed it to me in 1972. He got it from an employee who rescued it in 1953. It was a miracle that such a historical instrument was actually saved from the bandsaw. We will forever be indebted to their foresight.

The most remarkable variation from the 1952 production model—besides the unusual neck heel and sharp cutaway—is the pronounced, high arching up to the fingerboard and pickups. The thickness of the arched body rises up to 2 ^{1}/8" thick, exposing ^{3}/16" of maple not only in the cutaway, but on both sides of the neck! This higher arched plateau continues from the neck down, between the pickups, and tapers down towards the bridge. The binding follows upward, in typical Gibson fashion, along the side, showing the maple lamination beneath.

This prototype has a beautiful, one-piece, natural-finished, curly maple top. Others were done in their standard Cremona golden sunburst. Gibson generally stayed away from wide pieces of maple because of warping problems, yet this and many others have held up well. A rectangular, gray plastic piece supported the pickup selector switch mounted from the top in a small cavity drilled from the front.

The entire mahogany neck enters the body in a very unique manner. It fully traverses into the cutaway (to the binding) a few inches from where a small ledge of the body starts the cutaway portion. The body extends ^{3}/4" over the neck heel by an extra ^{1}/2" in thickness, creating a very deep heel, as on the larger archtops. Virtually the entire neck width (unlike a standard narrow tenon) is glued in five inches to the beginning of the pickup cavity. It is additionally secured with two screws that are cosmetically covered with pearl dots. (Gibson obviously simplified the neck attachment in many ways in later prototypes for production.)

The neck joins the body at the sixteenth fret of its 22-fret (which became the standard) length, on a slightly extended, unbound rosewood fingerboard. Gibson tried a few scale lengths during this embryonic stage. This guitar measures 24 ^{7}/8"—a transitional step towards the smaller body of the earlier, large-bodied, non-cutaway version that may have had the full 25 ^{1}/2" scale length (which, unfortunately for taller guitarists, was not an option during the '50s).

Its neck declination angle is [two degrees] similar to the first production models. However, the high neck set was taller, giving the necessary ^{5}/8" height for a normal bridge setup (the strings are actually ^{11}/16"). Essentially, the neck's height was brought down or sunk in deeper with the same declination to the top on the final first production Les Paul models.

A typical, early-'50s, deep-neck profile with an unbound, dot-inlayed rosewood fingerboard and medium/small early-'50s frets adorns this instrument. The width at the nut is a standard 1 ^{11}/16", but measures 2 ^{1}/8" at the 22nd fret—^{3}/32" narrower than production versions. The overall body is slightly smaller than production models, measuring 1 ^{7}/8" thick to the top of the binding, 12 ^{13}/16" wide, and 7" at the waist—^{3}/16" narrower—and 17 ^{1}/8" long. Its similarity to the recently introduced, smaller, three-quarter-sized 1949 ES-140 is quite apparent. There was a ^{1}/8" mahogany piece laminated across the entire back before the rear edge routing. This appears to be from its original construction, which is covering the rear channel routing—as it was under the original finish. While playing this instrument, if you get too wild, you can actually whack your wrist on this sharp cutaway!

Since no one can remember the exact bridge setup, an educated guess would suggest a metal compensated bridge on a rosewood or metal foot like a Bigsby Les Paul setup (thus the version pictured on page 58). Some 1920s F-4 mandolins actually used original aluminum bridges. Possibly, for sound considerations, an ebony setup may have also been experimented with. Les remembers that the prototypes he saw had a flat, trapeze tailpiece to secure the strings, such as those used on L-7, ES-350, and ES-175 models, but with a shortened bottom flange. He even used them for his experimentation.

(Above) Second incarnation, at a Prune Music guitar show, with a sunburst finish; added was a phase switch and stop/stud combination tailpiece bridge. *Courtesy Dale Wills*

They certainly were along the right path to a fully realized production version. Gibson's engineers got a lot of attributes almost right by the time they built this later prototype in 1951. According to numerous Gibson employees interviewed by Gil Hembree, many felt Larry Allers was the man most responsible for the overall design of the instrument. It's interesting to see the progression from this massive, early arching to the finalized, more subtle, stylized carve.

This 1951 prototype of the Gibson solid body shows the natural progression of the Les Paul model, and is the only surviving Gibson guitar of its type to be discovered. Many years after leaving the factory with a natural finish and gray P-90 pickups (as on some Gibson steel guitars), it was modified with humbucking pickups and various bridges/tailpieces while still in Kalamazoo. The instrument soon migrated west with a Kalamazoo guitarist, and was refinished to sunburst with a stop/stud tailpiece in Mill Valley, California in the late '70s.

(Left) First photographed in Kalamazoo in 1972 showing heel and exposed maple on topside. Note the original aged natural lacquer finish over the light-brown filler stain. The extensive weather checking shows it was exposed to a few cold winters up there. *Courtesy Ron Allers*

(Below) Here's the back cutaway view of a 1960 Standard (for comparison), and the 1951 prototype instrument with original finish intact. Note the unique pearl dots on the heel and maple top exposed in the cutaway.

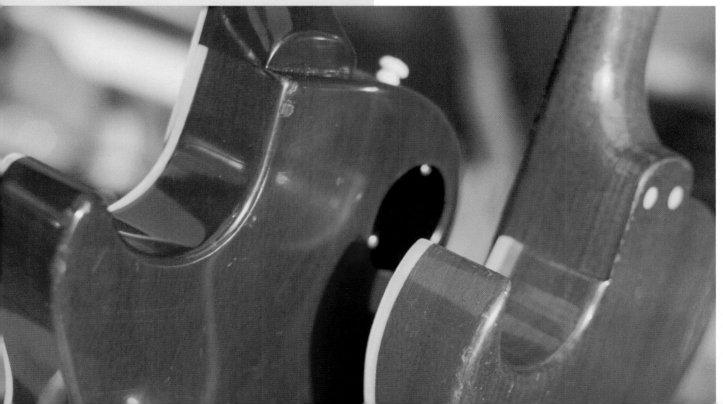

(Above) This back shot gives you an idea of how much neck wood is exposed into the cutaway, the apparent ledge, and ½" extended heel overlay. The pearl dots were replaced with a matching mahogany cap. Note the ⅛" complete back overlay. *Courtesy Warren Klein, 2000*

(Opposite) Portrait of the true "Prototype" Les Paul guitar, restored close to what we believe was the way it would have appeared in 1951–52. Black plastic pickups and a gray switch plate were originally on it (per Dale's later recollection), and early numbered "speed knobs," the ES-175 tailpiece, and a compensated (fixed) metal bridge assembly (ala Bigsby) gives you an approximated idea of how it looked in its day.

The instrument was sold to singer/keyboardist Lee Michaels at Prune Music, and was eventually purchased in Malibu, California by its current owner, Warren "Tornado" Klein. In 1983, Scott Lentz and David Flood expertly restored it back to a natural finish.

Acoustically and electronically, this special instrument sounds very bright, rich, and quite powerful—truly a notable footnote in the history of America's quest for the electric solid guitar.

When asked about what happened to all those dozen or so prototypes, Ted states, "Because we never finished any of those that we were working on. We build something in the raw and try it. And if it worked, fine." Then Gibson would usually put a finish on ones they were considering more seriously. (Imagine what an original sunburst or this natural prototype would be valued at today!) Gibson was creatively developing their own traditional solid-body Spanish guitar; yet, what were they going to call this new-fangled instrument?

Enter Les Paul

"I had been trying to get Les Paul to play Gibson guitars long before we ever saw a solid-body," continues Ted. "Except he made one out of a plank (4" by 4" that never went anywhere. He was an Epiphone player, and he knew the Stathopoulos that owned it, and he wouldn't change to a Gibson. I wanted him to play an L-5. So, when we got our solid-body guitar completed and were ready to put it on the market, we needed an excuse to make a solid-body guitar—because Martin didn't do it, Guild didn't do it, Harmony didn't do it, Kay didn't do it. None of them made a solid-body guitar in those days. We were the first big company to make one.

"Fred Gretsch, the uncle of the current Fred Gretsch, and I were personally good friends, and he called me and said, 'Ted, how could you do this? You know, now anybody with a bandsaw and a router can make a guitar. And that's the sort of thing that Fender is selling.' I said, 'Yeah, I know that. But he's also getting, he's cutting into the market, and we're going to give him a run for his money.'"

Many think Gibson originally considered not using their own name because it was a radical move for such a traditional company. According to Ted, that was not the case. He said that they had every intention of using their own name, and took great pride in doing so. Gibson's Nick Lucas and Roy Smeck signature artist models had met with success in prior decades. It was perfect timing to create a brand-new artist model. Collaborating with a known guitarist was great promotion for both the company's product and artist. The plan was to enlist the most popular electric guitarist—someone who had already championed the solid-body guitar.

Les Paul had already been a featured artist in Gibson catalogs in 1939 and 1949. He had recently won *DownBeat* magazine's top guitarist honors a few years in a row, and was on top of the field. Les was their man—seems his name was on the guitar before they built it! Incidentally, Gibson rep "Tiny" Timbrell told me that, when he was asked by CMI/Gibson what they should call the new guitar, he suggested Les Paul as the perfect player to endorse the guitar, because of his experiments with solid-bodies and his current popularity.

According to Les, Maurice Berlin asked his assistant Mark Carlucci to "Go find the kid with the broomstick and the pickups on it!" Then Maurice flew Les to Chicago for his first meeting with CMI, where they originally discussed his ideas for an electric solid-body. Gibson had already been working on their earliest prototypes. At first, Les figured it was to be with a simple flattop—but Maurice had another remarkable plan in mind. Then he took Les to his violin vault to see the real stuff—and how the arched-top really evolved. Les quickly agreed, and also wanted them to try to match the sound of his modified Epiphone "Clunker" with great action and a bright tone. His own guitars were also examined in Kalamazoo for ideas.

Ted continues, "So we made our solid-body guitar. Now we needed somebody with a reputation; a player to give it some publicity. So I went to Les… and that's when we went up on the mountain (and all the rest of that) and made a contract with him. We paid a royalty for the use of his name."

Gibson "Salutes" advertisement featuring Les and Mary, with their Epiphones, endorsing Gibson just prior to the release of the Les Paul model guitar.

Gibson SALUTES LES PAUL

Congratulations, Les Paul, on winning the Down Beat Guitar Poll. We're proud of the interest in guitars fostered by your artistry, and we're proud, too, of the wonderful Gibsons now under construction for you and Mary. We are confident these fine instruments will inspire you to new feats of wizardry in your musical accomplishments.

GIBSON, INC., Kalamazoo, Michigan

The Hunting Lodge Summit

Eventually it was time to show Les Paul the prototype guitar. Ted McCarty first flew out to New York to meet with Gray Gordon, Les's business manager, and discovered that Les and Mary had gone up near Stroudsburg, Pennsylvania, where they were busy recording at bandleader Ben Selvin's rustic hunting lodge in the beautiful Delaware Water Gap in the Pocono Mountains. Ted and Gray ended up driving over a hundred miles in a storm, up to the city, and stopped for dinner. They called Les, and bassist Wally Kamin came down to guide them up Tott's Gap Road in the dark to the secluded two-story lodge. There they found Les, Mary, and her sister Carol busy tracking in the makeshift living room/studio.

Ted had brought one of Gibson's latest sunburst prototypes, and soon strummed a few chords on the guitar. Les then played it and got very excited, calling out to Mary, "I think we should join them!" She quickly came downstairs to play the new instrument. After a few solos, they both knew it was time to be with the Gibson Company for good.

Ted tells us about the historic meeting: "Actually, the first time Les Paul saw that guitar was when I took it to Pennsylvania, to the Delaware Water Gap, where he and Mary were cutting records up on top of a mountain in somebody's hunting lodge, and showed it to them. And they liked it, so we decided to call it the 'Les Paul' model, put their name on it, and that was it."

Through the night, the three men discussed the guitar and a lucrative business arrangement as the coffee kept flowing. By the time the sun came up, the landmark deal was done, and they celebrated over a special breakfast.

It was a deal made in heaven for both parties. The details included a renewable five-year contract with a five-percent royalty of deferred payments (for tax reasons). This was dependent on the agreement that Les would publicly perform on Gibson instruments exclusively during the five-year period—or forfeit everything. The other stipulation was for Les to be a consultant for Gibson. This was integral to Les's creative and technical input in the future. In the end, it was so well written (freehanded, at that), the entire wording was left intact. Over the decade, the contract was extended to two five-year contracts. In the interim before the guitar arrived, Les was asked to put Gibson decals on his working Epiphones!

Les explains:

> We were still playing modified Epiphones and a Gibson L-12 at the Delaware Water Gap. Mary and I both played acoustical ones—clunkers, in other words—with the Epiphone name removed. It had three brads we took off and there was no name. We got some stencils from Gibson and put the logos on the guitars. It said Gibson, but they were Epiphones! (Laughs.)

A few important guitar details had to be worked out, too. First, Les felt that the sharp cutaway could be potentially dangerous to the player during high runs, stating, "It would knock your wrist if you weren't careful." Les asked for this to be changed for the production model. The sharp cutaway was then slightly rounded off, which also gave it a distinctively smoother look.

Les requested a brilliant gold finish, which he felt was extraordinarily different and exciting and would make the guitar appear rich and regal. Les ordered a custom-made gold ES-175 for a disabled patient in a hospital where Les and Mary had performed. This 1951 gold guitar was quite the sensation at the Gibson office, with all the top staff posing with it. That gold guitar quite likely became the impetus for the use of this rich and flashy new color. It looked absolutely great in all its radiance and gleaming sheen; why not use it on the new Les Paul model, too! Les asked for the gold finish because he felt it was rich-looking and unusual.

Les also wanted Gibson to use a combination bar bridge/tailpiece assembly that he had invented. Les had developed it back in 1945, and built the prototype at his neighbor Phil Wagner's garage metal shop. He had been using it successfully on one of his Gibson L-12 archtops, and thought it would work great on his new guitar.

Gibson went to work putting together and refining the original Les Paul model during late 1951 into 1952. Meanwhile, Les and Mary continued their amazing "Hit Parade" touring, and kept busy doing TV shows. After some recording sessions in New Jersey, they soon located their new dream home in the Ramapo Mountains near Mahwah. Les began work on his home studio and anxiously awaited Gibson's new "Les Paul" model. History was in the making.

Looking North from Winona Cliff.
Delaware Water Gap. Pa.

Here's a view of the picturesque Delaware Water Gap in the Pocono Mountains where the historic meeting took place in 1951. Note the famous Kittatinny hotel. Selvin's hunting lodge was up Tott's Gap Road where Les and Mary were recording.

New York Television magazine with Les and Mary playing the Gibson L-12, which featured a trapeze tailpiece, and Mary playing Les's "Clunker" special. (*Sunday News*, December 1951)

The New Gibson Les Paul Model

"The guitar everyone has been waiting for and asking about is here at last! It's the new and smart-looking gold finished Gibson Les Paul Model, a solid-body electric Spanish cutaway," exclaimed the new 1952 Gibson catalog.

In May of 1952, the Gibson Company courageously announced their original Les Paul Model solid-body. With traditional Gibson guitar styling and a rich, gold-finished top, this lustrous Les Paul signature model was completely new and exciting! The longstanding Gibson image was shaking and boldly jumping onto the wave of the future!

It was Gibson's first entry into the Spanish solid-body realm—a trend that would soon be adopted by many professional and amateur musicians across the country. With Les and Mary's multiple hit records soaring, sales were brisk and the guitar took off, right out of the gate, to be a winner! The dealers were already primed across the country, and everybody was quite eager to see the new guitars. It was the beginning of something big that the world was just starting to wake up to. Over the next few decades, the Les Paul model would become one of the world's most popular electric guitars. As we will see, its transformation into a cultural icon was eminent—it was soon to be an important instrument in many different musical fields, including jazz, country, and the soon-to-emerge rock-and-roll idiom. With Gibson's world-renowned construction and tonal characteristics built right into the Les Paul guitar, its rise to fame was soon at hand.

1952
$ 210.⁰⁰

LES PAUL MODEL

Original one-page flyer showing the new guitar in 1952.
Courtesy Mike Ladd, 1972

Les Paul Guitar

A spectacular instrument created by Gibson to the exacting requirements of this popular Capitol recording star.

The solid body with cutaway measuring 12¾" wide by 17¼" long rigidly supports the two pickups, thereby assuring clear sustaining tones in all positions.

Each pickup with individual pole pieces has controls for both volume and tone along with one toggle switch to facilitate rapid changes by the flip of a switch.

A truly magnificent instrument with its natural mahogany back and neck, while the top is in gleaming gold with contrasting ivory trim.

The 22-fret fingerboard with large pearl inlays is remarkably easy to handle and the very ~~ven the most imaginative guitarist.~~

~~bination tailpiece bridge, the famed Truss Rod,~~
~~d the name Les Paul on the headpiece.~~

~~ove—535 Faultless.~~

LES PAUL and MARY FORD really need no introduction. The sensational sales of their Capitol records recently is an indication of the popular reputation they have built up with their imaginative artistry on the guitar. The instruments they use were designed by Les Paul himself, and carefully built to his specifications by Gibson.

(Above) 1953 catalog description showing first-production model and case with nifty wrapped cord. This well-composed and lit photograph complemented the original Les Paul advertising.

(Left) Mary's guitar looks to be black, but that's just the reflecting contrast of the photograph. The caption actually states that Les and Mary's guitars were designed by Les Paul, which is partially true and good marketing!

It's Gold

The gleaming gold finish was entirely new for a Gibson guitar, and had a striking visual impact. It looked great in all its radiance and polished sheen, setting the stage for the introduction of this flashy new color to the world. Little did they realize that many of the '50s blues players would love these models and play them exclusively. It's an interesting coincidence that during the mid 1930s, Stella produced one of the world's very first production solid-body electric steel guitars painted in gold!

I asked Ted McCarty to elaborate:

RL: How did the gold finish come about?

TM: All right now, Les came to me and he said, "Can you make me a gold guitar? Finish it in gold; paint it." And I said, "Yes, we can; why?" He said, "I've got a friend in the hospital, and I want to give him a present, and I'd like to give him a gold guitar." So I said, "Okay, fine, we'll make one." So we painted one and gave it to Les, and Les gave it to his friend. I don't even know who the guy was. But anyway, that's how the gold started. But that guitar was all gold. We just made the one. Gave it away.

RL: The gold paint that was used for the Les Paul guitar and the ES-295 had brass in it.

TM: They all had brass in them. The finish in the guitar, the Goldtop, is bronze powder mixed in lacquer. That's what makes it reflective and brilliant. It's a very fine bronze powder mixed up in the lacquer and sprayed on. It's little flakes of bronze. But the metal parts—any of them that were gold-plated, were strictly 24-carat gold.

RL: What about the knobs—the clear knobs that were sprayed underneath with the gold?

TM: That's the same type of thing—bronze powder in lacquer.

RL: It turned green on the edges.

TM: Bronze is a combination of copper and zinc, isn't it? [Note: true bronze is an alloy of copper and tin.] And copper turns green when it oxidizes.

The Finishing Process

Finishing the maple top was a completely different process than that for mahogany. Due to the smooth nature of the dense maple, the wood didn't need a filler coating, but needed to be properly prepped. The tops received a few initial, thinned-out lacquer sealer coats that were lightly sanded and readied for the final finish. "On the Goldtop, they would put what they called a sealer on it," states Gibson's Aaron Porter, "which was just thin lacquer kind of thinned out. They put maybe two coats and then sanded it. They made sure there wasn't any pits or anything on there because it would show up underneath in the gold. If there was a scratch or groove, it would show right up. The gold lacquer mixture was then sprayed once or twice to make sure it was well covered."

The bronze powder was pre-mixed into the clear nitrocellulose lacquer for these classic models. The paint department soon discovered that the brass filings in the mixture were quite obtrusive. "In fact, when they were doing that at Gibson, they had a booth… that's all they did was gold," says Aaron. "Like a small room inside of a spray room, and they sprayed gold in there. And they used those guns and didn't take them out of there. They just took the guitars in there, put the gold on them, and then took them back out after they dried to keep from contaminating, because that stuff would get in the air and everything!"

Seeing how the oxidation of bronze turns green, often worn and weather-checked instruments show green in the lines, adhered to the prep coats, and also in some of the sealing topcoats. Unfortunately, the bronze/gold color under the finish didn't stand up too well to the rigors of constant use. It would often pit or become somewhat rough on the necks and top edges.

According to Aaron, "After you put the gold on and let it dry, you put a coat of sealer over that gold to kind of lock in that bronze powder. Then you scrape the binding before you put the clear on." The top sealer coat was often contaminated with the bronze particles left in the guns, giving worn guitars a greenish tint above the deep gold finish. The final coats of clear were done outside of the special "gold" spraying room. "They used four coats of lacquer," says Aaron. "They put on only two a day and they let them dry. After they get four on there, they sand it with that white 220 paper. And then they put one or two coats more and let it dry. It would set a day, or two, or three, and they buff it." They would fine color-sand the topcoat before the buffing procedure. In those days, the highly lustrous gold-finished Les Paul models and ES-295 guitars were quite outstanding to see when brand new.

All gold Les Paul guitars were made only occasionally into the mid '50s. The instruments certainly have an overall "regal" look to them. As the ES-295 production paralleled Goldtop production, some stores and customers ordered those entirely in gold as well. The finishes on many of those that have been played to some degree start to wear through the clear, and eventually turn green on the gold necks and body edges. Collectors and the factory today often refer to such guitars as "Bullion Gold" Les Pauls. Some called them "Anniversary Gold" models back in the '60s, after a 1958 custom special-edition model. There is said to be a 1950s Les Paul painted in real gold back in the day!

This example of Gibson's first-production Les Paul model shows the distinct variations that set it apart from the more common 1952/1953 versions. This includes the lack of binding on the fingerboard and offset mounting screws on the back pickup. Note the original pickguard's lighter cream plastic and wallpaper-type pocket lining unique to the first-style Geib case. *Courtesy Albert Molinaro, November 1993*

The P-90 Pickup

A CMI-NAMM show article stated: "Players will like this instrument's three-way toggle switch and four controls, including a separate tone and volume control for each pickup, which permit presetting the tone to any desired quality, and changing from one pickup to another instantly. Those who played it at the exhibit and at its pre-convention preview at the Waldorf-Astoria Hotel on July 24, said that all traces of feedback and overtone have been eliminated in the Les Paul Model Gibson. Those hearing it agreed that it produced a wealth of contrasting tonal effects, from brilliant treble to full, deep bass, with a good solid in-between voice for rhythm."

Gibson's contemporary pickup at the time was Guy Hart and Walt Fuller's 1940s-designed PU-90 model 480 single-coil, commonly known as the "P-90." It was a popular pickup with good volume, strong output, and reasonable fidelity. Rich tone with a good high-end gave it an overall big sound. Early versions had Alnico V magnetic slug polepieces; but by 1949, it went to ferrous steel Fillister screw polepieces with two magnets beneath the pickup coil.

The Les Paul version of the P-90 pickup had the same basic base plate without the side brackets. Gibson now set their pickups solidly into deep-routed cavities with two long wood screws. Its new inset, rectangular cover did away with the old "dog ears" attachment. In later years, these pickups were dubbed "soap bars" because of their rounded shape and ivory coloring. A few rare guitars were shipped with black or brown plastic pickup covers, too.

The pickups were wound with approximately 10,000 turns of 42 enamel-coated wire measuring around 8,000 ohms. Under the black plastic coil bobbins, two M55 (Gibson's nomenclature) Alnico III magnetically opposed magnets ($1/2$" wide, $2 1/2$" long, $1/8$" thick) straddle a center steel strip ($3/16$" by $2 3/16$" by $1/8$"), tapped to secure the screw polepieces. At one end of the base, a rubber grommet surrounds the hole, protecting the two black wires that are connected to the braided lead wire. A piece of masking tape is wrapped around the connection, while the metal braid is soldered to the zinc-coated base. Basically speaking, as the magnetism transfers up the polepieces, it registers the fluctuations of the strings in the field above. The width between the first and sixth poles measures $1 15/16$". P-90 coils measure $3 1/8$" by $1 3/16$", and are $3/8$" tall. The entire pickup is $9/16$" tall and $3 1/4$" wide, while the covers are $1 5/16$" by $3 3/8$" by $7/16$" tall ($1 3/8$" by $3 7/16$").

(Above) Final neck-to-body construction was simplified for production with a clean demarcation line as it meets the cutaway and top-bound body. Meanwhile, the fingerboards were unbound on these first Les Paul models. Frets were small by today's standards.

(Below) Decorative "crown" trapezoid-shaped inlays of "lumerith" pearloid became a mainstay of this model still in use today. Note the center-pocket inside wallpaper-type lining sometimes found inside Gibson amps from the forties. This early 1952 guitar is presented courtesy of Albert Molinaro.

As with other Gibson electrics, these pickups were set wide apart, nearly flush with the fingerboard, and close to the bridge. On the first production models, the treble (or back) pickup had two attachment screws on the outside corners, while the rhythm (or front) pickups used two center screws in between the polepieces. This was soon standardized, like the rhythm pickup attachment on later bound-neck versions. Most players raised the bridge pickup polepieces up to balance the output, since the rhythm position has greater natural volume. With the setting in the upright position, wonderfully rich and deep tones were obtained from the new Les Paul model. Very bright, stinging tones were achieved for cutting through in the down setting. Using both pickups together created a blend of the two, being full with a parallel-sounding high-end edge. Many would slightly adjust the volume on one of the pickups to their liking. Some guitars were shipped with one reversed magnet, resulting in a real plunky kind of tone when both were switched on together.

The P-90 was a very popular pickup during those times. Even today, many superlatives have been said about its tonal qualities. Great jazz guitar tones are easily obtained with good articulation and dynamics—nearly an acoustic timbre, some say. They can sound fat and round while maintaining that direct edge. A relatively rich, full-bodied tone can still be achieved when the volume is slightly backed off on the control. P-90 pickups can have a real honking and squawking grind when amps are up full-volume.

(Above) The P-90 model 480 pickup exposed shows the common oxidation that occurs and the normal masking tape on the connecting wires. *Courtesy Ken Hower, 2004*

(Right) Typical playing wear of the nickel on the Les Paul trapeze will expose the brass on these early instruments. Diagonal mounting screws on the treble pickup are unique to the original '52 production models. Note the lighter colored plastic often found on this early version's pickguard.

Electronics

Gibson's two-pickup circuitry was pioneered on the 1951 Super 400 and L-5 electrics. They featured two volumes, two tones, and a three-position Switchcraft toggle switch (#12010 nickel). The Les Paul model adopted this convenient setup. However, it was somewhat limiting in the combination setting for overall volume. Controls consisted of four 500K audio taper CentraLab potentiometers, and two .02 mmf waxed cylindrical Cornell Dubilier "Grey Tiger" capacitors for the tone circuitry. Often linear taper models are found, and 250K values were sometimes used for the tone controls. The pots for example, would be coded 134319, identifying the manufacture (134), the year ('53), and the week (19). CentraLab pots with side codes during these early years would often have a fine CRL in a diamond-shaped stamp on the back. Pickup leads and wiring to the switch used shielded (metal braided) black-cloth-covered (sometimes dark green-cloth-covered) 14-gauge wires. An amber-coated, cloth-braided protector was sheathed around the single-strand ground wire between the potentiometers. Inside the control cavity, a loose-fitting black plastic insulation tube was around the final wires from the toggle to the Switchcraft 1/4" output jack.

During 1952, volume and tone controls were the tall, cylindrical-style, 5/8" "barrel" or "speed" knobs made of clear plastic, sprayed a deep gold underneath, with white numbers. The shorter 1/2" "speed" knobs were begun in 1953. Customary metal pointers were attached to the pot stem to indicate where the setting was. (You must be careful with those sharp pointed things!) The pickup switch tip (lever knob #T12912) was an amber plastic during the 1950s, with some very early ones being ivory (#T12741). A knurled thumbnut simply fastened the toggle switch to the top surface of the guitar, as on their archtops. Electronic control and switch cavities were conveniently concealed with inset, brown Royalite plastic covers.

A slightly more refined, final-production version of the popular Les Paul guitar. The attractive maroon plush was a nice contrast during these early years. This exceptionally fine condition 1952 Goldtop is courtesy of Norm Harris, Feb. 1994.

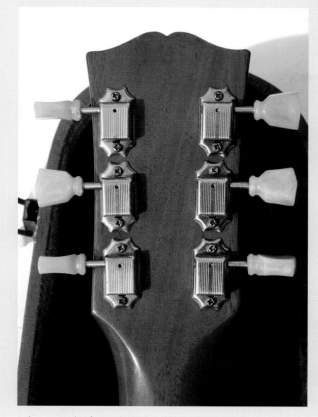

(Above) These 1952–53 models wrap-under-the-bar combination bridge/tailpieces gave the guitarist somewhat of a ledge to pick from while negating the muted techniques. It was, however, adjustable for height and relative straight-bar intonation. Note the nifty $5/8$" tall "barrel knobs" and matching cream plastics.

(Above) Lack of serial numbers kept a clean look for the first year of production. Kluson "Keystone" tuning keys were unmarked during the early fifties.

(Right) The front "soapbar" pickup is flush against the fingerboard for deep rhythm tones. This fine 1952 Les Paul guitar's finish has a radiant gold color with reddish overtones that come out in the sunlight.

(Below) Curved control routing soon became the standard. Cornell Dubilier caps and CentraLab potentiometers comprised the basic Gibson electronics. Note the leftover brown grain filler stain on the ledge.

Carved Maple

The original Les Paul model's main feature was its solid body and the unique Gibson arched maple top. At this early stage of the guitar's evolution, the laminated top's carving had finally been refined. The 1951 prototype's high neck-set dictated a fairly radical lengthwise arching. The final production model had a deeper-set neck with the same two-degree angle. This made the arching less steep between the pickups, causing it to gently flow into the upper region, meeting the fingerboard smoothly. It was certainly a more graceful arching for the original Goldtop. These early versions therefore had maple tops that measured approximately 1/2" thick. Consequent versions during the 1950s (with the later tailpieces and steeper three-degree angled neck) had slightly taller arched tops measuring between 9/16"–5/8" thick.

Construction

A Gibson Les Paul guitar body begins life as a 1 3/4", quarter-sawn, seasoned Honduras mahogany blank. Before the laminated maple cap is applied, the 1 3/8" switch cavity and control cavity are routed, along with a 1/2" slot that connects the two areas across the pickup area for the wiring harness. Early control cavities were trapezoid-shaped with rounded corners. They were soon configured around the four potentiometers, which also gave more room for the back-plate screws. An additional curved 1/2" slot was soon added for the grounding wire, from the control cavity to the tailpiece base, doing away with the long drilled hole.

Afterwards, the thick maple top is glued onto the mahogany. Switch, jack, and control cavity holes are then drilled. A large angled cut into the maple of the control cavity was done to slightly tilt the rhythm pickup controls for the curved face of the instrument. Two sides of the rounded cavity were chamfered away in the process. Inset cover-plate ledges were also added. Once this was all completed, the laminated blank was rough-cut to the template size.

Then two bodies are attached to the cutting table where an adjoining carving template is used to create the famous Gibson arched top. A roller moves over the template, guiding the cutter blades over the two bodies, effectively carving the maple into a bell shape. The first models were graduated to 1/2", and subsequent versions approximately 5/8".

(Above) Another nice example built in 1953 and shipped with the Lifton maroon case. Shows some slight playing wear on the nickel-plated bridge piece down to the brass. The bright gold logo script seems to light up in the sunlight as does the brilliant golden finish. The cases are works of art as well! *Courtesy Blue Guitar Workshop*

(Below) The gold silk-screened "Les Paul Model" proudly adorned the headstock of Les Paul's signature guitar. "Gibson" in abalone pearl was set deeply into the layout of the head during these years. The bell-shaped truss rod adjustment cover and tulip-shaped Keystone tuner grips completed the attractive peghead.

An overhead pin router then follows an attached template on the back of the body to cut the outer periphery and neck slot. The bodies are then slightly edge-routed for the front binding fitting. (Custom Les Paul bodies require a deeper cut on the front and back due to its thicker multiple-ply binding.) Once the binding is glued on, stretching rope is wrapped all around the body in different directions and it's left to dry.

Neck construction is one of the most critical procedures, and its process affects the overall playability of the instrument. Before the truss rod and maple spline insert is fitted into the mahogany neck blank, a rotary profile-shaper roughs out the desired neck shape. Then the final profile is performed with the periphery routed. It is carefully belt-sanded for uniformity prior to receiving the already prepared fingerboard and headstock veneer.

The fingerboard is inlayed, sanded, fretted, and bound prior to this operation, along with the inlayed abalone "Gibson" holly-wood headstock face. Multiple-blade circular saws cut the fret slots all at once to the exact specifications for its 24 3/4" scale length (technically 24 9/16"). After the frets are partially hand-hammered in, a large fret press is used to do the final, overall seating. The proper neck alignment is then checked with a metal pitch gauge before being glued into the body. After all these procedures are done and the neck is attached, the pickup cavities are routed. The top portion of the neck tenon is now milled away, exposing the inserted truss rod maple strip beneath the fingerboard. There is a small curved gap in the trough where the tenon ends. Final sanding takes place with 220-grit (or up to 400-grit) paper, and the instrument is left in the famous "whitewood room" before moving on to the finishing department.

Necks Specs

The Les Paul model necks were comprised of genuine Honduras mahogany throughout the 1950s. Ted McHugh's 1920 patented truss rod was still Gibson's mainstay, which kept the necks straight as could be expected. Neck shapes were fairly large by today's standards, but actually quite comfortably rounded as medium large. Of course, they varied slightly due to the hand-sanding processes used through the various years of production. Fingerboards were made of Brazilian rosewood for the Goldtop series, with a radius varying between 10" to 12". Nine crown-shaped, trapezoid, pearlescent plastic inlays adorned the fingerboard. These pearloid pieces are made from Herring fish scales in nitrocellulose. Side dots appear black, but in actuality, consist of very dark red translucent amber side dots on the bound models. Frets were medium/small-sized and standard for the era. The stated scale length of 24 3/4" was actually just a bit shorter, measuring 24 9/16" (12 9/32" to the twelfth fret).

First-production guitars can be easily differentiated from consequent versions by their lack of neck binding and their two adjacent pickup screws on the bridge pickup. Nickel-plated Kluson "Keystone" tuning machines were used as on other mid-priced guitars (No. 550 in the '50s parts catalog). Known technically as GS-320-V, vertical-style, "Deluxe" covered machine heads, Gibson special-ordered them with an "opal" plastic button. The greenish plastic grips had a single ring through the '50s. A stamp on the underside read "PATAPPLD" and "2356766." These early versions had no text branding on the backs, while later ones during the 1950s said, "Kluson Deluxe" in one line down the center. Ferrules (or collets) to secure them on the face were stepped with a ledge profile and knurled on the hidden outer edges. Early '52 versions had hex-shaped collets.

An original first-production instrument in for a neck reset at the Blue Guitar Workshop in 1999. Yuris Zeltins carefully removes the neck and a portion of the fingerboard to work his magic as he has on countless vintage Martins over the decades. This is one way to accurately rectify the neck declination problem for use with contemporary bridges and get better down-force for coupling the string pressure. Note the truss rod construction with the flame maple filler insert and brass greening effect in the finish.

An exceptionally fine 1953 example (in pristine condition) owned by Les Paul. We traded this beautiful guitar to Les for a large box of old guitar pickups and parts from his basement back in 1974. He and Wally Kamin had torn up so many guitars back in the fifties, so it was a good trade for Les to have an all-original version Goldtop to pose with. It's been in numerous articles over the years since, and seen in our special Grammy's tribute film in 2001. Guitar is courtesy of the late Phil Pierangelo. Photographed at Matt Umanov's apartment in Park Slope, Brooklyn, August 1975.

The Les Paul Tailpiece

During their historic meeting at the hunting lodge, Les suggested that Ted use his trapeze tailpiece. So Les went back to Gibson with his tailpiece invention, which was the last item to be incorporated before the actual production models began. Les developed it back in 1945, and built the prototype at his neighbor Phil Wagner's garage metal shop. It featured a combination bridge and tailpiece all-in-one unit, and was connected with two long, slender rods attached to a flange at the bottom edge of the guitar. The solid steel bar design gave the bridge a good sustain factor. Les particularly liked the sound of the thick steel bars for bridges. This early bridge did not compensate for individual strings, but was adjustable for height and relative intonation lengthwise.

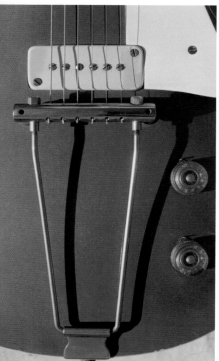

(Above) This early ES-295 Les Paul model trapeze tailpiece shows the Gibson Les Paul logo, which is rarely seen on these units.
Courtesy Steve Soest, November 1973

(Left) This close-up of the original Les Paul solid-body features Gibson's production LP trapeze bridge tailpiece. It had shorter arms and was designed to have the strings wrapped beneath the bar which created a ledge to pick from.
Courtesy Albert Molinaro, November 1993

Combined Bridge and Tailpiece for Stringed Instruments

Lester W. Polfuss, Hollywood, Calif., assignor to Gibson, Inc., Kalamazoo, Mich.

Application July 9, 1952, Serial No. 297,874

The combined bridge and tailpiece of my invention comprises the upwardly bowed or curved body member desirably formed of rod stock of uniform circular section, and having a spaced series of bores deposed horizontally there through to receive the ends of the strings which are passed over and rest upon the top of the bridge...

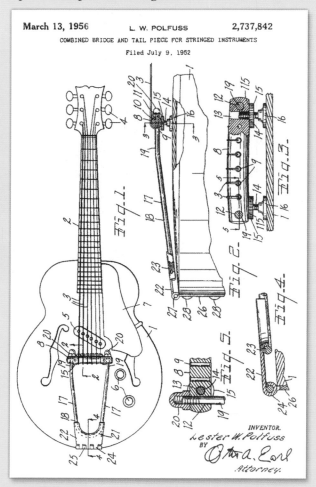

Although Les Paul had developed and used this special combination bridge/tailpiece for a number of years prior, his patent was finally filed in July of 1952, just as the new Gibson guitar was being introduced. The stylized guitar featured in the patent drawing looks much like an ES-300 with its slanted bridge pickup. Curiously, they didn't show the strings being used underneath as on the concurrent guitar model. The patent was finally granted in 1956 while the two acoustic/electric 225 and 295 models were in production. Its patent number, 2,737,842, was used as a smokescreen for pickup patent details in the '60s.

The patented Les Paul "trapeze" tailpiece was designed as a combination bridge and tailpiece assembly to help increase the sustaining power of the guitar. It was first intended for use on large-bodied guitars like his Epiphone and Gibson archtops. "That was my invention," says Les. "I had my neighbor across the street, Phil Wagner, build it for me in his workshop back around 1945–46. You'll see [hear] the tailpiece on 'It's Been a Long, Long Time' with Bing. There was no vibrato on there."

The tailpiece was constructed of a solid bar to which the strings were anchored and then wrapped over the bar. Two support pedestals suspended the bridge with screws and thumbnuts for adjusting the height. Relative intonation was accomplished with twin hub nuts for lateral movement (under loose tension). The long trapeze arms extended down and were hinged to the base flange piece. This assembly was anchored with three or four screws at the bottom of the guitar with the strap button. It became standard equipment on production ES-295 models in gold, and later ES-225 models during the 1950s. This model, in its original configuration, is now known as the "wrap-over" trapeze tailpiece. The LP trapeze was made of brass and was nickel-coated for protection. With long-term playing, the plating often wore through, showing the brass beneath. The 295 description spoke highly of the new item: "The combination bridge and tailpiece, by shortening the distance from the nut to the tailpiece, releases about 25 percent of the string pressure on the body, adding to the sustaining power and brilliancy of the instrument, and giving faster and lower action. Every note in each chord has equal power and rings true without an abrupt ending of the tone." This may have been true on an archtop with the strings over the top.

In its advertising, it was touted as the "greatest step forward since the introduction of the electric guitar," and the "miracle tailpiece designed for you by Les Paul" (supposedly so that other musicians could get the famed Les Paul muted tones). However, adds Les, "The first ones that came out had the strings under the bar instead of over the top, and you couldn't muffle or mute the strings."

Here's what Ted remembered in 1995 regarding the Les Paul trapeze tailpiece:

RL: *Now, you went ahead and used Les Paul's tailpiece right?*

TM: *We started out with a regular trapeze tailpiece, and Les had the idea of this one with the round bar, and said, "Would you use that?" And so we said, "We'll put it in there." Didn't make that much difference.*

RL: *But the strings went underneath instead of over the top, like Les designed it.*

TM: *Look… how Les designed anything, I wouldn't know. Well, you know, we were the designers and the guitar-makers, and Les had some ideas about this, that, and the other thing.*

Unfortunately a serious oversight occurred with the original production. The strings were now going under the bridge bar instead of over the top. His famous muffled "Les Paul tones" were virtually impossible with the tailpiece the way it was utilized.

Les talked with me in 2000 about the introduction of the Les Paul model with his tailpiece:

RL: *Tell me about how excited you were when the Gibson Les Paul guitar came out?*

LP: *Well, they weren't excited for sure because… they made four: one for Mary, and one for me, and two for them. So they made four. Then they made a hundred. And then they may have made a thousand. But they were all screwed up.*

RL: *Because of the wrong neck tilt and string placement on your tailpiece.*

LP: *Yes. The trapeze tailpiece. There were a million things wrong with it at the time.*

RL: *It wasn't utilized properly.*

LP: *Well… see, I don't use big words (laughs).*

RL: *You were busy with Mary…*

LP: *'Course I was (laughs).*

RL: *On tour all over the world, you were busy, and the guitar was in production with the wrong neck tilt.*

LP: *That's okay. We straightened it out.*

RL: *In '53.*

LP: *Well, there were a lot of changes. There were some we didn't catch right away, some we caught later, some are collectors' items and very precious.*

In their excitement, Gibson went ahead with the instrument's initial design plans. The expense of all the ordered bridges and tooling may have had something to do with it. But how could such a great guitar have the neck tilt and bridge so off? Les knew his samples were incorrect and evidently figured Gibson would remedy the problem soon; he always modified his personal guitars extensively anyway, and figured they would take care of it. He and Mary's busy schedules had them all over the map, and they were soon to be on the *Queen Elizabeth* heading to England. This was a classic case of miscommunication and inaction it seems. Les continued experiments with his Gibson solid-bodies while Gibson sold this great (almost perfect) instrument to many unsuspecting players.

Evidently, the importance of muting the strings over the top, as Les did, didn't carry much weight at Gibson. They wanted to seat the bridge pickup deeply into the body and keep the string-height low. Therefore, Gibson's engineers used the same neck pitch as the '51 prototype model, yet set it lower into the body—and then inadvertently put the strings underneath the bar, not considering the muting technique or necessity of playing near the bridge. They really wanted to get the tone of the body's presence with it directly attached to the solid wood (which was slightly sonically detectable). Later, they found that the suspended adjustable pickups were more neutral in picking up the strings oscillations without the body's vibrations interfering.

One evening in 1975, during my slide show, Walt Fuller and Julius Bellson explained the way it happened. Their recollection of Gibson's reasoning was that they wanted to place the pickups down deep inside the cavities, and secure them firmly with screws directly onto the wood for the body vibrations. The P-90 pickup's short height also had something to do with it, since a mounting ring like the one on the ES-5 would be too bulky. They therefore wanted to get the string action down close to the body with streamlined pickups. To compensate for all of this, they simply reversed the stringing of the tailpiece—and thus disregarding right-hand muting techniques. The height below the bar bridge was already $1/2"$ because of the supporting leg brackets. For a bridge designed to be that tall, a high neck inset or a steeply angled neck was required. This is radical on a smaller-sized guitar but fine for a full-sized 16" box, like the 295 and 225 models. This is one reason why some of the prototypes (with old-style bridges) had such tall neck insets before they discovered they could angle the neck back instead.

Gibson naturally wanted to make Les happy by using his tailpiece (which was intrinsically too tall). The cost of redesigning and retooling for a more trim profile trapeze was evidently out of the question. It was, unfortunately, now impossible to mute the strings with the fleshy part of the hand, like is necessary to achieve the "chicken pickin" sound Les was famous for. Another symptom of this design was that the tailpiece would slide around on the top when played, due to the lack of adequate down force. This would end up knocking the guitar a little out of tune and sometimes mar the top surface. Some would put sticky two-sided tape under the legs to keep them steady, losing the direct energy contact. Many players just lived with it, while some modified their bridges by milling them down considerably, or putting on other makeshift versions. I've even seen guitars with the tops gouged out in order for the bridge to sit down low enough!

Meanwhile, Les and Mary were touring constantly, unaware that the problem wasn't rectified immediately. I estimate that around 3,000 Goldtops were produced into mid 1953 this way (1,716, plus half of 2,245). Les simply put on a traditional ES-175/350 tailpiece (Gibson part no. 938), as others did. Then he used Doc Kauffman's vibrolas (made by Rickenbacher in the 1930s) with simple rolled-bar bridges on his other guitars. Note the photo with Les and Mary sitting on an oversized guitar, and the advertising shots showing Doc's long-armed vibrolas. Back in the early days, country star Ray Price's Cherokee Cowboys guitarist, Pete Wade, used this 175/938 setup with a thin, compensated bridge.

The earliest shipped guitar naturally went to case manufacturer, Geib. (The April 25 order for a fitting read, "1 Les Paul Model Gtr., Geib, Inc., 1 case.") Less than a month later, May 20, Gibson shipped two Les Paul models to Mahwah, NJ. Les and Mary now had their first, true Gibson solid-body models! Les continues, "I don't even know if I got the first one from Gibson. For instance, they make a new model, they make a run of three or four thousand, and before I ever get mine, in many cases, they say, 'How do you like your new model Les Paul?' I said, 'I haven't seen it yet.' We agreed on how to make it, and they went ahead and made it and put it out, and then, when I would see it, I would say, 'Jeez, you know, maybe you ought to do this and do that.' They're great people to work with, Gibson. They try very hard to do what the public wants, what the designer wants. It's important; and when you talk about quality control, they are all the time trying to make the quality control better. Every company has those problems."

(Left) The working man's Gibson guitar and Fender amp rig. This Pete Wade setup (shown here on a Ray Price Band break with unidentified pianist) that shows the switched-over Gibson trapeze and thin compensated bridge with round thumbnut screws for his Goldtop. These Fender Pro amps (1-15" Jensen-equipped) were the popular choice during the early 1950s.

(Right) This is one of the first Les Paul guitars highly modified by Les and Wally Kamin over the years. It even has holes for large slanted pickups. Today it has low-Z pickups, a Bigsby and Sunburst finish by Gibson. *Courtesy Les Paul, Mahwah, NJ, July 1972*

(Right) Here's a close-up of Mary playing one of the original guitars now modified with a bar bridge and 175 tailpiece.

(Below) Here is the famous, big Goldtop promotional picture that graced many Gibson catalogs and magazines during the 1950s. This clever composite pose was achieved by photographing Les and Mary sitting on a sawhorse, then superimposing the shot over a blow-up of Les's modified early Goldtop. Note the DeArmond Gretsch Dynasonic rhythm pickup (which fits perfectly in the P-90 hole), Gibson 983 trapeze tailpiece, pointer control knobs, and top-mounted output. The simple bar bridge was conveniently obscured as usual! Les and Mary were obviously quite happy riding on their big Gibson model guitar and phenomenal hit record parade!

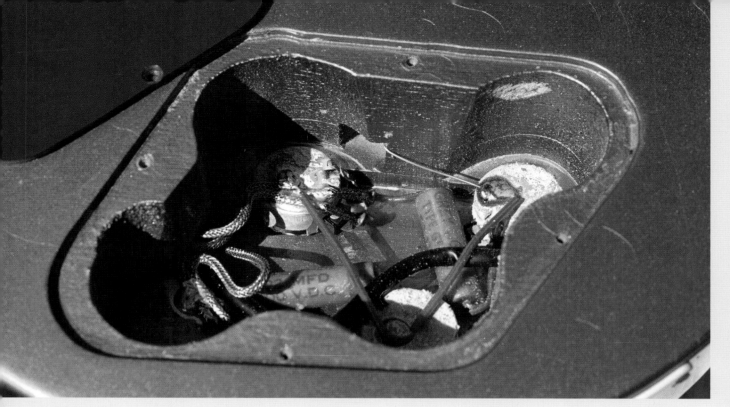

(Opposite page, below left and above) This all-gold Les Paul model gleams in the sun from all directions! Owner guitarist Dave Amato is especially proud of this very clean golden wonder. Its clear coat has yellowed somewhat (especially apparent over the Gibson logo), giving the guitar a real golden-colored bullion look in the sunlight. Note the ground wire runs into the routed channel running back to the tailpiece, and Grey Tiger tone capacitors. From the Amato collection, 2004.

(Below left) 1953 Les Paul Goldtop, photographed at George Gruhn's GTR shop (George, Tut Taylor, and Randy Woods), selling for $650 in 1972.

(Below right) A very rare left-handed version of the Les Paul model. Note they continued to apply the silk-screened gold logo in the same direction, which is upside down as you view the guitar from its playing position. Guitar courtesy of Lloyd Chiate, photographed in Mill Valley, circa April 1973.

Sales

> *"News and Notes—Our feature item for this issue of the GAZETTE is the sensational LES PAUL MODEL guitar. The demand for this instrument has been amazing, and judging from the first few months of sales, it looks like it will be one of the most popular guitars ever produced by GIBSON. We're proud of the addition to the GIBSON line, and we're proud, too, of the way you dealers have been selling it."*
>
> (Clarence Havenga's Gibson Gazette, November/December 1952)

This *Gazette* review is quite an understatement, considering that the Les Paul guitar was, and is, one of the most popular guitars of all time!

The *Gazette* also included a print of the guitar's two-page flyer literature, which stated: "We know that some of you haven't had a chance to see the LES PAUL MODEL yet, and want to know more about it, so we've enclosed an illustrated multi-print which describes its outstanding features..."

Added by Clarence was, "IMPORTANT! The men up at Kalamazoo are working overtime to fill all the orders for the LES PAUL MODEL guitars and amplifiers, and delivery is definitely promised in December if you place your order now." It was basically a six-week turnaround for orders of the solid-body hit. Demand for the new guitar was quite surprising. Gibson got production rolling soon after Les and Mary received their guitars. Every few weeks, a few dozen would go out to various stores around the country. For example, seventeen left the factory on June 30, and twenty-six on July 2. Then twenty-two went out on July 9, and twenty-four on July 11, etc. Production in 1952 alone was for 1,716 guitars that were shipped beginning in June of that year, and 2,245 during 1953. Shipments totaled 1,504 in '54, and 862 in '55.

Its popularity and sales were greatly affected by Les and Mary's hit records and regular live performances. "Your favorite stars, and their favorite guitars," was often seen in the leading magazines, as well as record shops, theaters, and in airline literature. "The famed Les Paul model guitar is following in the wake of its designer... its exciting Les Paul tone, beautiful design, and many magical features have put this Gibson right at the top of the guitar parade," boasted one ad. Les and Mary kept a large chart to graph the guitar's sales, as well as their record sales, as the two sets of figures mirrored each other throughout the 1950s.

(Above) Here's a glimpse of Gibson's 1952 logbook listing of a group of LP guitars sent out around the country. As shown on the top, Golden Regal ES-295 models were also produced concurrently. *Courtesy Walter Carter and Gibson, 2003*

(Right) This picture was proudly displayed in Gibson's hallway by the President's office for many years.

They're News!

LES PAUL, MARY FORD and their GIBSONS

Your favorite stars, and their favorite guitars, are featured headliners in the leading magazines, as well as in record shops, theatres and on the airlanes. The famed Les Paul Model guitar is following in the wake of its designer . . . its exciting Les Paul tone, beautiful design and many magical features have put this Gibson right at the top of the "guitar parade."

For information . . . Les Paul Mo . . .

GIBSON, Inc., KALAMAZOO, MICHIGAN

(Left) "They're News!" says the Gibson ad featuring caricatures of Les and Mary with their Gibson guitars, creating headlines on the newsstands. The actual magazines pictured featured articles on Les and Mary playing their new guitars.

(Below) 1953 Gibson Les Paul model ad, "It's a Sensation," with Les playing the Emperor's guitar... can't you see it?

Gibson Les Paul model

It's a Sensation!

Designed by Les Paul—produced by Gibson—and enthusiastically approved by top guitarists everywhere. The Les Paul Model is a unique and exciting innovation in the fretted instrument field; you have to see and hear it to appreciate the wonderful features and unusual tone of this newest Gibson guitar. Write Dept. 101 for more information about it.

Gibson, Inc., Kalamazoo, Mich.

ELECTRIC SPANISH GUITAR (Cutaway) SOLID BODY

*LES PAUL MODEL	Guitar, Solid Wood Body, Cutaway, with two built-in pickups and toggle switch	$220.00
535	Faultless Case (Flannel) for above model	41.50

(Above) Interesting how in March, they had already set a price for the new Les Paul guitar months before it was ready to ship! This March 7, 1952 pricelist shows the Les Paul model "Solid wood body" guitar, which cost $10 more for shipping west to Zone 2 in California. Note the mistaken flannel-lined case reference.

The new gold Gibson solid-body listed for $210, and came with a brown leather shoulder strap. Its beautiful hard-shell case was an additional $39.50. Per the March 7, 1952 zone 2 (West Coast area) pricelist, the cost was $220 for the guitar and $41.50 for the case. Prices remained the same in 1953. The original-style "Faultless" 535 cases, manufactured by Geib, initially had a flat top and were covered with Gibson's light brown "leatherette" case linen (a material that was also used on their late-1940s suitcase-style amps). The company soon switched to two-tone leatherette as was used on the early-1950s amplifiers. The cases were constructed of lightweight but sturdy birch plywood, and featured a convenient center pocket for accessories, cords, and a strap. These fine cases featured either a brown burgundy, rose, or more commonly, a light pink-colored plush lining. Soon afterwards, another brown case style was offered, made by Lifton Manufacturing in Chicago. It was hourglass-shaped with an arched top, and featured a narrowly curved center pouch with a deeper magenta "American Beauty"-type plush lining.

Meanwhile, Les and Mary were busy performing with the new, although slightly modified gold guitars, and Les was heading back in the studio. Some of the first hit records featuring the new Gibson Les Paul models were released during August and November of 1952. Les remembers, "Many of the songs that really sounded great was done on a Goldtop. One of the best guitars I used was on 'Meet Mr. Callaghan' (which went to No. 5 on the charts) and 'The Best Things in Life Are Free' (No. 11). 'My Baby's Coming Home' was a Goldtop."

Chicago's Geib case manufacturers would often affix decorative plaques onto the center pocket beneath the neck yoke. This MasterKraft Geib emblem is emblazoned on the brilliant, hot-pink plush lining we all love.

Here's the Geib Company's truck at the busy CMI dock in Chicago.

Having a good ol' time at home with their gold Gibson Les Paul guitars!

"Built Like a Fortress" was the Lifton company motto. From experience, I know that their strong cases can, even if driven over, protect and spare a Les Paul guitar's life without any damage to either item... save for the tread marks! The top arching and side construction is particularly rigid. Their pink plush was a very close match to the famous American Beauty plush of the original Super 400 cases.

(Right) Musician Bill Dalton plays his early '53 Goldtop with the Royal Teens in the *Let's Rock* movie of 1958. Their hit song was "Short Shorts" (Al Kooper was in the band too) before his memorable keyboard work with Bob Dylan; Michael Bloomfield; and Blood, Sweat & Tears.

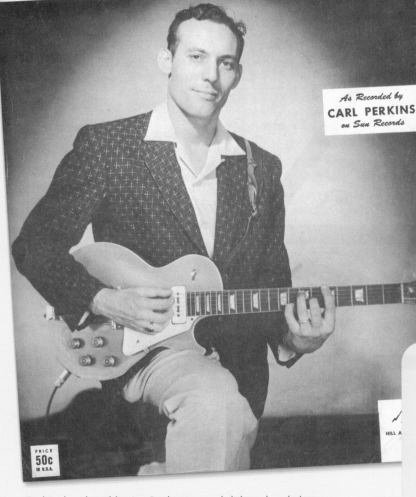

Carl Perkins loved his Les Paul guitar and did much to help popularize the instrument. His "Blue Suede Shoes" tune was one of the biggest hits of 1956. He was often known to say that you could swing your way out of a barroom brawl with a Gibson Les Paul guitar!

Gibson and Les had an idea—and with divine guidance and wisdom.

The Les Paul guitar had providence, it had a purpose... and it meant business.

A harmony of mathematical precision and tonality was achieved.

Emergence of a new guitar with high-volume capabilities was an inevitability of its nature.

Efficient parameters of perfection in wood... initially and undoubtedly created a new level of electric freedom.

The 1952 is the fundamental archetype. Its predecessors gracefully expand the profound effect on guitarists.

An emotional force happens from a quintessential musical design.

The New Combination Bridge and Tailpiece

Ted McCarty eventually saw the drawbacks of their first Les Paul guitar. He also felt that the trapeze wasn't adjustable enough, and wanted to anchor a bridge to the top of the guitar, since it was solid. Ted's next patent incorporated an all-in-one, new combination bridge/tailpiece simply attached with two large screws. His engineers went ahead and developed the idea into a working model with lateral inset screws for an easier method of intonation. This not only solved the previous neck/bridge problem, but also raised the strings to a more comfortable height above the body. They tilted the neck four degrees with Ted's new tailpiece, and finally rectified the earlier problems.

Many called it the "stop," "stopbar," or "stud" tailpiece, for obvious reasons—the bar stops the strings, and two studs screw into the body to anchor the unit. The bridges were cast of a lightweight aluminum alloy weighing just over one ounce. Both stud screws were made of heavier brass. All parts were nickel plated for durable wear. Many today call this combination bridge/tailpiece the McCarty "wrap-around" unit.

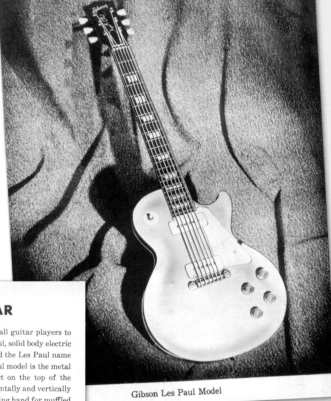

Gibson Les Paul Model

(Above and left) 1953 promo for the "improved" Les Paul model.

LES PAUL MODEL GUITAR

Gibson's new and smart-looking Les Paul Model now enables all guitar players to achieve the special effects that made Les Paul famous. This beautiful, solid body electric has a gold-finished, carved maple top, mahogany body and neck and the Les Paul name in gold script on the peghead. A unique, new feature of the Les Paul model is the metal combination bridge and tailpiece with the strings making contact on the top of the bridge. With this new style bridge and tailpiece, which is both horizontally and vertically adjustable, the player may dampen the tone with the heel of the picking hand for muffled "Les Paul tones."

Further valuable Gibson features include the 3-way toggle switch and four controls, including a separate tone and volume control for each pickup, which offer the player additional advantages of presetting the tone to any desired quality and changing from one pickup to another by a flip of the toggle switch. The 22 frets on the fingerboard assure marvelous, clear, sustaining tones in all positions—with no dead notes. Annoying buildup of synthetic tones or feed back have been eliminated in this new Les Paul Model Gibson guitar and the player can count on wonderful contrast of tone, sharp brilliant treble, fine in between balanced tone for rhythm, and deep basses when desired.

Body length, 17¼"; body width, 12¾"; scale length, 24¾".

LES PAUL SOLID BODY ELECTRIC
SPANISH CUTAWAY GUITAR $210.00

CASE 39.50

GIBSON, INC., KALAMAZOO, MICHIGAN

Chicago Musical Instrument Company • Distributors

(Opposite) A beautiful, all-gold 1954 Les Paul model #4 3284, with its original tag, in a rare "American Beauty" plush case. *Courtesy Buzz Jens, October 1975*

These early versions measured 4" by $^{3}/_{4}$" and are $^{3}/_{8}$" thick. The two outside flanges (or ears) that attached to the stud posts measured $^{3}/_{16}$" thick. The bridge assembly was positioned at an angle and screwed into knurled inserts pressed in the body. It used two inset Allen screws for further (relative) intonation of the instrument. An arched design was necessary to compensate for the fingerboard radius. Now everyone could truly get the famed Les Paul muted tones—hooray! Many felt that this simple but effective design gave the guitar its ultimate resonance and timbre via a direct coupling that transferred the strings' energy into the body. Being a curved bar with a moderately formed peak, it sometimes created an ever-so-slight drone sound that is more apparent on the high (non-wound) strings. It produces a unique tone somewhat like that of a sitar bridge, but with far less buzzing. Without a definite sharp edge to focus the point of contact, a slightly unclear sound was naturally created with the strings over the more rounded stopbars.

The January 1954 Gibson *Gazette* stated, "Notice the unique metal combination bridge and tailpiece with the string making contact on the top of the bridge. With this new style bridge and tailpiece, which is both horizontally and vertically adjustable, the player may dampen the tone with the heel of the picking hand to achieve the muffled 'Les Paul tones' and special effects that made this great guitarist famous." Editor Clarence Havenga asked storeowners to take advantage of Les and Mary's radio and TV show publicity and order blow-up ads for extra promotion. (Where are those Les and Mary displays now?)

The patent was applied for on January 21, 1953; the Les Paul models received this new bridge tailpiece in mid 1953. Some original '53 transition guitars were released with the early shallow neck angle and factory installed "stop/stud" bridges. Evidence of the drilled ground wire hole to the bottom of the trapeze could sometimes be seen. String action was very high by today's standards, even with the tailpiece completely lowered. Evidently, a number of these transition guitars left the factory with medium-high action; yet, it would be virtually unplayable today (or, you could say they were already set up for bottleneck playing!). Some were factory "adjusted" to use up pre-made, old-style bodies with mahogany shims under the tenon and lower portion of the fingerboard.

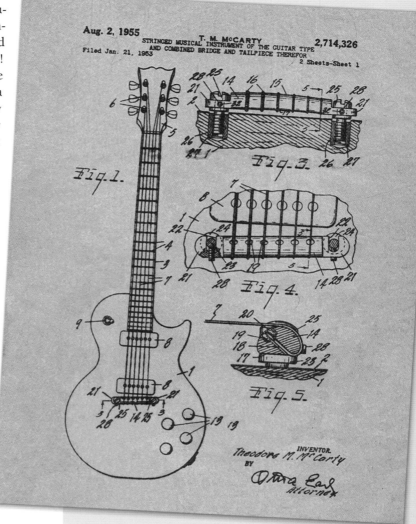

This is Ted McCarty's patent for the famous combination bridge/tailpiece, filed in January of 1953. This popular "stopbar" unit has been used for decades on many different Gibson models. Note the angled string entrance put to use on their steel guitar models.

Here are examples of various McCarty "wrap-around" bridges shown with a 1957 Century steel guitar in Bittersweet pink. String spacing was wider on these steel guitar models. Get a load of those cream knobs and pink P-90! The gold bridge was Les Paul's personal one from his early Custom with slight string- and hand-wear showing. Note the tapped holes in the thin arms. The nickel stop/stud is from the late fifties and is a bit more sturdy in design.

A nice 1954 Goldtop #4 2575 showing a little oxidized brass area. *Courtesy Albert Molinaro, 2005*

Variations on a Theme

During the early 1950s, the first Les Paul models went through a number of big and small construction changes with respect to cavity routing, neck set, arching and top thickness, grounding wire methods, and cutaway details. After the transition in '53, they used the remaining earlier channeled bodies (with the proper neck-angle adjustment). For a short while, ground wires were put through another small hole from the control cavity to the bridge stud insert. This drilled hole was left intact, but abandoned in '54 in favor of a different route. A short hole was drilled from the stud to the lead pickup cavity and soldered to the braided shield nearby.

With the neck angle and tailpiece change in 1953, the final thickness of the actual maple cap increased to roughly 5/8", according to the final sanding. Originally, only a small amount of maple was visible under the binding in the cutaway on trapeze models. As the neck angle increased, the top became more pronounced, with a slightly higher arch in the center, neck, and cutaway area. This also meant that a longer maple strip was revealed—a characteristic that continued through the years.

Small differences with the cutaway horn design appeared during 1953 into 1954. Later models had a slightly shorter and less pointed horn. The cutaway tip was ever so slightly brought in, too. These very subtle changes occurred to finalize the instrument as they refined it. Even changes in the pickup covers occurred with thicker plastics and artistic swirled effects.

This rare, multi-colored swirled cover (similar to the ES-295 version) was made of the slightly thicker and more brittle plastic material used in 1953.

A fine example of a 1954 Les Paul Model #4 1796 showing how the three-piece maple top can show its laminations. Most don't have such a dramatic demarcation as this near mint condition guitar. *Courtesy 4 Amigos, Pomona, August 1993*

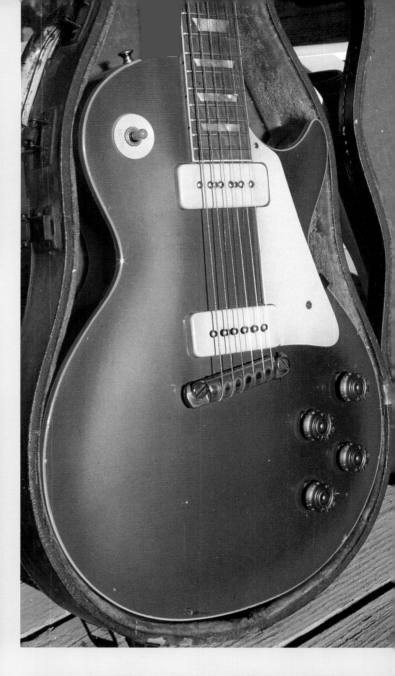

(Above) Typical of aged Gibsons, the lacquer that covers the pearl logo shows the yellowing of the clear coat, and some flaking of the finish that didn't adhere as it does on the holly overlay.

(Right) A nice player's '54 Goldtop.
Courtesy Warwick Rose, 2003

(Below) Uncovered switch cavity revealing the rear of the Switchcraft toggle. Routing was 1 5/8" across until later years.

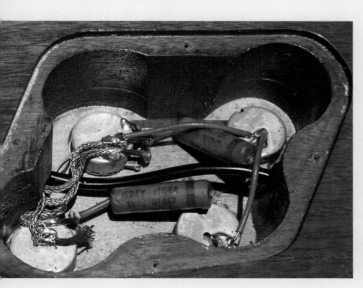

Close-up of control cavity clearly showing the Grey Tiger caps and green-cloth-clad lead wires. Note the ground wire now goes towards the rear pickup.

This cutaway shot shows the maple cap strip and some heel stress present.

A circular, ivory plastic surround with "RHYTHM" and "TREBLE," labeled in gold, was added to the toggle switch. It protected the guitar's finish from the metal thumbnut and added to the attractive styling. Plastic control knobs by Gibson during the late '40s finally had numbers and were painted various colors from beneath—similar to the attractive Gibson steel guitar plastic parts. The original, 1952 $5/8"$-tall gold "barrel" knobs were modified to $1/2"$-tall "speed" knobs during 1953. They were basically sprayed gold, and often would fade a few shades, from light gold to a darker tone (some even becoming deep orange). Many would turn green around the edges from the brass oxidation. Eventually, they were streamlined into easy-to-grip, small bell-shaped or "bonnet" versions during 1955/1956. "They were made like little hats," says Ted. "We had our own dies for it."

Smooth-action Bigsby B-7 true vibrato units were available for Gibson Les Paul models in 1953. In 1955, they retailed for $50. Bigsby tailpieces were natural-polished aluminum that would dull (become lackluster) over the years. Early versions were fixed-arm units without rocking bridges; then they were available with a swinging movable arm by the mid 1950s. The inside portion of the casting was painted black around the logo, and design patent #D169,120 writing. A tall, circular spring was used that would often oxidize, with white powder coming off. They soon came with a complementing compensated rocking bridge, and were available throughout the '50s. Carl Perkins later used a Bigsby vibrola on his original Goldtop during the '50s.

(Right) An all gold Les Paul (# 4 0989) with a fixed-arm Bigsby vibrato tailpiece. These early vibrolas came with a matching aluminum compensated bridge that simply sat flush on its arched "dog bone" saddle. Later, improved units had swinging arms and rocking bridges on thumbscrews. The Bigsby units for Les Paul models used this extra roller bar to give a good angle over the bridge. Note the typical white oxidation on the spring.

(Left) Serial numbers are sometimes seen with pre-stamped ghost numbers.

(Below) Some early Goldtops like this one (#3 1662) were later equipped with a movable Bigsby and compensated bridge setup, doing away with the limited trapeze setup. *Courtesy Ken Hower, 2003*

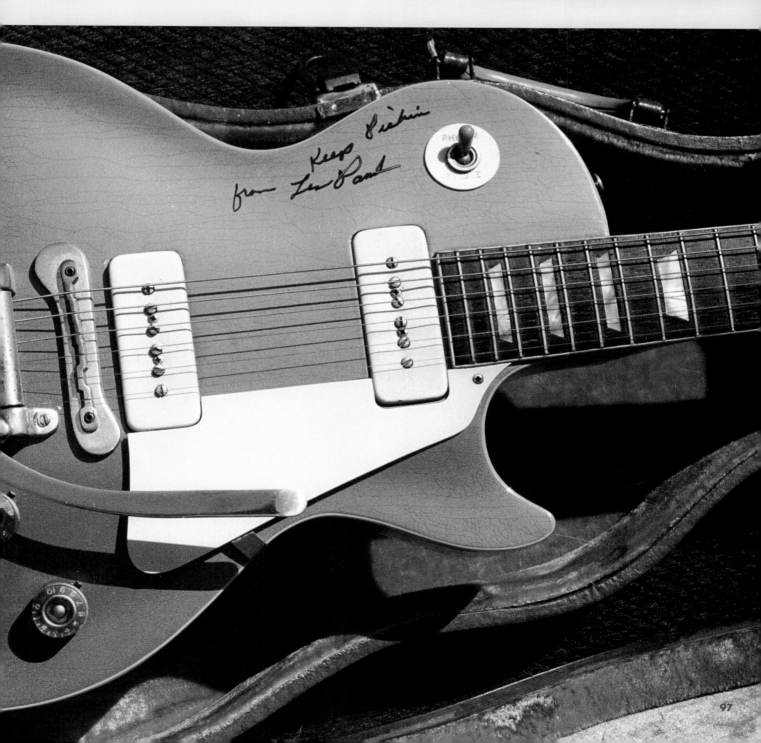

(Above) A late model, stop/stud, all-gold Les Paul model #6 9466 in exceptional condition. *Courtesy Albert Molinaro, September 1993*

(Below) The dark reflection on the back gives it a molten effect while showing the sparse, long weather checks from rapid temperature change.

An early stamped serial number "3 2379" in the new, improved Les Paul model. *Courtesy Steve Soest, February 1975*

Serial numbers were issued starting in early 1953 on the trapeze Goldtop models. The stamp set is size 1 1/2". They are quite easy to decipher. The first digit is the last digit of the year (i.e., '53), and the last four are generally consecutive production numbers (i.e., 1359, for a serial number of 3 1359). In 1954, the serial numbers reached up towards 5000; then Gibson simply resumed that high 5000 sequence when production resumed in 1955. Eventually, the serial numbers went up over 9999, so Gibson simply added a 1 (and then a 2) after the first digit. Some late guitars in 1956 added the 1. Unprecedented high production in 1959 and 1960 included a 2 and 3!

Not all of Gibson's serial numbers were entirely sequential, since you can find a trapeze tailpiece on a #3 14xx number and a stop/stud tailpiece on #3 13xx. They were serialized in batches of ten to fifteen (normally producing 40 at a time), and would often overlap. In later years, the transition from the P-90 to the humbucker during 1957 also had overlaps with the serial numbers.

Prices were up to $235 in zone 2 on the West Coast in 1954, and jumped to $250 by 1956. The Gibson *Gazette* sometimes called the guitar a "Les Paul Regular," while the September 1956 pricelist was the first reference to officially give the guitar its ultimate name of "Les Paul Standard," prior to the 1960 catalog. These magnificent Les Paul Goldtops with the classic stopbar bridges were released into 1956 and a few in 1957.

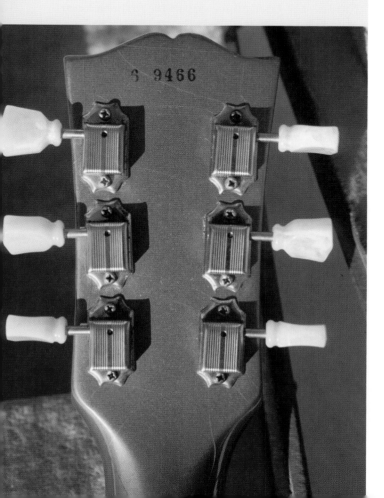

Artists

The list of influential blues artists who played the P-90 Les Paul Goldtop is long. With greats like John Lee Hooker, Muddy Waters and his second guitarist Pat Hare, Eddie "Guitar Slim" Jones (who owned the first LP in New Orleans, which is supposedly buried with him), B.B. King, Hubert Sumlin (with Howlin' Wolf), Buddy Guy, Bobo Jenkins, Sister Rosetta Tharpe, Link Wray, Michael Bloomfield, Jerry Garcia, Alan Wilson, and Johnny Winters all played the seminal gold Gibsons.

As part of the shining blues giants of the King triumvirate, Freddy King's emotional vocals and quick-fingered guitar technique garnered a multitude of young guitar followers during the sixties. Originally from Texas, he first started guitar at six, learning from his mother and her brother Leon King. After moving to Chicago at sixteen, he began absorbing influences like T-Bone Walker, Eddie Taylor (who taught him to use finger-picks), Robert Lockwood, Magic Sam, and Otis Rush, After playing clubs during the fifties, Freddy finally broke out in the early sixties scene (on Federal Records) with such hits as the instrumental "Hideaway" and the memorable "Have You Ever Loved a Woman." His crying vocal delivery and burning guitar technique (plus wicked vibrato) put him in a special class all his own—earning him the nickname "Texas Cannonball." Adopting the Gibson's great tones early on, Freddy set the world on fire with awesome picking prowess on a Les Paul Goldtop. In later years, he also used the ES models. His influence on Mike Bloomfield and Eric Clapton indirectly helped change the guitar world during the late sixties.

I caught up with Freddy backstage after a killer set at Hollywood's Starwood Club in 1976:

RL: I mentioned before about Michael Bloomfield telling me you were the first guitar player with the sound of the Les Paul guitar.

FK: Yes, in the fifties. There were guys who had it before me. But I was the first one he saw. Muddy Waters and other artists like Joey Williams was the first one I think I saw with one. I think that was '55.

RL: It was a popular blues guitar.

FK: Yeah. Everybody was playing the Les Paul, the gold-model guitar. And it was really good. It sounded good and it really played good, you know. That's it. I've got a Les Paul guitar now.

RL: What did you like about the qualities of the guitar?

FK: It's just the neck, the frets, and the way it sounds... everything. It had feeling. But also now I play in the studio a 355 and a Custom Les Paul. Both of them are heavy, you know. So, I love Gibsons, period.

RL: Was the Les Paul guitar the first solid-body you ever picked up?

FK: Yes. The Les Paul Junior was the first one I ever picked up.

RL: Did you prefer the Goldtop over the Junior?

FK: Yeah, right.

RL: What did you think of the sound of the two-pickup guitar?

FK: The Junior was a nice-playing guitar. The action was nice, you know. The action was really good. The other, it had more bite.

Since the late thirties, singer/guitarist Sister Rosetta Tharpe's impact in the Gospel field was enormous beginning with the 1938 Decca best sellers "Lonesome Road" and "Rock Me." She performed with a National Duolian and Gibson L-5N for many years prior to her use of this early Les Paul Goldtop.

FREDDY KING SINGS

HIGH FIDELITY
KING
762

LONESOME WHISTLE BLUES
YOU'VE GOT TO LOVE HER WITH A FEELING
HAVE YOU EVER LOVED A WOMAN
YOU KNOW THAT YOU LOVE ME (But You Never Tell Me So)
YOU MEAN, MEAN WOMAN (How Can Your Love Be True)
IT'S TOO BAD THINGS ARE GOING SO TOUGH
IF YOU BELIEVE (In What You Do)
LET ME BE (Stay Away From Me)
TAKIN' CARE OF BUSINESS
I LOVE THE WOMAN
I'M TORE DOWN
SEE SEE BABY

(Above) Blues great Muddy Waters used the classy Gibson Les Paul Goldtop back in the day.

(Above) Freddy King Sings LP featuring his well-worn Goldtop that influenced many English and American guitarists.

(Left) Alan Wilson, guitarist with the American blues band Canned Heat, is shown here playing his 1954 Les Paul guitar. Alan was also a blues musicologist, having transcribed material for folklorist Harry Oster. He played with his fingers and sometimes in open tunings. This guitar can also be seen on the "Playboy After Dark" show. After Alan's unfortunate death in 1970, Bob Hite used the guitar with the band (in open tuning), and it soon acquired a smell of whisky and sweat. It now sits restored in a place of honor at the Boogie House Museum in Belgium. *Courtesy drummer Fito de la Parra*

Tune-O-Matic Bridges

For many years, Gibson players wanted their instruments set up so they could be played in accurate tune throughout the entire register. Everyone lived with the wooden compensated bridges, and intonation was always slightly off—and especially off with any radical change in string gauges. The advent of the solid-body instrument demanded far more accurate intonation for recording artists and other performing professionals. Thus the critical need for a better bridge, due to the inherent clarity of solid-guitar construction. Enter the revolutionary Gibson ABR-1 Tune-O-Matic adjustable bridge!

April 3, 1956   T. M. McCARTY   2,740,313
BRIDGE FOR STRINGED MUSICAL INSTRUMENTS
Filed July 5, 1952

(Above) This is Ted's patent on the groundbreaking Tune-O-Matic bridge, filed in July of 1952. In reality, it was developed right along with the original Les Paul guitar, yet they reserved this new invention primarily for the upcoming top model. These patent papers were a gift from Ted McCarty in 1975.

(Left) Here's a spectacular 1956 Goldtop with the Tune-O-Matic Lifton "hourglass" case. *Courtesy Norm Harris*

Originally designed in 1952 (as the first Les Paul guitars appeared), it was initially reserved for the upcoming top Gibson models, and purposely held back from the lesser ones. Though the production of the Les Paul Custom began in 1954 with the new Tune-O-Matic adjustable bridge, it became an incorporated item on the Les Paul Regular in 1956. Although we even see them in '55, many combination stop/stud models were built into '56 and '57.

By this point in time, Gibson began shipping the two Tune-O-Matic-equipped Les Paul models with strings that went through the anchoring bar, instead of over the top. This, more than likely, would have initially been for cosmetic reasons. Possibly a setup person tried stringing through the bar, thought it looked better, so management capitulated. Most players have accepted it that way since. The sharper string angle gives more down force on the Tune-O-Matic and can brighten the tone in the upper register. With hard playing, it certainly contributes to concaving the bridge, and will break strings far easier. Most players raise the stopbar slightly to maintain reasonable body contact and a slight bend over the edge of the bridge. Two prominent players who always used this over-the-bar, tailpiece stringing were Duane Allman and Billy Gibbons. Tone purists still gravitate to the earlier stop/stud models for the extra sustain, though.

The intonation afforded by the innovative Tune-O-Matic bridge was a welcome addition for the professional musician desiring the golden precision tones of a well-tuned Les Paul model. (More on this story later.) It has become such a standard in the industry, most professional Gibson players couldn't imagine owning a Les Paul without one.

Prices for the Goldtop Les Paul model in September 1955 (zone 2) was $250 and $43 for the 535 Faultless case. By July 15, 1957, the zone 1 price was only $247.50, and $257.50 in zone 2. Production was 862 in 1955, and 920 in 1956.

"*Tune-o-matic*" *Bridge* — Complete answer to intonation problems, the ingenious Gibson "Tune-o-matic" bridge has six individual saddles which are adjustable by means of small screws, so that the playing length of each string may be set to give an accurate scale throughout — regardless of the gauge of strings used. Available in nickel, or in gold plate.

"*Tune-o-matic*" *bridge in Nickel plate*
"*Tune-o-matic*" *bridge in Gold plate*

(Above) The catalog's Tune-o-Matic depiction with box and handy flathead screwdriver. List price for the nickel ABR-1 bridge was $13.50, and $21.60 for the gold-plated ABR-2 in CMI's 1957 parts price list.

ELECTRIC SPANISH GUITARS (Cutaway) SOLID BODY

Les Paul Custom 537	Guitar, Solid Body Cutaway, Black Finish, with two built-in pickups and toggle switch	$375.00
	Faultless Case (Gold Plush) for above	47.50
Les Paul Model 535	Guitar, Solid Body, Cutaway, Gold Finish Top, with two built-in pickups and toggle switch	247.50
	Faultless Case (Plush) for above	42.00
Les Paul Special 535 115	Guitar, Solid Body Cutaway, with two built-in pickups and toggle switch	179.50
	Faultless Case (Plush) for above	42.00
	Durabilt Case for above	13.50
Les Paul TV 115	Guitar, Solid Body Cutaway, Natural Finish, built-in pick-up	132.50
	Durabilt Case for above	13.50
Les Paul Jr. 115	Guitar, Solid Body Cutaway, with built-in pickup	120.00
	Durabilt Case for above	13.50

(Above) Zone 1 East Coast price list effective July 15, 1957. "All prices subject to change without notice" and "we reserve the right to change specifications without notice" were two sayings always included on price lists so Gibson could constantly keep improving and make ends meet.

(Left) Specially constructed to recreate those high-pitched, lightening-fast runs for which Les Paul was known on his popular recorded novelty tracks, Gibson made up two of these 1956 ½-sized, gold-topped, cute little Lesters! Sporting a cream "soap bar" P-90, TOM bridge, a single master volume, a 15 ¾" mandolin scale length with a 22-fret rosewood fingerboard, this miniature Goldtop delivered pure Gibson ringing highs!

THE POPULAR "LES PAUL" SOLID BODY GUITAR

The famed "Les Paul tones" can now become a reality for all guitar players with this beautiful, solid body Les Paul guitar, incorporating many unusual Gibson features. Striking in appearance with its gold-finished, carved maple top, mahogany body and neck, the Les Paul name is in gold script on the peghead of this model.

Double combination Bridge and Tailpiece is another Gibson first . . . Tailpiece is adjustable for height, nickel Tune-O-Matic bridge adjustable up and down, and individual fine tuning adjustment for each string. This combination provides a new high in sustaining tone quality and precision pitch adjustment.

- Two pickups have separate tone and volume controls.
- Three position toggle switch activates either or both pickups.
- Tone can be pre-set to any desired quality and change from one pickup to another can be accomplished by a flip of the toggle switch.
- No dead notes—clear, sustaining tones in all positions with the 22 fret fingerboard.
- No buildup of synthetic tones or feed back.
- Body size—length, 17¼"; width 12¾"; scale length, 24¾".
- Gibson Adjustable Truss Rod neck construction.
- Padded leather strap included.

Les Paul Solid Body Electric Spanish Cutaway Guitar
Case: 535 Faultless

(Above) Catalog description of 1956 Les Paul model. This Goldtop photo was not retouched as most were in these now-classic brochures.

(Right) An early Tune-O-Matic-equipped 1955 Goldtop. *Courtesy Albert Molinaro, 2005*

(Below) Another exquisite 1956 Goldtop Standard #6 6916. Note the reversed contrasting plastic and unfaded lower portion from its original display stand. *Courtesy Bill Feil, 2005*

Improved Goldtop Models... "Humbucking" Pickups

A major milestone in guitar electronics was introduced in 1956—the "humbucking" pickup. In early 1957, they became standard on the Les Paul Goldtop and ES-175 models. It was soon added to other top models in the Gibson line.

The principle wasn't exactly new, since Seth Lover and others had used the opposing, out-of-phase transformer idea in amplifiers with choke circuits. The earliest examples actually go back to the late nineteenth century for other applications. Even Leo Fender had his 1953 Stringmaster Hawaiian steel guitars on the market with dual single-coil pickups wired together with the humbucking principle that was enabled when both pickups were mixed together. He used the same idea on the modern split-pickup Precision Bass in 1957.

The necessity to have quiet electrical instruments for concerts, TV broadcasts, and, especially, recording sessions was an important requirement. Having to constantly angle yourself to minimize the hum always took away from the player's spontaneity. Nearby external lighting fixtures and local power tools in the neighborhood could easily create an electronic disturbance.

Ted McCarty recalls its origin:

> **TM:** *Actually, we picked up the humbucking principle from the clavinet, which was a French instrument. It was one that fit on the keyboard of the piano. But the first clavinet[s] had a hum in them, and the hum created a problem. I went to Paris and talked with the engineer that had made the original design of it. He worked on the hum. And he came up with… it had a couple coils in it, and he reversed the coils and eliminated the hum, which was the humbucking thing.*
>
> **RL:** *The way the coils are set, they're turned the opposite way.*
>
> **TM:** *That's right, so the hum of one is cancelled by the hum of the other. It "bucks" the hum right out—you reverse the coil and they cancel the hum. So when I found out what he had done with the clavinet and killed the hum, as soon as I got back, I got a hold of our engineers and told them, "look, let's see what we can do to come up with a double-coil pickup, then reverse it," which they did. The "humbucker." Well, it's been copied by everybody now.*

After Ted returned from Europe in 1954, he soon prompted Seth Lover (under Walt Fuller's supervision) to get started designing a new pickup that could solve the unwanted noise from their popular P-90 single-coil pickup. This 60-cycle hum had plagued electronics since the inception of the electric guitar.

A close-up of the first experimental dual-coil humbucking pickup's back. Note the folded cover flanges and Seth's 9200 output writing. *Photo by Seymour Duncan*

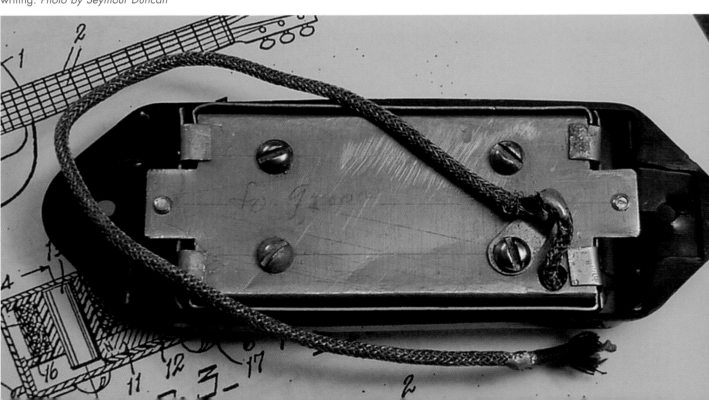

The following is from my 1973 interview with Seth Lover:

SL: I said, "Let's make one that gets rid of some of the problems we presently have. Hum pickup from an amplifier, whenever you get close to the power transformer, is a problem." So with that in mind, I developed the humbucking pickup. We applied for a patent on it, and, oh, ninety people ahead of me had designed humbucking pickups of various kinds. Oh yes, you'll find if you look at the patent I got on it finally, for Gibson, there was only one patent allowed on it. And I disclosed a number of different ways making it; but on the back of the patent, they always cite previous attempts at the same problem. And there were all kinds of variations of humbucking pickups. Some of them, instead of using magnets, they actually had DC passing through coils to create a magnet, and hooking it up in a humbucking construction. So we were probably lucky to actually get a patent on it.

RL: Where did you get the idea of the humbucking pickup?

SL: This hum was bothering us, so the idea was for us to make a pickup that does not have… that cancels out the hum pickup. So you put the two coils, and they are wound in such a direction… they're both wound in the same direction, but they're connected so that they're out of phase as far as the start; the two starts and the windings connect together, and the two ends. One is the "hot" side and the other is the "ground" side, or the output. *Those two coils, since they're both wound in the same direction, will pick up identical voltages from external fields. But because of the connection, they cancel the hum that's picked up externally. The string vibrating over them induces voltage of one clarity in one coil, and the opposite clarity in the other coil. But because they're wound in such a manner and connected in such a manner, those voltages add. The external fields away from the string cancel. And that way, we were able to get the very strong pickup, because we had two coils picking up energy, adding the voltages.*

The use of the cover material was important in how that thing performed. With the cover on, it always has a slightly different sound; but if you were to use some types of materials for shielding there, it would sound like you'd turned the tone control down. And so the material selected for that is very important.

RL: What year did you first start working on the humbucking pickup?

SL: I guess it was back around 1954, '53. I think we applied for the patent around 1955. I was working for Gibson at the time.

RL: And how many turns—what were the specifications?

SL: Seems to me each coil had around 4,000–5,000 turns—something like that.

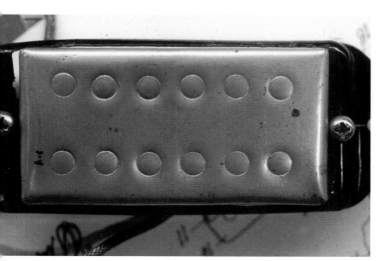

This is Seth Lover's original hand-built 1955 prototype humbucking pickup, set into a P-90 "dog ears" cover. Note the semi-punched holes above the polepieces on the hand-formed cover. *Courtesy Seth Lover and Seymour Duncan*

It took them until well into 1955 to develop the new pickup. Seth's prototype pickups proved the idea worked well. They applied for the all-important patent #2,896,491 on June 22nd, and basically let it sit temporarily while introducing other Gibson products. One known experimental 1955 Les Paul Goldtop surfaced with two prototype humbucking pickups with handmade covers and bezels. Once Gretsch unveiled their new Filtertron pickup in 1956, Gibsons was soon to prepare theirs. Now they needed a production unit with a suitable cover for encasing the coils, a mounting ring to suspend and maneuver it, and the extra sales feature of adjustable polepieces.

'55 "Humbucker" Goldtop

The saga of the first humbucking-equipped Gibson goes back to this mid-1955 Les Paul Goldtop. Designer Seth Lover coined the famous moniker as he slid the first prototype across the table to Ted McCarty: "Here's your humbucker!" Seth's initial creation (with its dog-ear surround) was experimented with on their testing setup first. Ted said to proceed and put some on a guitar to hear them. Then two more sample pickups were built and hastily covered with hand-fashioned metal covers. Engineers naturally chose the premier solid-body, with its clear and distinctive pure string tone, to use as a test-bed instrument.

They pulled an unfinished Les Paul model from the whitewood room and partially routed the pickup cavity slightly deeper to receive its new-fangled pickups prior to the golden gilding. With hand-built surrounds (surprisingly similar to the final version), craftily made up in the model-maker's basement facility, and a trimmed pickguard, the world's first "humbucker"-equipped Gibson arose! In-house electronics man Seth Lover also reverse-phased the pickups and added some shielding to the control cavity for extra noise reduction. Afterwards, in-house guitarist/endorser Rem Wall demos the instrument for the Gibson brass to evaluate. It was a thumbs up all around as they decide to put it into production. First it was necessary to give it a cosmetic facelift (add adjustable polepieces for a more commercial appeal) and start dye molds for the coil, cover, and surround parts.

Enter Flint Michigan guitarist Gil Hembree, who had an idea (or a "vision," as he put it) to advertise locally in Kalamazoo (in the *Yellow Pages*?) to find a vintage Gibson in the homeland. With a chance call from the son of the original owner (evidently someone outside the factory), Gil tried to ascertain what this newfound treasure might be. After some initial confusion and be-wonderment, Gil headed for Kalamazoo to check out this puzzling instrument in person. Lo and behold, it turns out to be the "real deal"— the original factory, humbucking-modified test guitar from 1955. It's presented here while on display at the winter 2004 NAMM show in pickup specialist Seymour Duncan's booth, accompanied with other Lover artifacts of wonder.

An attractive display of Seth Lover's humbucking pickup evolution from his first prototype, the test-bed 1955 LP Regular, pickup winding machines (Lover's and Duncan's), and various incarnations of the hugely popular pickup. *Courtesy Seymour Duncan and Gil Hembree, 2005*

(Opposite) This is Gibson's first test-bed guitar for the newly developed 1955 "humbucking" pickup. Sporting hand-fashioned nickel covers, cutout solid plastic rings, two Filister screws (their polepiece variety) for height adjustment and pickguard screws to hold the new units on—the modern Les Paul icon we know today took shape. *Courtesy Gil Hembree, 2005*

The prototype's old-style "dog ear" flange setup was soon abandoned. An attractive, trim-looking, rectangular raised-plastic surround bezel was designed to securely mount the pickup with four flush flathead Phillips screws. You could adjust the overall pickup height easily with two slotted, roundhead screws. A new pickup base was also developed with $1/2"$ legs and tapped $1/4"$ flanges extending into the body. It was formed of stainless steel and nickel-plated for low conductivity. This whole setup also created a sonic suspension with the two spring-loaded screws, compared to the solid-mounted P-90 setup. It gave the pickup a more neutral stance in relation to the body's vibrations and string movement. The pickup being suspended was advantageous for a more accurate and focused sound.

Molded pickup bezels had reinforced tube-like supports in each corner that were drilled for the various screws. The taller bridge bezel ($3/8"$+ to $1/2"$ tall) reads "M-69" and "8" (for height) on the treble-string side. Its bass side has pickup designation "MR-490," and a manufacturer's symbol (a stylized "H" over an "I"), resembling a TV antenna. One extended tube is slightly smaller than the other three. Neck bezels (measuring $5/32"$ to $1/4"$) read "M-69" and "7," while the other side reads "MR 491." Within the next few years, 492 and 493 molded versions were also used. The bezels, molded by Hughes Industrial Plastics, were cast out of a plastic resin that was somewhat flexible. Neck units were flat and naturally curved along the arching, while the bridge bezel was molded with its curve. As the tooling wore, slight variations occurred. Early humbucking-equipped Goldtops used black M-69 pickup bezel surrounds. After a few production runs, they soon switched to the original cream color scheme as used on the 1955 test-bed guitar. These cream-colored parts were only used on the LP Standards, late ES-295s, and some Ultratone steels.

Covers

To shield against electrostatic interference, a metal casing was necessary—and also good protection for the exposed coils. Seth specified a thin, non-conductive metal, since a thick cover would muffle the pickup's tone. The non-magnetic material most appropriate was stainless steel that was nickel/silver plated. This coating, often called "German silver," was non-conductive and easy to solder. Early experimental metal covers were sprayed in an unusual orange/gold-colored paint that didn't hold up under the rigors of strumming or time. Plain nickel/silver versions appeared soon afterwards, which still have the finely brushed finish to help the earlier paint adhere. Sharp, squared edges visually characterize these early covers. Late-1957 and onward versions were shiny, nickel/silver-plated, and had more rounded edges. I've even seen these thin metal covers completely worn through from years of intense playing! Gold covers were thinly plated over the nickel and would easily wear off to the nickel.

A fine pair of early humbucking pickups from #7 3746. Note the slight string abrasion in the reflection.

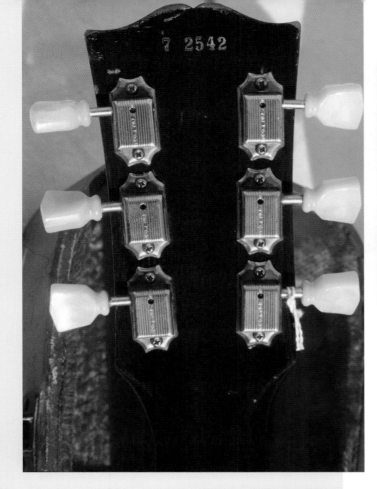

(Above) Typical underside of early "pre-PAF" humbucking without sticker affixed. Note M-69 surround and nickel Phillips coil screws.

(Below and left) This early 1957 humbucking-equipped production Les Paul Standard #7 2542 sports original black plastic parts and dark back. *Courtesy George Gruhn, Texas, May 1994*

Very nice Goldtop LP Standard #7 3746 showing early humbucking pickups and exposed neck tenon in cavity routing. *Kind courtesy of the late Ben Fisher, 1994*

(Above) A great-sounding 1957 Goldtop Standard with original Bigsby vibrato tailpiece and no stud holes. Aerosmith's Brad Whitford bought this fine guitar from this author and used it extensively during the seventies. *Courtesy then-owner Buzz Jens, Laguna, CA, 1973*

Coils & Magnets

Coil bobbins were originally molded from a black butyrate plastic material. Each coil received approximately 5,000 winds of 42-gauge copper wire. This very fine wire was enamel-coated and had a slightly maroon color. With the cover off, you can see the copper wire through the small, single square hole on each coil. Dark olive/black paper tape was wrapped around the coils. An M-55 Alnico magnet (Gibson's term) was placed directly beneath the twin coils, in between the polepieces. They were purchased from General Electric as before with the P-90. Higher magnetic strength was reflected in the increasing Alnico numbers (II, III, and IV) with different mixtures of aluminum, nickel, and cobalt. These various strengths were used during the 1950s, and also affected the brightness, warmth, and output. One preferred combination reads around 8K with Alnico IV magnets for a more overall robust sound and better-defined high end. Alnico V was begun during 1960 with a slightly shorter M-56 magnet. This stronger magnet gave it a brighter tone and more overall output. A small maple-wood spacer was inserted to stabilize the coil with the extended slug polepieces. A tapped strip of cold drawn steel received the ferrous steel Fillister screw polepieces on the other coil.

To achieve this type of quiet pickup, both coils are wound in the same direction and connected in series to increase the output. Then the coils are both wired out-of-phase electrically, and set up magnetically to silence the outside interference. The screw pole bobbin is oriented south while the slug coil is north. Some were reversed for three-pickup special effects. Electronically, the tail end of the coil leads are connected together (with black-coated 28-gauge wire), while the start of the adjustable coil was grounded to the base. This left the beginning of the non-adjustable coil to be attached to the center of the 22-gauge lead wire. Its braided shield is then soldered to the pickup base and exits through a hole in the base.

DC resistance output was specified to be around the 8,000 mark as before. Often pickups would vary in output due to accidental under- or over-wound coils. They would read out between 7–9K or more according to how long the worker was distracted! Hotter (over-wound) pickups would compress the frequency width, increasing the midrange output but losing definition and dynamics. Usually, four to six coils were wound at the same time. Around 2,000 winds a minute was the rate— and without a counter in those days. Some coils would be mismatched slightly with some inherent noise present. These pickups with varied wind combinations actually sound a little brighter (less muffled) than the evenly matched coils. This factor can be considered a plus for use with effects. Micro-phonic feedback (a high-pitched squeal) is sometimes noticed at the advent of super high-gain amplification. The minute airspaces in the coils would create high-volume squealing, and could be solved with careful wax potting. High-volume static occurs when metal filings (i.e., steel wool) gets drawn deep into the coils.

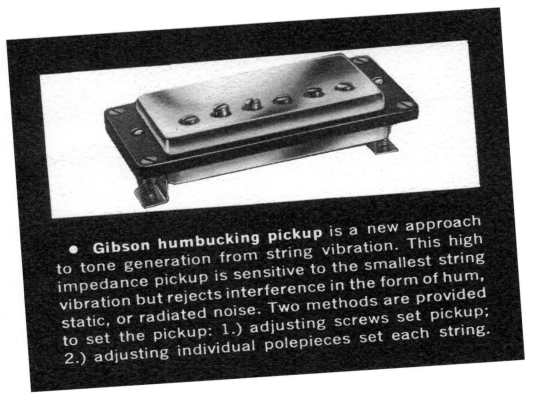

• **Gibson humbucking pickup** is a new approach to tone generation from string vibration. This high impedance pickup is sensitive to the smallest string vibration but rejects interference in the form of hum, static, or radiated noise. Two methods are provided to set the pickup: 1.) adjusting screws set pickup; 2.) adjusting individual polepieces set each string.

Pickup catalog depiction used into the sixties. Note this early version with slotted screws for bezel attachment, sharp cover corners, and raised Filister pole-piece screws.

Gibson's *Gazette* article announcing "Another Gibson First!" with the new model 490 humbucking story. Shown here is an ES-175 guitar. The 490 is also stated as a standard item on the Les Paul Regular, among other models… try one!

Seth's new design actually created a very full-sounding pickup. It didn't, however, have quite the same highs and rich low-end of the P-90, due to the nature of the design. Humbuckings naturally tend to have a darker tonality (blocked high frequencies) because the string is sensed at two separated magnetic points—a compromise that can be an advantage in another area. The P-90 is considered to have a clear, yet gutsy, tone at volume, whereas the new humbucking has a remarkably smooth, fat midrange and strong sound. Coupled with the Les Paul's brighter maple top, it was a true success story in the making.

Seth elaborated on the humbucking pickups:

SL: *Actually, I think when we first started out, we glued the forms together with celluloid to make our initial models of it.*

RL: *Do you have any original humbucking pickups with you?*

SL: *I have one of them. The original one has a different cover. That was back in the time when the pickup was designed and no one else had anything like it on the market, and so you couldn't get much action out of people to get it produced, put on the market. Just as soon as competition brought one out, in one of the trade shows one summer, Gretsch had what they called a "humbucking pickup." Then the sales force says, "How come we never had anything like that?" Well, we've got it all there; all you've got to do is make up your mind what kind of cover you want to put on, how you want to decorate it.*

RL: *What does the cover have to do with the performance of the pickup?*

SL: *Well, metal encloses it to keep out electrostatic pickup. The winding will eliminate your electromagnetic pickup, but if you have an open winding it's subject to so many amps, and you get close to that source of noise and you'll get a pickup with the noise in there. And while it might be some cancellation of it, generally you find that one coil picks up a lot more than the other. And you'll get some of the "hashy" noise.*

Generally it's the one closest to it, because all humbucking cancellation problems, if the coils are exactly the same distance from the source, you have exactly the same cancellation. But, say, one is off to one side and a little bit closer to the first coil than the second, so there's going to be a differential between them. Say there's a noise source over there and you have a pickup here; one coil is wound here, one there. This one is closer to it. So the one closest to it will induce more voltage than the other one. Now they do not equally cancel. It's like a little antenna on a radio receiver. You turn it for maximum pickup if you want to receive a station, but if the station's bothering you, you try to put it in a position to mellow it out. The idea on these coils is that if they're both the same distance from the noise source, they both induce the same voltage in the coil. But physically, two cannot occupy the same space, so if the noise source is off to the side and one is closer than the other… if it's straight away from the thing in a horizontal position, then you have no problem.

Here are the important points of Seth Lover's patent:

2,896,491
MAGNETIC PICKUP FOR STRINGED MUSICAL INSTRUMENT

Seth E. Lover, Kalamazoo, Mich.,
assignor to Gibson, Inc., Kalamazoo, Mich.

Application June 22, 1955, Serial No. 517,171

This invention relates to improvements in magnetic pickup for stringed musical instrument. The principal objects of this invention are:

First, to provide a magnetic pickup for a stringed musical instrument which is not affected by adjacent electrical devices and which does not pick up and transmit at the amplifier the hum of such devices.

Second, to provide an electromagnetic pickup for stringed musical instruments with magnetically opposed pickup coils that neutralize the effect of currents induced by adjacent electrical devices...

Magnetic pickups for stringed musical instruments having steel strings are well known and heretofore have consisted essentially of a coil wound around a permanent magnet core with a string of the instrument passing in proximity to the core so that vibration of the string will vary the magnetic field through the core and induce an electrical current in the coil capable of being amplified and passed through a loud speaker for amplifying the sound of the

instrument. Stringed musical instruments and magnetic pickups of this type have been subject to the undesirable creation of hum noises in the amplifier by reasons of electrical devices in proximity to the pickup, which create undesired, interfering currents in the coil. The present invention eliminates the undesirable hum by neutralizing undesired induced currents in the pickup coil before they can be amplified and reproduced...

The permanent magnet system created by the permanent magnet 11 and pole pieces 13 and 13A establishes north and south poles at the exposed ends of each pair of the pole pieces in proximity to the superimposed metal string 2 of the instrument and opposite poles are accordingly induced in the metallic string. Vibration of the string causes it to move over the ends of the pole pieces creating a variation in the magnetic field through the coils in a well-known fashion. Since the pole piece 13 has a north pole at its upper end, variation in the strength of the magnetic field will tend to create a current in the coil 15 in the direction indicated by the arrow 23 in fig. 6 and concurrent vibration over the pole piece 13A will tend to induce a current in the coil 15A in the direction indicated by the arrow 23A. The currents in the two coils thus are added together to provide a strong signal in response to the vibration of the string. The pickup thus filters out or eliminates the hum of unwanted interfering devices and creates a strong electrical impulse from the vibrating string for accurate reproduction of the sound of the instrument.

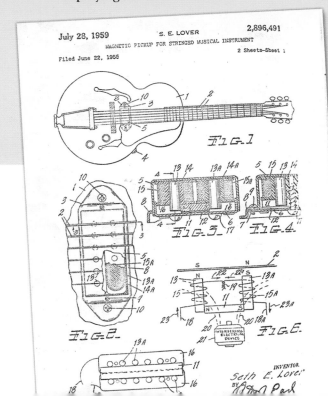

Gibson's landmark patent #2,896,491, filed on June 22nd and granted in 1959 to Seth E. Lover for his humbucking pickup principal. The inclusion of extra novel variations insured that the patent would go through, since so few others had been granted since 1870.

An exceptional Les Paul Standard Goldtop #7 3749 (*courtesy of Doug "Prof" Suman, tech for the group America, October 1996*). Note the small stamped "2" for "factory second" above the serial number. Possibly dented after finished since no flaws were found. These decorative brass Gibson logos were often put on cases.

Seth Lover's patent depicts twelve soft iron cylinder poles, with the magnet bar in between, charging each row either north or south. Besides the deleted outside flanges and added adjustable screw poles, the humbucking has basically remained the same. It was a remarkably simple idea that became a major breakthrough. However, one slight flaw existed that usually is overlooked. GE generally manufactured their long magnets with a different orientation. Past employee Bruce Fellows worked at GE during the 1950s and '60s, and personally invoiced and processed orders for Gibson. (He shared some of his observations with Dan Attillo, who purchased magnets from him for DiMarzio Pickups during the early '80s.) Bruce had then left his position at GE to manage the PerMag Corporation, selling custom-made magnets in later years. He recalled that, at the time, the preferred magnetized orientation direction was along the longitudinal axis of the rod. Gibson, on the other hand, specifically used magnets oriented across the width (along the short dimension) with the north on one edge and south on the other edge. They would stick them in the magnetizer at a 90-degree angle to the normal axis (preferred orientation). Therefore, the long edges were polarized opposite to affect each coil differently.

The aluminum, cobalt, and nickel were melted and cast in molds in various shapes and strength combinations for industrial use. Originally, these particular permanent magnet rods were 36" to 48" long. After milling, they measured $1/2$" by $1/8$" by $2 1/2$" long. The heat-treating process would naturally arrange the magnetic domains in a preferred direction of orientation. Since these particular magnets preferred long magnetism to short, Gibson's procedure would occasionally facilitate slight anomalies or weird holes in the field (strong and weak areas).

Bruce would often magnetize them and pack them to ship to Gibson, and sometimes bring them home to wrap for shipment.

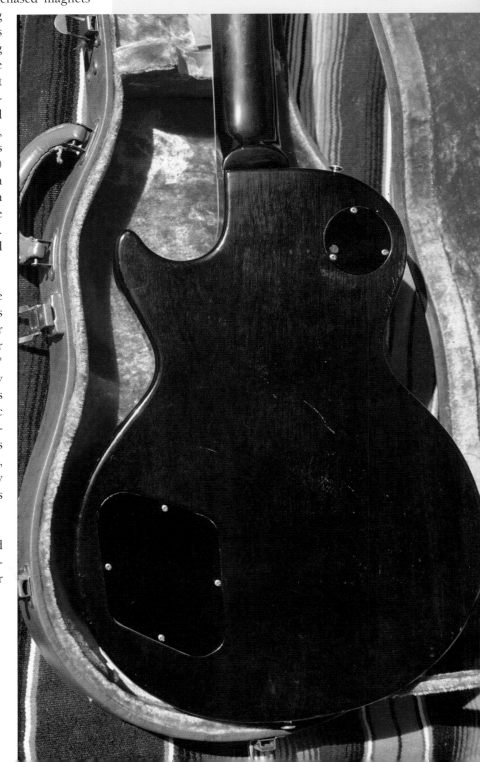

A fine 1957 Goldtop #7 3763 with walnut-stained back (Arlington, Texas Guitar Show, November 1993). Note the yellow serial numbers and black plastic back plates.

The following is from my 1975 interview with Walt Fuller:

RL: Did any of the specifications change on any of the humbucking pickups through the '50s? I don't really know if the coils deteriorate that much… do they?

WF: *No. The coils, if anything, about the only thing that would be possible to change would be the magnets. The magnets lose some of their flux density through their age. Each time you put on a new set of strings, why, you magnetize the strings from the magnet; and over a period of time, why, you're bound to lose something from it. Because, each time you throw those strings away, you are throwing away some of the magnetic force from it. That's about the only thing.*

RL: Do you run a spectrum test or anything like that for comparison from the old pickups to the new pickups?

WF: *Only that we've done power output tests and impedance tests like that.*

RL: Is the power the same? Don't they vary in between 7.5–9 pretty much?

WF: *Do you mean the DC resistance?*

RL: Yes. Some of them would measure 8.5 and up to 9; some went down to 7.5.

WF: *Well, that means actually the number of turns. The more turns that you put on, the higher the resistance would measure. Also, one of the things that enters in there is the size of the wire. For instance, 42-gauge wire—the standard that we wind the coils with—can vary from 42-gauge, two and half thousands in diame-*

ter. It can vary from about two thousands to about .027 or .028 because, as they are drawing the wire through the dies, the dies wear and the wire then gets just a bit larger. And when it gets so large, why, then they have to clear new dies. So when they put in new dies, why, now it gets much smaller. So, from one shipment of wire, maybe to the next shipment of wire, there is a tolerance of difference between the wires. And this is what makes your difference in reading. You can have the same number of turns, but due to the size of the wire, the DC resistance is apt to change. But normally it doesn't vary more than ten percent.

The wire gets its hardening—you might say, work hardening—from drawing it through the dies. It starts off with a rod, actually, and happens to the end when it gets twenty feet long. They keep drawing it smaller and smaller and the wire gets down to .02 thousands.

RL: So what makes certain pickups more powerful than others?

WF: *Your power comes from the number of turns. If you still have the same number of turns, why, there may be a little difference in the DC resistance that would put your AC impedance changes the same. You can also change the power by the range within the magnets and the material that you make the magnets out of.*

RL: The aluminum, nickel, cobalt.

WF: *You can use all nickel Alnicos I, II, III, IV, V, VII, and VIII; they've got 8H now. It's all due to the different alloys of the manufacturers.*

Gibson released the first humbucking pickups in late 1955/early 1956 with their eight-string Consolette, Multiharp, and Electraharp Hawaiian steels prior to the electric Spanish models. These 16-polepiece, large steel pickups were mounted in a different manner. The standard, six-string, 1957 humbucking pickups had the nickel/silver base surface underneath with four nickel, round-head Phillips woodscrews to secure the bobbins. They changed to brass screws in later years. During late 1957, a new black-and-gold sticker was added, that read "PATENT APPLIED FOR," supposedly to temporarily stymie the competition. Some early 1960s versions read "Pat. Pend." shortly before adding "Pat #2,737,842." This erroneous patent number was actually Les Paul's trapeze patent number that kept them all wondering!

A pair of original "Patent Applied For" pickups. *Courtesy Randy Peterson, Seattle, 2008*

(Left) This 1956 Gibson Electraharp has one of the earliest humbucking pickups on an eight-string steel guitar. Note the exposed slug polepieces, height adjustment screws, and partial pickup surround, which serves a cosmetic purpose.

(Below) A typical black and gold decal affixed to the back of the humbucking pickups. Some decals show the double-shadowed gold lettering and have the appearance of looking somewhat out of focus.

Improvements in the performance of Gibson amplifiers are being made continually by qualified engineers in the Gibson laboratory. Complete and modern test equipment includes Oscillators, Voltmeters, Analyzers and Oscilloscopes to thoroughly check amplifier performance. In the photo at the left tests for determining changes in power output are being analyzed.

The Gibson laboratory is staffed with qualified engineers, and functions on a full time basis to analyze, design and develop. Here, a camera attached to the Oscilloscope records the frequency standards for correct placement of the instrument bridge.

(Below) Side view of open humbucking showing coils, wood spacer, and magnet.

(Above) Seth Lover (top) and Walt Fuller (bottom) in their electronic labs. From the 1958 Gibson catalog.

Although prototypes and special samples were produced in 1955 and 1956, the Goldtop was officially fitted with the new Humbucking pickup in the spring of 1957… and the rest is history. Original vintage guitar collectors ten years later would often use the term "Golden Anniversary" and "Golden A"—referring to these early humbucking Les Pauls. On February 17, the first ES-175 with humbuckings was stamped "#A-25000 H.B. Pickup starts here," in the logbook. This is quite an auspicious number in the scheme of things! Humbuckings soon began to be regularly fitted on Les Paul Standards. Some P-90s continued and overlapped, even up towards #7 3800—though most early humbuckings started in the #7 2000 range. A few players still ordered some with P-90s. Through these years, Gibson kept different containers with the various types of original humbuckings using them for the proper application into the mid '60s. Generally, the guitars were numbered a few weeks before leaving for their destinations.

Many heralded this new invention, and it quickly caught on with a multitude of professional players. It was especially well received in the jazz circles; like with Wes Montgomery and others. Some players I spoke with during the mid 1960s, however, weren't particularly attracted to the new humbucking pickup's tone. At the time, they preferred the wider frequency P-90, just as some do today. Regardless, the "PAF" mythology soon began in the late '60s, once rock players realized their smoother high-gain signal for overdriving amplifiers. They also noticed the unique, slightly distorted (sort of edgy), but very smooth tonal variations of these early versions compared to the later pickups with the patent number decal. With high volume, rock players noticed that they could keep the volume backed off for playing rhythm and then simply turn up full for that ripping, burning tone for solo lead playing. Session guitarists with many types of music oftentimes find the inimitable Gibson Les Paul humbucking sound indispensable for creating a full-bodied tone for recording dates. Many landmark albums were recorded with original PAF-equipped Les Paul guitars. Its mystique continues today as the "cow with the bell," as many others have strived to recreate its magic authentic tone. Seth Lover's masterpiece pickup was a true breakthrough, and is still a benchmark for guitar electronics into the 21st century.

(Right) While traveling in Europe in 1985, I had the wonderful pleasure of visiting with some avid guitar enthusiasts who kindly let me photograph their collections. This 1957 Goldtop was photographed as an F-104 Starfighter buzzed 100 feet overhead. *Courtesy Erhard and the Bochen family in Munderkingen, Germany*

(Above) A 1957 Goldtop with pink case reflection. *Courtesy Harvey Moltz, Tucson AR, October 1977*

(Below right) A 1958 Les Paul Goldtop from another great collection photographed in Germany. The traditional, locally brewed *Hefe Weizen* wheat beer accompanied much of our memorable music sessions. *With gracious courtesy of Alfons Baumann, Munchen in Bavaria, 1985*

Wood and Finish Variations

Some all-mahogany Standards were made in 1957, and are fairly rare birds. Naturally, their tone was richer—like a Custom. Some Goldtops were made with one-piece maple tops, even though it was thought that they could warp or cup easily. They've held up fine since, however, so it was a feasible idea. Finish colors for the back of these Goldtop Les Paul guitars would often be of different shades during the mid 1950s. They used a walnut brown and dark brown lacquer in addition to the light beige sealer stain models, regardless of black or cream pickup and pickguard colors. The darker colors would often have yellow serial numbers and black plastic cavity covers. The workers would basically follow a color scheme that they felt would please the salesmen and customers.

Production of the gold Les Paul Standard dipped down to 598 in 1957. A quarter portion of the new humbucking models accounted for the 434 built in 1958. The 490-equipped Goldtops were produced for about a year altogether. Its arrival marked a major breakthrough, and eventually became one of the most dominant electronic pickups in the history of electric guitars. This now-powerful golden guitar set the stage for the next major version of the Les Paul Standard.

(Above) Here's a fine Goldtop Les Paul with an all-mahogany body. Fine grain lines can be seen under the gold, much like you would see on a black Custom. This guitar was used by Laurence Juber on some of Paul McCartney's tours during the seventies. *Courtesy Laurence Juber, 2004*

(Below and right) A very late Goldtop 1959 model #9 0225 with heavy weather checking. This extremely rare instrument was photographed at a Texas guitar show.

RL: Who were your influences musically?

BC: My influences were Albert King, Grant Green, George Benson, Jimmy Nolan, and Al MacKay (when he was in Dyke and the Blazers). I listened to Michael Bloomfield with Butterfield and with the Electric Flag. "East West" on Butterfield's album was kind of interesting. I also listened to Bloomfield's instrumental version of Howard Tate's vocal tune "Stop" on the Super Session album. Prior to that I listened to Hendrix and to Eric Clapton when he was in Cream. I got a lot of my rhythm from Jimmy Nolan, James Brown's guitar player on "Popcorn," "I Got That Feeling," all the main rhythm stuff was him. Actually I was taught to play rhythm guitar by an organ player. I just listened to the other guys, but he's the one who gave me the techniques. Playing two-handed organ comping on the B-3 taught me how to strum guitar and put little accents in. I had switched from bass to guitar and spent a lot of time learning how to solo on the guitar as opposed to how to comp. He would tell me, "Naw, you got to learn how to comp." So I started practicing on that, which helped me out a lot with my career.

RL: You definitely have that percussive thing going strong. It's especially tight with all those syncopated songs.

BC: Yes, you had to be real exact with your parts in that band 'cause it was a busy band, but yet it didn't sound busy… if that makes sense.

Bruce Conte's well-worn 1957 all-mahogany Goldtop Les Paul. He even wore through the original metal pickup covers! *Courtesy Bruce Conte and Cal Vintage, 2006*

Here's Bruce Conte in sync with the "soul/funk" horn group Tower of Power playing his trusty '57 Goldtop at San Diego's Balboa Stadium in 1973. Players pictured include Chester Thompson on B-3, Francis Rocca Prestia on bass, and David Garibaldi on drums.

A 1957 Goldtop Standard on display at Milwaukee's Discovery World Les Paul House of Sound, 2009.

The Les Paul Amplifier

Shortly after the new guitar's introduction, Gibson's engineers developed the first in a series of five different signature model 1-12" combos. In October of 1952, the Les Paul Model GA-40 amplifier was finally released. It utilized a popular Williamson power amplification design with a Bauxendal equalization circuit. To further complement the GA-40, it also featured a special tremolo circuit by Gibson electronic engineer Seth Lover. They naturally tried to match the guitar's electronics to the amplifier's in order to produce a pleasing tonality that would complement the beautiful tone of the new solid-body guitar.

GA-40 – Version I

These original Les Paul model amps were very distinctive, with the monogram "LP" over the speaker grill. Its brown plastic was quite decorative, and doubled as a speaker protector along with its checkered cloth grill. A raised Gibson logo in flat gold adorned the top portion, and a dark brown "Les Paul" model script logo, like the guitar's headstock, was stenciled on the right side. It was a fairly small amp, measuring 22" wide, 16 1/2" tall, and 8" deep. The cabinet was covered in a two-tone design with a dark brown, "buffalo-grained," heavily textured top portion, and a gold piping that separated it from the lighter brown, "leatherette" linen bottom covering (similar to that on the Geib guitar cases). These 1950s GA series amplifiers were very attractive then and today. Its cabinetry consisted of lightweight but sturdy lock-joint redwood construction. On top was a recessed leather handle also unique to a Gibson amplifier of this era.

A top control panel in the rear featured one mic input, three guitar inputs, and four controls with maroon-brown Bakelite pointer knobs on a brown enameled chassis. Tube sockets were suspended with rubber grommets as on the sophisticated Hi-Fi gear. Seven tubes (or valves) were used, giving it twelve watts of power through a 12" Concert Series Jensen P-12P loudspeaker. Its tubes consisted of a 5Y3GT rectifier, twin 6V6GT power tubes, two 5879 preamp pentodes (one for each channel), a 12AX7 driver (phase-inverter), and a metal 6SQ7 (with an octal base) for the tremolo oscillator circuitry.

A new built-in variable tremolo circuit by Seth Lover created the amplitude modulation using two sides of the twin diode/high triode 6SC7 tube. The two controls activated the "min/max" depth and "low-to-high" frequency being operated by a 15' remote wooden foot pedal.

Les Paul GA-40 amplifier nestled in the tall grass of the San Francisco highlands. The distinctive "LP" monogram sets it apart from all other amplifiers. Original set-in handle replaced. *Courtesy Glen Quan, 1973*

An original GA-40T with Jensen P-12P and wooden footswitch. *Courtesy David Swartz, CVG, 2004*

Les Paul Amplifier

An extremely versatile general purpose amplifier with unique design and fine performance.

Features—
- 8 tubes suspended in rubber.
- 12" Jensen Concert Series speaker.
- 12 watts Output.
- Built-in tremolo circuit with foot actuated control pedal.
- Top control panel for easy accessibility with 4 inputs jacks including microphone and 4 control dials.

The very attractive luggage case is handsomely tailored in two-tone brown leatherette with gold line trim and the monogram "LP" on the grill.

1953 catalog description of the original Les Paul GA-40 amplifier.

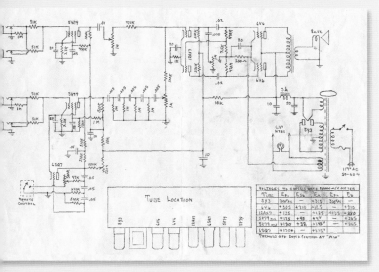

Circuit diagram for the GA-40. The 6SQ7 tube was for the tremolo circuitry, making this a GA-40T in actuality.

A clean GA-40T and original box shipped to Fife & Nichols in Hollywood, which became Wallichs Music City in later years. *Courtesy Dave DiMartino, Guitar Center Hollywood, 1973*

Seth recalls: "I did a lot of work on the Les Paul amplifier to bring it out, put the tremolo circuit in it. I designed a number of different tremolo circuits in amplifiers. One of the ones they used on the old GA-50 [twin speaker GA-50T suitcase model] after the war, I designed it between '45 and '47, right after the war. And it wasn't in production then; but when I came back to work in '52 for Gibson, it was already in production. That was kind of a balanced, modulator-type system, where I modulated two stages out of phase, and then the tremolo voltage as such would cancel in the output circuit, but the signal voltage of the guitar would remain there. In the early days when we had vacuum tube amplifiers, this was always a problem. They always wanted a great deal of intensity variation. But as soon as you've got a lot of intensity variation, you've got what we call a 'putnoid,' or 'thump.' So you have to turn that down a little, and you're never quite satisfied with the amount of amplitude variation, but you just had to stop somewhere. Well, that was one method that helped to reduce the 'thump.' But it was expensive—it cost you an extra tube to do it."

Using sharp-cutoff miniature 5879 pentodes was similar to later low-powered Vox amps. Its first channel (mic or instrument) had a flat response without any tone control. The second channel used a multiple stage RC (resistance-capacitance) filter network equalizer circuit for its Gibson voicing. This type of tone shaper had a varying effect on different frequencies as the tone changed. The five sections of the filter acted as a low-pass filter, passing the low frequencies and attenuating the high frequencies, creating a bass boosting effect.

The power supply had a choke, and all B-plus current, including the output tube current, flow through this three-Henry choke. This type of pie-section rectifier filter is considered a smoothing filter because it's better filtering the DC current, giving cleaner amplification with less hum and distortion. The output 6V6 stage is much like a Fender Deluxe amp with the 12AX7 phase inverter. This type of Williamson circuit was basically designed for the best hi-fi systems of the day.

Gibson and Les Paul basically tried to introduce an amplifier that was matched in price to the original gold model guitar. It was well received as a guitar outfit, and was also popular with harmonica players in later years. The GA-40 Les Paul model amp listed for $169.50, and was $178 in zone 2, west of the Rockies.

GA-40 – Version II

The 1956 Gibson catalog stated: "GA40 'Les Paul.' An extremely versatile general purpose Amplifier with remote controlled, built-in tremolo."

The next Les Paul amp was upgraded in a few important areas. A considerably larger cabinet measured 22" wide by 20" tall, and 9"–10 1/2" deep. Construction was 3/4" redwood with lock-jointed corners. The new cabinet had a similarly attractive, two-tone covering consisting of a maroon-brown "buffalo-grained" fabric and rough-textured top section (separated by a thin gold piping), with a contrasting two-tone (light pink and maroon) smoother fabric that visually resembled a woven-rug material. Gibson simply referred to this scheme as two-tone "buffalo-grain" fabric. It actually resembled a pinkish oatmeal with the dark top portion being a very heavily grained material like rough animal skin.

An "acoustically transparent" Saran grill, made of woven brown, maroon, and yellow nylon strands, was used on Gibson amps of this period. It was similar, but slightly different, to Fender's mid- and late-'50s grill. A single P-12 Q blue Alnico V Jensen was the upgraded speaker capable of handling a little more wattage than the previous P-grade speaker. Some were equipped with a GA-30 twin speaker setup (same cabinet design), adding the 8" Jensen. Nominal output stated in the catalog was 14 watts, but it sounded more like 18 watts. Tonally, these amps had a fat, yet crispy, tone. And with its classic Gibson tube sag, it very well could have been the beginning of that elusive "brown sound." They are fairly reminiscent of the early Fender tweed Deluxe 5A3-5B3 amplifiers. Its weight was quite light for its size— only 34 pounds due to its light transformers and redwood construction. This is arguably the most attractive incarnation of Les Paul amp, cosmetically speaking, and it also has a beautiful tonality. Cost was $203.50 in 1955 (zone 2) and $199.50 in 1957 (zone 1), with an additional $7.50 for the light brown "Artistic" cover provided by Artistic Products Company of New York City.

The majestic GA-40 in two-tone "buffalo-grain" fabric from 1955, with the elusive "brown sound" that was produced from its P-12 Q speaker.

Top view close-up of the chassis inputs and famed Les Paul logo.

THE POPULAR LES PAUL AMPLIFIER WITH BUILT-IN VARIABLE TREMOLO

Professional in performance, size and appearance, this Les Paul endorsed amplifier, complete with built-in variable tremolo, provides a top quality "High Gain" instrument with a clear, brilliant treble response. Powerful 7 tube chassis; 14 to 16 watt output; top mounted control panel; 12" Jensen speaker with Alnico No. 5 magnets.

A wide range of effects is possible with the built-in tremolo regulated by separate intensity and frequency controls and on-off switch mounted in foot pedal. Two channels; channel one with two volume controls; combination bass-treble voicing control. Channel two with two instrument inputs; separate inputs for microphone or additional instruments; wood lock-joint construction covered in dark brown buffalo grain and contrasting mottled brown and grey; slanted front panel; extra large speaker baffle, colorful dark grille of woven saran; jeweled pilot light; protective three amp fuse; off-on switch. Size: 22" wide, 20" high, 10⅛" deep; weight 34 lbs. The amplifier case is of sturdy, compact solid ¾"

GA-40 Les Paul Model Amplifier. 40-C Cover for Above Amplifier.

1956 catalog depiction of the revised GA-40 amplifier, with its larger cabinet and updated styling.

Back removed to show the completely original hand-wired circuitry, Gibson RCA tubes, blue bell Jensen speaker, and foot switch. From my personal collection, thanks to David Petrie.

GA-40 – Version III

The third type of GA-40 (1957–59) was basically the same mid-'50s amplifier chassis and cabinet with a slight facelift. It was covered in two-tone material of dark brown sharkskin with contrasting lighter tweed or cream vinyl. The lower portion of the two-tone cabinet switched to an amber-yellow, woven tweed fabric and, most noticeably, a larger (4" taller) speaker baffle area differentiated it from its predecessor. It retained the textured brown top, gold piping, woven Saran grill, and "Les Paul" model logo plaque at the bottom. Some early versions used a cream-colored vinyl instead of the woven tweed covering, and came without the Les Paul Model plaque (#54812). Its chassis was soon changed from brown to the new chrome-style with black markings. The addition of a sturdy plastic and metal swivel handle, and a new shiny, metallic-gold raised Gibson logo completed the late-'50s Les Paul model amplifier. The catalog description states its output now at 16 watts. It listed for $199.50.

GA-40T – Version IV

The new GA-40T Les Paul amp "with built-in variable tremolo" was introduced in late 1959, and sported a major facelift. Once again, Gibson changed the whole range of their amplifiers to a new cosmetically pleasing look; this time, featuring the popular airplane-luggage linen look of their competitors on the West Coast—a tweed or "twill" covering, as they called it (named after a British weave). Gibson's woven material was similar, but had a much thicker plastic coating, making it more durable and very shiny. The diagonal pattern of yellow "wheatstraw" and brown stripes followed a pattern that angled up to the right. Gibson had used an attractive-looking tweed style called "Aeroplane" luggage linen on their amps and cases during the late 1930s and early '40s; and it seems this tweed-like material was popular for suitcases on through the '50s.

Its cabinetry consisted of $^{13}/_{16}$"-thick redwood lock-joint construction that still measured 22" wide by 20" tall, but was now uniformly 9 $^5/_8$" deep. Its new baffle board consisted of a 1" slanted back for sound dispersion, with the entire frontal area covered with the same maroon, brown, and yellow Saran grill; and with the oval brown "Les Paul" plaque at the bottom. A nifty metal and plastic handle with imbedded tweed material, as well as the Gibson logo, adorned this version of the GA-40 Les Paul model amplifier.

THE POPULAR LES PAUL AMPLIFIER
WITH BUILT-IN VARIABLE TREMOLO

GA-40

This Les Paul endorsed amplifier has built-in variable tremolo, and brilliant treble response. 16 watt output; top mounted, chrome-plated control panel; 12" Jensen Auditorium speaker.

Tremolo regulated by separate intensity and frequency controls, on or off switch mounted in foot pedal. Two channels; channel one with two inputs for microphone or additional instruments; channel two with two instrument inputs; separate volume controls; combination bass-treble voicing control. Colorful dark grille of woven Saran; jeweled pilot light; protective three amp fuse; on-off switch. 22" wide, 20" high, 10½" deep; weight 34 pounds.

GA-40—Les Paul Amplifier............. $199.50
No. 30-C—Cover 7.50

(Above) GA-40 type III amplifier description in the 1958 catalog. Power rating went up to a big 16 watts! The taller baffle area was increased with this half tweed-covered model. The early versions of this amp used the brown chassis while the brochure mentions a chrome-plated chassis transition model.

(Below) 1960 catalog description of the revamped GA-40T in "twill" covering.

GA-40T LES PAUL MODEL
With built-in variable tremolo

Endorsed by leading artists for its thrilling tremolo and brilliant treble. Outstanding in its price range for power and distortion-free sound reproduction, for flexibility and ease of handling.

Features: Handsome case with top-mounted control panel ......
...woven Saran grille cover...jeweled pilot light. Tremolo with separate intensity and frequency controls...on-off switch in foot pedal. 12-inch Jensen speaker...7 tubes. Two channels...separate volume controls for each...bass-treble voicing control...two inputs for each. Polarity switch eliminates interference. 16 watts output.

22" wide, 20" high, 10½" deep

GA-40T Les Paul
80-C Cover

If you ever built model cars as a kid, you'll remember the chromed plastic as used on the late fifties raised Gibson logos.

A clean Les Paul model GA-40T amplifier in "twill" with chromed chassis and solid Gibson handle. *Courtesy David Swartz*

The chromed chassis with a new polarity switch completed the Les Paul combo. Original tubes were made exclusively by RCA for Gibson, with both their logos, and with the same prior configuration—a 5Y3GT rectifier Gibson RCA, two 6V6GT power tubes, a black metal 6SQ7, a 12AX7A, and two 5879 preamp tubes. Controls were the same, consisting of a volume for each channel, a single "voicing" for bass and treble equalization, and depth and frequency adjusters for the tremolo circuit. All these Les Paul amps sounded very sweet, with only 16 watts of power delivered to the blue P12-Q Jensen Alnico V loudspeaker. They sounded much like the similar GA-45 Maestro amp, but with four 8" speakers. (However, some say that the GA-40s had more wattage than this—and some custom versions may exist, like the Johnny Rivers amp.) It is surprising that Gibson didn't make a more powerful version, with 40 or 60 watts and multiple speakers, like some of their other amps with two or four 6L6/5881 power tubes. List price in 1959 was $215, and $8.75 for the cover.

Les Paul Model GA-40 Amplifier Production

1952	1953	1954	1955	1956	1957	1958	1959	1960
329	1774	1158	929	957	650	501	615	623

GA-40T – Version V

By far, the most unusual of all Les Paul amplifiers is the early-1960s version. Gibson amps did a complete overhaul in late 1962, with front facing access control panels and brown embossed vinyl covering. They were smart-looking and practical, too. For small venues and home use, the old 18-watt amps were adequate. These rare amps finally featured 45 watts with dual 6L6 power and could easily keep up with a rock drummer.

Some of their combos emulated the new piggyback enclosures, with a specially tuned "tone chamber case design" that they said was "designed to smooth out resonances and project full, rich sound." The controls were on the top of the front panel for easy access when standing close to the amplifier. They still had the "Les Paul" writing on the front for a few years. Although this Les Paul amp is not in the normal amp catalog, the GA-40T continued into the mid '60s without the Les Paul name.

Les Paul Model GA-40T Amplifier Production

1961	1962	1963	1964	1965	1966
515	413	345	184	29	14

The extremely rare early sixties Les Paul GA-40T amplifier with front mounted chassis. Gibson. This very attractive amplifier had a thick brown vinyl covering, insert red pointer knobs, and a nifty regal crown emblazoned on the front. *Courtesy Gary Hernandez*

Les Paul Junior & TV Amplifiers GA-5/GA-7

A companion student amp was provided for both the Les Paul Junior and TV model outfits. These nifty little amps started off many young guitarists on the road to greatness. Later catalogs renamed the Junior amp as a "GA-5" model, which became the "Skylark" amp in different cosmetic guises. Gibson's production records called the short-lived TV version the "GA-7."

Both featured an even-bordered, or old-style, TV set-like front panel with rear-mounted, slanted chassis controls. Brown faceplates had a simple layout with two inputs, a volume, a fuse holder, an on/off switch, and a red jeweled pilot light (measuring 12 $9/16$" by 2 $7/8$"). The TV's Gibson logo was cleverly set inside the depiction of a television set! Junior amps measured 13 $1/2$" wide by 11 $1/4$" tall, with a 7" base and a 4 $1/2$" top, and a $3/4$" redwood construction and $7/16$" birch ply base. TV amps were 15 $5/8$" wide by 13" tall, and with almost the same lower depth and a 4" top.

The 1954 Les Paul Junior GA-5 amplifier.
Courtesy David Swartz

GA5 "LES PAUL JUNIOR" Presenting a low power, but well built Gibson Amplifier at an unusually low price, this model features two inputs with volume control and uses a regular transformer operated power supply—making it safe for even a young child to operate. THREE TUBES. Nominal output—4 watts. Special oval type 5" x 7" p.m. speaker. DIMENSIONS—13½" x 11½" x 7". Weight—12 lbs. Finished in light brown, grained fabric with gold coloured grille.

GA5 "Les Paul Junior"—60 cycle, also available for 25 cycles at extra cost.

1956 catalog description of the Junior amplifier.

The rare Les Paul TV amplifier with cool pink and grey simulated rug covering and tan "wheatstraw" Saran (sonically transparent) grill.

The winning Les Paul combination for students in 1956.

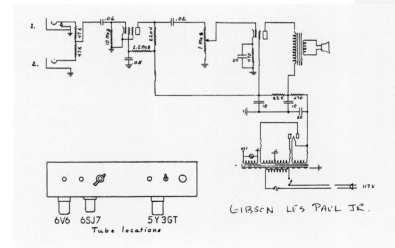

Simple schematic for the LP Junior amp.

Les Paul Junior Model GA-5 Amplifier Production			
1954	1955	1956	1957
1153	2947	2834	3481

Les Paul TV Model GA-7 Amplifier Production		
1954	1955	1956
1	244	224

The Junior was covered in "light brown, grained fabric," which actually appeared to be a light bone- (or cream-) colored linen with a simulated fine brown woven pattern. The TV version was covered in a creamy, almost oatmeal-type, grained material similar to the concurrent GA-40 pink and grey lower section. The Junior speaker grill was a loose-knit burlap material sprayed a brilliant gold color. Later models had a dark-brown flocked material or the brown and maroon Saran grill. Meanwhile, the TV model featured a tan-colored woven Saran grill with brown highlights. Both had the famous Gibson logo in brown lettering on the front. Juniors had a silver 5" by 7" oval Rola speaker with an outboard output transformer, while the upscaled TV had a larger 10" silver Rola with the attached transformer. The rear panel had a 9 3/4" by 5 7/8" opening for cords and tube cooling.

Its tubes consisted of a 5Y3GT, a 6V6GT, and a 6SJ7 putting out a big 4 1/2" watts of pure Gibson Les Paul power! This simple, low-powered class A amplifier (virtually a small Fender 5C1 Champ practice amp) weighed only 12 pounds. Catalogs stated that it "...uses a regular transformer-operated power supply—making it safe for even a young child to operate." Besides the normal 60-cycle model, Gibson amps were also available in 25-cycle overseas versions at an extra cost.

Rear view of the amp and '56 Jr. headstock hiding its oval speaker and outboard output transformer. *Amp courtesy Steve Rodriquez, now in Les Paul's collection.*

The Junior/GA-5 amp debuted in 1954 and sold in the thousands for a few years. It eventually became the Skylark amp during the late 1950s, and is still the most popular student amplifier by Gibson. Les Paul TV amp production began in late 1954, along with the 3/4-sized TV guitar. Only one amp was shipped that year. In its three-year run ending in 1956, 469 were shipped. It was a novel idea to release this student amplifier with a 10" speaker and TV moniker to go with its matching guitar. Naturally, these are quite rare and a must for the avid TV model collectors! Hmm... I wonder why they didn't build an LP Special Amplifier with two 10", or a 40-watt LP Custom amp with four 10" speakers?

Rear view of the TV motif and 10" Rola speaker. Personal collection.

6

The Les Paul Custom Models '54–'61

The Les Paul
Custom Models '54–'61

Les Paul and Gibson both felt the need to give the amateur, as well as the professional, guitarist a wider range of fine quality instruments to choose from. Just as Schwinn bicycles and Chrysler automobiles offer wide arrays of product diversity, Gibson was also known for their great variety. In the high-end range, a more lavish model with fancy binding and gold appointments was introduced—the Les Paul Custom. After prototypes were developed from late 1953 into the spring of 1954, they took it to the summer trade show, and production models began shortly thereafter.

First of all, this new top-of-the-line solid-body Gibson introduced the groundbreaking Tune-O-Matic adjustable bridge. Other features included a powerful new Alnico V pickup, and a special L-5-style customized ebony fingerboard. The model was officially nicknamed "the Fretless Wonder" because of its extremely low, smooth frets and easy playing action. At the time, these small frets were considered advantageous for the jazz players of the '50s. With extra low action, players' hands could virtually fly across the fretboard.

The Custom model was constructed out of a one-piece, solid Honduras mahogany body with a carved top, and finished in an "ebony" black lacquer. Contrasting white pearl inlays and bright 24-carat gold-plated metal fittings gave it a lavish and refined look. Although this costly solid-body instrument had all the fancy ornamentation, for various reasons, the featured Les Paul model's sustaining maple laminated top was absent. Ted McCarty had this to say:

> **RL:** *Eventually, you did the Les Paul Custom in black, but without a maple top. Why?*
>
> **TM:** *(Laughs.) 'Cause it was cheaper and it was good enough—it sounded good! It was more expensive than the regular Les Paul.*

Cost may have been one consideration, but achieving a different tone was more likely the reason. Gibson was aware that not everybody felt the need for a brighter tonality, so they left that for the standard model. The Custom, however, was geared towards a richer sound for the sophisticated players on the day's bandstands. Solid mahogany construction naturally created a deeper resonance and made for a very tone-full Les Paul Gibson. They also felt that their newly introduced electronics created versatile tonal qualities, regardless of the expensive maple cap construction. The Customs were considered to be somewhat of a jazz guitar from their inception. The slightly dampened tone (i.e., diminished brightness) of the one-piece mahogany body was enhanced by the clear-sounding ebony fingerboard. In comparison to the inherent maple sustain and brightness, it was better suited for the darker tone preferred by many jazz artists.

In those days, many popular jazz guitarists preferred the laminated ES-350 and ES-175 maple models, and avoided the brighter sound of the spruce-top models. This included Barney Kessel, Tal Farlow, Howard Roberts, Jim Hall, and Tommy Tedesco, to name just a few. Some of these top players adopted the new Custom Les Paul for recording dates and performances. In later years, Les, however, felt that the maple top should have also been used on the more expensive Custom models.

1955 Gibson catalog description of the "Fretless Wonder" Les Paul Custom.

"THE FRETLESS WONDER"—
THE INCOMPARABLE LES PAUL
CUSTOM GUITAR

Here is the ultimate in a solid body Gibson Electric Spanish Guitar . . . players rave about its extremely low smooth frets and playing action, call it the "Fretless Wonder." Features clear, resonant and sparkling tone, with widest range of tone colorings.

Solid Honduras Mahogany body with carved top, size 17 ¼" long, 12 ¾" wide, 1 ¾" thick with graceful cutaway design; bound with alternating white and black strips on top and bottom of body. Mahogany neck, with exclusive Gibson Truss Rod neck construction; ebony fingerboard; deluxe pearl inlays.

Two powerful magnetic type pickups specially designed and engineered for this model; individually adjustable gold colored magnets, gold plated polepieces. Double combination Bridge and Tailpiece is another Gibson First . . . adjustable both horizontally and vertically, plus the Gibson gold-plated Tune-O-Matic bridge, adjustable up and down, and individually for each string length. This combination provides a new high in sustaining tone quality and precision pitch adjustment.

Three way toggle switch selects either front or back pickup, or both simultaneously; each pickup has separate tone and volume controls; finest individual gold-plated Kluson machine heads; gold plated metal end pin and strap holder. Finished in solid Ebony color for rich contrast with gold plated fittings. Padded leather strap included.

Les Paul Custom Guitar
Case: 537 Faultless

An early Les Paul Custom, circa 1954... believed by owner Larry Henrickson to possibly be a 1953 model due to its early arching and potentiometer dates.
Courtesy Larry Henrickson of Axe-in-Hand, Dana Point, 1993

143

This is from the first of the big size catalogs for 1956 and 1957. It mentions that the Les Paul Custom "Fretless Wonder" has unique frets for "the lightest action ever developed on any guitar." It's debatable as to whether they were that popular during its heyday. Some players did take advantage of the extremely low action and precision fret milling. Trying to bend notes was another story altogether! Most jazz guitarists weren't pushing up a whole note, so it wasn't an issue.

LES PAUL MODELS

LES PAUL and MARY FORD

LES PAUL "CUSTOM"—This is a further development, by Gibson technicians, from Les Paul's original design, and it approaches the ultimate in solid bodied Guitars. Using extremely low frets and elaborate care in alignment it has been possible to provide the lightest action ever developed on any Guitar. As a result, the Les Paul "Custom" model is incredibly fast—it must be tried to be believed. The ingenious Gibson "Tune-o-matic" bridge removes intonation difficulties completely, making it possible, easily, to bring all six strings in tune throughout their playing length no matter what gauge strings are used. Fingerboard has 22 frets—16 clear of the body—scale length 24¾". The solid, carved-top body is dramatically beautiful in gleaming black lacquer, with contrasting ivoroid binding and pearl inlays. Body dimensions— 13" wide by 17¼" long and 2" deep. All metal fittings, from the Kluson "Sealfast" machine heads, to the heavy bridge are in gold plate. Fitted with two special pickups—each with its own volume and tone controls—and a toggle selector switch.

Les Paul Custom Guitar

#537 Faultless case, plush lined

A good day in the factory, with Les Paul admiring a new Custom model while Ted McCarty looks it over. Meanwhile, superintendent John Huis is checking inventory and a happy setup man beams with joy over working on the greatest guitars. Note the rack of limed Specials and/or TVs getting ready for shipment. *Photo courtesy Les Paul*

A 1955 Les Paul Custom with the original 537 black and gold plush case. This clean instrument has the high six-digit yellow serial number. The regal and attractive headstocks on these models have always been their forte.

The Tune-O-Matic Bridge

The Les Paul Custom featured the revolutionary new "Tune-O-Matic" bridge. Intonation discrepancies soon became quite apparent with the solid-body's more distinctively clear tone compared to the acoustic electric. Gibson's compensated wooden bridge and the new stop/stud bridge were adequate for most guitars with the heavier gauge strings of the day. More precise tuning was deemed necessary for this particular upscale instrument. It soon proved to be a valuable (necessary) invention for guitarists and still quite popular today.

The Tune-O-Matic bridge was originally designed by Ted McCarty with his engineers under strict guidance. They had evidently been working on it just as the first Les Paul guitar was finalized. "I designed that," states Ted, "and I have the patent on that, too."

Ted's patent was filed in July of 1952, and was eventually granted in April of 1956. This new adjustable bridge eventually graced all higher-grade Gibson electrics over the next decade, and was a popular aftermarket item. "The ingenious Gibson 'Tune-O-Matic' bridge removes intonation difficulties completely, making it possible, easily, to bring all six strings in tune throughout their playing length no matter what gauge strings are used," stated the 1956 catalog.

This new bridge utilized individual, adjustable metal string saddles for the precise intonation of each string. They were beveled to allow maximum travel, and tapped for the six lateral screws to allow easy adjustment without releasing the tension of the strings. To follow the fingerboard radius, compensated height for the individual bridge pieces was cast into the bridge base. Like prior bridges, it was also adjustable for overall height by two thumb wheel nuts. The Gold version of the Tune-O-Matic was designated as the ABR-2 bridge in the parts catalog. Later nickel versions, as used on the Goldtop, are known as the ABR-1. They were cast of brass, machined, and tapped. Both bridges, however, were cast ABR-1 underneath.

While holding the Tune-O-Matic in its original orange Gibson box, Ted recalls, "Now, this base was designed so that it would fit on an archtop guitar. They put the instruction sheet (how to install it), package it... this was the screwdriver which made it possible for you to adjust them. It was the first adjustable bridge that you could adjust under tension. So many of them, you had to loosen the string and then adjust the bridge, and hope that you have it. But with this one you could actually adjust it under tension."

INSTRUCTIONS
TUNE-O-MATIC BRIDGE*

What it does:

Makes it possible to tune your guitar to perfect accuracy on each individual string, at the bridge.

Permits precise adjustment for intonation, regardless of string gauge.

Saddles can be reversed individually, for full range of tuning.

Easily raised or lowered to suit individual preference for solid or feather touch action.

Makes possible longer sustained tones, and increases the playing life of each string.

Allows precise adjustment of each string even under full tension.

Reduces distortion caused by imperfect intonation.

Adds to the beauty and appearance of your guitar.

How to install:

1. Remove old bridge and place Tune-O-Matic bridge in same relative position on guitar.
2. Be sure to have the individual saddle adjusting screw heads towards the fingerboard.
3. Tighten the individual strings to approximately correct pitch.
4. Adjust action height with the thumb nuts in the usual manner. The action height may vary with instruments and players.
5. Now tune the guitar to perfect pitch.
6. For fine tuning, pluck the harmonic at the 12th fret, and then depress the same string to produce the true octave. If the harmonic is sharp, turn the screw for that string counterclockwise until the octaves match. If the harmonic is flat, turn the screw clockwise.
7. Repeat No. 6 for each of the other strings.
8. If you prefer you may notch the saddle top very lightly with the edge of a file.
9. If necessary to remove or change saddles, snap out by pushing on the screw head with your thumb.

Your Tune-O-Matic bridge is precision made of finest materials and with reasonable care should give you a lifetime of trouble-free service.

Product of

GIBSON, INC.
Kalamazoo, Michigan

*Patent Pending

Ted McCarty's Tune-O-Matic bridge instruction sheet. Its practical design merits have been enjoyed for many decades and is still a standard of the industry.

● **Gibson Tune-O-Matic bridge** makes it possible to tune your guitar to perfect accuracy on each individual string, at the bridge. It permits precise adjustment for intonation and each saddle can be reversed individually, for full range tuning. Easily adjusted for fast, low action.

Catalog depiction of the Tune-O-Matic bridge.

To complete the assembly, the new bridge was used in conjunction with the stop/stud tailpiece—this being generally placed 1 9/16" behind the center of Tune-O-Matic bridge to anchor the strings. Today, many people are unaware that, originally, these items were depicted in the catalogs and shipped normally with the strings over the top of the tailpiece (the way it was designed). This original stringing method is naturally comfortable to rest your hand on at the bridge area. With the studs screwed in deeply for full vibratory string-to-body contact, the guitar's overall sound is enhanced as it was intended. It also helps to prevent the strings from breaking as easily on the sharp metal edges. Furthermore, instead of the tension just pulling on the stud screws laterally, when wrapped around the stop bar, it torques the tension in the body differently (as inherent with the Goldtop's big tone). The original method results in more body resonance and better acoustic tone. Some players improvise with the strings from the back, using a series of ring washers and tightening the studs to get better contact and body tone.

Gibson sold the Tune-O-Matic bridge as an aftermarket item that many guitarists put on various brands. Shown here are the standard nickel and gold ABR-1 models. Instructions and a yellow-handled screwdriver were also in the box.

Trim & Appointments

The top and bottom edges of the body have multiple bindings, consisting of alternating white and black celluloid strips. Fancy binding naturally adds a refined elegance to the instrument, yet leaves a fairly sharp edge on both sides. Twenty-two small frets, filed low, with a 24 $^9/_{16}$" (24 $^3/_4$" in the catalog) scale was the requisite for the "Fretless Wonder." Its mahogany neck featured a bound ebony fingerboard with large square mother-of-pearl block position markers. Some came with slightly V-shaped necks through the years. Custom headstocks had similar multiple bindings and a Super 400-style, pearl-inlaid, split-diamond design below the pearl Gibson name. The "rolled," black-and-white laminated PVC plastic truss-rod bell caps (showing fine little ridges) read "Les Paul" in script, and "CUSTOM" was engraved into the white. Headstocks measure nearly $^1/_2$" wider than the original Goldtop models, adding a little more mass at the other end of the instrument. Gold-plated Kluson GS-503-V Super "sealfast," ridged machine heads with Keystone "Tulip" plastic grip buttons were utilized on this model into 1958. Custom pickguards were of laminated (four-ply) black plastic with the black border shown in the beveled edge.

From 1954 into 1955 and 1956, serial numbers were left off the back of the fancy Custom headstocks—Gibson didn't want to mar the beauty or the simplicity of the instrument. Ted McCarty remembers, "For many years, they had no serial numbers... we didn't put serial numbers on them if we could help it. The factory used to fight putting serial numbers on them because you destroyed the appearance of the thing." During 1955, they capitulated, however, and began using a yellow or white ink to imprint numbers for identification purposes. Only a few known early Customs have small imprinted numbers on the top edge of the headstock.

The Finish

Many naturally called this model the "Black Beauty" because of its striking elegance and dark color. The traditional Gibson ebony black satin finish actually dates back to Orville's handmade instruments, and was a standard color for a few decades. At Les's request, they painted it a stylish "tuxedo" black for stage contrast. Like the Goldtop's finish, it was unusual at the time for an electric guitar. "Gold and black—nobody I know was using it," says Les.

After sealing and filling the porous mahogany grain properly, six coats of black lacquer were applied over the entire body and neck. Then the binding was carefully scraped, followed by a few clear coats with a fine sanding in between. A final buffing and some polish created the lustrous ebony nitrocellulose (a chemical compound produced by the reaction of nitric and sulfuric acids on cellulose) finish. With this elegant black-piano-type finish, it was virtually the Steinway of the Gibson range. Sometimes a Custom would have a slight green or grayish hue to the black. This was due to the effect of humidity when painted during certain times of the year.

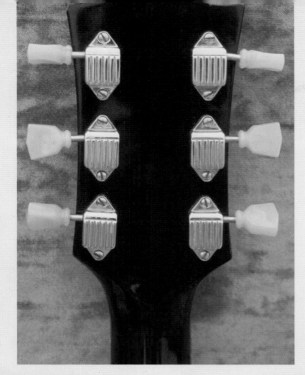

A beautiful 1955 Les Paul Custom with original-style stringing over the tailpiece. Note the lack of a serial number and attractive Kluson "sealfast" enclosed machine heads. *Courtesy Steve Soest, 1973*

Once the new models arrived, Les and Mary adopted the Customs as their mainstay instruments, and left the gold guitars at home. Gibson shipped a number of them to New Jersey over the years. Like the earlier Goldtops, eventually, they were modified in one way or another—some of were even flattop versions for ease of electronic applications. (Gibson also sent out a few special-ordered white-finished ones in 1958.)

"We carried two white ones and two black ones," states Les. "Not very often did we use gold ones… the white and black ones we always used on the stage. The reason for the white and black guitars was because of whether I was wearing a white formal tux or a black one. If I was wearing a black tuxedo, I played my white guitar; and when I wore my white jacket, sport jacket, or whatever (in the summertime), then I would use the black guitar. When we're at the Paramount, your hands are white and they show up real good against that black. And even though the white guitar used a black pickguard, they could see the hands move faster."

(Above) A 1957 Alnico V-equipped Les Paul Custom used for one of my first recording dates at Wally Heider's Hollywood studio. The stair-stepped Grovers were added. *Courtesy Gary White, May 1973*

(Left) This "White Beauty" possibly came with triple P-90 pick-ups. It has been played here in the states some, and eventually made its way over to Europe. *Courtesy Erhart Bochen, 1985*

(Above) A snappy pose of Les and Mary performing with their Les Paul Custom "Black Beauty" guitars.

(Right) This is one of Les Paul's original Customs that was developed (regularly customized) into a "Recording" model by Les and Wally Kamin. I had the pleasure of playing it for months while staying with Les in 1975. It has an early version of his novel microphone input and extra volume on the top by the toggle switch. Wally's specially hand-wound, low-impedance stacked pickups sound simply amazing through the LP-12 low-Z amplifier! It has the individual controls with phase and bypass switches (plus decade control) and a fancy gold Bigsby vibrola. The case is actually from his original Goldtop with the 1952 *Queen Elizabeth* steamship sticker attached. Quite the vintage recording machine!!

151

Electronics

The new Custom models used the newly standardized 1951 Gibson layout with dual volume and tone controls. A gold Switchcraft, three-way pickup selector switch—BDB (bright dip brass) #12011—and a black tip T12742 with a plastic rhythm/treble surround was on the upper bout. Both the switch and ¼" input jack used gold-plated nuts. Four CentraLab 500K potentiometers were complemented with two .022 mfd Cornell Dubilier or interim Mallory Plascap capacitors for the volume and treble roll-off circuitry. During 1956, Gibson models began using the Sprague "Bumble Bee" .022 400 volt caps.

During the first few years, black see-through "speed" knobs were featured, until the switch to the black "bell-" or "hatbox"-style knobs were incorporated in 1955. Over the years, some Customs were special-ordered with other interesting electronic layouts. Both Johnny Gray and Mickey Baker had some of theirs built with triple pickups and three volumes with a master tone control on top.

Les can sing, too, but only Mary's voice is heard on their recordings

(Above) Les is having a ball singing and playing along with Mary in this great 1955 *Hi-Fi* magazine photo in the control room. The rack behind them holds four Goldtops with various unusual and mysterious modifications.

(Right, top) Great Gibson advertisement pushing the merits of Les's hi-fi recordings for the selling of the two styles of instruments.

(Right, bottom) Another wonderful Gibson plug for their guitars with the radio and television theme. Note the gold records, Black Beauties, and vintage microphones.

(Above) A rare Bigsby-equipped LP Custom (with compensated Bigsby bridge) shown at the Dallas Guitar Show.

(Right) Late 1956 Custom #612376 control cavity with interim Mallory Plascap capacitors.

Alnico V Pickups

The 1950s were a very fertile period of pickup development within the various guitar companies; hence, an entirely different rhythm pickup was newly introduced on the Les Paul Custom. One recent innovation at Gibson brought about a new pickup design... the Alnico V.

The Alnico V featured six powerful rectangular magnets that produced a big, rich tone. It was originally designed by Gibson's electronics engineer Seth Lover in 1952, and used exclusively on their upper-end electric models (Super 400, L-5, and Byrdland) during the mid '50s. Seth was temporarily in the Service when Ted McCarty asked him to evaluate a popular new DeArmond pickup; he therefore had him come up with something new and competitive for Gibson.

Of course, Walt Fuller's trusty P-90 from the early 1940s was already an excellent pickup, which utilized Alnico III- and IV-strength magnets. Gibson had recently improved it by switching from slug poles to adjustable Fillister head-screw polepieces with two magnets in 1949. It was time to try something new and install the Alnico V on the upcoming flagship Les Paul Custom.

The Alnico V rhythm pickup had the same 10,000 winds of 42-gauge copper wire, but a higher output with the magnetic Alnico V poles to sense the strings' vibrations. Seth also wanted to be different by using a unique chamfered rectangular magnet. They were striving to give the guitarist a richer bass response with this new unit. Many love its warm, beautiful tonality. It was similar in design to the day's Gretsch "Dynasonic" pickup by the Harry DeArmond company. Les was already using a Dynasonic on his early Goldtop! Both pickups had a hidden structure inside with springs around the adjustment screws to raise

and lower the Alnico magnets. Gibson's ad stated that the new pickup would "Give greater sustaining power."

The following is from my interview with Seth Lover:

> **RL:** *What other pickups did you design that came out in production on the Gibson guitars?*
>
> **SL:** *There was one that had some rectangular magnets; the magnets were adjustable up and down.*
>
> **RL:** *Those were on the Les Paul Custom models, L-5s and Super 400s.*
>
> **SL:** *It could have been on some of the custom models. This is where the magnet actually moved up and down. That one you had to be very careful with because the magnets were so strong that if you tried to get them too close to the strings, you would get dog tones, wolf tones, on the tone on that string.*

Gibson's Alnico Vs were fine-sounding pickups, but you had to be extra careful about the proximity to the strings. The 1¹⁄₈"-long magnets were so strong they could actually hamper the larger wound string's oscillating vibration. The harmonics would get jumbled up (slurred) with bad overtones and not ring true. Therefore, these large polepieces were always adjusted low enough so as not to get so-called "wolf tones." When adjusted properly, they still had a good output volume, yet it was a careful balance.

"Then we came out with a rectangular magnet, which was very, very strong," remembers Les. "The question that came up was to whether it was so strong it actually stopped the string from vibrating if you get it too close. Very, very, potent, strong magnets."

1956 Les Paul Custom with fine weather checking and a high serial number of #612376. Note the "staple" polepieces and nearby adjustment screws on the Alnico V rhythm pickup. *Courtesy Fort Worth Guitar Shows*

The following is from my interview with Walt Fuller:

> *RL: The pickup that utilizes the individual poles with adjustable screws on the early L-5 CES was on the early Les Paul Custom. Seth told me he developed that pickup. And because the magnets were so powerful, it would produce "wolf tones," so to speak. Is there a technical name for that?*
>
> *WF: Well, most musical terms are, let's say, manufactured names. What was actually happening was, the magnets were so strong that it made a nodal point at that part of the string, and so, of course, the string was vibrating back and forth while it wanted to actually stop at that particular point. It hampered the vibration of the string—especially if they were adjusted up close.*
>
> *RL: Right. I was doing a recording session at Wally Heider's and borrowed one of those Custom Les Paul guitars. It just didn't quite sound the way I wanted it to. So I lowered the poles down and it sounded a lot better.*
>
> *WF: It was very expensive to produce. If you ever took one of them apart you'll find the long pole and a spring that moves around with a fine magnet. You will notice they are all ground and beveled around on the top.*

Many call these pickups "Alnico" or "staple" pickups because of the magnets used and their shape. They had small adjustment screws in between the poles that floated the large poles. Each connecting portion (between the screw base and pole) was individually grounded. Alnico coil flats were most often made of a laminated black/white/flat plastic, while the bridge pickup was solid black. They were attached firmly to the body like the early Goldtop lead pickup with two corner screws. Routing was slightly deeper in the neck position to accommodate the long polepieces. A clear plastic insert shim was sometimes used between the pickup and cover. Some early covers didn't have the openings for the screw adjustments. The back pickup, however, was the same as the original cream P-90 480 model pickups on the Les Paul model, but with gold Fillister polepiece screws. The black cover had the underside stamp "UC-452-B" with a "2" on the other side of the holes.

Les had numerous innovative ideas for developing his own guitar pickups around this time. He noticed that modern studio microphones had far more natural fidelity and less hum. In his quest for tonal excellence, his involvement with customized, low-impedance guitar electronics was right around the corner. Les elaborates: "I'm on the road. Mary and I are performing, so all I know is the guitars are selling like mad, and they're good guitars. Now, you realize that with every one of those guitars, immediately I pulled out my electronics and I used that guitar, but with my electronics, which are low impedance."

Les's early Custom was soon modified with an extended pickguard to hide mysterious pickups. Like his modified gold guitars, Les always used a master volume and tone with pointer knobs. The two tone-control holes were often utilized for an extra switch and a front output jack (thus keeping the cord from being pulled out easily). Les Paul's tone noticeably changed on his recordings during the later 1950s.

The Alnico V pickup exposed to see the grounded polepiece elevator mechanisms. This somewhat corroded "staple" magnet pickup was photographed courtesy of Seymour Duncan.

Sales

The Les Paul Custom model was introduced in July of 1954 at the Chicago NAMM music trade show. It was well received, and numerous orders were taken. Ninety-four were shipped that first year, and things picked up, with 355 the following year. 1956 saw 489 logged out, while 283 were shipped in 1957, with about half of those featuring the original pickup design. (Incidentally, the Custom was originally going to be called the "Deluxe" model, which eventually was used on a later model; but that idea was abandoned when production began.) The list price was originally $325 in 1954, and soon went up to $375 in 1955, where it stayed into 1957 (in zone 2, west of the Rockies). Gold-plated Bigsby True Vibrato units were also available with a compensated Bigsby bridge or special rocking Tune-O-Matic bridge saddle for $90. A hard-shell, "textured buffalo skin," black-covered Geib 537 "Faultless" with golden-yellow plush lining was the standard case. Many were shipped with white wrapping paper along with the tags and instructions in the case.

July of 1957 Zone 2 price list for the Les Paul series showing the Custom at $375 (its price from 1955 to 1958) and Goldtop model at $247.50.

ELECTRIC SPANISH GUITARS (Cutaway) SOLID BODY

Les Paul Custom 537	Guitar, Solid Body Cutaway, Black Finish, with two built-in pickups and toggle switch	$375.00
	Faultless Case (Gold Plush) for above	49.75
Les Paul Model 535	Guitar, Solid Body, Cutaway, Gold Finish Top, with two built-in pickups and toggle switch	250.00
	Faultless Case (Plush) for above	44.00
Les Paul Special 535	Guitar, Solid Body Cutaway, with two built-in pickups and toggle switch	182.50
115	Faultless Case (Plush) for above	44.00
	Challenge Case for above	14.50
Les Paul TV 115	Guitar, Solid Body Cutaway, Natural Finish with built-in pick-up	131.50
	Challenge Case for above	14.50
Les Paul - Jr. 115	Guitar, Solid Body Cutaway, with built-in pickup	119.00
	Challenge Case for above	14.50

Jenkins Music Co. window display featuring Gibson products. This fine display, which was arranged by Mr. Frank Burgard, Display Manager, drew a lot of attention in Kansas City and proved profitable in its promotion of Gibson products.

Jenkins Music in Kansas City pulls out all the stops with an almost full-line Gibson promotion window display. Note the blow-up ads and vintage Gibson banners. All the Les Paul guitars except the TV model are shown.

JOHNNY GRAY

BOBBY GIBBONS (WITH TENNESSEE ERNIE FORD)

BILLY STRANGE

MICKEY BAKER

Popular Artists

Some of the many Gibson artists to use and endorse the Les Paul Custom models during the 1950s were Mickey Baker and Johnny Gray (who ordered special triple-pickup versions with unique controls), Francis Beecher (with Bill Haley and His Comets), Bob Gibbons, and Billy Strange. Jim Hall (with Chico Hamilton) used his Les Paul Custom for many years before he sold it to Howard Roberts. Rock 'n' roll innovator Chuck Berry played an early Les Paul Custom on many of his hit recordings. Jimi Hendrix also performed with a Custom Les Paul occasionally.

(Above) Popular session guitarist Mickey Baker did some great instruction books back in the day. He was known for playing a few different Les Paul Customs, including one with three single-coil pickups.

(Below) Teaming up with the beautiful and talented Silvia Robinson, this couple had some well-loved tunes in the late fifties and early sixties. Mickey Baker's memorable guitar lines in their 1956 hit "Love is Strange" still rings in many of our minds.

Gibson artists who played Les Paul Custom models were (top to bottom) Johnny Gray (with his specially wired triple-pickup Custom), Bobby Gibbons, Billy Strange, and Mickey Baker.

Gibson GAZETTE

Editor   JULY, 1957   Dick Mueller, Copy Editor

HALEY'S COMETS TOPS IN ROCK N' ROLL

In the crazy, mixed-up world of music, nothing is really new any more. But certainly the dynamic rise of the rock 'n roll trend, and more specifically, the tremendous success of Bill Haley and his Comets is a wonder to behold. Few orchestras or musical combinations have aroused as much interest—and controversy—as has the fabulous Bill Haley.

Not only in the U. S. has the Haley brand of rock been a success, but in all the appearances he has made throughout the world—and these are many —the reaction has been as great. Apparently even those who come to mock stay to behold the sight of the one-time local guitarist who built a musical style into a million-dollar business.

Gibson, too, is in on this great musical phenomenon. Bill Haley and his Comets are exclusive Gibsonites.

It all started in a suburb of Detroit, Michigan, where Bill Haley was born in 1927. The first seven years of Bill's life were spent in Detroit, and then his family moved to Booth Corner, Pennsylvania. His parents were consider- ably musical and Bill himself began his musical way on a pasteboard guitar —strumming and singing. At an auction mart not far from his home, Haley began working professionally and began, too, to build up a combo. His first tour was through New England with a group called the "Down Homers." After this tour he and two others decided to strike out on their own. From there on the Comets experienced a more or less steady rise, success following success both in playing engagements, and in numerous record hits.

(Continued on page 4)

Haley and his Gibson Super 400 CN as seen in recent movie, "Rock Around the Clock."

This 1957 Gazette features Bill Haley and His Comets, with Fran Beecher on the Les Paul Custom. Once "Rock Around the Clock" was released in the 1956 movie, their careers, and rock 'n' roll, took off.

Original Artist Fran Beecher

One of the most visible users of the Les Paul Custom guitar was Francis "Fran" Beecher of Bill Haley and His Comets. The 1954 song, "Rock Around the Clock" virtually became the first rock 'n' roll hit to overturn the music world. Although Fran joined the group shortly after the song was recorded (by guitarist Danny Cedrone, who passed away), he performed it for years with the popular group. Both Bill Haley and Fran endorsed Gibson during the 1950s. Bill had a cutaway Super 400 and a black L-7, while Fran played the Custom Les Paul model.

When growing up, Fran was first inspired to play guitar by the popular cowboy stars, and eventually, Charlie Christian caught his ear. He studied Charlie's playing so much that he wore his records out (and his parents' patience, too), learning every solo note for note. His first guitar was a $50 Gibson, and he soon saved up for a brand new L-5 back in 1939.

I caught up with Fran Beecher in Hollywood in 1997 and thoroughly enjoyed the original Comets' lively performance. Today, he plays a vintage 1958 blonde Byrdland Gibson, and sounds great as he tours with one of the most famous of all rock 'n' roll bands ever.

RL: When the Les Paul Custom guitar came out, what attracted you to the guitar?

FB: It's hard to say. I went through different models of different Gibsons. I guess it was because of the responsiveness. No feedback and so forth… and less bulk. Before, I was used to the thick bodies. They are a very responsive instrument. You can do a lot on there that you can't do on the type of instrument I'm playing (Byrdland). The fingerboard is not appropriate; you have to work too hard (laughs). The Fretless Wonder (frets) I didn't like.

RL: Why did you pick the Custom model?

FB: I don't know; but once I got it, I liked it. I kept it. That's a long way back. That's forty years… over forty years.

RL: Did you go to a store and buy it or did Gibson give it to you?

FB: One of the Gibsons, our manager, bought for me. That's how I got it. He called Gibson and made the deal.

Fran Beecher with the famous Comets performing in Hollywood. Known for playing an early Les Paul Custom during the fifties with Bill Haley, he still plays his 1958 natural Gibson Byrdland with the band, circa 1999.

Besides his Stratocaster guitar, Jimi Hendrix also played a few Gibsons, including this 1950s Les Paul Custom. His upside-down playing fashion didn't seem to hinder him much in this very emotive photo at Madison Square Garden. *Courtesy Elliot Landy*

The Les Paul Custom '57–'61

In November of 1957, the new "Les Paul Custom" guitar, featuring three gold Humbucking pickups, was introduced. A very bold statement was indeed made with all that contrasting gold metal. Like the ES-5, electronically, Gibson pulled out most of the stops on this version (some were even made with the big switch and six knobs). The modern facelift further enhanced its alluring mystique. You could call its new stature luxurious, affluent, chic, glamorous… or maybe even downright extravagant with so much gold. The Les Paul Custom now looked quite impressive and showy—right in the winner's circle!

A nice example of a 1958 Les Paul Custom "Black Beauty" in a Bavarian setting. *Courtesy Alfonse Baumann*

"The Fretless Wonder"
THE INCOMPARABLE
LES PAUL CUSTOM GUITAR

Here is the ultimate in a solid body Gibson Electric Spanish Guitar—players rave about its extremely low, smooth frets and easy playing action, call it the "Fretless Wonder." Now with three humbucking, adjustable pickups, this new and improved "Les Paul Custom" guitar has increased power, greater sustaining and a clear, resonant, sparkling tone, with the widest range of tonal colorings. Finished in solid ebony color for rich contrast with the gold-plated metal fittings.

Solid Honduras mahogany body, graceful cutaway design with carved top; bound with alternating white and black strips • mahogany neck with exclusive Gibson Adjustable Truss Rod • bound, ebony fingerboard with deluxe pearl inlays • Three powerful, humbucking magnetic pickups • individually adjustable gold-plated polepieces • separate tone and volume controls • three-way toggle switch provides a new method of tone mixing: top position selects top pickup for rhythm; center position activates the center and lower picks simultaneously for extreme highs and special effects; lower position operates lower pickup for playing lead. Tailpiece can be moved up or down to adjust string tension • Tune-O-Matic bridge permits adjusting string action and individual string lengths for perfect intonation • gold-plated Sealfast individual machine heads with deluxe buttons • gold-plated metal end pin and strap holder. Padded leather strap included.

SPECIFICATIONS
12¾" wide, 17½" long, 1¾" thick, 24¾" scale, 22 frets

Les Paul Custom—Ebony Finish..........................
No. 537 Case—Faultless, gold plush lined.................$375.00
No. ZC-CLP Zipper Case Cover........................... 47.50
21.50

The great "Wizard" cameo of Les Paul graces this 1958/1959 catalog page for the prestigious Les Paul Custom, now with three humbucking pickups.

With a little binding missing and some burn marks, you can tell this headstock has seen the hands of a working musician over the years.

Standard 1958 serial numbers with a "6" that looks almost like an "8." Note the typical crooked Grovers on the first and third tuners.

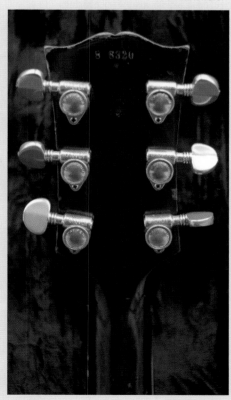

(Above) Here Eric Clapton is captured playing his 1958 Custom Les Paul. The hit single written by Jack Bruce and Pete Brown, "Sunshine of Your Love," was recorded with this guitar. You can hear the distinctively different tone achieved from this all-mahogany body in comparison to a maple-top Les Paul—even cranked through 100–watt Marshall stacks. *Photo from Getty Images*

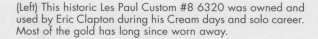

(Left) This historic Les Paul Custom #8 6320 was owned and used by Eric Clapton during his Cream days and solo career. Most of the gold has long since worn away.

The switching setup was quite unique. When switched to the middle pickup position, the volume dropped down slightly, producing a somewhat brighter, reverse magnetic induced tone; then the volume would increase slightly when the volume was reduced! A Gibson *Gazette* article states: "The addition of the third pickup gives a much wider range of tone coloring. Looking for extreme highs for special effects. This guitar has it with the 3-way toggle switch in center position. It is a new method of tone mixing." Mixing both middle and treble pickups together created a nifty, out-of-phase sound for the fifties. They simply reversed the bar's magnetic polarity for the center pickup to create a novel tone.

Many players asked repairmen to fix these guitars for them, not knowing why the middle position sounded so "honky"—much like Peter Green's out-of-phase Les Paul sound on old Fleetwood Mac tracks. Gibson Stereo ES-345 and 355 models purposely used this reverse

New "Les Paul Custom" Guitar

Here is the ultimate! The new and improved "Les Paul Custom" Guitar. Now with three humbucking adjustable pickups. Greater sustaining, sparkling, clean tone while reducing hum and extraneous noises from electrical disturbances. The addition of the third pickup gives a much wider range of tone coloring.

Looking for extreme highs for special effects? This guitar has it with the 3-way toggle switch in center position. It is a new method of tone mixing. The Les Paul Custom has always been the choice of players seeking the finest in solid body guitars. They rave about its low, smooth frets and playing action, call it the "Fretless Wonder." Other features are tune-o-matic bridge which permits adjusting height of string action and each individual string length for perfect intonation. Available with the famous Bigsby true vibrato unit if desired, at additional cost.

Price: $375.00
Case: 47.50

(Left) This November 1957 *Gazette* exclaims, "Here is the Ultimate!" with a description of the new pickups, special wiring, and optional Bigsby tailpiece.

(Above) Here's a rare 1957 Custom with three straight controls and a master volume in place of the toggle switch. *Courtesy Larry Henrickson, LA Vintage Guitar Show, circa 1980*

(Below) 1959 Les Paul Custom #9 1368 in a 535 brown and pink case. Buzz Jens had this gem back in the early seventies.

magnetic humbucking in their rhythm position. By reversing or flipping the magnet over edgewise, the adjustable coil was reoriented to south polarity, which put both the rhythm and center pickups back in magnetic phase. (Don't have this done if you want your guitar to be completely unaltered and original.)

As great as it looked, there was one drawback: Where do you pick? Most guitarists play in between the twin pickups. With three, the center pickup most often gets in the way. Some would adapt while others would simply lower it for adequate clearance (I've even seen a black plastic cover put over the emptied hole). A few astute customers ordered the new Custom model with only two humbucking pickups—as a young Johnny Winters did. Generally, the middle pickup's polepieces were oriented towards the rhythm position. Laminated pickguards were now cut straight across. Weight was slightly increased with the extra pickup.

Gold-plated Grover Roto-Matic tuning machines became standard trim during 1958, replacing the lighter Kluson Super machine heads. They were considered an improvement, making tuning a pleasure. Slightly heavier and more bulky, they gave the guitar a distinctively different feel and punch. They read "Pat. Pend. USA" and "Grover" on the back, had dual collar rings, and used the "kidney bean" grip buttons. Many appreciated the smooth feel and extended turning ratio. Similar Grover Imperial deco-styled tuners were popular on other brands, including Gretsch and D'Angelico guitars. In addition to the extra mass, the screw-down grommets, if too tight, could create compression on the mahogany peghead, also affecting the neck's resonance and feel on the strings.

The small "Fretless Wonder" frets were used during the entire production into 1961. In later years, most players preferred the larger, 1959-style frets, and jokingly called them "fretless blunder" frets. They were contemporary for players at the time, yet medium or large frets could be custom ordered. This rather low fret was curiously continued into the 1970s on the Custom model. Ted McCarty had the name trademarked (#626204) in 1956—which was good for only 14 years. Many Custom Les Pauls have been re-fretted with medium or larger frets for modern ease of bending.

This is one of three white Customs sent to Les Paul in 1958 for his low-impedance electronics. The bright white stood out on stage for their performances with dark outfits. Two of these were special flattop versions for ease of installation with the various gizmos. Mary often played the flat version without a vibrola. They used these on the *Bell Telephone Hour* broadcast. This arched one has an unbound fingerboard, Bigsby vibrato (without the Paulverizer attached), and the unfinished ground frets he prefers. Originally, they had the early, small-sized, low-Z pickups with black plastic covers when used during the fifties. *Courtesy Les Paul, 1972*

This is a nice example of a '59 Custom Les Paul that's been played but not abused. Most of the gold has naturally come off the pickups and stopbar. Note the original low, wide frets and fine weather checking. From the Dave Amato collection, 2003.

LES PAUL CUSTOM

Here is the ultimate in a solid body Gibson Electric Spanish Guitar—players rave about its extremely low, smooth frets and easy playing action, call it the "Fretless Wonder." Now with three humbucking, adjustable pickups and the adjustable tailpiece, this new and improved "Custom" guitar has increased power, greater sustain, and a clear, resonant, sparkling tone with the widest range of tonal colorings. Three-way toggle switch provides a new method of tone mixing: top position selects top pickup for rhythm; center position activates the center and lower pickups simultaneously for extreme highs and special effects; lower position operates lower pickup for playing lead. Finished in solid ebony color for rich contrast with the gold-plated metal parts. Deluxe, padded leather strap included.

- Slim, fast, low-action neck—with exclusive extra low frets, joins body at 16th fret
- One-piece mahogany neck, adjustable truss rod
- Ebony fingerboard, deluxe pearl inlays
- Solid Honduras Mahogany body with graceful cutaway design and carved top
- Adjustable Tune-O-Matic bridge
- Three powerful, humbucking pickups with unique wiring arrangement
- Separate tone and volume controls
- Three-way toggle switch specially wired

12¾" wide, 17¼" long, 1¾" thin . . . 24¾" scale, 22 frets

Les Paul Custom Ebony finish

Les Paul Custom with gold plated Bigsby
537 Faultless gold plush-lined case

ZC-CLP Deluxe zipper case cover

- Slim, fast, [extra low fr]
- One-piece [truss rod]
- Rosewood [
- Graceful cu[
- Adjustable [
- Twin power[with separa[controls wh[
- Three-posit[activate eit[

12¾" wide, 1[. . . 24¾" sc[

Les Paul Star[

535 Faultless [

ZC-LP Deluxe [

(Above) 1960 catalog depiction. This particular single-cutaway Custom model was made into early 1961. Nice artist's touch-up rendition from the original photograph.

(Left) A hybrid Switchmaster Les Paul Custom with ES-5 electronic switching. *Courtesy Alan Rogan, 2000*

This fancy headstock sure looks great in the pink-lined case.

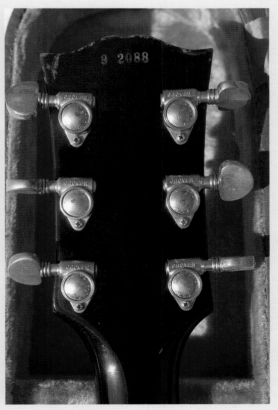

"Pat. Pending Grovers" and "#9 2088" in yellow numbers complete the package.

167

(Above) A fine-condition 1959 Custom Les Paul with unusual early-style Kluson "sealfast" tuning machines. *Courtesy Lloyd Chiate, 2004*

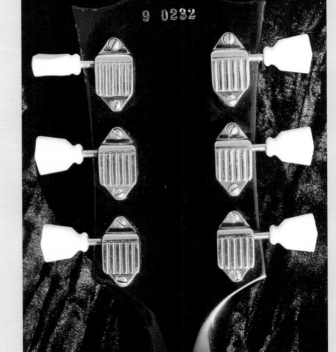

(Opposite) A rare and beautiful two-pickup 1959 Les Paul Custom special-ordered for easy playability. *Courtesy Rich Stillwell, 2004*

(Above and below) This particular guitar was originally built in 1954/55 and was returned to Gibson for twin Pat. # humbuckings, a short Bigsby vibrola, larger frets, and a new finish in the mid sixties. Note the very tidy conversion they did with added ledges for the pickup surrounds and clean routing technique. Les signed this guitar at the HOB-Hollywood in 1992. Thanks to later owner Andy Brauer, this guitar was also used by John Fogerty at the Rock 'n' Roll Hall of Fame show in 2000. *Courtesy Barry Dubin, 1993*

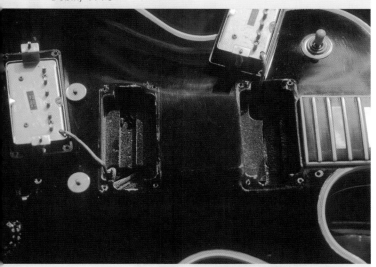

(Opposite) Another real head turner! Gibson's sparkling burgundy finish (generally for ES-345s) was applied to this 1959 Les Paul Custom in the mid sixties. Like the extra "Custom Built" plaque or pearl inserts over the stud holes to go with a Bigsby vibrola, this has a specially configured factory plastic piece to conceal the Bigsby holes! Chrome hardware and a newer ABR-1 bridge were also added. Previously owned by guitarist Ray Gomez. *Courtesy SRC guitarist Gary Quackenbush, 1978*

Custom Color Finishes

As with their usual custom-ordered option, various colored versions were ordered over the years. A few cherry-finished Les Paul Customs were built and sent to England in 1960. Phil Manzanera, the guitarist with Bryan Ferry's group Roxy Music, has owned one for many years. (This author set it up, along with Manzanera's other guitars, during Roxy Music's American Avalon tour). At the time, its finish was a fairly dark-cherry color. The unique instrument played and sounded very nice. Most Gibsons sent overseas and to England during this era have a very faint but distinct "MADE IN USA," in small letters, imprinted on the backs of the headstocks near the serial numbers. Incidentally, an all-gold, triple-pickup Les Paul Custom is known to exist with cream parts. With all that gold, you'd best put on your shades!

Another unique custom order took place in 1959 in Costa Mesa, California, when CMI rep John Levy ordered two maple-top, cherry sunburst Les Paul Customs for his customers. His father, Jack, had been a longtime CMI representative since the 1930s, handling National and Gibson. While at Coast Music in Newport Beach, he recalled that these particular Custom models had twin gold pickups, nicely figured flame maple tops, and were very beautiful when finally arriving at the store!

Pricing went up to $395 (zone 1) by February 1959. Many were shipped with gold Bigsby B7G vibrato tailpieces for an overall deluxe package.

Danny Gatton

Guitarist extraordinaire Danny Gatton was keenly interested in Gibson guitars when he started playing. As a child, his ears were already tuned in to Les Paul's guitar playing. Danny recalls getting his first Gibson guitars and the love affair he enjoyed with the Les Paul Custom model:

Les was the big influence on my guitar playing. I started listening to him when I was about three. He was the first guitar king that absolutely destroyed me. By the time I was 12, I was making multi-track tapes like Les Paul. I did my own echo and all that.

I got a Gibson ES-350 for my birthday in 1957. It cost $375, my old man's bonus money. It was my second choice. I didn't care about that small neck. They didn't have much else in the store. What I really wanted was either a 295 or a blonde 175. Actually, I really wanted a Les Paul Custom. We went looking and we found one. So I played one in the music store one day. I vividly remember an ES-5 that was so cool you couldn't look at it. It was hanging up, brand new. Later, that one went off the rack and I played the Les Paul and I really liked it. My old man said to me, "You can't hear it if it ain't plugged in. What good is that? You'd better get one you can strum and hear it." So, I wound up getting the 350.

But I still really wanted a black Les Paul Custom. By the time I figured out that's what I needed, they had just quit making them, the triple pick-up one with the humbuckers. Eventually I acquired a whole bunch of those, real nice ones for nothing back in those days, 300 bucks. They were great, all of them. Some had Bigsbys, some of them didn't. I always loved Les Paul guitars because I always loved Les Paul.

Danny used to keep the action on his Customs so low without buzzing that it amazed even the Gibson technicians who examined his guitar at the factory when he visited.

Danny Gatton tearing it up on his 1961 Les Paul Custom 1990. The novel "Dingus box" attachment for organ-like sounds was inspired by the Paulverizer. *Courtesy Steve Wolf*

Peter Frampton

British guitarist Peter Frampton first became known with the Herd and soon recorded with Stevie Marriot's Small Faces, which then created the popular Humble Pie group. With jazz influences like Kenny Burrell and Django Reinhardt, his style of rock guitar takes on another flavor with songs like "Stone Cold Fever" on "Rock On." His live solo album *Frampton Comes Alive!* was released in 1976 and became one of the top-selling albums of all time. I interviewed Peter for Guitar Center in Hollywood during a Ringo tour while at their 1997 Rock Walk induction ceremony.

Robb: I saw you playing a Les Paul Custom with Humble Pie at the Hollywood Bowl.

Peter: *It was the black one that was on the front cover of* Frampton Comes Alive!, *a '54 Black Beauty that a friend of mine in San Francisco gave me. He had sanded it down for refinishing, and had taken off the original P-90.*

He had removed the Alnico V and routed it for humbuckers because he had seen a Smokey Robinson and the Miracles cover. He liked that, so he made it into a 1957 Custom. Back then I was playing the Fillmore West with Humble Pie and had an SG, but I swapped it for a 335 just before we played. And every time I played a solo (we played so loud) I wacked it up and—whew, whew—feedback, you know. So I could never play a solo with Humble Pie that night. Then a guy named Mark Mariana came up to me and said, "I noticed you're having some problems. Would you like to try my Les Paul tomorrow?" I said, "I'm not big on Les Pauls. I had a bad one before, but I'll try anything." He said, "I'll tell you what. I'll meet you at the coffee shop tomorrow morning." So he brought this thing and opened the case, and I said, "Oh, my God. This is beautiful." I picked it up and it fit right into my hands because he had shaved the neck. My fingers aren't very long, so I need a thinner guitar neck. It was like the instrument was handmade for me. I played it that night and I think I touched the ground only a couple of times. Most of the time, I was about two inches above the stage. It was unbelievable. It was great plugged straight into a 100-watt Marshall amp. After the first set I came offstage and asked Mark, "Would it be okay to use it for the second set?" He said, "Yeah." I said, "You wouldn't think about selling this would you? This is my guitar!" He said, "No, I want to give it to you." So that's the happy story.

RL: Which guitars are you using now?

PF: *I'm using pretty new Les Pauls. I have one that's called a Florentine. It has a denim color and f-holes.*

RL: Sort of like a 335 semi-solid.

PF: *It's great, so I'm using it for one number. I'm also using a Classic '60 reissue that's just beautiful. In fact, I'm using Les Paul guitars for just about the whole show. The Classic '60 has a slender neck that they worked on for me. I live in Nashville, so my local candy shop is Gibson. If the wife can't find me, she just speed dials Gibson. "Oh, sorry darling. I kept my hands in my pocket. I didn't buy anything!" (laughs)*

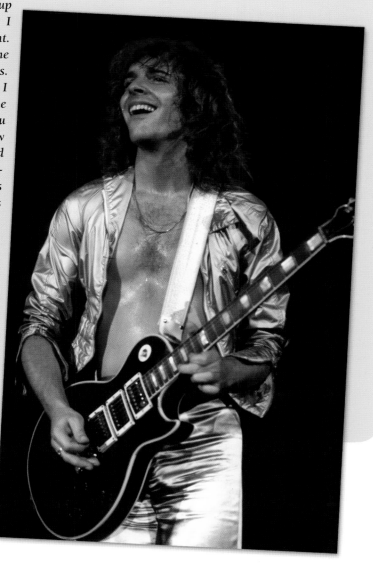

Peter Frampton playing his favorite Les Paul. He used this guitar for the best-selling album *Frampton Comes Alive!*, recorded just before this picture was taken. *Courtesy Neil Zlozower, c1976*

Albert Lee

British country favorite Albert Lee has been winning countless polls for his exemplary guitar playing. With influences from James Burton and Jimmy Bryant, he took off into the country field like wildfire. Early efforts like Head Hands & Feet started his stellar career, and his memorable stint with Eric Clapton brought rave reviews. His accompaniments with the Crickets, the Everly Brothers, Rodney Crowell, Emmylou Harris, and Bill Wyman are always crowd pleasers.

Although generally known as a Telecaster player, Albert has an extensive collection of instruments that ranges from Everly Brothers acoustic Gibsons, mandolins and Stringmaster steels, to a vintage 1958 Les Paul and a Ferrari 250. After borrowing a Les Paul Jr., then acquiring a '60 Custom by paying off its loan, he traded it for a Super 400. With that Les Paul, he inspired Jimmy Page to get his first LP Custom. Later, Eric Clapton gave Albert one of his own. Albert remembers the Gibson instruments arriving in England and tells some great stories about his mates.

Robb: Tell us the story of how you influenced Jimmy Page to play Les Paul guitars.

Albert: We used to play together around the West End of London. There was a little coffee bar called the Two Eyes where we played four or five nights a week. We each were paid a pound a night. On the weekends, we'd go out and do club gigs. So I was working as a professional musician at 17, playing at the Two Eyes.

Jimmy Page played a Gretsch at the time. I had the Les Paul, and he loved it. I also had a Supro with a 15-inch Jensen, which he loved. Jimmy went out and bought a Les Paul, and a Supro as well. He didn't buy the big one; he bought a smaller one. I heard he used that Supro on a lot of the Zeppelin tracks. It's in the Rock and Roll Hall of Fame. He bought that amp because he liked mine. So that's how that came about, but I don't know how long he had it. I guess he had it a couple of years, and then everyone was after the Les Paul Standards. So he probably traded it in for a regular Les Paul Sunburst. Everybody wanted them. So that's the story of Jimmy Page.

Shortly after I joined Eric Clapton in 1979, I happened to have some guitar photographs with me at a rehearsal. I showed him one and said "I used to have this Les Paul. It was a great guitar." It was a funny picture. I was pulling a strange face and he kind of laughed. He said, "Oh, I've got one of those at home

somewhere." The next day, he brought it in and gave it to me. It was a '58 Les Paul. That's the one I have. I've still got it. It's a great guitar. He said that he'd used it with Delaney & Bonnie. He had it around that time.

RL: And then you played the guitar live with Eric?

AL: Yes. I took it on the road with me, on most of the tours, I'm sure. I took it to Japan, used it on "Just One Night." I had a flight case made straight away because it wasn't in a hard case. So I used it on the other two albums I did with him, Money and Cigarettes and Another Ticket. I'm pretty sure that I would have taken it, because when you do an album like that, you like to have an array of guitars around.

RL: And you also used it on your own recordings?

AL: Yes, two or three of my solo albums. I played it on "One Way Rider" on my second album, Seventeen Summer, on one of my instrumental records, and on "Montenido."

RL: What do you like about the sound of the guitar?

AL: It reminds me of a grand piano… just the black ebony. And I love piano, and it's like a guitar version of a of a nine-foot Steinway grand. It's just got so much body and substance to it. It's really well made—and pretty, too.

Albert Lee is proudly holding his 1958 Custom Les Paul given to him by Eric Clapton in 1979. This instrument was previously used on *Disraeli Gears* and sessions with Delaney & Bonnie.

The Les Paul Junior, TV, Special, Melody Maker, and EB-0

The dynamic impact of the Les Paul model in late 1952 stimulated Gibson to expand both its basic production and variety. Interest continued to grow in electric instruments, and it was a good time to introduce other solid-body versions to expand their line. Having a broader product line insured more of the overall electric market and reached out to many new customers who wanted Gibson instruments.

In the early 1920s, for each of their guitar, mandolin, and banjo lines, Gibson developed "Junior" models—low-budget instruments targeted specifically at beginners and individuals on meager wages. Gibson sold these successfully during the '20s, helping to start off many aspiring musicians. "An innovation, therefore, that will be welcomed by those who are desirous of owning a Gibson is the offering of the Junior line, which will give you practically all that is desirable in a Gibson, lacking only some of those refinements, which at present, you may feel you can not afford," read an excerpt from Gibson's Junior instruments catalog.

Developed expressly for the student and amateur, the 1954 Les Paul Junior was an entry-level, economy model that made available the solid-body tone with Gibson's high-quality and lifetime guarantee. They were simple, single-pickup, flattop solid-bodies without binding, available in a standard scale length of 24 3/4" (actually closer to 24 9/16"). Soon afterwards, a shorter 3/4-sized model with a scale length of 22 3/4" was available for youngsters and individuals with smaller hands.

Les recollects the instruments: "What range do we want? From a Rolls to a Volkswagen. We wanted to cover the whole range, give the amateur guitarist to the professional his needs. Finest quality instruments for its price, a moderate price. Encourage them to be a musician... instead of using a cheap instrument."

Gibson and Les Paul especially wanted the beginners to have an inexpensive solid-body that was easy to play and appropriately fitted to the youngster. Good neck action and tone would definitely inspire them to continue playing, and, eventually, to buy more expensive models when they were ready to move up.

LES PAUL JUNIOR OUTFIT

LES PAUL JUNIOR GUITAR—Solid body Electric Spanish Guitar with fine tone, playing action and performance, at an unbelievable price for this instrument. The solid hardwood body is 17 1/4" long, 12 3/4" wide, and 1 3/4" thick, with cutaway design. Slender Mahogany neck with exclusive Gibson Truss Rod construction, Brazilian rosewood fingerboard with 22 nickel silver frets, pearl position dots; powerful Gibson magnetic pickup with individual adjustable polepieces; new metal combination bridge and tailpiece, adjustable horizontally and vertically; separate tone and volume control; Kluson machine heads; Gibson Golden Sunburst Finish on top, dark brown Mahogany color on back, rim and neck. Complete with leather padded strap.

Les Paul Junior Guitar; No. 115 Challenge Case

LES PAUL JUNIOR AMPLIFIER—Amazing quality and f workmanship, performance and guarantee. Sturdy, comp covering, size 13 1/2" wide, 11 1/4" high, 7" deep. Sl accessible control panel; three tubes, two instrument in volume control and on-and-off switch.

Les Paul Junior Amplifier
5-C Cover

(Above) First-year catalog description in 1954.

(Right) Early *Gazette* ad for the "limed oak" TV model Les Paul.

Les Paul TV Guitar

Designed to emphasize the latest in modern design . . . beautiful limed-oak finish, low action, slender neck, single pickup unit with separate tone and volume controls. This solid body Electric Spanish Guitar is similar to the "Les Paul Junior" and offers fine tone and outstanding performance. The solid hardwood body is 17 1/4" long, 12 3/4" wide, and 1 3/4" thick, with cutaway design. Slender Mahogany neck with famous Gibson Truss Rod construction — Brazilian rosewood fingerboard with 22 nickel silver frets — pearl position dots — powerful Gibson magnetic pickup with individually adjustable pole pieces — new metal combination bridge and tailpiece, adjustable horizontally and vertically — Kluson machine heads. Complete with leather, padded strap. Immediate delivery.

Les Paul TV Guitar............$122.50
#115 Challenge Case............13.50
(Slightly higher west of the Rockies)

production at a low price, true Gibson
ck plywood construction, attractive beige
panel, top mounted chassis with easily
Oval Type speaker; jeweled pilot light,

(Below) A very serious female student playing with her early natural TV model. From the 1957 CMI product catalog.

(Left) Two extremely rare 1955 Les Paul TV models with the unique light-washed "natural" finish. *Courtesy David Swartz/CVG*

Prototype Junior

This early prototype Les Paul Junior model was constructed in 1953. It has a considerably higher neck inset with less neck angle. Unlike all later flat-topped Les Paul models, the side of the neck runs flush into the cutaway body with unusual multiple mahogany inserts. An early "dog-ear" P-90 pickup cover is in the period's ES-175 style, and is slightly smaller than later production versions. It also utilized the Goldtop's pickguard shape, but is a bit larger, and attached flush with four screws. The rich 1953 Cremona Sunburst with wider brown shading was also continued into some early 1954 production models. No serial number is present while the gold Junior silkscreen looks to be original. This is a very special and unique instrument. Courtesy George Gruhn, July 2003

First-year production Les Paul Junior model #4 5067 with the bright-yellow sunburst top finish. This 1954 Junior has a beautiful Brazilian rosewood fingerboard, "speed knobs," Kluson strip tuners, gold Gibson decal logo, and gold silk-screened "Les Paul Junior" wording. From the collection of Dave Amato, 2003.

As on other entry-level Gibsons, the Honduras mahogany body and neck featured a dark walnut filler to color the back of the instrument, with a built-up, light- or dark-tinted brown lacquer coating over that. To achieve the golden sunburst finish on the top, very dark brown (almost black) shading was done over a nearly opaque, brilliant yellow, creating the dramatic sunburst effect on the top of the body. Some early versions and 3/4-sized guitars used a lightweight Western maple for the bodies instead of the customary mahogany. Early-1954 models had wider dark shading on the top with an almost orange-yellow hue in the center. Some later versions had an orange, almost red mixed in between the bright yellow and dark brown. Backs varied in medium to dark walnut-brown filler stains with darkened edges, heels, and head-stocks. The 1950s catalogs show the mahogany student's model being cut out in the factory.

A Gibson worker carefully cuts out a pre-routed, laminated Junior or TV body. The routs made previously were for the control cavity, pots, and neck slot. The bandsaw cut is about 1/4" from the final periphery routing.

The Les Paul Junior and TV models used a new "dog ear"-style P-90 pickup cover redesigned slightly larger, and which was to be used on a flat surface. These powerful single-coil P-90 pickups were 8K, and sometimes higher, if the winding continued. When coupled with the extra body mass and the simple stop-bar bridge, it produced an inherently strong tone that bordered on the raucous and gutsy. It was still smooth-sounding, yet had an extra punchy sustain when turned up through high-gain tube amplifiers. Pickups were repositioned 1/2" away from the bridge during late 1956 in order to reduce the bright output of the single pickup.

An original 1956 Junior model #6 7120, stamped for export. Just above the yellow serial number, a "Made in the USA" stamp was added after finishing, which slightly shattered the lacquer finish. *Courtesy California Vintage, 2003*

Plain black, single-piece, truss-rod covers and pickguards were used for these models. 1954–55 versions used the short, golden "speed" knobs, and switched to the "bell"-style knobs during 1956. Early versions also used the original thinner stop/stud wrap-around combination bridge tailpiece up to mid-1955. Kluson Deluxe covered "3-on a plate" G-301-V strip tuning machines with ivory plastic buttons were utilized for the whole economy series. The Kluson Deluxe branding down the center of the sealed back was begun in 1956. Bushings (or collars) were the rounded style. Instead of the Gibson logo inlaid in pearl, a sharp gold Gibson decal sufficed, with a silk-screened "Les Paul Junior" in gold.

(Above) A fine 1956 Les Paul Junior (not stamped for export) in Munderkingen, Germany. *Courtesy Erhard Bochen, 1985*

(Below) CMI's 1957 guitar accessories catalog depicting the P-90 pickup unit and cover, No. 480, which listed for $32.40.

This 1958 Junior sports an original white pickguard (which sometimes came on tradeshow Juniors) and has a wide three-color shaded sunburst with a very opaque yellow. *Courtesy Guitar Center, Hollywood, 2004*

185

"To fill the needs of players who prefer a guitar with a smaller reach, Gibson had three models of ³/₄-sized guitars. The unusual ease and speed in fingering is due to the low string action and short scale of these instruments. Following in the footsteps of the famous Les Paul Junior guitar is Gibson's new ³/₄ model. This solid-body guitar is 17 ³/₄ inches long, 12 ³/₄ inches wide, and 1 3/4 inches thick, with cutaway design," stated the 1957 Gibson *Gazette*, which also introduced the thin ES-140, LG-2 ³/₄. Gibson's ledgers, however, show ³/₄ models were shipped in 1956. These 22 ³/₄"-scale guitars were actually available beginning in 1954 with the first "TV" versions.

List price was initially $99.50, and went up to $120 in 1957—great value for the money (Gibson's bread 'n' butter!). Prices were slightly higher west of the Rockies. The Les Paul Junior models substantially out-sold all Gibson electrics except the ES-125 models. With the Gibson quality and workmanship inherent in these budget models, beginners certainly got more "bang for the buck" in the '50s.

(Above) Here are two ³/₄-sized Gibsons together. The rare 1954 TV model (#4 4799) is constructed of a light maple for the body and a mahogany neck. They were not on the shipping records or in any catalogs for a few years. The matching Les Paul Junior (#7 0796) features an entirely different opaque yellow. *Courtesy Larry Henrickson, August 1993*

(Below) This ³/₄-sized TV guitar has an unusual translucent yellow finish, which would be naturally brighter with its maple body for Les and Mary's popular television show. They obviously rethought the color scheme a few times while developing the natural and the "limed oak" finishes. Note the yellow finish over the serial number and strip Klusons before the deluxe imprints.

The Les Paul "TV" Model

"It's the Les Paul Show! Yes, we call it the Les Paul show with Mary Ford—you can call it transcribed because here it is... hot out of the recording machine... and here's the guitarist himself... Les Paul." Five times throughout the day, that five-minute spot would air on television, showing Les and Mary comfortably sitting around their newly remodeled house in Mahwah, NJ, and Les getting Mary to sing a song with him. Listerine mouthwash sponsored these popular short television shows to advertise their product. And to go along with the show, Gibson joined the bandwagon and decided to feature a new model guitar—the Les Paul "TV" model.

"No doubt you are already aware of the new Les Paul-Mary Ford TV and radio commercials. They're on several times daily, coast-to-coast; check your local newspapers for time and station. Here's wonderful free publicity for you... not only for the Les Paul model guitar, but for every Gibson instrument in your stock. Take advantage of these programs being seen and heard by your customers and potential customers—we suggest you order one of the Les Paul-Mary Ford blowups and fasten a banner across it, giving the time and station of the program in your city." (Clarence Havenga's "Editor's Notebook," Gibson *Gazette*, January 1954)

Another rare 1954 ³/₄-sized TV model (#4 4804) with a two-piece light maple body. These early versions had the pickup placement in the same spot as that of the later 1957 Juniors and TVs. Note the pronounced ledge in the cutaway and darker mahogany neck coloring. From the Albert Molinaro collection, April 1998.

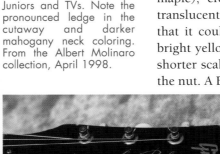

[From Les Paul's Notes: Milwaukee radio shows WTM and TV, 5:55 P.M., five minutes long, five times a day, at 7:00 A.M., 12:00 P.M., 5:55 P.M., 11:00 P.M., before sermonette, before the news.]

"We had the TV show, 'Les Paul and Mary Ford at Home,' four years—'54 to '58," says Les. "So they would go out and buy the TV model and associate the two. I had a little vignette, 'I'll get my TV model,' to launch the whole thing, to get it started," says Les.

Essentially, the TV model was a sales idea to promote a new version of the Les Paul Junior. It featured a brilliant yellow finish that easily stood out on television. In those days, black and white television sets were becoming common in American households. The relatively new color sets, however, were still in their infancy and quite expensive. Nevertheless, viewers watching on both types of sets could easily see the lighter natural (yellow, on color TV sets) finish. Its color was quite similar to the Heywood Wakefield bleached-looking mahogany furniture of the day. (Actually, during May of 1952, some special "bleached mahogany" Hawaiian Console steel guitars were shipped as samples to CMI. Going back even further, a wartime acoustic was made with yellowish/blonde finish for Zeke Clements. So this type finish was around and being used.) A late-'50s catalog states, "Designed to emphasize the latest in modern appearance with beautiful limed-mahogany finish, and incorporating unusual quality, features, and performance at a popular price."

Incidentally, Gibson endorser Tal Farlow special-ordered a brilliant orange/red ES-140 for a prior color-broadcast television performance. It had a matching plastic fingerboard made with the paint's pigment. Tal's striking instrument may have helped instigate the Les Paul TV guitar idea, too.

The earliest TV models built in 1954 were ³/₄-sized versions with nineteen frets (joining the body at the 14th fret), and a 22 ³/₄" scale. Bodies were still full-sized and made of a special Western maple (a light resonate type of maple), creating a bright yellow color with the first translucent yellow TV finish. There is some speculation that it could have been a light poplar wood, too. This bright yellow stood out on the television quite well. The shorter scale neck had a slightly narrower 1 ⁵/₈" width at the nut. A Brazilian rosewood fingerboard with pearl dots set on a Honduras mahogany neck completed their first TV guitar. For example, the Les Paul TV #4 4804 had a two-piece maple body and measured 13" wide (not 12 ³/₄"), 1 ³/₄" thick, and 17 ¹/₄" long.

As on the Junior, the smaller TV had the same P-90 setup and electronics. The pickup was moved slightly away from the bridge on these $^3/_4$ models compared to the standard models. As with the Junior, full-sized models eventually had the pickup moved $^1/_2$" from the bridge in 1957.

Standard, medium-scale 24 $^3/_4$" (actually, 24 $^9/_{16}$") models identical to the new Junior models were available in 1955. Light maple was also used in '55 for full-sized TV and Junior models. Some very early full-sized versions were simply finished with a natural filler and clear coating as on the Goldtop backs. The 1955 pricelist quoted them as having a "natural finish." A 1956 *Gazette* ad referred to the finish as a "beautiful limed-oak" because of the popular stained furniture nomenclature. Later catalogs correctly renamed it "limed mahogany."

This complex, tinted lacquer finish became the standard on the mahogany TV guitar, with slight variations of a pale yellow/green tint with beige coloring added. Some were much more on the beige or tan side of the spectrum, however. In early collectors' circles, it's always been known simply as the "Les Paul TV" model. Because of the light finish, modern collectors mistakenly refer to it as the "TV Junior," with the same misnomer "TV Special" for the original "Specials."

The official production totals (compiled by Gibsonian Kenny Kilman in the early 1970s) showed TV models being manufactured and sold from 1954 onward. Only five were shipped in 1954, and 230 in '55. 1955 pricelists left them off entirely, while a Gibson *Gazette* finally featured the guitar in 1956, when 1,345 were sold. The TV then listed for $122.50, which went up by July of 1957 to $132.50 (both in zone 1). 1957 saw only 552 shipped, with even fewer in the transition year of 1958. As with the Junior model, a "Challenge" #115 soft-shell, brown alligator-style case was supplied for $13.50. Additionally, the guitar and a Les Paul TV model student amp (similar to the Junior amps) were occasionally sold in sets for a few years.

This 1956 Les Paul TV model (#612867) features the "wheat" limed mahogany finish. Some were even a lighter brown color. *Courtesy John Nelson, August 1995*

A bright yellow 1956 Les Paul model with the pickup moved away slightly. *Courtesy Dave Amato, 2003*

The Les Paul "Special" Guitar

"This new addition to the range of Les Paul models has been introduced to make available the advantages of the design at a lower price. The object has been achieved by simplification in trim and in the less essential details," stated the Gibson catalog. The new Les Paul "Special" was an economy twin-pickup model without the frills. Moderately priced between the $120 TV price and the regular $235 for the Les Paul model, the Special was a reasonable $169. Its unbound flattop (non-arched) mahogany body actually measured 1 7/8" thick, 13" wide, and 17 1/4" long. Those measurements are on spec with the large 1956 catalog, which is a 1/4" wider and 1/8" thicker than the 1954 specs.

OUTSTANDING VALUE IN A SOLID BODY GUITAR

The new LES PAUL SPECIAL solid body Electric Spanish Cutaway Guitar incorporates the features that have made the Les Paul Model famous—tone, versatility, slender neck and low, fast action—with a moderate price. The appearance is rich and attractive . . . solid Honduras mahogany body and neck finished in limed mahogany shading . . . contrasting brown Royalite pickguard and unit covers . . . nickel plated parts . . . 22 fret, bound rosewood fingerboard with pearl dot inlays.

Other features of the Les Paul Special: Two powerful Gibson pickups with separate tone and volume controls for each; Alnico magnets and individually adjustable polepieces for each string; two position toggle switch activates either or both pickups; unique combination metal bridge and tailpiece, adjustable horizontally and vertically; individual Kluson machine heads; adjustable Gibson Truss Rod neck construction; padded, adjustable leather strap.

Les Paul Special Solid Body Electric Spanish Cutaway Guitar

Cases for Above Instrument: 535 Faultless, 115 Challenge

The 1955 catalog depiction of the original Les Paul Special that featured brown Royalite plastic and a natural limed finish that soon switched to the TV's "limed mahogany" shading mentioned here.

An immaculate 1956 Les Paul Special (#615252). This instrument is all-original, down to the Sprague "Bumble Bee" capacitors. This guitar courtesy of Mick Mars (who actually named his son after Les!), February 1995.

Here's a close-up of a Special's stopbar/stud bridge and P-90 pickup. You can see the brown filler stain in the grain under the yellow limed finish, flat-wound strings, and beveled edges on the outside of the laminated pickguard.

This nice 1957 Les Paul Special came with the deluxe Lifton Faultless 535 pink-lined case. *Courtesy Steve Soest, October 1975*

Neck joints, however, weren't flush on the cutaway as on the Goldtop and Custom models. A small, squared body ledge was left to simplify the production (except the finish sanding). The neck set was also taller, compensating for the lack of an arched top. Kluson Deluxe, G-301-V, 3-on-a-Plate (with brass posts), enclosed machine heads were also standard on Special models. Gibson, however, used the nicer bushing as on the Goldtop. Unlike the Junior and TV, the Special also featured single-ply binding on its Brazilian rosewood fingerboard, and a pearl-inlaid Gibson logo. An adjustable stop/stud "wraparound" bar bridge/tailpiece was also standard. A few are known to have been special-ordered in 1956 with the addition of a Tune-O-Matic bridge.

When introduced in 1955, Specials first featured a light natural finish. Soon afterwards, they adopted the "striking modern tinted finish," as on the finalized TV models. Variations occurred in coloration between the standard pale yellow, with an almost greenish tint, to a beige cream wheat color—all with the stained mahogany grain showing through in different degrees. The first catalog stated that a "limed mahogany" shading was used, much like the full-sized, lightly "limed" TV models. Additionally, a few sunburst- and cherry-finished, single-cutaway Specials were made. One rare cherry single-cutaway guitar (aka "Buddy," #9 1230) that was found is one of five that was made with small frets on a more slender neck. It came with a crispy clean 535 case, and puts out 9.3K at the neck pickup!

Pickups and electronics were identical to that on the Goldtop versions, but with black "Royalite" plastic pickup covers and switch surrounds. Although the early ads stated that, "contrasting brown Royalite pickguard and unit covers" were standard (as were brown "speed" knobs), they were used on the guitar pictured in the catalog, and a few early production versions. Pickguards were comprised of four-ply, laminated black-and-white PVC plastic, partially angle-cut to show the white borders. 1955 Specials sported black "speed" control knobs, while black "bell" versions were standard on later models. Lastly, the three-position Switchcraft pickup selector utilized a matching black plastic surround, as used on the Custom. Some Specials used the rubber grommet floating-toggle surround as found on the L-5CES.

The cases that were supplied with the instruments were generally the brown alligator-style "Challenge," or later, the "Durabilt" #115 Geib soft-shell cases ($13.50). Many Specials were shipped with brown hard-shell "Faultless" 535 Liftons (touted as being "built like a fortress") cases ($42–$43) with the striking pink interior plush. List price in September 1955 through July 1957 was $179.50 (in zone 1) and $182.50 (in zone 2).

In its first year, 1955, 373 products were shipped. The Special soon outsold the Les Paul regular (Goldtop) in 1956, with 1,345, and nearly three times as many in 1957, at 1,452! It slacked off a bit in 1958 before the new models took over. It was quite a popular model of the Les Paul series and is still affordable and appreciated today.

Notable players of the Special during the 1950s included Silvia Robinson (of the Mickey and Silvia duo). Carlos Santana's first album in 1969 featured numerous tracks recorded on a single-cutaway Les Paul Special. John Sebastian also favors an old Special single-cut. Reggae star Bob Marley played a well-worn and refinished Special for many years. Jimi Hendrix's incredible recording of "Voodoo Chile" was done on a single-cutaway Special, accounting for those amazing bends and that thicker Gibson tone he achieved.

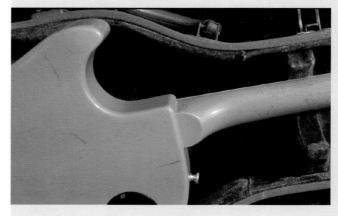

This very rare 1958 tenor Les Paul Special guitar (one of three) is ready for the player who doubles on banjo or mandola and bends notes with lots of sustain! Bow-tie style inlays are on other models instead of the simple dots. Playing a solid body in fifths can be enjoyable. Note the twin decorative inlays on the P-90 covers and individual white button Kluson tuners. *Courtesy Gary Hernandez, Del Mar, 2004*

(Above). By 1958, the Special had a light-yellow finish that was more opaque over the filled grain. This clean Les Paul (#8 5336) shows some slight edge-wear, where you can see the lighter beige coloration under the coats. *Courtesy California Vintage G&A, 2004*

(Right) The 1956/57 large-format catalog page with the Special, GA-40, and Junior outfit.

LES PAUL MODELS

LES PAUL "SPECIAL" GUITAR—This new addition to the range of Les Paul models has been introduced to make available the advantages of the design at a lower price. The object has been achieved by simplification in trim and in the less essential details. The clear sustaining tone, rapid action, and freedom from feed back make this "Special" model really outstanding value. The solid mahogany body has a flat top and a striking modern tinted finish, highly polished. Body dimensions 13" wide by 17¼" long and 1⅝" deep. Pearl dot inlays add sparkle to the rosewood fingerboard which has 22 frets — 16 clear of body — and 24¾" scale length.

All metal parts including the heavy one piece bridge and tailpiece are brilliantly nickel plated.
Fitted with 2 pickups—separate tone and volume controls and toggle selector switch.

Les Paul "Special" Guitar — #535 Faultless case

LES PAUL AMPLIFIER—An excellent general purpose amplifier with remote controlled, built-in tremolo. One of the four inputs has separate volume control for microphone use. Wide range voicing control. Eight tubes produce about fourteen watts. Twelve inch "Concert Series" Jensen speaker. Complete specification under "Amplifiers" on Page 23.

*Les Paul Amplifier — 60 cycle,
also available for 25 cycle
at extra cost.*

LES PAUL "JUNIOR" — Developed expressly for the student, who can now enjoy the benefits of this very successful design at a price he can afford, the "Junior" is similar to the "Special" above but has one pickup, with tone and volume controls, and is finished in rich dark brown with sunburst. BODY is solid mahogany with flat top and measures 13" wide by 17¼" long and 1⅝" deep. Rosewood fingerboard has pearl dot position markers, 22 frets — 16 clear of body — and gives a scale length of 24¾". Heavy one piece bridge-tailpiece and all metal parts are in nickel plate.

Les Paul "Junior" Guitar   *#115 case*

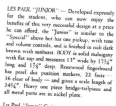

LES PAUL JUNIOR AMPLIFIER—This well designed low power amplifier was developed to provide a good performance at the lowest possible price. It has two inputs with volume controls, uses three tubes and produces about four watts of audio power. Full details under "Amplifiers" on Page 24.

*Les Paul Junior Amplifier — 60 cycle
also available for 25 cycle at extra cost.*

15

193

Artists

(Left) Dave Pevrett of Foghat performs with his old Les Paul Junior at the San Diego Sports Arena, 1973.

(Below) Green Day guitarist Billie Joe Armstrong graciously poses with his well-worn 1956 Les Paul Junior. Behind him are his new signature models in Gibson's booth at the 2006 NAMM show. His use of the LP Jr. model helps keep the ever-popular Jr. and TV models in the limelight.

(Left) Steve Howe of Yes enjoys many Gibsons, and this 1955 Les Paul Junior #5 6856 is one of his favorites. Taken at the San Diego Sports Arena, circa 1977.

(Below) A colorful Steve Miller is performing here with a wildly painted SG (Les Paul) Special in San Diego, circa 1974.

Double Cutaway Models '58–'61

A completely new double-cutaway design was unveiled in late 1958. This revolutionary development gave the guitarist complete ease of access to the furthest reaches of the entire fingerboard. It was an added comfort for those who used the 22-fret neck in its entirety. Many felt that these new double-cutaway designs opened up a whole new playability to their electric guitar line, and made it "a snap to hit those high notes!"

"The much lauded double-cutaway body is ultra-modernistic in appearance and practical in performance. It gives these instruments a sleek, well-balanced look while providing maximum access to all 22 frets." (Gibson *Gazette*)

(Above) Gibson's best electric solid-body seller was the cherry-red 1959 Les Paul Junior. Note the unusual grey-swirl pickup cover. *Courtesy David Swartz, 2005*

(Left) The "Exciting News!" *Gazette*: the announcement of the new double-cutaway Junior and TV models was great news for many players who wanted full and effortless access up to the 22nd fret. It also introduced the cherry-red finish for the new Junior model and an improved brighter yellow for the TV model.

pre-set — three way toggle switch to activate either or both pickups.

Les Paul Guitar—
  Cherry Red Finish $247.50

No. 535 Case—
  Faultless, plush lined...... 42.00

NEW DESIGN AND FINISH FOR LES PAUL JUNIOR AND TV MODELS

Both the Les Paul Junior and Les Paul TV guitars have taken on a brand new look — double cutaway body design plus a lovely new finish for each.

The much lauded double cutaway body is ultra-modernistic in appearance and practical inperformance. It gives these instruments a sleek, well balanced look while providing maximum access to *all* 22 frets. This is a feature every guitarist desires — to reach full chords down the entire length of the neck. All music becomes easy and effortless with the new double-cutaway.

Beautiful, new finishes further enhance the stream-lined looks of these guitars. The Les Paul Junior shows off a solid cherry red tone, which will now be its standard finish. With this brilliant coloring the Junior is sure to be a 'stand-out' in any crowd! The Les Paul TV is being finished in a brand-new shade of limed mahogany, much finer than the former one.

Other features include powerful pickups located near the bridge for clarity of tonal response. Individually adjustable polepieces to balance each string. Separate tone and volume controls. Combination bridge and tailpiece that adjusts both horizontally and vertically. Strings are set close to the fingerboard for easy low playing action.

Les Paul Junior Guitar—
  Cherry Red Finish $120.00

Les Paul TV Model—
  Limed Mahogany Finish... 132.50

No. 535 Case—
  Faultless, plush lined...... 42.00

No. 115 Case—Durabilt 13.50

(Prices slightly higher west of the Rockies)

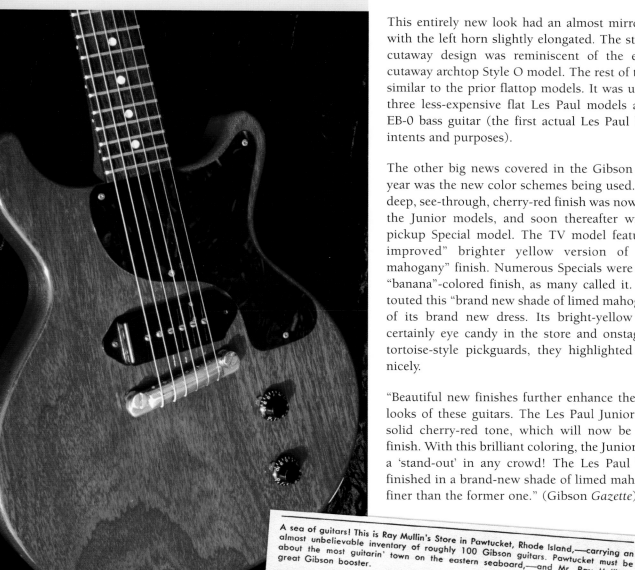

This entirely new look had an almost mirror symmetry, with the left horn slightly elongated. The straight-across cutaway design was reminiscent of the early Gibson cutaway archtop Style O model. The rest of the body was similar to the prior flattop models. It was utilized on all three less-expensive flat Les Paul models and the new EB-0 bass guitar (the first actual Les Paul bass—for all intents and purposes).

The other big news covered in the Gibson *Gazette* that year was the new color schemes being used. A gleaming, deep, see-through, cherry-red finish was now standard on the Junior models, and soon thereafter with the twin pickup Special model. The TV model featured a "new, improved" brighter yellow version of the "limed mahogany" finish. Numerous Specials were done in this "banana"-colored finish, as many called it. The *Gazette* touted this "brand new shade of limed mahogany" as part of its brand new dress. Its bright-yellow tinting was certainly eye candy in the store and onstage. With the tortoise-style pickguards, they highlighted the yellows nicely.

"Beautiful new finishes further enhance the streamlined looks of these guitars. The Les Paul Junior shows off a solid cherry-red tone, which will now be its standard finish. With this brilliant coloring, the Junior is sure to be a 'stand-out' in any crowd! The Les Paul TV is being finished in a brand-new shade of limed mahogany, much finer than the former one." (Gibson *Gazette*)

(Above) A stamped "2" was later added to this late 1959 Junior. #927396 to indicate a minor imperfection.

(Right) A sea of Gibson guitars in Pawtucket, Rhode Island! This Gazette picture shows Roy Mullen's store inventory of 100 guitars with lots of double-cutaways and some singles. It must have been breathtaking to waltz into their showroom and smell all that Gibsonian freshness!

A sea of guitars! This is Ray Mullin's Store in Pawtucket, Rhode Island,—carrying an almost unbelievable inventory of roughly 100 Gibson guitars. Pawtucket must be about the most guitarin' town on the eastern seaboard,—and Mr. Ray Mullin a great Gibson booster.

IMPORTANT NEWS FLASH:

All the beautiful and exciting new guitars and amplifiers pictured in the enclosed four-page circular will be available for shipment in January. Be sure to place your order now in order to insure prompt shipment. 1961 should be the greatest guitar year ever, and you won't want to start out understocked!

197

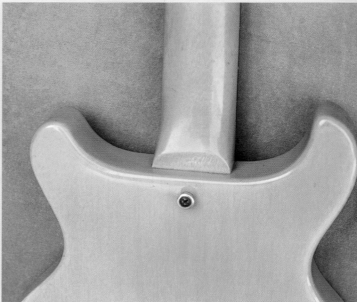

A strikingly bright-yellow color became the norm for the newly styled TV model. This 1958 Les Paul TV #8 5819 is a desirable example of Gibson's economy winner. *Courtesy Jeff Lund, 2004*

TV

The graceful double cutaway design emphasizes the latest in modern appearance with beautiful limed-mahogany finish and incorporating unusual quality, features and performance at a popular price. Its easy, low playing action, slender neck, and clear sustaining tone make it a favorite with students and advanced players. Bright nickel-plated metal parts and quality machine heads. Leather strap included.

- Slim, fast, low-action neck—with exclusive extra low frets joins body at the 22nd fret
- One-piece mahogany neck, adjustable truss rod
- Rosewood fingerboard, pearl dot inlays
- Combination bridge and tailpiece, adjustable horizontally and vertically
- Powerful pickup with individually adjustable polepieces
- Separate tone and volume controls which can be pre-set

12¾" wide, 17¼" long, 1¾" thin . . . 24¾" scale, 22 frets

SG TV Limed-Mahogany finish

535 Faultless plush-lined case

ZC-LP Deluxe zipper case cover

115 Durabilt Case

(Above) This beautiful-condition 1960 TV model has the slender blade neck and a more subdued, creamy TV finish with nice grain. According to the catalog, it is technically an SG TV without the Les Paul silk-screened logo—but some were still shipped with the logos anyway. I should have kept this one! *Courtesy John and Mark, The Black, February 1975*

(Right) The 1960 catalog description showing the SG TV (Les Paul) model.

Electronically, these new versions basically used the same pickup layouts and controls as previous models. Early Specials had a pickup selector switch set between the rhythm pickups knobs, which was soon moved close to the bridge for easier use. This proximity may have been a problem for those reaching for the volume and some wide and crazy strummers. CentraLab 500K pots and Sprague "Bumble Bees" continued with the switch to "Black Beauty" caps in 1960.

The following is from my 1975 interview with Walt Fuller:

> **RL:** *One thing I have always wondered about. When you take the old Goldtop guitar and compare that pickup output with the Les Paul Junior pickup, the Junior pickup seems more powerful. Isn't the pickup pretty much the same?*
>
> **WF:** *Yes, it is. It uses the same coil form, the same magnets, the same polepieces.*

The Junior and TV models naturally gave that ballsy/gutsy grinding tone so desired in loud rock 'n' roll—*a là* the tone achieved by Mountain's Leslie West in later years. The classic "dog ear" P-90s, with their pickup bracket directly attached to the top of the body, gave a different tone. Specials were somewhat more subdued-sounding with their pickups suspended into the body, just as the earlier Goldtop's tone was a bit mellower than a Junior's or a TV's. It's thought that the combination of pickup mounting, tenon length, and extra body mass makes up the big difference in tones between the single- and double-pickup models. Be that as it may, they all sound wonderful and different for a wide variety of musical styles.

(Right) Although the Junior and TV models were first to feature the new double-cut design, the Special was soon released a few months later and first advertised in this 1959 Gibson *Gazette*.

(Opposite page) This early version of the double-cutaway Les Paul Special (circa 1959) has the toggle switch between the rhythm controls. Its beautiful, curly mahogany would have been obscured by a standard limed finish. The back view reveals the nicely-flamed wood and exposed cavity with original CentraLab pots and Sprague caps. *Courtesy Mark Hays, 1995*

6

Introducing—
The NEW Les Paul Special

A familiar and highly popular model for years, the Les Paul Special now has a brand new dress — that wonderful double cutaway design plus a gleaming finish of limed mahogany. This should make it the perfect instrument for the guitarist who wants beauty plus Gibson quality at a moderate price.

Les Paul Sp.

The Les Paul Special combines tone, versatility, slender neck, low fast action, — with the much lauded double cutaway body. It gives the guitar a sleek, well balanced look while providing maximum access to all 22 frets —something that every guitarist desires. The finish is a brand-new shade of limed mahogany. A last-minute notice from the factory tells us this guitar will also be available in the new cherry red finish at no extra charge.

Other features include Gibson Adjustable Truss Rod neck, bound rosewood fingerboard with pearl dot inlays. Two, powerful pickups with individually adjustable polepieces to balance each string. Separate tone and volume controls. Combination bridge and tailpiece that adjusts both horizontally and vertically. Strings are set close to the fingerboard — as every guitarist wants them.

Les Paul Special Guitar........$179.50
No. 115 Case 13.50
No. 535 Plush Case 42.00

With the new Special's front pickup next to the neck, their rhythm position provided an extra-rich rhythm tonality, but some problems arose. This proximity, and the considerable amount of neck tenon removed, created a somewhat weak neck-to-body joint, which became its Achilles' heel. The stability of the neck soon became an issue, as some necks even broke loose on minor impact. An accidental dropping of the instrument (even in the case) could have resulted in a heel fracture, due to its light mahogany construction. (This is true of most Gibsons, for that matter, so always be very careful!). They were fine instruments, regardless of their fragility.

A prime example of a late-1959 Les Paul Special (#921331) in the limed mahogany finish. Note the thin plastic piece between the neck and rhythm pickup. The updated electronic layout puts the toggle switch near the bridge with an elongated control cavity. The shape of the curved routing is reminiscent of a racecar track! From the collection of Norm Harris, June, 1995.

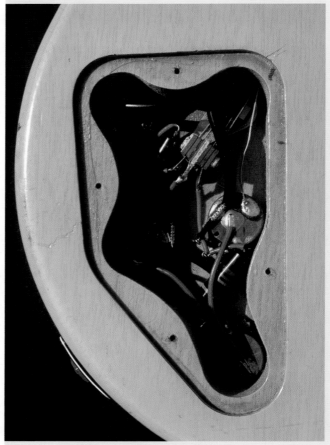

THE LES PAUL JUNIOR, TV, SPECIAL, MELODY MAKER, AND EB-0

To give the Special a more sturdy design, the rhythm pickup was brought back a good ¹/₂" to give it more integral wood support. By late 1959/early 1960, a redesigned pickup layout and pickguard accompanied this transition. Some transitional models were made with the pickup halfway back. Compared to the strong heel strength of the earlier single-cutaway, a double-cutaway's higher access was a compromise worth taking for the careful musician. Tonally speaking, there are distinct sonic differences between the two models. Some feel that the single-cut has a stronger acoustic tone with more mass, while others enjoy the double-cutaway's unique looks, great tones, and incredible playability.

In the beginning, a few rare models were built with identically shaped horns. Two-piece body Specials and Juniors were also produced. The edge-routing radius around the bodies varied on these models. They were fairly sharp at first, and became quite rounded through the years, at ³/₁₆" radius.

During 1960, the Les Paul name designation on the Special and TV was dropped from the catalog and headstock. The new moniker was announced as an abbreviation for "solid guitar," or simply "SG." It was the first use of this name for a Gibson that was not actually shown on the instrument. Occasionally, one will see a later version (into 1961) with the Les Paul silk-screen, originally shipped as such. Many who began playing during the 1960s still call these thick, double-cutaway models "Les Paul" guitars anyway!

The next Special version sports a revised pickguard and pickup placement due to structural neck issues. This 1960 "Les Paul" Special #0 2272 (since it does say "Les Paul" on the head) has a limed finish that really lights up in the afternoon sunshine. It also came with a beautiful 535 plush case.
Courtesy Barney Roach, 2003

Even with the medium 24 $^9/_{16}$"-scale (supposedly 24 $^3/_4$"), double-cutaway model necks were quite long to begin with. Nut width was still the standard 1 $^{11}/_{16}$". They featured a comfortably rounded, '50s profile (fairly large) in 1958 with smaller frets, and in 1959, with the new larger jumbo frets. As with the other higher-up models, the mid-1960 neck profiles became considerably more slender in depth for extra ease of playability—or so they thought. These "blade" necks sacrificed some sustain for their lack of mass, however. Playing for long periods of time on later versions caused less strain on the thumb for some players, though.

The very cute, $^3/_4$-sized, double-cutaway, cherry red-finished Les Paul Special and Junior guitars were introduced in 1959 for students and guitarists with small hands. As on the earlier $^3/_4$ Les Paul models, the scale length is 22 $^3/_4$+" and measures 1 $^5/_8$" at the nut. Its total new design set the back pickups and bridge far down into the body, while the neck joined the body at the 15th fret. This made it an entirely smaller package for the smaller guitarist, but provided for little upper access! The Special's selector switch was oddly placed way up on the top horn, while the four controls were in the standard location. It could take the vote for the strangest non-futuristic guitar from the 1950s. Plus, it didn't sell too well at first, and most of the Specials built in 1959 were actually shipped in October of 1961. Now they are both a curiosity and a Gibson novelty. Ninety-eight Specials were shipped between 1959–61, while 366 3/4 Juniors went out during the same period.

A sight most people never see! A full Bigsby B5 setup on a double-cut Special (SG-R) with the factory-modified neck-angle tilt. *Courtesy the Texas Guitar Show, May 1992*

This clean, cherry-red 1960 SG-R Special has the slim neck and Grovers added. Note the great Flamenco tapestry. *Courtesy the Bowen Brothers*

SPECIAL
SPECIAL 3/4

Two ways new! A lovely new finish in a new shade of limed mahogany or Gibson's new cherry red . . . an ultra-modern new shape—the solid body double cutaway design that provides easy access to *all* 22 frets. Outstanding for its tone, versatility, and low fast action at a modest price. Very graceful and sturdy with beautifully finished, nickel-plated metal parts. Enclosed individual machine heads. Leather strap included.

Available also with three-quarter size neck and fingerboard that joins the double cutaway body at 15th fret.

- Slim, fast, low-action neck—with exclusive extra low frets, joins body at 22nd fret
- Rosewood fingerboard, pearl dot inlays
- One-piece mahogany neck, adjustable truss rod
- Combination metal bridge and tailpiece, adjustable horizontally and vertically
- Twin powerful pickups with separate tone and volume controls which can be pre-set
- Three-position toggle switch to activate either or both pickups

12⅜" wide, 17¼" long, 1¾" thin . . . 24¾" scale, 22 frets

SG-R Special Cherry-red finish
SGC Special Cream finish
SG Special ¾ Cherry-red finish
535 Faultless, plush-lined case
ZC-LP Deluxe zipper case cover
115 Durabilt case

(Left) 1960 catalog description with the "SG Special" name. Note that it refers to the red guitar as a "SG-R" and the cream model as an "SGC." A ZC-LP zipper case for the 535 Faultless is also listed.

(Above) The unique Les Paul Junior ³/₄-sized student guitar. With its bridge set back like the bass guitar's, there are only fifteen frets clear of the body... but how many students wail solos past the high E? It makes for a more compact travel guitar, too! This 1960 model (#0 3439) has nice grain, somewhat like an ash body. *Courtesy John Nelson, August 1995*

(Right) This 1959 *Gazette* features the latest "Convention Snapshots" that depict the new double-cut Junior, TV, and Special, along with the now-famous Flying V. Note the white pickup on the Junior and extended white pickguard on the new prototype Les Paul Melody Maker.

(Left) This clean little 1959 Les Paul Special wonder has it all for the small-handed rocker. It even comes with a ³/₄-sized 535 Faultless case. *Courtesy Kim Shaheen, 2003*

CONVENTION SNAPSHOTS

This is for the benefit of our dealers who didn't quite make it to the N.A.M.M. convention—a few pictures of the Gibson display rooms. Our photographer tried to catch as much of the exhibit as possible.

Amplifiers by Gibson, with a few solid body guitars on the left.

Those wonderful electric guitars, including the new Flying V.

Thrilling New EB-0 Bass

"A new, economy-priced bass by Gibson—that's wonderful news in the world of frets." Bass-wise, the EB-0 (a pseudo Les Paul double-cutaway bass) was introduced in 1959, and replaced the original EB-1. It utilized the same standard 30 1/2" scale with twenty frets and a rosewood fingerboard. Translucent cherry-red was the specified finish, and most that we've seen had the sharper radius edge rout. The control knobs were adjacent to a nickel bridge set down at the end of the body.

The bass humbucking pickup (also by Seth Lover) as first used on the EB-2 had the dual-coil "Sidewinder" design, with poles set in the middle and a black plastic cover. "The bass pickup was one of the most difficult to design," say Ted, "because you wanted to get that very low response, and the average pickup wouldn't do it. It had to be a special kind of pickup." Each coil received a whopping 12,500 turns, and all were set on their sides. This massive output restricted the highs and gave the instrument a deep and powerful tone—especially being placed by the neck.

EB-0

A new, economy priced bass by Gibson—it offers clear sustaining bass response, easy and fast playing action, and modern cherry-red finish. Double cutaway body brings the entire length of the fingerboard within easy reach. Expensive bass style machine heads further enhance the value of this instrument. Once you hear its throaty bass tone and feel the quick easy response, you'll agree—the EB-0 gives the professional artist the quality he wants.

- Slim, fast, low-action neck joins body beyond 17th fret
- One-piece mahogany neck, adjustable truss rod
- Rosewood fingerboard, pearl dot inlays
- Combination bridge and tailpiece, adjustable horizontally and vertically
- Powerful humbucking pickup with separate tone and volume controls

13" wide, 16½" long, 1¾" thin...
30½" scale, 20 frets

EB-0 Cherry finish
127 Durabilt case

EB-O

(Above) 1960 catalog description of the EB-0; it almost looks like a long-scale from this view.

(Left) An original 1959 EB-0 (Les Paul bass!) in nice shape with its warmly-faded cherry finish. *Courtesy Guitar Resurrection, January 1975*

A rather large, single-ply pickguard covered the lower portion of the body—even though most of the playing was done on the topside! Expensive (according to the *Gazette*) Kluson "Waverly"-style banjo tuning pegs adorned the headstock into 1960, when the standard big-keyed nickel Klusons arrived. The banjo pegs were somewhat difficult to negotiate, with their heavy tension and the particular ratios used. Original cast-style, fixed-stud combination bridge/tailpiece with small screws for relative intonation was standard. One bass found has an early version of the adjustable bridge and separate anchor bar seen on the later Thunderbird series. They were even shipped with "flat-wound strings to insure smooth fingering and natural bass quality." During 1959, 123 were built, while 342 were shipped in 1960. One fun bass!

Prices for the new models began at $120, and $132.50 for the Junior and TV models. The Special was $179.50 when it premiered in 1959. EB-0 models were "priced at only $180," with the 127 Durabilt case for $19.50. Of course, "prices slightly higher west of the Rockies" was always the situation. Cases were available with either the 535 pink-plush hard-shells for the Specials at $42, or the lightweight Durabilt 115 brown imitation alligator cases for $13.50.

Here's a 1960 EB-0 (#0 0480) with the Sidewinder humbucking pickup, set by the neck for booming solid-body tones. Note the Kluson banjo peg geared tuning machines with opal buttons. *Courtesy Ken Collins, 2003*

Melody Makers

Last but not least, the "All NEW Les Paul Melody Maker." Yes, the little 1959 Melody Maker was actually a Les Paul model in the very beginning (according to an early *Gazette*). This wonderful little economy student guitar came in both ¾-sized (22 ¾"-scale) and soon after, full-sized models. The smaller version's neck joined at the 12th fret, while the normal-sized one joined at the 16th. Dual-pickup MM-D versions were announced in late 1959 and shipped in 1960.

Basically, these guitars were thin-line, single-cut Les Paul Juniors that measured 1 ⅜" thick with a ⅞" Skylark single-coil steel guitar pickup. During 1960, a smaller ⅝" nylon-coiled pickup was used. Its large, thick pickguard incorporated the controls and either pickup configuration, much like Fender's easy component construction. The old-style Junior finish with dark brown to bright yellow (with a red grain filler) sunburst top was resurrected as well. The most notable visual difference was the narrow, straight-lined 2 ¼" headstock, which remained a characteristic of this model through its various 1960s double-cutaway versions. The Melody Maker never had the silk-screened signature, since its name was on the pickguard near the neck. Gibson dropped the advertised "Les Paul" moniker when it hit the catalog in 1960. They were soon available in double-pickup models for the more adventurous young player.

All NEW Les Paul Melody Maker

- Solid mahogany body with graceful cutaway
- Slim, short neck and short scale for easy playing
- Mahogany neck, adjustable truss rod
- Powerful pickup near bridge with separate tone and volume controls
- Rosewood fingerboard with pearl dot inlays
- Combination bridge and tailpiece
- Sunburst finish
- 12¾" wide, 17¼" long, 1⅜" thin
- 22¾" scale, 19 frets

Everyone's excited about the Melody Maker — players, teachers, students! They're impressed with its fine sound, big tone, sensitive pickup, feather-light touch, and beautiful finish. "Finest electric guitar I've seen for the young player," say teachers. A ¾ guitar especially for students and those with small hands, its short neck joins the body at the 12th fret, bringing the complete fingerboard within comfortable reach. Small in size, big in quality and value! Also available in standard scale with neck joining body at 16th fret Only $89.50.

No. 114 Durabilt case $10.00

(Above) Here's a solid-body cutie! The original 1959 Melody Maker ¾ (Les Paul MM) has a real kinship with the discontinued Junior single-cutaway, sans the narrow headstock. Guitar courtesy of Steve Soest, October, 1975.

(Left) "Finest guitar I've seen for the young player," says the teacher in this *Gazette* ad for the original Les Paul Melody Maker. It was a ¾-sized instrument with a 23 ½" scale length, nineteen frets, and was a very thin 1 ⅜" thick... essentially, a miniature Les Paul Junior, for all intents and purposes.

Its cost was only $89.50, and $10 for the 114 Durabilt soft case. With Gibson's famous construction standards, these students had a fabulous neck and great tone for next-to-nothing. "Small in size, big in quality and value!" Only the Les Paul Junior model outsold it, with 1,397 full-sized and 1,676 ³/₄-sized Melody Maker models in 1959; and in 1960, 2,430 and 424, respectively. In late 1961, a symmetrical double-cutaway version was introduced with the same 16th-fret neck-heel access. Subsequent cherry-finished versions in 1965 had a slightly pointed body shape with better neck access—before Gibson adopted the sculptured SG body shape in 1966. It was a high-volume, budget guitar that started off a whole generation of players who, it was hoped, would buy other Les Paul models.

MELODY MAKER
MELODY MAKER 3/4

Greatest value ever in a Solid Body electric with full-size neck and scale length. Acclaimed by players, teachers and students for its fine sound, big tone, sensitive pickup, feather-light touch, and beautiful sunburst finish. Expert workmanship and finest materials are used throughout to produce this top quality low-priced instrument. Nickel-plated metal parts. Cutaway style. Leather strap included.
Available also with three-quarter size neck and fingerboard that joins the body at the 12th fret.

• Slim, fast, low-action neck—with exclusive extra low frets, joins body at the 16th fret
• One-piece mahogany neck, adjustable truss rod
• Graceful, cutaway design
• Rosewood fingerboard, pearl dot inlays
• Combination bridge and tailpiece, adjustable horizontally and vertically
• Powerful pickup near bridge with individually adjustable polepieces
• Separate tone and volume controls

12¾" wide, 17¼" long, 1⅜" thin . . . 24¾" scale, 22 frets

Melody Maker Sunburst finish

114 Durabilt case
Melody Maker D with two pickups

Melody Maker ¾ Sunburst finish

114¾ Durabilt case

(Above) A clean 1963 Melody Maker double-pickup version with a Maestro vibrola. *Courtesy Don Underwood, Riverside, July 1974*

(Left) By the time the 1960 catalog came along, the Les Paul name had been dropped from this model, which was now a full-sized instrument with an optional MM-D double-pickup version.

Two single-pickup Melody Makers from 1960 and 1962 with the thinner pickups, May 1973.

The Sunburst Les Paul Standard Models '58–'60

The Sunburst Les Paul Standard Models '58–'60

"A beautiful red cherry sunburst finish is the news here! This guitar now has a rich, rubbed appearance that cannot be equaled at any price, and the new look that is tops with today's guitarist! If the illustration above were in color, you would see exactly what we mean—this instrument is a true beauty. In the future, all Les Paul guitars will be shipped in cherry sunburst finish. There will be no increase in price." (Gibson *Gazette*, 1958, announcement for the new sunburst Les Paul.)

First introduced in August of 1958, the eye-catching, cherry-red sunburst Les Paul was a wonderful new addition to the already impressive Gibson solid-body lineup. The company had finished the first officially designated "sunburst" on July 31, and presented it at the summer trade show to observe the reaction. And as the sales of the 1957 and '58 Goldtops had slowed considerably, Gibson thought that they might be able to pick up the pace by applying the traditional sunburst finish to the instruments that previously featured a concealed maple top… only this time, the sunburst would be in a gleaming cherry red!

As previously mentioned, in 1950–51, Gibson had originally made a few sunburst prototypes, as well as having built a few special-ordered Cremona-shaded Standards (Les Paul Regulars) throughout the years. They experimented with a solid, bright cherry-red in early 1958. This red stain was concurrently introduced on the lesser expensive Junior model; the stunning sunburst finish over the attractive light maple really stood out. This new color scheme on the Les Paul guitar, with its fancy, curly (figured) maple top and cream-colored plastic, was quite the eye candy! To complement the sunburst top, the mahogany back and neck was finished with a deep cherry-red stain.

A gorgeous deep red 1958 Les Paul Standard #8 6761 with a nice, curly maple top in a Stone 535 case. This was bought from GTR Guitars in 1973 for market value of $1,400 by Ralph Perry. Full cream ES-175 pickups were added. Note the original deep red finish on these 1958 guitars. *Courtesy Ralph Perry, La Jolla, 1975*

(Right) Early '58 sunburst Standard with 1958 Bassman combo. This tonal combination didn't get any better for a few years. My first "Sunburst" Les Paul experience was with this very guitar. *Courtesy Mike Duerr and Paul Cowie, 1971*

(Below) This 1958 Gibson *Gazette* made one of the most important announcements of the twentieth century: "Exciting changes in Les Paul Models." With great pride, Gibson introduced the Les Paul Standard guitar in cherry-red sunburst. It was an inevitable move from the gold since the beautiful maple tops were generally always covered up. Gibson was known for their wonderful sunburst finishes, and this one was shaded a gleaming cherry. As with the introduction of their Lloyd Loar Master 5 models and superb Mastertone banjos, they were a little slow to get it in gear... but better late than never! For just over two years, Gibson produced this true gem of the solid-body guitar world, and this simple flyer gave us the heads-up in 1958.

LES PAUL GUITAR IN CHERRY RED

A beautiful red cherry sunburst finish is the news here! This guitar now has a rich, rubbed appearance that cannot be equalled at any price, and the 'new look' that is tops with today's guitarists. If the illustration above were in color, you would see exactly what we mean — this instrument is a true beauty. In the future all Les Paul guitars will be shipped in cherry sunburst finish — there will be no increase in price.

All other features of this wonderful guitar will remain exactly the same. Two, powerful humbucking pickups give the instrument increased sustain and a clear sparkling tone. Any guitarist will appreciate the wide range of tonal colorings produced by the Les Paul. Tune-O-Matic bridge permits adjusting string action and individual string lengths for perfect intonation. Graceful cutaway design with attractive inlaid rosewood fingerboard. Separate tone and volume controls for each pickup that can be

Werlein's for Music down in New Orleans staged a big extravaganza late in June, — invited Les Paul and Mary Ford to demonstrate Gibsons for the folks in the deep south. Over 500 people were present at the two hour show given by Les and Mary. Parham Werlein was so pleased with their playing he went to hear more of same at the Roosevelt Hotel where Les and Mary also appeared.

(Above) This *Gazette* issue has the only known picture of Les Paul playing an original sunburst Standard while they were in production. He and Mary were performing in June of 1959 at Werlein's music store in New Orleans, Louisiana for a crowd of 500 people. Mary is playing a new double-cut Special, and Les is picking on a Standard with a hang-tag on it! Surprisingly, Les never did receive an original sunburst Standard back then.

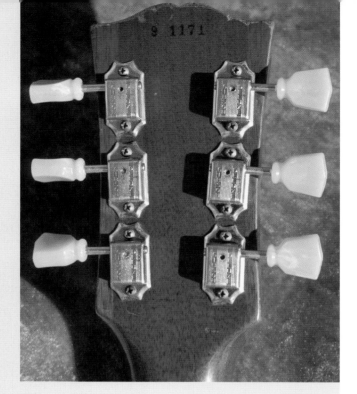

Maple Revealed

The final icing on the cake was the gorgeous, figured maple "chatoyant" (having a changeable iridescent luster or color with an undulating narrow band of white light; such as a gem) effect, which featured so many unique and individual patterns. Many were quite beautifully flamed with varying degrees of fiddle-back ribbon, large tiger stripes, curly bird's-eye maple, and even combinations thereof. Not all late-'50s Standards were figured, however, as the supply wasn't always consistent (and, therefore, curly maple was not specified in Gibson's advertising literature). Most of the Gibson guitars that featured maple construction had nice figuring, and the new Les Paul generally had some. But others were spectacular!

The two-piece, "book-matching" effect that was used was accomplished by cutting the quarter-sawn maple in half and opening it like a book—which gave it its symmetry on both sides. Sometimes the same piece of book-matched maple would go from quarter-sawn to half-sawn graining depending upon the particular area of the tree that was cut (which is why it can be quite flamed in one

(Above) Billy with Pearly in action! This picture is from their concert later that night. It shows a hard-working musician paying his dues, Texas style.

(Facing Page and Above) This is certainly one of the most visible Les Paul Standards. It's been on tour for many years with that lil' ol' band from Texas... namely ZZ Top. Here is Billy "the Reverend" Gibbons's favorite '59 Gibson #9 1171, nicknamed "Pearly Gates" after his 1936 Packard that paid for the guitar. This tightly figured top Les Paul has one of the nicest, beautifully deep tobacco-shaded finishes. Billy let this author take the instrument outside after a sound check for this photo session back in 1974. As evident in these series of pictures, Pearly was in near mint condition and didn't have any wear on the back. Tone-wise this expressive guitar is all anyone could ever ask for in a great Les Paul, an integral part of Billy's soul, which generates that absolutely great tone they are famous for... heavenly! *Courtesy Billy Gibbons, 1974*

> "'Pearly Gates,' a fine example of the famed Les Paul Standard Sunburst from 1959, possesses the mysterious qualities that highlight the fiercely attractive power of the design...makes this one of the wicked ones!"
>
> —Billy F. Gibbons

spot and somewhat plain elsewhere). Not all tops were fancy wood patterns however. While many were downright plain, others were quite dramatic, and appeared to have a 3-D reflective effect, as though you could look deep into the wood. Because of the chatoyant effect, in the right light, the most spectacular of these would virtually "trip the light fantastic!" No wonder they are the crown of Gibson solid-bodies.

Mostly sugar maple (*Acer saccharum*; also called rock maple or hard maple) was utilized to ensure the solid tonality of the instrument. Some silver (*Acer saccharinum*) and red rum (*Acer rubrum*) maples were occasionally used, too. These light-colored, smooth-textured hardwoods took the traditional Gibson nitrocellulose finish quite well.

The following is from my interview with Ted McCarty:

RL: Could you tell me about when you were picking out these different kinds of woods?

TM: See, mahogany you buy from an importer. Mahogany is a very stable wood and a hard wood. It takes a finish very beautifully and it machines well. So we had always used mahogany for the backs and sides of flattops, and for the Les Pauls. Maple you have to hunt and hunt for. You buy it wherever you find it because curly maple is one of those things that nobody seems to know ahead of time that it's going to be curly. This is your fiddle-back maple for various things.

Mr. Huis and I made a study with the Forestry Department of the Michigan State University on curly maple. Their man, a fellow by the name of Stump, became a forestry man. He and I and John Huis, to the best of my knowledge, are the only three people alive who can look at a maple tree and tell you whether it's curly or not before you cut it down. It's the bark. We used to go over to Michigan State; they have a big forest there and a good deal of it maple. We would stand back with a pair of binoculars and look at the pile and say the third one down from the left is curly. We were too far away to see whether it was curly or not, and then have somebody over there pick it out and it would be curly maple. And we even went up to… they have a big forest up near the Sioux… and picked a hundred standing trees, which they were going to forest. They agreed—they have a sawmill there in East Lansing, part of the University. They were willing to work with us, and they cut those trees, brought them down here, and logged them. And out of a hundred trees we had 99 of them that were curly maple. The question is, is the curly maple a species? Is it a sport? What causes it? Why? And you don't find a grove of them—you find a tree here and a tree there.

RL: What about the quilted maple effect? Can you tell that from the bark?

TM: The quilted maple is basically a similar type of thing, but it grows in a different part of the country. You don't get any quilted maple that I know of around Michigan.

RL: Where do you get it?

TM: Oregon; the state of Washington. We never would buy it. We used to stay away from it. At times, we could have bought whole carloads of it when we were dying for this kind of [fiddle-back] maple, and our sales department wouldn't even attempt to sell a guitar made out of quilted maple. It wasn't traditional.

RL: My '37 L-5 had very quilted maple wood, but that was a pre-war instrument.

TM: They made some of them. That's a beautiful piece of curly maple. But it's that bark formation; that's why we took the picture of it (pointing to the '39 catalog cover).

RL: What would be the difference between that and a flame maple?

TM: That is a flame. It's just a different name. It depends on how you cut it, too. If you cut it across this way, flat-saw it, you're going to have a different figure in the maple than if you quarter it. It's a very interesting thing. Wood in itself is a study—a study all by itself. I think that Rollo Werner, purchasing agent at Gibson, is probably as knowledgeable on woods as almost anybody you'll find. He learned it there from some of the old-time boys. And old fellows like Ed Rosenburger… he was still working there when he was in his seventies. Wood is a very peculiar thing you have to know.

This 1959 Les Paul model has a wonderful, tight flamed fiddle-back maple top. Over the years, many amber-colored switch-tip knobs would crack or break off from bouncing around in the case. *Guitar courtesy of the late Jimmy Parks, 1973*

Solid-Body Sonics

The true sonic magic of the late-1950s Les Paul model—affectionately know as the "Burst"—emanates from its many important attributes: first of all, its incredible acoustical tonality is derived from its combined construction of well-seasoned tone woods. The resonant Honduras mahogany neck and body, coupled with its ⅜" carved maple top, give the instrument a unique singing quality with an incredible sustaining power—the notes truly sing out and chime. The two woods, married as such, produce a full mid-range with a shimmering, upper harmonic. Natural variations occurred with denser woods, which gave the instrument more sustain, while lighter versions were very open and resonant. The actual seasoning, or aging, effect is created when the wood's natural fluids slowly evaporate in its arteries, giving it an aerated effect, while at the same time lightening it and giving it a more lively resonance. Whether used for recordings or live performance, no other solid-body guitar has such a vibrant, rich, deep, and full-bodied sound—truly another great Gibson tone machine!

> "Those old ones were fine instruments," states Ted. "They had more sustain than any solid-body that has ever been built since then."

This rare Gibson "action" tag says the instrument is set up for "light pick" action, and to raise the action for a harder stroke.

Professionals Attention

This guitar has been adjusted for professional usage (light pick action) which enables the guitarist to fully develop and use his technique. If you use a hard stroke and do not wish to change to a light pick action, raise the bridge slightly to eliminate string rattle. We advise the use of Gibson hi-fi strings for low action settings.

Gibson, Inc.

This big tone is especially noticeable in the studio, where it can be easily captured and appreciated with a substantial amplifier. All those acoustical properties, coupled with their trusty "Patent Applied For" humbucking pickups, add a smooth and powerful electric sound to complete its overall tone. Some speculate that perhaps the lack of the heavier, metallic, brass-finished top also gave these instruments a slightly different and more open tone than the earlier humbucker-equipped Les Paul Goldtop versions. (Inspired by an essay by Bernard Ayling.)

(Above) Les Paul Standard #9 2340. Owner Bernard Ayling (ex-Guitar Trader employee) expounds the complex and majestic tonalities of the "Burst" and equates it to the solid-body "Stradivarius" of our times. How true!

Electronics

Sunburst Standards maintained the tried-and-true, four-control, and three-way switching setup. CentraLab 500K potentiometers continued to be the featured volume and tone controls, with some occasional 250K tone pots. Sprague's .022 400V "Bumble Bee" was still the capacitor of choice. However, during early 1960, Gibson ran out of the Bumble Bees and substituted white Astron caps before resuming with the Sprague's new, red-banded "Black Beauty" caps. Two ground wires were used to connect the stud inserts; one went from the control cavity through a small drilled hole to one knurled insert, while the other came off the lead pickup's braided shield straight to the other stud. Evidently, two connections were more effective to thoroughly ground the instrument with the nickel-plated aluminum stop tailpiece.

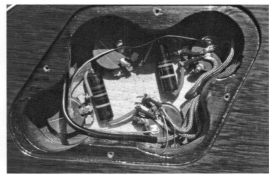

Original wiring components with the contemporary CentraLab pots and color-coded Sprague "Bumble Bee" caps (that look like big resistors).

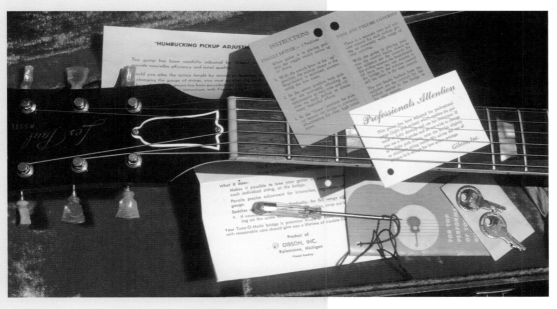

(Left) The "case candy" shown here is original to this guitar.

221

PAF City

The Holy Grail of pickups, the "PAF" (Patent Applied For) humbuckings, are exceptionally smooth-sounding. Quite a mystique surrounded these famous pickups. Coupled with an already superior-sounding guitar, these awesome pickups created a majestic tone with ample amplification: i.e., a high-powered 5F8 Fender Twin of the day, or a mid-1960s Marshall JTM-45. Imagine the first electrifying moment, when plugging a Les Paul Standard into a Fender tweed Bassman or Bandmaster, and turning up towards full volume!

Most PAF humbuckings have a warm tone that is very desirable. Over these years, some of these pickups varied according to how even or mismatched its two coils were wrapped. A pickup that included one coil that was over- or under-wound would produce a brighter-sounding tonality—often a plus if on a heavier- or richer-sounding instrument. Once Gibson started with the Alnico V magnets in 1960, the resulting extra strength gave even more output and high-end (and as such, players will often back off the volume slightly in order to get less over-modulation for a cleaner sound).

A few British players, including Eric Clapton, Jeff Beck, and Alvin Lee, started taking their electrostatic nickel covers off their PAF pickups. They and many others were exposing the twin bobbins and to get a brighter, grittier tone. Besides using the standard, black, molded bobbins, a light plastic was soon introduced. Seth Lover elaborated:

RL: *Were you aware that they [Gibson] were using ivory plastic for some of the humbucking pickups around 1959?*

SL: *No, but it wouldn't surprise me, because every once in a while, they would bring out a change of the color of the plastic… which didn't mean too much.*

The M-69 cream pickup surrounds have an "MR 490" designation with a "7" for the taller rear, while neck bezels read "MR 491" and "8." Many Les Pauls were shipped with the rhythm pickup's narrower pole spacing.

Gibson began incorporating molded cream-colored coils during late 1958—a trend that lasted into early 1961. Most often, when both coils are cream-colored, they're called "double whites" or "full-cream pickups" (and in Memphis, good ol' "crème coals"). Sometimes, pickups had both colors, resulting in the popular coil monikers "half white" or "Zebra" coils. Because of the rarity of cream coils and their attractive matching color scheme, they have become very desirable and valuable to collectors. Speculation that the lighter material vibrates the tone differently always comes up in vintage guitar circles.

(Below) Close-up of the full cream PAF and rhythm pickup's back side showing brass screws and the "PAF" decal. Many covers have been unsoldered looking for the sacred cream coils. Cream surrounds will often absorb the cherry finish in the neck position. Also note how some decals have double image lettering.

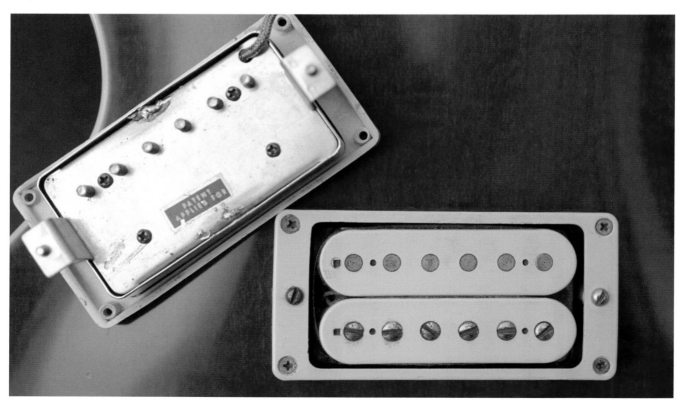

Walt Fuller adds:

RL: *Did any of the specifications change on any of those pickups through the '50s?*

WF: *Some of these things get started… for instance, the original coil forms on the Les Pauls are made of black kenic, and the people who were molding them ran out of black material. So they asked us if they could make some out of cream; and it didn't make any difference to us because they are all covered up. But the molders don't like to run cream because it means that they have to clean their machines each time, because there's always some black residue left in there. So, the first coil forms that came out were kind of cloudy and mixed, you know, with black material, so they don't like to change back and forth. But in order to keep us going, why, they run coil forms out of cream and…*

RL: *This is during the late '50s. Even during the early '60s.*

WF: *Yes… well, it's even happened several times through the years. Actually, the myth got started that the cream ones sounded better than the black ones… and they're exactly the same.*

RL: *Of course they are! Some people think they sound different because they are a different density. It probably doesn't make any difference at all. I found through the years that the pickups take on a different characteristic of tonality [not because the specifications changed that much; it seems as though the suppliers of the raw materials changed].*

WF: *Well, I think if you take and play the instruments unamplified, you would find the same characteristic differences are there. The more you play a variety, the easier it is to play, the more responsive it gets.*

RL: *True. You become more accustomed to the instrument.*

This 1959 Standard retains it deep cherry coloration. Guitar courtesy of Mike Slubowski. *Photographed by Steve Pitkin*

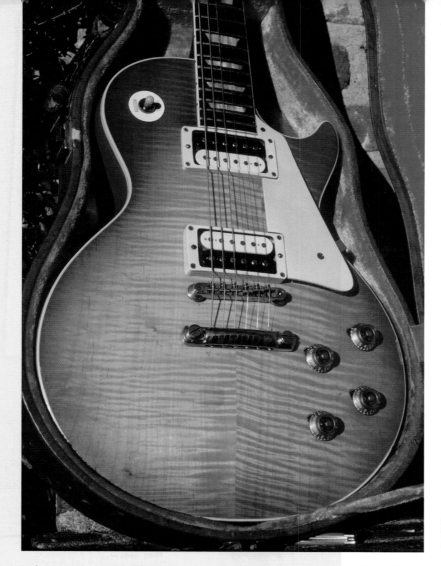

(Left) A true fiddle-back, flame-maple top graces this warmly lite, beautiful 1959 Standard. *Courtesy of the Bergen Brothers, Oakland, January 1975.*

(Left Page) The spectacular "Main Squeeze" Les Paul Standard #9 0597 with great tiger flame maple. An all-time favorite photographed at one of the first Texas Guitar shows. *From the collection of John Clardy*

(Below) Another Texas knockout! Les Paul Standard #9 0905 shot at the same show over by the pool. Great flame-maple with some good color left. Definitely a keeper! *Courtesy Jimmy Wallace*

Definitely one of the more favored guitars of Sunburst Les Paul aficionados, this wonderful instrument (#9 1876) has flame-maple with real charisma! The real story goes… "One day I woke up with a letter and picture of this guitar from Dave Dingus who read my '73 "Rarebird" column in *GP* magazine. Was I still dreaming? It was definitely a dream come true! He was less than five miles from my home, so I called and went right over to OB, California. Dave was interested in trading it for a Gibson jazz guitar… so I located an ES-295 from Steve Soest, and we went over to trade plus some money and a Pignose amp. He had accidentally left it near a furnace and showed us where the blisters were by the input jack. Otherwise this lightweight guitar was a great Les Paul… even with its big neck. A number of our friends had the pleasure of owning it, including Steve, Phil Pierangelo, Paul Cowie, and Peter Criscoulo. Then we sold it to Paul Stanley of Kiss, and it eventually ended up on the cover of another fine book." The "Dingus" 1959 Les Paul Standard has very deep chatoyant curly maple with subtle shading that creates an overall flaming butterscotch effect. *Courtesy Paul Cowie and the late Peter Criscoulo, October 1975*

Finishing

To begin with, the original Les Paul Goldtop models used a "natural filler" paste on the mahogany. It came straight out of the can with a light brownish-yellow tint, and was used for filling the light-colored mahogany instruments. Later Goldtop and Junior models used a walnut-colored filler with a darker brown stain added. The back of the new Les Paul Sunburst, Special, and Junior models were covered with a special "Les Paul cherry" filler stain, which was basically a wash that was rubbed into the grain. A special organic substance called "tow" was used exclusively to wipe the excess material off the porous mahogany.

Past Gibson employee Aaron Porter, who began at Gibson in 1962 and did final assembly, was kind enough to share his knowledge of the finishing procedures and furnish the following information. Back in the early 1960s, Aaron asked Gibson's best finish man all about the early finishing processes:

"First off, the mahogany grain was filled with a natural filler. Mahogany is always filled. What they call a 'filler' is like a paste. The 'natural' was just light brown like you see on a Les Paul Goldtop. There was a stain mixed in with it. It's called a 'filler stain.' Then they had a red stain that they put on the later Les Pauls. The filler went on the mahogany and it would dry to a haze, and then they would wipe the excess off with tow and let it dry overnight. We used the tow just to soak up most of it. They would go across the grain when they wiped it off so you wouldn't wipe it out of the grain. 'Tow sack' is like a cotton material that comes out of a plant [a short or broken fiber, as of flax or hemp, that is used especially for yarn, twine, or stuffing]. It's kind of like a burlap but real coarse. Gibson used it because it was cheap and you could throw it away. They would wipe the excess off with most of that. Then they would take a rag and would wipe it until it was smooth, let it dry, and then start putting sealer over it—clear and everything else. A sealer was put on before they started with the heavy lacquer, just to let it lock up, because that sealer penetrates the wood more and it kind of makes the lacquer stick better."

When the new 1958 cherry-finished Les Paul models were first developed, the sprayers became quite creative with their guitar-finishing artistry. The red filler was most often augmented with extra shadings of cherry-red lacquer coats along the edges, neck joint, and headstock—similar to the earlier walnut side and neck shading. This was necessary to even the blending, due to the different absorptions of the filler stain. Aaron elaborates:

"They would over-shade a back that was red, too. You get up around the neck or somewhere where it didn't look dark enough or didn't match. Now the filler and red stain on the rims and end grain is going to look a lot darker. And on the side, it doesn't go into the grain as much and looks lighter. So they might over-shade it and blend it to look the same color all around the rim. You can do a lot with a lacquer gun."

Gibson had a special department where the red filler was applied. Aaron adds, "They had a sign in there labeled 'Les Paul Red' on the big container. But it was just red—it was brighter; more of a bright red than the modern ones." These beautiful red-colored aniline dyes are derived from the indigo plant, and are used chiefly in organic synthesis for dyes. Certain ones were more prone to fading than others, which soon became apparent in the sun's ultraviolet rays; as the cherry finish fades to a lighter orange color over the years, you can see small pockets of red filler stain still deep in the grain.

(Above) The cutaway always shows a portion of the maple top between the mahogany and binding. The deep cherry filler highlights the mahogany's pores for a rich and contrasting finish.

(Below) Superlative fiddle-back flame-maple sets this early 1959 Standard into the full eye candy department. This special guitar was at the Mill Valley Prune Music guitar show in its original box. *Courtesy Kosta Kovachek, 1975*

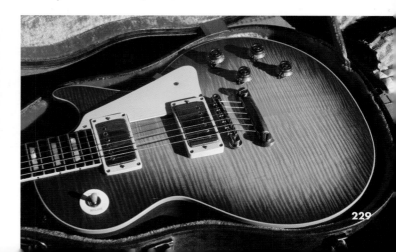

229

Cherry Sunburst Finish

The illustrious cherry-sunburst finish is another story entirely. There were variations in colored dye supplied throughout the years, and some painters mixed their own favorite colors. This led to a wide variety of hues and fading characteristics that made up the Les Paul sunburst palette. Carl Kopp was the main Gibson sprayer during this golden solid-body era. His many years of "sunbursting" expertise is an art we admire and cherish today.

After much meticulous inspection and cleaning in the white (unfinished) wood room, the guitars were prepped for Gibson's famous lustrous sunburst effect. The maple tops were first sprayed yellow over the sanded sealer coats. Then the graduated cherry shading was "bursted" around the edges. Clear coats followed to seal the colors in. As with other Gibson guitars, darker shading also occurred to cover up wood imperfections.

Examples of bright cherry-red colors were done in all three years, as on the cover's 1958 guitar. 1959 saw a variety of colors, including the standard ES-175 Cremona finish, often miscalled "tobacco" burst. Other '58s and '59s sometimes had a ruby or purplish merlot-wine tinge to them.

Cleaning line—all instruments are cleaned before spraying.

White (unfinished) wood inspection and final cleaning.

Carl Kopp.—Spraying on that famous Gibson finish.

Final assembly and inspection.

(Above) A time machine look into Gibson's 1959 factory where the final cleaning takes place in the white wood room before the lacquers are sprayed by Carl Kopp in the finishing department. This is where the final magic happens… the application of the variations of sunburst finishes. After they cure and get color-sanded, the instruments head to the final setup room shown here. Then they come to life… brand spanking new!

(Left) The dark cherry-bursting with good coloration, full-cream pickups, a Bigsby tailpiece, and moderate, fine flame-maple give this Les Paul Standard #9 2794 guitar a unique flavor all its own. *Courtesy Bill Stapleton, January 1975*

(Above) Here is John Clardy's "darkburst" 1959 Standard with an apparent "Bigsby beard" cherry coloring left over. Full-cream PAFs complete this "Texas" special. Thanks, John.

One favorite color is the beautiful "darkburst." As the story goes, a sprayer who normally did archtops didn't particularly favor the Standard's new cherry-bursting, and added the traditional dark brown to the final cherry-shaded combination. Thinking that that was a more proper Gibson color scheme, he conveniently used up leftover brown paint (before having to return to the specified routine). When not too faded, the darkburst finish left a distinctive inner red-burst that blended nicely into yellow. This unique artistic detour in late 1958 and 1959 created a deep combination rarely seen.

For the most part, the official color was cherry sunburst. In actuality, it was a new color-scheme departure for Gibson that was initiated in the late 1950s. Some beautiful cherry-bursts were very dark red on the outside edges. (Many I've known over the years have actually faded since these pictures were taken. Color photography and the printing process often misrepresent the way the finishes really looked. Many are still cherry-red when viewed in person, compared to the flat, faded images on the printed page. Depending on the type of light source, amount of exposure, and particular angled view, subtle variations in the colors and figuring occur with photography.)

(Left) Here is an all-around, really nice sunburst Les Paul with strong cherry color and excellent flame maple... the epitome of a sunburst Standard.

(Above) Wonderful shot of Duane Allman playing his favorite Les Paul, which he named "Hot 'Lanta," with its signature flame-maple top. *Photo by Michael Dobo/Getty Images*

(Right) Twiggs Lyndon proudly displaying his Les Paul, which was previously owned by Duane Allman, circa 1977. He told the story about trading a car to Greg Allman and how the famous "Duane" frets ended up on the back. Kurt Linhoff and Christopher Cross were originally instrumental in Duane getting this historic instrument. Years after this photo session, Steve Morse said he kept the guitar sealed in his studio wall until Duane's daughter was old enough to inherit it.

(Right Facing Page) Presenting one of the most famous and beautiful sunburst Les Paul Standards of all time... Duane Allman ("Skydog") named this guitar "Hot 'Lanta." I had the great pleasure of photographing it with Twiggs Lyndon (past guitar tech for the Allman Brothers Band). It needed some neck restoration during a 1977 Dixie Dregs session. The rare dark sunburst coloring was put over the dramatic "seagull wing" flame-maple top. This instrument recorded some great timeless songs with the famous Allman Brothers Band and on Eric Clapton's *Layla* album. Gibson Custom Shop's Edwin Wilson and Tom Murphy did a special reissue of this historic instrument in 2003. A true Holy Grail Les Paul Sunburst of our music age.

Many sunburst Standards exposed to sunlight over the years have completely faded to yellow—which is also attractive today. Most cherry colors faded easily, so Gibson even had a "Mr. Dealer" card reminding dealers and customers to keep their instruments out of direct sunlight. Many have turned to attractive "honey" colors (caramel, ice tea, etc.), and even greenish/gray hues. Under the pickguard, pickup surrounds and switch rings in the original cherry color can most often be seen.

Mr. Dealer:

In order to preserve the delicate coloring of this beautiful Gibson instrument, avoid displaying in show windows where it will be subjected to direct or excessive sunrays.

(Above) Gibson soon discovered that their red colors would fade if subject to long sun exposure in storefronts, so they sent these "Mr. Dealer" cards out with the Les Paul Standards of the late fifties to remind dealers to spare the instrument from direct sunlight displays. This is the last and most expensive collectible accouterment for your real Burst.

Les Paul Standard #9 2308 formerly owned by Peter Green and Gary Moore. This is the instrument Peter used with John Mayall and with his Fleetwood Mac group. He later gave lessons to Gary Moore whom he sold the guitar to for a very reasonable price. Today it's one of the most valuable celebrity guitars in the world.

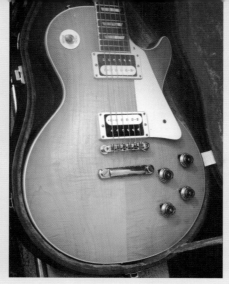

(Above) A typically faded-to-almost-green 1959 Les Paul Standard with factory Bigsby (with original pearl dot inserts) and half-white PAFs.

(Above) Faded sunbursts take on a beauty all their own, even without much maple figuring. The half-white, inside-coil exposed pickups add a nice flavor to this all-original Les Paul Standard (January 1986).

(Above) The $125 Burst! This faded beauty #9 3177 was bought from an overseas Navy man's local wife who needed groceries! Note the "California Girl" Lifton case with a larger upper bout and original red color around the toggle switch. *Courtesy Jim Young, 1974*

(Above) A very greenish, faded 1959 Standard with (half from this angle) tight flamey top.

(Above) A beautiful LP Standard #9 0643. *Instrument and photo courtesy Billy Straus*

(Below) This is an early Les Paul Standard in our camp. It was traded straight across for a very nice gold P-90 LP model after Memphis's Mike Moffitt woke up on the wrong side of the bed! My bandmate Michael Sterling was the proud owner until his 1959 Flying V was discovered flying on wires (like the Gazette display) in a Palm Desert music store. Local San Diegan guitar and blues advocate Paul Cowie then let this lightweight, faded flame-top #9 0639 go to our brother Bobby Z in 1971. And it's still in the family! *Courtesy Robert Zinner*

(Below and Right) Keith Richards' original Les Paul Standard #9 3182 with Bigsby tailpiece (and added Grover machines) shows its fine quarter-sawn ribbon maple and lightly faded coloration. The Rolling Stones' rise to popularity in 1964 with Keith playing this guitar exposed many young musicians to the Sunburst Les Paul's beauty and tonalities world-wide. *Presented here courtesy of Symbolic Motor Cars of La Jolla, CA*

(Above) An unusually deep-orange colored center hue characterizes this highly flamed 1960 Standard with full cream humbuckings. *Courtesy Mac Yasuda*

(Above) A nice faded '59 Standard #9 0897 with attractive figuring. It shows some local checking from playing use. *Courtesy Albert Molinaro, 2005*

A striking 1959 Standard dubbed the "Sunset Burst" with its rippled cloud-like chatoyancy and coloration. *Guitar courtesy Byron Goad*

(Below) This 1959 Standard darkburst reveals that its red has faded, but still retains a dark-brown coloring. Note the Stone Company emblem at the somewhat squared end of the case. Photographed in a Bavarian garden. *Courtesy Alfonse Baumann, July 1985*

(Above and Below) This well-figured, somewhat faded Les Paul was brought to the Santa Monica Civic 4 Amigos guitar show in 1995. It is the only original Standard I've seen without a serial number!! *Courtesy Louis "Uncle Lou" Gatanas*

One of the earliest 1960 Standards #0 0608, which carried over the same characteristics of the '59 models with a medium-sized neck. This gem was owned by Michael DeTemple for many years, and ended up in the Chinery collection. It is also another book-cover guitar, and is shown here with lots of added case candy. *Courtesy David Swartz, 2004*

Early 1960 versions continued with 1959's fade-prone colors until the improved dye of the "tangerine" red was introduced soon afterward. These new versions held their red color quite well, but developed a definite orangey hue to them as they faded. Some were very bright red during the last production runs.

An early 1960 Standard #0 3191 posed with an indoor skylight. *Courtesy Bill Feil, Malibu, 2005*

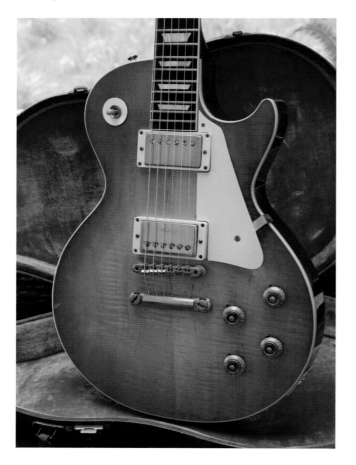

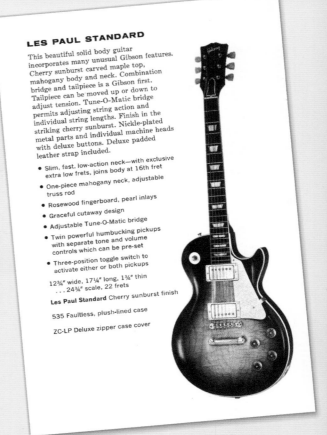

LES PAUL STANDARD

This beautiful solid body guitar incorporates many unusual Gibson features. Cherry sunburst carved maple top, mahogany body and neck. Combination bridge and tailpiece is a Gibson first. Tailpiece can be moved up or down to adjust tension. Tune-O-Matic bridge permits adjusting string action and individual string lengths. Finish in the striking cherry sunburst. Nickle-plated metal parts and individual machine heads with deluxe buttons. Deluxe padded leather strap included.

- Slim, fast, low-action neck—with exclusive extra low frets, joins body at 16th fret
- One-piece mahogany neck, adjustable truss rod
- Rosewood fingerboard, pearl inlays
- Graceful cutaway design
- Adjustable Tune-O-Matic bridge
- Twin powerful humbucking pickups with separate tone and volume controls which can be pre-set
- Three-position toggle switch to activate either or both pickups

12¾" wide, 17¼" long, 1¾" thin . . . 24¾" scale, 22 frets

Les Paul Standard Cherry sunburst finish

535 Faultless, plush-lined case

ZC-LP Deluxe zipper case cover

(Above) This 1960 catalog depiction shows the Les Paul Standard sunburst during the last year of its production.

(Below) A pair of 1960 flame-tops basking in the Berkeley sunlight. Robbie Dunbar's Standard is on the left, and my "Tiger top" Standard #0 2192 is on the right. Note the tall barrel knobs that were in vogue for us early Burst collectors. After jamming with Humble Pie at the A&M Chaplin soundstage, I let it go to England with "Clem" Clemson. After a British dealer bought and sold it to Rod Stewart's then-guitarist Jim Kriegen, it made it into the first full-color guitar book.

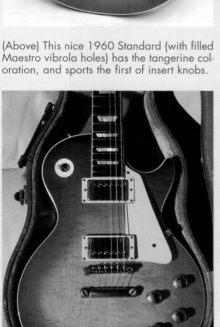

(Above) This nice 1960 Standard (with filled Maestro vibrola holes) has the tangerine coloration, and sports the first of insert knobs.

(Above and Right) Steel guitarist Ed Black (now deceased) treasured this Les Paul Standard #0 9259 for many years until it was unfortunately stolen from his home in Beechwood Canyon, Hollywood. It has the typical late-1960 attributes, but the headstock has the black "Stinger" back (to hide a wood flaw) with yellow numbers. *Courtesy Ed Black*

(Left) This near-mint, late-1960 Standard #0 7168 has a deeper cherry coloration to it. Along with the lettered insert knobs, the Kluson tuners now have the double-collared Keystone grips. *Courtesy Phil Pomeroy, June 1995*

(Below) A stunning 1960 flame-top Standard played by guitarist Paul Warren during the seventies. The exceptionally fine figured maple comes through with a tangerine orange-red coloration on this beautiful instrument. It was professionally re-necked (with the original fingerboard) by Yuris Zeltins after an accident at an SIR rehearsal. *Courtesy Paul Warren, April 1976*

Intrinsic Sunburst Attributes

Whether it's played acoustically, amplified cleanly, or turned up with great natural amplification, you know that these original Les Paul sunbursts mean business. It is definitely the most seriously constructed and beautiful-sounding solid-body guitar produced during Gibson's golden vintage years.

The real magic ingredient is the multitude of years of Gibsonian craftsmanship and loving care put into each instrument; given that, it's then the energy and soul that the player imparts to the instrument. The visual impact of Gibson's traditional Spanish guitar styling with the striking cherry-sunburst, book-matched flame maple—accented with cream-colored plastic, nickel hardware, and golden "bell" knobs—aesthetically add up to a strikingly gorgeous instrument. The cherry-finished back nicely complements the overall effect. The final touch is the mottled-brown leatherette Lifton or Stone Faultless 535 case with the plush magenta or velvety hot-pink lining.

Part of the mystique for the sunburst's high-desire factor is the human, emotive response to its sheer beauty overall. Our brains react physiologically to the visual orientation of the natural symmetry, vivid colors, and, in this instance, the wood's figure patterns. (The brain's "reward circuit pathway" is comprised of the ventral tegmental, nucleus accumbens, and prefrontal cortex—three receptor sites that make a circuit that, when engaged, causes a chemical response that results in feelings of euphoria and other pleasurable emotions.) "It's truly beautiful!" one says as the compelling stimuli permeate the imagination. Different people, of course, have their own definitions of beauty—which accounts for the diversity we all enjoy.

Speaking of which... a sunburst Les Paul is always something truly special to behold. As it sits in its case, gleaming away, simply to look into the guitar's radiant sunburst color-shading over its stunning, curly-maple figuring is a mystical experience all its own—it's like a big piece of delicious exotic fruit waiting to be picked and eaten! Each one has its own character, and is unique in its own way—whether moderately flamed or featuring a deeper variation of Cremona with cherry-shading added.

(Above) Taken with a flash to show the extra flame depth.

(Below) The Burst Extraordinaire #9 2218 affectionately known as "Gladys" by its proud owner Joe Ganzler. *Photo courtesy Martin G. Miller*

Even faded versions consisting of mostly amber-yellow, honeyburst, or a greenish tint still have much character and a distinguished, aged look. All this special magic is culminated in the original Gibson Les Paul "Sunburst" Standard. No wonder it is the most prestigious and expensive electric guitar in the world!

Jim Gentry's beautiful dark burst Standard #9 2312 and the lovely "Carmelita" LP #9 1953 named for its unique shading. *Carmelita photo by Martin Miller, 2005*

Artists

In the heyday of the late '50s Les Paul Standard model, Gibson endorser Al Hendrickson played his custom-ordered, cherry-red Standard in a big band context with Bob Crosby's Bobcats. In Memphis, a 14-year-old guitarist named Travis Wammack bought his Bigsby-equipped 1960 sunburst Standard brand new. He soon recorded two instrumentals, "Firefly" and the 1964 hit "Scratchy." He commented, "When I played it, I just loved the low end on that thing" (quote courtesy of Jeff West-LP Forum). "Scratchy" was a twangy, distortion-laden, sped-up version of "Coming Home Baby" with a bizarre backwards vocal section in the middle. Wammack's fiery style was also fueled with the early use of a light-gauge, plain banjo G string. He went on to do some great session work at Muscle Shoals and to perform with Little Richard. Another popular artist, Johnny Horton of "Battle of New Orleans" and "Sink the Bismarck" fame used a sunburst Standard while they were in production.

(Above) A young Memphis guitarist Travis Wammack playing his 1960 Standard.

During the mid 60s, John Sebastian of the Lovin' Spoonful used his '59 sunburst Standard for their live performances and for recording popular hits. British artists embraced the instrument early on, too. Rolling Stones guitarist Keith Richards made his appearance with one on the TAMI Show filmed at the Santa Monica Civic in Oct. '64. "Satisfaction" was released in June of 1965 and is still one of the greatest rock hits of all time—recorded with his '59 Standard (with Bigsby vibrola) and Gibson Fuzztone. Other guitarists who brought the Gibson Sunburst solid-body into the limelight are presented here in more detail.

Mike Bloomfield: An American Icon of the Electric Blues

Michael Bloomfield was, without a doubt, one of the greatest exponents of American blues music in the rock field. His inspired riffs started many a young and impressionable guitarist off on a greater appreciation of America's true blues roots. Michael had a few different Les Paul guitars through the years, including some early Goldtop models. Here's an excerpt from my filmed interview with Michael that was used for the *Wizard of Waukesha* documentary movie in 1980. Robbie Dunbar graciously brought over his 1960 Standard flame-top to Norman Dayron's home. Michael had these words to share about his experiences with Les Paul Gibson guitars:

(Below) Michael Bloomfield poses here with LP Standard #9 1876 at his home during our interview in Mill Valley, 1974.

(Below) Michael Bloomfield preparing for our *Wizard of Waukesha* film interview in Mill Valley,

MB: *This is a cherry Les Paul sunburst guitar. It's one of the greatest rock 'n' roll guitars ever made, and I've enjoyed playing one for years and years, though it's not the first Les Paul guitar that I've ever played. The first Les Paul guitar that I ever did play was a black "Fretless Wonder" that was given to me by my guitar teacher, a man named Tony Tanaglio in the suburbs of Chicago, in Glenco, Illinois. And for years—about a year preceding the time that I got that guitar—I used to love to pore through Gibson catalogs, and the Les Paul section was my favorite section of the catalog because those were indeed the flashiest guitars.*

Right around the time I was using this I started noticing that in Europe, guitar-players were picking up on this model guitar as well. Keith Richards had played one in the past and Clapton was currently playing one. When the Butterfield Band went to Europe in '66 we noticed—I noticed—that Peter Green was playing a red Les Paul guitar like this sunburst cherry one. And Eric Clapton was playing one, and I wondered to myself, "How did they know that his guitar had all the inherent qualities of sustain volume and tone that was just better than any other possible rock 'n' roll guitar at that time?" They had known, the word had gotten out. They experimented by using and trying the guitars. And so we found ourselves, this little triumvirate or quartet of very influential American lead guitar players all playing the same guitar, never mentioning amongst themselves and saying, "Well, my God, I wish that... this is a good guitar, Eric; maybe you should get one, too. All of us, unbeknownst to us, were playing the same model guitar.

I don't know if this particular guitar is Les's guitar of choice. I've always sort of fantasized that Les Paul, when he would play, that he had the souped-up guitars that were guitars that you just couldn't get then. Like what Chet Atkins had. He would do things to his guitar that just were not on the market.

The 1974 Home Interview

MB: *In Chicago, when I was watching blues guitar-players as a teenager, there was a guy... a few of them that were really excellent, and I noticed their instrumentation. Freddie King and Hubert Sumlin shared in that they both played gold Les Pauls. And there were two kinds of gold Les Pauls differentiated by the tailpieces. There may have been more, but the*

two kinds I knew about were differentiated by the tailpieces. They had cream-color pickups. And one of them had a tailpiece that is like the Les Paul tailpiece that we are all familiar with. And the other one had a tail, you know, a tail to the tailpiece. It came down to the bottom.

RL: *That's the trapeze.*

MB: *That's the trapeze. Now the characteristics that made that gold guitar different from the black Les Paul, from the sunburst Les Paul, definitely different from the Strats and Teles, is that it had a thing that I called "sprounkiness." Sprounkiness is a tone it had. And you especially get the tone on the second pickup [position]. And the tone is a most definable sound if you listen to any of the Freddie King instrumentals that he made that are very famous: "Hideaway," "San Jose"; that sprounky tone is there. Hubert Sumlin is this guitar player who backed up Howling Wolf on dozens of records. He too had this identical tone. I can duplicate the tone on a Stratocaster by putting the toggle switch between the third and fourth positions out of phase. The only way I can call it a sprounk is if it sounds like someone sprounky. It's a very electric sound, a very nice sound. It sounds entirely different than the sound of Chuck Berry. Gibson put on the treble pickup. This was definitely a combination of pickups sounds. So I wanted this gold Les Paul 'cause it was not only loud, but it had sprounk.*

Then, as time evolved, I was told the best Les Paul one could get was this black Custom called the "Fretless Wonder." I found that not to be the best Les Paul ever. Why? One, the neck was not natural. Two, it had three unusual tones; it had ultra-treble… it was so shrill it was almost unusable. It had a lead switch and rhythm switch and a special tone. One super treble, one is normal and one is a muffled bass effect. It didn't have the blended sounds that I thought. I didn't like that guitar because it didn't have a blend tone.

RN: *The Custom's middle pickup was magnetically out-of-phase, and the Goldtop pickups were in-series.*

MB: *Exactly. I think the bright sound was because it was a combination of pickups of the Goldtop. Now as it turns out, the sunburst—this is what I was leading to—was the loudest of them all. You sacrifice a little sprounk, but you had volume without feedback, or a certain kind of… you didn't have the feedback other f-hole guitars had with humbuckers, the 400, the Byrdland…*

Jeff Beck

Jeff Beck sprang onto the British rock scene in a big way with the hit group The Yardbirds just as Eric Clapton exited. His inventive and flashy style turned quite a few guitarists' heads in the day with their LP *Over, Under, Sideways, Down.* With early influences from Les Paul and Cliff Gallup, Jeff went on to do his own solo efforts with blazing tones from the Les Paul guitar on *Truth* and *Beck Ola.* His landmark instrumental 1975 album *Blow by Blow,* done with Beatles producer George Martin, set a precedent. On that tour, Les Paul, his son Bobby, and I went to meet Jeff at Avery Fisher Hall, since Jeff had previously told me he always wanted to meet him.

Although Jeff was known for the incredible Les Paul sounds he got on his landmark *Truth, Beckola,* and *Blow by Blow* albums, he later used the Gibson for some recording sessions like Stanley Clarke's album *Modern Man* on the track "Rock 'n' Roll Jelly" (my 1959 cherry Les Paul pictured in this book).

RL: *What attracted you to the Les Paul guitar?*

JB: *It was the thickness of the sound as opposed to the Tele that I was using. Everyone was using Strats and Teles. I saw Eric with the Bluesbreakers going through a Marshall. It sounded pretty blown and whipped, but the low-end of it sounded more like a cello… you know, like a lower bass with a fat upper-register, too. With a trio it sounded really good. It sounded meek using a wiry, thin guitar; it sounds empty. The Les Paul sounded very impressive, so I had to have one of those.*

RL: *How many years did you use it?*

JB: *On and off. It was quite hard to get off it really, because it was such a soft guitar to play. I mean soft in [that] it didn't make mince meat of your fingers like the others do. It's heavy; but nice action with very, very thin strings on. And then when I saw Jimi [Hendrix], I realized that wasn't going to be the way things were going to be. He played my guitar and told me it wasn't playable. We swapped guitars. Well, he used one of my guitars when we were playing one night. He said "You won't be able to play this thing,*

with rubber bands on it." I said, "Yeah, I know… after six weeks of touring, the strings will get thicker (laughs)." Jimmy Page plays with thinner strings. You can't even see his!*

RL: *When did you get a Les Paul Sunburst?*

JB: *I think I got it near the end of the Yardbirds, beginning of the Stewart Band [The Jeff Beck Group]. Can't be too sure when I got it. Then it was stolen.*

RL: *How much did you pay for it?*

JB: *I paid about 140 quid. About 300 bucks.*

RL: *Wow, what a deal! Well, back in the late sixties here in America, they were going for $250 to $400.*

JB: *I mean, you know, it was a fair chunk of money, but I still think it was a desirable guitar even then.*

RL: *Was this the only Burst that you had then? You had a yellow one, too.*

JB: *I only had one at a time. I replaced that one with another one.*

RL: *You had one with black pickup surrounds on it. Was that a different guitar?*

JB: *Yeah, a different guitar. I have that one at home, which I stripped the front off. It's just the bare natural wood color underneath. Pale limey color. And I still got that.*

RL: *And you had kind of a yellowish one, didn't you?*

JB: *Yeah, that's it, that's the one. It used to be sunburst and I stripped the sunburst off; a 1959.*

RL: *I remember the dark brown one… you used that on the* Blow by Blow *stuff.*

JB: *I still got that. It was a converted Goldtop with a fixed bridge on it.*

Jeff Beck playing his Oxblood Les Paul in San Diego. *Courtesy Martin Miller, 1975*

Jeff Beck on the *Blow by Blow* tour in the Navarro Hotel with Binky Phillips's '58 Les Paul sunburst.

Peter Green

Peter Green reflects on his tenure with the Les Paul guitar. Teaming up with John Mayall after Eric Clapton left the Bluesbreakers was quite a challenge. Peter adopted the Les Paul guitar with some hesitation and did a fine job. Then he went on to form the popular Fleetwood Mac group, and virtually rivaled Jimi Hendrix for his sheer intensity and brilliance of execution… all on a 1959 Les Paul Standard. I caught up with Peter in 2000 just after a Ventura Theatre concert, and he had these reflections on his years with the Gibson solid-body:

RL: *What attracted you to the Les Paul guitar?*

PG: *It was the salmon-pink color. And the way Eric Clapton was playing it. The way Eric Clapton was holding it and playing with it. He let me try his on. He let me use it. And I got one of them. It wasn't as good as his. I bought it for 100 pounds, ten English pence.*

RL: *That was your original sunburst Les Paul.*

PG: *Sunburst, cherry! Gibson Les Paul Standard. They called it "cherry."*

RL: *And what did you like about the sound of the guitar?*

PG: *It sounded like Eric Clapton playing, but it wasn't. It was me!*

RL: *It was you. And you did a great job, too!*

PG: *I had to sort of cover Eric's shoes. I felt like it wasn't very true, because you can't wear or fill someone else's shoes. But I had to do it with certain tunes that he did with the Bluesbreakers. "Key to Love" and those tunes. So on "Witchdoctor"… I had to get the feedback (sings the notes). I couldn't do it as good as him, obviously. Maybe, but not the same. Somehow he had a certain command over his guitar. But that's what I got to do those tunes. If I had it to do over again, I would have kept the guitar I had. It was a Harmony Meteor. It was much better for blues than the Les Paul was.*

I think one day the Les Paul will go back to where it came from. It won't be such a… rock icon. I don't know what it is about the Les Paul. It's a lovely guitar. You should treat it nicely like a Les Paul. Plays it all like a jazz guitarist, like pretty nice. I think it should be treated more like that than… in the pop world.

RL: *It is like a solid jazz guitar. I've used mine occasionally as a jazz guitar.*

PG: *It was originally, to my knowledge, a jazz guitar. In France, Les Paul is a babe… a jazz guitar.*

(Below Left) Mick Taylor is playing the Les Paul that he used with the Rolling Stones. His slide stylings are some of the very best blues-rock playing ever done. He sits here performing with John Mayall. *Courtesy Martin Miller, circa 1989*

(Below Right) Peter Green performing with his Fleetwood Mac group in Orebro, Sweden in November of 1969. *A sincere thank you goes to Bela Stephens who has supplied the book with valuable personal information. His passion for Peter Green's music is manifested on the website www.thebluepearls.com. © Bela Stephens*

(Above) Paul Kossoff played with great passion this night at the Starwood Club in 1976. He did his final performance with his Back Street Crawler group in Hollywood; unfortunately, he passed away the next day. Old bandmates Paul Rodgers and drummer Simon Kirke were on hand, and we all jammed a bit backstage. His signature riffs from "All Right Now" with Free will permanently carve his epitaph in rock history.

(Above) Dickie Betts is performing here with the revised Allman Brothers Band in San Diego, circa 1973. They dedicated the show to brother Duane, and played a burning three-hour show with an intermission. Meanwhile, Dickie showed me his ported Marshall cabs with JBLs during the break.

(Below) Mick Ralphs proudly shows his '60 LP while cooling off after a Bad Company gig in San Diego.

(Below) Eddie Van Halen, known for his tapping/dive-bomb antics, also owns a real Burst. *Coutesy Neil Zlozower*

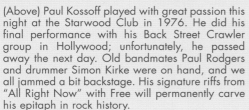

(Top) Here the great Martin Barre is playing his beautiful Les Paul Standard at the San Diego Sports Arena, circa 1973.

(Bottom) Humble Pie's Clem Clemson performing with #0 2192 on the 1972 *Smokin'* Tour.

253

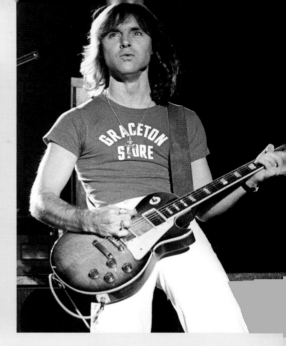

(Above) Rick Derringer is playing Ralph Perry's '58 Standard in the garden of the Beverly Hills Hotel.

(Above) REO Speedwagon's original guitarist Gary Richrath with his 1959 Les Paul. *Courtesy Neil Zlozower*

(Above) Ronnie Montrose broke out on his own after performing with the Edgar Winter Group. Here he's playing at the San Diego Sports Arena in 1973 with his beautiful 1959 sunburst Les Paul.

(Facing Page Left) Jimmy Page playing his favorite Les Paul Standard 1959, found for him by Joe Walsh. He's performing in Dallas, Texas, circa 1975. *Courtesy Steve Epeneter (RIP)*

(Below) Joe Walsh is captured here warming up backstage for a gig in Philadelphia with Johnny Winters and Rick Derringer, circa 1975.

(Below) Joe Walsh playing his favorite Les Paul sunburst (awash in red lights) with his Barnstorm group in San Diego, circa 1973.

Steve Lukather

Steve Lukather—"Luke," as we affectionately know him—is a noted Los Angeles studio musician who worked his way through the ranks with the talented Porcaro brothers, playing on numerous hit records over the years. Along with these *crème de la crème* of studio musicians, he formed the Grammy-winning group Toto, recording their own hit albums and movie soundtracks. His love for playing Gibson Les Paul guitars gave the world many memorable recorded solos. I caught up with Luke at home just after the 2006 Les Paul & Friends concert.

SL: *My first really great guitar was a Les Paul Deluxe my dad bought for me in 1970 or '71. He finally realized, after I'd been playing for about seven years, that I was dead serious about it. I was going to study and try to become a real musician.*

RL: *What attracted you to the Les Paul Sunburst?*

SL: *Oh man, Jimmy Page, Eric Clapton and Peter Green, all the cats from that era. That sound! I wanted to get the big, fat sound like that. Plus, that was the rave at the time, having a Sunburst. A '50s Sunburst with PAFs in it was just the guitar to have. It was like the Holy Grail to have this guitar. I've played it on a lot of recording sessions from '79 to '84. I also used it on some of Don Henley's stuff, including my solo on "Dirty Laundry."*

RL: *Did you use it mostly for lead or for rhythm parts?*

SL: *Both, clean and dirty sound. It had a great sound for doing little skank parts like all the pseudo-funk, pop music that was coming out of L.A. at the time—Randy Crawford's records, for example, which were a cross-pollination between rock and funk.*

RL: *What do you like most about the guitar?*

SL: *It's one of the easiest guitars I've ever played. Just the neck itself is so smooth, it's unbelievable. I've forgotten since I've put it away for a while. I don't want to take it out of the house because it's so valuable. If I do, I always keep one eye on it. I make sure I'm always grabbing distance from it. I would never take it on tour now.*

I bought it through Paul Jamieson. He was the first guy to get me into it. He got

me into Goldtops and some other instruments I've had come and go throughout the years. He said, "Look, you've got to buy all that you can." I was making some bank, but three- or four-thousand dollars for a guitar was insane back then! We were in Phoenix in 1979. Someone was asking five grand for this guitar and I begrudgingly bought it. I loved the way it played and I dug the way it looked. I didn't have a 'Burst, so I grabbed it. Now I'm sitting on a gold mine. My son will probably inherit it from me because he's a guitar player and it will be a family heirloom. It will probably be worth a million bucks in 25 years.

RL: *The big tone. You like the way it sounds.*

SL: *You heard it… I just plug into a Marshall and—bang!—it sings. It's in the wood. I broke it out inside that arena and hit one note, and it resonated in the wood of the building! There's something going on there, but I'm not quite sure what it is. There's something about the way they made things back then. Maybe it's the type of wood, the density of the wood, the age of it, the smokiness of it—it being played and sweat on a lot. It's got a little soul to it because of that. Some are better than others, but it's all in the way you play, too. It's all pretty much one big package. If you can get one, get one!*

RL: *What do you want to say to Les Paul and the Les Paul crowd here?*

SL: *My dear Les, it's an honor to play this guitar. Thank you for inventing such a beautiful piece of history. Lord knows, it's one of the greatest guitars ever, for every style. You're one of the greatest guitarist ever, and it's a great honor to be a part of your incredible history. Thank you and God bless you.*

Waddy Wachtel

RL: *What was your first instrument?*

WW: At nine years old I had a little Kamiko, and at ten years old, a gorgeous Gibson L-7 that had a beautiful sound. When I was ten, I went away to camp for the summer, and this guy had a black three-pickup Les Paul. After that I kept telling myself, "I don't like my big guitar anymore." All I could think of from that time on was a Les Paul solid-body. Boy, I like that thing. All those pickups on it were really cool. It didn't matter that my father had already bought an amp, and I had a DeArmond pickup on it. It was gorgeous, but it didn't matter to me. I had to have a Les Paul. My father wasn't rich by any means. So my grandmother said, "Write to your uncle. He has a lot of money. He'll buy you a guitar." I said, "Yeah, really?" So I wrote him a letter. A few days later my father called me from his shoe store. He said, "Get over here right now!" So I went over there and he said, "Get in the back room. Just get in there." He came in the back and said, "Did you have the nerve to write to your Uncle Harry and ask him to buy you a guitar? What is the matter with you? Are you insane? Where do you come off with that kind of nerve?"

He was really dumping on me. I said, "Well, I don't know. Grandma told me to do it." I thought he couldn't afford it. He was yelling at me and he left the room for a minute. I was sitting around and in the corner I saw part of a guitar case. So he came back and he was still yelling. I said, "Knock it off. That's enough. Come on,

let's go." It was a TV model. The yellow double cutaway is what he got me. So when I was 11, I had a Les Paul. It wasn't black with three pickups, but I wasn't annoyed. Kids are rotten, you know! I had this gorgeous little tweed Vibrolux and I started playing this Les Paul.

RL: *Did you like the sound?*

WW: Oh, yeah. I played that one forever until the Beatles came out. All of a sudden the Gibson wasn't looking quite as hip as the Country Gentleman. So I ended up selling my little one to Leslie West. It's probably the guitar he played "Mississippi Queen" on. We lived in the same building and spent a lot of time together playing guitar. So I got a Gretsch.

Some years went by and we moved to L.A. The Gretsch broke in my hand one day. So my band's manager, Dolph Rempp, opened a rehearsal studio in the back of their (S.I.R.) building off of Vine Street where they rented instruments. David Ray suggested that they open up the two rooms in back. The only bands that rehearsed there were my band and Crosby, Stills and Nash. One day we rehearsed in their room and there were a million Les Pauls in stands. They were beauties. I said to Steven Stills, "Would you want to sell one of them? I'd love to get another Les Paul." He said, "Take your pick—whatever one you want." We rehearsed and I tried every Les Paul in the room and this was one of them. It was the loudest one. That's why I picked it. It was the most trebly one and the loudest one. There was a three-pickup one but I didn't dig it. There was no room to pick and it was dark-sounding. This one was real bright compared to those and it had the Bigsby on it. I ended up getting it for $350! I told my father, "I need some money." He said, "For what?" "To get a Les Paul." "You had a Les Paul. You sold it to Leslie West. I'm not getting you another." I said, "Yes, you are. I need the money." It took a while, but I got the money. So anyhow, that's how I got this one.

RL: *It's an early '60. Do you like the slim neck?*

WW: I love this neck. It's the best neck they've ever made as far as I'm concerned. It's not fat like the real thick baseball bats they made earlier.

This one, you can't play badly on it. It's unbelievable.

Guitarist Waddy Wachtel is a longtime Les Paul player. His playing can be heard with Linda Ronstadt and the classic "Werewolves of London" track with the late Warren Zevon. He did an interview with this author at the Joint in Hollywood, 2005.

Close-up of 1958 Standard #8 6761 with its deep cherry coloration.

This beautiful 1959 Standard Les Paul came down from Pat O'Donnell in the Northwest. It shows some slight fading and nice fiddle-back flame on the quarter-sawn side portions. From the collection of Phil Pierangelo and Barbara Sutherland.

Sculptured Les Paul Models
and the SG Guitar '60–'63

Sculptured Les Paul Models and the SG Guitar '60–'63

This striking new Gibson model for the '60s was a radical departure for the Les Paul range. The distinctive Les Paul Standard (SG-style) model was first introduced in late 1960, and is still a popular classic today. Shortly there-after, the whole series of Les Paul solid-body models were to follow suit in 1961. According to the 1962 Gibson catalog, "This dynamic Les Paul series is an exciting new approach to the solid-body guitar. Beauty in gleaming white or cherry-red that must be seen. Wonderfully clear, bell-like tone that must be heard. Fast action that should be tried… soon. By Gibson, of course."

This new guitar line had a very thin, 1 5/16" lightweight Honduras mahogany body. It featured a beautiful full, double-cutaway design, carefully sculpted and comfort-contoured. The stylish silhouetted shape had novel bevel-ing around most of the body to create a shape that was very comfortable to hold and play. Its slightly offset, sharp Florentine cutaways gave the player full access to the highest registers up the neck (22 frets clear of the body).

(Above) An early sculpted Les Paul Standard in excellent condi-tion, shipped in 1960 with an ink-stamped "0 8779" serial number.

(Below) Gibson's "Solid Hit" ad for their new guitars. Since the series did quite well, Gibson wasn't too far off the mark.

(Right) Columbia release of *The Fabulous Les Paul and Mary Ford* LP, circa 1962. One of a few memorable poses from a studio session with Harry Parker.

Electric Spanish Guitars

SOLID BODY MODELS

LES PAUL CUSTOM

rs call it the "Fretless Wonder" for
remely low frets and fast action.
t's more wonderful than ever with new
design and new features. Ultra
and contoured, delicately balanced,
sts into a natural comfortable
position for any guitarist, with or
strap. With three humbucking
ble pickups, Tune-O-Matic
and new Vibrato* . . . with increased
greater sustain, and a clear,
sparkling tone, the "Custom"
the widest range of tonal colorings
ts. Three-way toggle switch
a unique method of tone
op position selects top pickup for
center position activates center
pickups simultaneously for
ighs and special effects;
tion operates lower pickup for
d.
d in gleaming white for smart
ith gold-plated metal parts.
dded leather strap included.
hand contoured, double
ody
slim, fast, low-action neck—with
xtra low frets—joins body
et
mahogany neck with adjustable

rboard, deluxe pearl inlays
Tune-O-Matic bridge
ful, humbucking pickups
wiring arrangement
one and volume controls
ecially wired

ibrato*—operates in
ck stroke; swings out
thm playing
ong, 1⁵⁄₁₆" thin . . .
e frets

ld plush-lined case
per case cover

LES PAUL STANDARD

An established favorite with completely
new modern styling . . . with thinner,
lighter weight contoured body, and deep
double cutaway that provides easy
access to all 22 frets. The new Gibson
Vibrato* and the extremely slim,
fast, low-action neck make this guitar a
joy to play. Tone is clear and bell-like
throughout its entire range. The
perfectly balanced solid body makes
playing comfortable in any position, sitting
or standing. The Tune-O-Matic bridge
permits adjusting string action and
individual string lengths. The finish is a
beautiful cherry-red with nickel-plated
metal parts and individual machine
heads with deluxe buttons. Deluxe
padded leather strap included.

- Ultra thin, contoured, double cutaway body
- Slim, fast, low-action neck—with exclusive extra low frets—joins body at 22nd fret
- One-piece mahogany neck with adjustable truss rod
- Rosewood fingerboard, pearl inlays
- Adjustable Tune-O-Matic bridge
- Twin powerful humbucking pickups with separate tone and volume controls which can be pre-set
- New Gibson Vibrato*—operates in direction of pick stroke; swings out of way for rhythm playing
- Three-position toggle switch to activate either or both pickups

12¾" wide, 16" long, 1⁵⁄₁₆" thin
. . . 24¾" scale, 22 frets

Les Paul Standard
Cherry finish
0537 Faultless, gold plush-lined case
ZC-CLP Deluxe zipper case cover

(Above) A radical new look for the Gibson Les Paul. This 1962 catalog depicts the attractive Custom in gleaming white, and a deep cherry-red Standard, both with a new-styled vibrato. Meanwhile, Les is still playing his old Goldtop, now airbrushed sunburst!

The overall shape, with its feminine sexy curves and sharp points, is somewhat reminiscent of a classic shield or family crest—or almost downright fiendish-looking with its twin horns, depending upon how you view it. The twin-horn-shaped cutaways actually harken back to the old Mirecourt, French-designed guitars. Some perceive it as evocative of Neptune/Poseidon's all-powerful, three-pronged trident spear as he rises from the sea on his dolphin. The guitar will undoubtedly create some of its own mythology in the future!

Nevertheless, the sculptured Les Paul SG is certainly a very distinctive, original design, and actually quite comfortable, balanced, and attractive (certainly in direct competition to the popular Fender contoured models). It is evident that Gibson put some real thought into creating an ergonomic and aesthetically appealing instrument—which, at the time, was an actual breakthrough for the company! Touts an SG ad: "Now it's more wonderful than ever with new body design and new features. Ultra thin, hand contoured, delicately balanced, it adjusts into a natural comfortable playing position for any guitarist, with or without a strap."

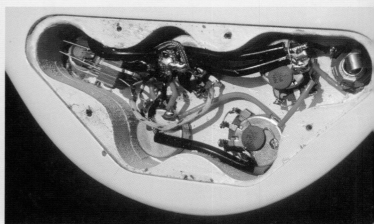

A very beautiful 1961 Les Paul Custom that is shown here gleaming brilliantly in the sunlight! This attractive guitar is actually a light cream color, which is highlighted by the 24-carat gold trim. The engraved plaque proudly states the guitar's "Custom" status. Note the filed-down frets and tidy electronic wiring. *Courtesy James Nabors, February 1975*

Naturally, Gibson derived the simple "SG" name from the acronym for "solid guitar." (Similarly, "EB" stood for the "electric bass," as "ES" signified "electric Spanish.") As previously mentioned, the original SG guitars were the late-1959, double-cut Special and TV models—which had been considered the "Les Paul" SG. The popular "SG Les Paul" name was eventually given to these later sculpted models. (It may be a little confusing, but easier to understand once you comprehend the timeline and nomenclature. Many prefer to call them "SG/Les Paul" guitars, while using "early" or "thick" Les Paul SG for the previous models.)

During the late 1950s, Gibson's new semi-solid ES-335/345/355 models drew some of the buying public away from the higher-priced Les Paul Sunburst and Custom models. That was to be expected; yet, they still sold respectfully. Meanwhile, the new cherry Junior models actually broke previous sales records in 1959. Ted McCarty adds, "Then we produced that up until the time the sales department again felt that we had to have something different and new and modern. So we went to these sculptured models [the double-cutaway], and dropped the single-cutaway." Another face-lift was in order to pick things up—which Gibson certainly did by 1961.

The transition in production—from the top single-cutaway to the sculptured models—was a process that began in 1960 and was completed in 1961, with a few concurrent production runs overlapping in both years. With the already successfully introduced double-cutaway models prompting interest, these new sculpted models were the freshest and most exciting instruments on the scene.

Many 1950s players complained about the sharp bound edges, the lack of balance, and the 8.5 to 9-plus pounds that the instrument weighed. Completely abandoning the original $^5/_8$" maple top, the new contoured guitar was now just over an inch thinner overall ($1\,^5/_{16}$"), which substantially lightened the instrument—ideal for standing and sitting musicians. Virtually aerodynamic with its new shape, the guitar was a welcome change (to some, anyway) in its own right.

Its consequent lack of maple, thin body, and softer tonality was the main reason that Les Paul, in later years, didn't favor this model as much as the more substantially weighted originals. This reduction in body mass was a big sacrifice in the Les Paul's full tone and long sustain—yet the lighter body had a sweet and vibrating tonality, too, prompting the ads to claim: "Tone is clear and bell-like throughout its entire range." The high-output humbucking pickups, coupled with this light-body acoustic tonality, was much like a Flying V setup—it still produced a warm tone, but without the full, massive bottom of the heavier Les Paul or Explorer models. (Many say that the compromise between a light and heavy guitar is exactly where electric guitars' best acoustic tonalities are derived.)

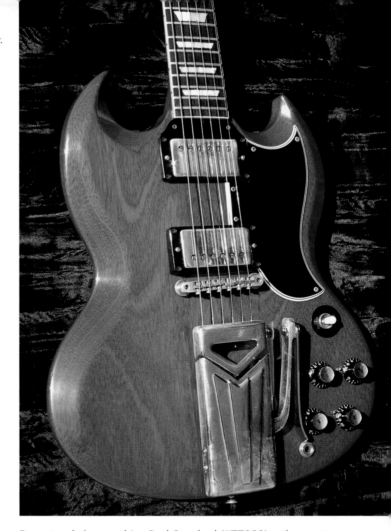

Exceptional cherry-red Les Paul Standard (#77892) with attractive grain patterns. *Courtesy Rich Stillwell, 2004*

New-style Les Paul instruments were fairly well-balanced, due to their lighter bodies. Sitting with the bottom-heavy, single-cutaway models generally required that the player hold onto the neck to keep it balanced in the lap. The neck was now extended outward, due to the redesigned waist placement, giving the illusion of a longer neck. The new guitar's waist is located near where the back pickup is, while the old model's center was in between the pickups (with the overall scale length set farther in).

The stylish, beveled silhouette shape naturally let the player hug the guitar close into the body. This ergonomic factor further enhanced the playability. Basically, a 25-degree angle was chamfer-cut around two-thirds of the body's edges to relieve the sharpness. Like a finely tailored garment, the sculpted solid-body Gibson was now easier to hold, without jutting into your arm or chest (as on traditional guitars). In addition, its back was also slightly beveled toward the neck heel across both horns. This original contoured design is arguably the most comfortable body shape that Gibson has ever come up with. Its sleek, new lines had a simple yet attractive elegance, quite a unique and innovative shape for this long-standing guitar and mandolin company.

The Particulars

Earlier appointments to the solid-body line continued into the '60s, with variations on neck styles, P-90 and humbucking pickups, Tune-O-Matic bridges, combination stop/stud bridges, and new vibrato tailpieces. Prices stayed the same—at $365 for the Custom and $265 for the Standard—even though the lack of maple and body binding cut costs slightly. Bridge placement pushed the Les Paul SG's overall length to 39", just ¼" longer than the single-cutaway models of the 1950s. The body remained at 13" wide, while the length was an inch shorter, measuring 16 ¾".

Neck

Depth-wise, the neck shapes were still quite slender for the first few years, and filled out some in 1962 and 1963. Besides

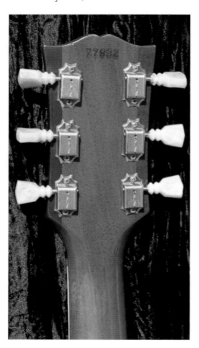

the now-popular 1959 profile, many feel that 1961 and 1962 were truly phenomenal years for neck shapes, with a seemingly wide (still 1 ¹¹/₁₆" nut) and very comfortable medium slender profile. Slight inconsistencies naturally occurred in the neck shaping-and-sanding process, accounting for some variations. The Standard headstock was widened to previous Custom specs, being enlarged ³/₈" at the bottom and ³/₁₆" at the top, to add some more

Nice, smooth heel transition with virtual unique sunbursted neck coloration. Imprinted serial numbers (size 2) and double-collar Kluson Deluxe tuners complete this fine example.

mass and complement the new body style.

Variations with the neck heel occurred each year. Originally, a smooth transition into the body (somewhat like the original Flying V) sufficed. Soon, a small ledge was introduced that made construction easier, while slightly reinforcing and defining the neck joint. This ledge became even more pronounced

Slightly wider headstocks graced the new series.

in later years. Still, this model guitar had its obvious Achilles' heel: after being accidentally dropped, many would fissure, split, or completely snap off from the fragile, almost brittle, (however sonorous) tropical Honduras hardwood.

Very early versions of the Standard in 1960 maintained the classic gold-script silk-screen "Les Paul" logo. An abalone pearl inlaid crown motif (i.e., as on the ES-350 and ES-5) was now put in the center of the headstock. The script "Les Paul" name was handsomely engraved into the black-and-white laminated (rolled; slightly rippled) plastic truss-rod cover. The "Les Paul Custom" name was now transferred from the truss adjustment cover to the laminated plastic plaque between the neck and front pickup. Pickguards were of the three-ply, white variety on the Custom, and four-ply, black on the Standard and Special. Beveled edges revealed the contrasting-color outline. Standard models used a thin, single-ply, black plastic piece to conceal the neck tang. A two-ply laminate pickguard (that would sometimes warp) was used on the single-pickup guitars. All guitars followed color suit on rear control cavity covers.

Pickups

P-90 pickups with similar specs continued on Special, TV, and Junior models, but with M56 magnets (now 2.359" long and 0.495" wide). Humbucking pickups went from the "Patent Applied For" decals on early versions in 1960 and 1961 to "Patent Pending" later in 1962 (quite rare pickups). During late 1962, a slightly different version began with a "Patent #2,896,491" sticker affixed beneath. (The number actually was Les's trapeze tailpiece patent. Seth says he wasn't aware of this fact for many years, and later said that Gibson knowingly did it to throw off competitors. Some speculate that it was actually due to the fact that his patent was granted for the other novel forms of humbuckings included, and not the same six-string design used. Regardless, the competition didn't find out, so it didn't make any difference.) Original PAF stickered pickups show up as late as 1964, and even 1965 in ES-345/355 and Super 400 models, often due to their narrower pole spacing.

These pickups still used the dark-olive tape on the coils into 1963. The two black coil wires were switched to having one white and one black. The "Pat. No." pickup's tonality had almost the same richness and over-modulation, but a little cleaner and brighter edge to its sound. Coils were wound more consistently during the early 1960s, and the shorter Alnico V M-56 magnets were used. Some of the stored PAF/Pat Pend pickups had been originally supplied on guitars in the rhythm position (especially ES-355 and SG Customs) into 1964. Pickups were specified as "PU-490 1N" for the back position, and "PU-490 2N" for the front on the Standards. Customs used a 3G for the center. The mounting ring for the Custom middle pickup was a MR-493, as opposed to the 490 and 491 on the Standards.

Rhythm pickup placement was set back due to the necessitation of adequate wood to insure a solid neck joint, as was done on earlier double-cutaway, solid-body models. Therefore, the rhythm pickup was moved back $^{11}/_{16}$" from its previous position—which still sounded "good enough" (as Ted would say), but certainly not as rich harmonically. The lead pickup was moved $^{1}/_{4}$" closer to the bridge, resulting in a $^{1}/_{2}$" closer arrangement of the dual pickup Standard. The Les Paul Special, Junior, and TV models used the P-90 pickups with little variation from the earlier 1950s guitars.

Controls

Gibson's standard dual-volume and tone layout continued, but was moved nearly two inches farther away—to just below the new toggle-switch placement. All four controls were tightly ganged together—$^{1}/_{2}$" closer than before. The TV's and Junior's controls were set in the far corner of their bodies.

Custom three-pickup wiring again featured the "unique method of tone mixing" in the middle position. With the center pickup's magnet purposely reversed to the field of the treble pickup, an out-of-phase, high-pitched "doinky" tone was achieved. This novel sound could be an advantage in cutting through the mix of instrumentation at times—but it lost its normally blended tonality, which was the sound most often desired. Simply turning the pickup around didn't solve the situation. Removing and reversing (flipping over) the magnet is the true phase remedy, but it can also disrupt the overall magnetic field if the whole pickup is magnetized originally. (To deter-

mine if just the magnet was treated, test the pole's magnetic field strength. This quick fix reinstates the normal phasing effect to warm up the blended combination tones. If you prefer total originality, leave it be, and don't unsolder the pickup's cover to attempt this.)

CentraLab 500K potentiometers continued to be used for the volume and tone controls. A right-angle #12016 BDB Switchcraft gold three-way pickup selector switch was used on Customs. The nickel/chrome #12013 toggle was for Standards and Specials, as it fit within the thin profile of the guitar. Switch tips (lever knobs) were changed to the white T12745 version. Sprague's "Black Beauty" (.022 mfd, 400-volt) capacitors were used at first in the tone circuitry; then the orange (.022mfd, 50-volt) flat ceramic disc caps were utilized.

Bridges

The "ABR-1" Tune-O-Matic bridges soon started using a thin wire insert bracket to hold the bridge pieces intact if a string broke. As their die tolerances slightly changed through the years, the small bridge pieces would easily fall out if a string broke without this wire support. The wire was attached into two small holes and traveled over the adjustment screws. White nylon bridge (plastic insert) pieces were instigated during 1962, and slightly muted the strings' tonality in comparison to the brighter-sounding, nickel-plated brass inserts. A special ABR-1 "T.O.M." with a rounded bottom surface to rock more freely on the flat thumbnuts was produced to complement the vibrato. The parts catalog stocked these separately as ABR-5NP (nickel/plastic) and ABR-5GP (gold/plastic) for the Standard (regular) and Custom. The stop/stud combination bridge tailpiece (TPBR-85N-A) on the Special, TV, and Junior models soon received a raised compensated bridge (offset) to help maintain their relative intonation—for the medium-gauge Sonomatics strings of the day.

Control cavity exposed with .02 caps and yellow-covered ground wires.

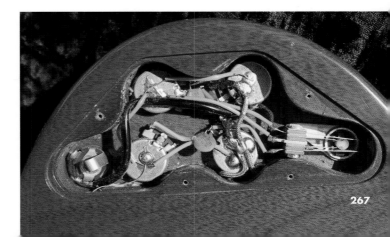

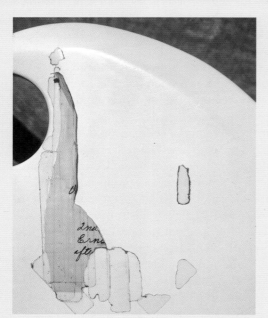

Mary Ford's personal Les Paul Custom, which she used in the early 1960s. This guitar later resided in Pasadena, California with her white Gretsch Penguin, and somehow lost a few of its pickups when the Penguin flew the coop. The refined Custom headstock is a statement in itself. Grover machines top off this instrument. Its serial number, "103367," is very faint, but definitely there. *Courtesy Greg Corronna, Mary's nephew, 1993*

(Left) Notice the remnants of Mary's old songlist still on the back.

A classic pose by Bruno of Hollywood of Les and Mary with a slightly modified white Custom. Their formal attire goes well with the custom black pickguard that hides the removed middle pickup. (Mary Ford was quite the doll in those days.)

This Gibson truss cover with "Mary Ford" written in script came off of an original white Les Paul Standard (SG) that was bought by a New Jersey music store during the 1970s. The guitar may have been special-ordered by a fan of hers. *Courtesy Mike Shaw, 2004*

Vibrato Tailpieces

"New Gibson Vibrato* [patented] operates in direction of pick stroke; swings out of way for rhythm playing," states the catalog. The odd and unconventional sideways vibrato first seen on the ES-355 (and sometimes on the ES-335) was standard fare on the new Custom and Standard Les Paul models. The arm would conveniently swing up and over for use. It often would get a little loose and have to be tightened regularly. Its covered, dual-spring, cam-activated mechanism worked somewhat stiffly and was prone to going out of the tune easily. Fine adjustments of the six nuts are necessary to help it operate smoothly and evenly. (Many joke that these vibratos will go out of tune just by looking at them.) They can be locked down easily by tightening the two spring nuts so as to make the vibrato inoperable.

Jim Hutchinson started at Gibson in the early sixties and wore many creative hats. His pattern-making skills are still utilized by Gibson today. He remembers, "We used to make those in the machine shop where I worked. These were molded (cast) parts. We called it the 'Sidewinder.' It never worked!"

(Above) Instruction sheet for the "Sidewinder" vibrola tailpiece; the tailpiece is adjustable only under string tension.

(Above Right) A clean 1962 Les Paul Standard with B-5 Bigsby vibrato. *Courtesy Diggy Pickett, 1973*

(Lower Right) A regal Les Paul Custom in a pretty setting near the Danube River. *Courtesy Erhard Bochen and his most gracious parents, 1985*

(Above) Fine lightweight Honduras mahogany was used throughout the sixties era for these resonant Gibson solid-bodies. Some like this have grain patterns that complement the lines of the guitar well. This exemplary 1961 Les Paul Standard guitar belongs to Lloyd Chiate (2004).

(Below) Another rare Les Paul Standard with a B5 Bigsby vibrola tailpiece. These Bigsby vibrolas are great to use live with a band at high volume. *Courtesy David Swartz, 2004*

(Above) The gleaming white finish truly stands out on this excellent Les Paul Custom model, shown here in its brown and hot-pink 537 case. *Courtesy Rich Stillwell, 2004*

(Below Right) This "Black Beauty" was ordered with dual humbuckings and a B5G Bigsby vibrola tailpiece. Rarely do you see these without the third pickup. *From the collection of Paul Waroff, March 1993*

(Below) Wow! What an SG Custom! This beauty from late 1963 has the gold Bigsby vibrola and simply says "Custom" on the neck tenon spacer. The neck profile is fairly substantial, too. *Courtesy Rich Stillwell*

Some erroneously refer to this particular tailpiece as a "Lonnie Mack" vibrato, even though Lonnie always used a unique suspended Bigsby setup on his trusty Flying V Gibson. Nevertheless, the main tuning problem was the string binding in the nut, of course.

Some short-tail Bigsby horseshoe-style B5 and B5G vibrato tailpieces were ordered on various Custom and Standard models. They certainly worked adequately, and looked quite attractive with the new body style. These rare Bigsby-equipped versions are understandably more desirable than the normal sideways models. Curiously, they didn't regularly produce the simple stopbar tailpiece setup. British catalogs, however, depicted one without it being truly available.

A complete switch in vibrato tailpieces was eventually made in 1962 and 1963, to the spring-blade vibrato, now simply called the "Gibson Vibrola." It was hinged into an attractive ebony flat block, inlaid with pearl pieces, and screwed onto the top of the guitar's body. Some of the last Standard and Custom models shipped in 1963 (and into the mid 1960s, after the official name change) used the attractive, long "Deluxe Vibrola" tailpiece. Its cover was engraved with the "Gibson" block logo and lyre (which were also featured on the '63 Firebird V), and utilized the same knife-edged mechanism. These later (GV-55N and GV-75G) long-tailed versions featured a comfortable, mottled plastic handle similar to the mottled, creamy Opal Kluson tuning grips. Special, TV, and Junior models used a similar short version or the cam-loaded, small Maestro vibrola, similar to those on the solid-body Epiphones. These Maestro-equipped models kept the guitars in reasonably good tune for creating desired variations in pitch modulation.

Hutch continues, "We made the Lyre tailpiece in our own factory, too. I made that [up] in the machine shop. We did all the silver soldering. We had milling machines and screw machines and that sort of thing. The original plastic ones [arms], the tips on these things broke. Like fifty percent of what we put on broke. They went back to just the plain flat handle. We made all these [metal] parts including the plastic inserts that went in the Tune-O-Matic bridge. Then we went back to brass inserts."

(Right) A creamy white Les Paul Custom SG with short ebony-inlayed Maestro vibrato.

(Lower Right) This close-up of the neck heel reveals an artistic, smoothly blended shape with the customary ledges on the sides. Note the great burnt orange plush case. *Courtesy Barney Roach, 2003*

(Below) Two Les Paul SG models with the long Lyre Gibson vibrolas as shown at a Las Vegas guitar show. The White LP Custom and cherry LP Standard are courtesy of Gary's Classics, 2002.

(Opposite Top Left) John Cipollina's Les Paul Standard SG, highly customized at various guitar shops in the San Francisco Bay area. This was John's main guitar for most of his gigs and memorable recordings with the Quicksilver Messenger Service band. Thanks, John, for your great inspiration through the years. (Mill Valley, 1971)

(Below) London Records' Phase 4 1968 release of *Les Paul Now!* showing a rare dual-pickup Les Paul Custom.

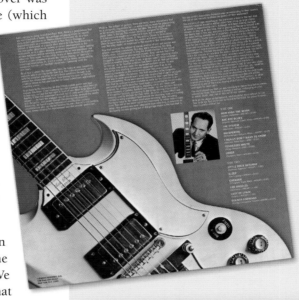

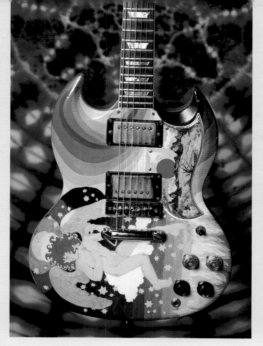

(Above Middle and Right) This is Eric Clapton's famous psychedelic SG Standard, artistically transformed to a cultural icon of the sixties by Dutch artists Simon and Marijke of "The Fool" in London, England. A similar oil-based Day-Glo paint scheme was done to Jack Bruce's Fender Bass VI and Ginger Baker's bass drum head. The original Patent number pickups, six-screw pickguard, and Lyre Vibrola date it to the mid sixties. Eric used it on *Disraeli Gears*, *Wheels of Fire*, and for many live performances with Cream. His famous wooing "Woman Tone" was achieved with this guitar by using both pickups with the rhythm tone completely off and at full volume, accented with the wah-wah pedal backed out three-quarters. After the painted finish began flaking off the neck, Eric had the rest of it removed, exposing the bare wood. It eventually changed hands to Apple artist Jackie Lomax, who let it go to Todd Rundgren in 1972. Todd told this author the neck virtually fell off in his hands one night. He had the instrument properly restored, the painting touched up, and a larger bridge and stopbar added a few years later. The historic Cream "Fool" SG was eventually sold at auction in May 2000. *Psychedelic photographs courtesy Jay Blakesberg, 1991*

(Below) A deep cherry-red Les Paul Standard SG with the attractive and functional ebony block and pearl-inlaid short Gibson vibrola. Note that you could change the arm's length if necessary. *Courtesy Buzz Jens, 1973*

(Above) A very rare cherry-red Les Paul Custom with the long Lyre Maestro vibrato, set off nicely in a pink plush case. Guitar courtesy of Greg Loeb, and is now in Waddy Wachtel's collection. This is Keith Richards's favorite jamming guitar when at the Joint.

Early-'60s Color Finishes

The Les Paul Standard, SG, Special, and Junior models maintained the bright translucent cherry-red finish that was produced with both the red-tinted (Les Paul cherry) filler and the cherry-red overshadowing effects around the neck, etc. In the early 1960s, a deeper red color with a much glossier sheen was developed. This particularly beautiful, darker finish was almost a true cherry color from the aniline dye color used. Sometime during 1962–63, a slight bleeding-pink effect occurred on the neck bindings, due to the residual in the last clear coats from the earlier cherry overshadowing.

The Les Paul Custom and SG-TV models now featured a beautiful white, nitrocellulose finish; a color that was an option for the SG Specials. White Les Paul SG Standards were also built. The TV ads described the color as a "beautiful cream;" the logbooks for the SG Specials called it "cream." With minimal exposure to sunlight and some slight aging processes, these models withstood the test of time fairly well. Gibson's white finish maintained its bright color (much like their Alpine off-white variety), with little yellowing or fading of the clear coat. (The brilliant white Gibson A-3 mandolin models of the 1920s kept their color very well, albeit without a yellowed clear coat.) The PPG Forbes Company supplied them with high quality fillers and lacquers for many decades. Shown in this book are a few rare variations of Custom models in cherry-red and black. Another seen by this author in 1971 (while performing in Newport beach) was an authentic, specially ordered golden sunburst 1962 Les Paul Custom.

SG-TV and Special models also sported the earlier 1958 "improved" limed-mahogany finish (some featuring an even more opaque and glossy yellow lacquer without the contrasting brown filler stain). The catalog description for the Special reads, "Two ways new! A lovely new finish in a new shade of limed mahogany or Gibson's new cherry red…" These beautiful "banana-finished" versions certainly are "Rarebirds" of a different feather.

Custom colors became a more popular option with Gibson during the sixties, especially as the Firebird series took off. Other known colors on SG and Melody Maker models included "Pelham blue" and "Cardinal red."

(Above) The Junior and Melody Maker (now in its double-cutaway guise with a natural finish) are shown in this 1962 depiction.

This close-up of the yellow finish shows the brown grain filler and some weather checking. *Courtesy the Four Amigos, Pomona, 1995*

This is a rare Gibson 1961 SG TV (#31550) in limed mahogany.

Sales and Production

Although Les Paul's contract with Gibson expired during 1963, Gibson still had the Les Paul guitars included in the revised September 1963 price list. This list of zone 1 suggested prices had the Custom retailing for $450, the Standard at $310 ($47.50 for the 0537 case), the Special for $235, and the TVs and Juniors for $155 (with a 316 Archcraft plush case at $24). Only 513 LP Customs were shipped in 1961 (minus the few "old-style" single cuts), while the LP SG Standard sold a whopping 1,662, 1962 saw 298 Customs and 1,449 Standards go out the door. 1963 was almost the same at 264 Customs and 1,445 Standards. LP Juniors were flying with 2,151 shipped in 1961 (minus some thick bodies), 2,395 in 1962, and 2,318 in 1963.

These Les Paul Junior SGs sold in the thousands during the early 1960s. Note the larger "Les Paul" logo on these SG versions. From the collection of Dave Amato, 2003.

22462	LP Custom - Black	11	29	61
22463	LP - Custom - white	9	18	61
22464	LP - Custom - white	9	18	61
22465				
22466	LP - Custom - White	9	18	61

| 7160 | LP - Custom - new | 2 | 27 | 61 |

6744	LP new	3	15	61
6745	LP new	3	14	61
6746	LP new	4	10	61
6747	LP new	3	20	61
6748	LP new	3	23	61
6749	LP new	3	15	61
6750	LP new	3	17	61
6751	LP new	3	14	61
6752	LP new	3	31	61
6753	LP new	3	21	61
6754	LP new	3	20	61
6755	LP new	3	14	61
6756	LP new	3	20	61
6757	LP new	3	14	61
6758	LP new	3	17	61
6759	LP new	4	6	61
6760	LP new	3	17	61
6761	LP new	3	17	61
6762	LP new	4	6	61
6763	LP new	3	22	61
6764	LP new	3	15	61

5610	LP. Spec.	3	10	61
5611	LP Spec	3	1	61
5612	LP Spec	3	3	61
5613	ES-330.TD	4	13	61
5614	LP Spec.	3	16	61
5615	LP Spec.	3	10	61
5616	LP Spec.	3	9	61
5617	LP Spec.	3	9	61
5618	L.P. Spec	3	9	61
5619	LP Spec.	3	9	61
5620	LP Spec.	3	10	61
5621	LP Spec	3	9	61

325	LP TV cream	3	1	61
326	L.P. TV cream	2	28	61
327	LP TV "	3	1	61
328	LP TV "	3	1	61
329	LP TV "	3	1	61
330	LP TV "	3	1	61
331	LP - TV cream	2	28	61
332				
333				
334				
335	LP Jr	3	22	61
336				

(Left) Here's a view into Gibson's logbooks for 1961, showing the widespread numbering sequencing between the three-digit LP TV models of February and March to the 22460 Customs in September and November. Note the "LP new" designation in March for the sculptured Les Paul Standards. Completion dates often vary by weeks and sometimes months for the same initial production model. Dates and models are filled in by the stamped number as the instrument is finished. Occasional color variations like the black Custom show up every few pages. Sincere thanks to Walter Carter and Gibson for this glimpse into the records of the vintage SG models.

ELECTRIC SPANISH GUITARS—Solid Body

Les Paul Custom	GUITAR, Solid Body, Double Cutaway, White Finish, *three built-in humbucking pickups and Gold Gibson Deluxe Vibrola*	450.00
Les Paul Standard	GUITAR, Solid Body, Double Cutaway, Cherry Finish, *two built-in humbucking pickups and Nickel Gibson Deluxe Vibrola*	310.00
0537	Faultless Case (Plush) *for above models*	47.50

*Special Order—Custom Instrument Dept.

Les Paul Jr.	GUITAR, Solid Body, Double Cutaway, Cherry Finish, *one built-in pickup*	**155.00**
116	Durabilt Case *for above models*	15.00
316	Archcraft Case (Plush) *for above models*	24.00
0537	Faultless Case (Plush) *for above models*	47.50

(Above) This price list from 1963 actually listed the Custom, Standard, and Junior models as Les Paul models... and some of the instruments were even still labeled as such. Though Les Paul's contract ran out in 1963, he was unaware that this practice was being continued.

Popular Artists of the SG Models

Link Wray

Hailing from North Carolina, this ³/₄-bred Shawnee Indian guitarist began playing guitar during the late thirties. His early days were spent playing western music with Wild Bill Elliot, Ted Ritter (High Noon), and by the early fifties, Jimmy Dean's band. In 1956 he penned the classic rock instrumental "Rumble," inspired by an audience brawl. It was recorded on St. Patrick's Day 1958, with a mid-1950s Goldtop on a one-track Grundig with his three-piece band, the Wraymen. Although banned on radio, this Cadence 45 sold over four million records. By 1959, his version of "Rawhide" on Epic sold one million records and garage rock was born.

After playing a longhorn Danelectro guitarlin and Supros with rows of knobs during the late fifties, Link adopted the Les Paul Standard (SG) guitar just as it arrived on the scene for his brash and bold style. His previous use of punctured speakers with his Premier amp paved the way for the modern raunch of later years. Using amp tremolo and a wild vibrato, this artist shook up a lot of young guitarist during the fifties and sixties. As the years pass, some consider him the Godfather of Punk.

Barry Melton played his Bigsby-equipped Les Paul Standard with Country Joe & The Fish during the late sixties. This Gibson Gazette shot shows Barry with a large Afro, contemplating his next lick.

California SG Artists

After moving to San Francisco from Mexico, Carlos Santana broke out on the scene in a big way with the new Santana Blues Band and his Gibson SG Special at the Fillmore West and Woodstock Festival. His burning Latin-flavored rock with the P-90 sound through Marshall amplification captivated millions worldwide, setting a star in motion. Many other popular guitarists enjoyed the sculptured-style Gibsons. Among them was Robby Krieger, who played an SG Special with the short vibrato with the Doors. Although Jim Morrison sang "Light My Fire," it was Robby Krieger who penned the song and shared it with the group. His avant-garde soloing during the sixties was quite unique during the Doors' heyday. Guitarist Sam Andrew with Janis Joplin played a decorated Les Paul SG during her heyday with Big Brother and the Holding Company. Other San Francisco guitarists who popularized the Gibson Les Paul SG models during the musically rich and very psychedelic sixties included Barry Melton with Country Joe McDonald and the great guitar duo of John Cipollina and Gary Duncan from Quicksilver Messenger Service. Jerry Garcia was also known to play an SG during the furtive years of the Grateful Dead.

Great pose of the legendary Link Wray performing with his Bigsby-equipped Les Paul SG Standard. *Photo by Chris Walter/Getty Images*

John Cipollina
From an interview at his home in Mill Valley, 1973:

JC: *My first flash of reality, I guess what the big guys used, was one of those Les Pauls. Anyway, I guess the way it started was... around Christmastime, Mickey Baker put out a song. Mickey and Silvia did "Love Is Strange." And I heard this thing, man... (plays riff with his signature vibrato) and I went, "Whoa!" (laughs) I heard that and I said, "Hey Ma, what's that?" And she said, "That's an electric guitar." And that's how I got started. Whew!! So all of a sudden, "Okay Ma, where's an electric guitar? Let me see what they look like! Can I comprehend?"*

I had a mother who was real crazy. She would always take us to see battleships or missions and stuff like that. "Let's all go to the museum." So anyway, we're going around and here's this door saying "no admittance," and I hear this electric guitar. And the guy's sitting there playing it and it sounds good. Sounds better than the guys around the school in teen dances, school bands, and stuff. So I braved it and went inside to hear these two sailors. Each one of them has a cherry-finish Les Paul Junior with a double-cutaway—the real radical one—and matching Fender Champ amps, tweed ones. On both handles of the Champ amps are tags. Off the pegheads of the guitars are tags, man—brand-spanking new! And it looked so bad and sounded so cool. I couldn't imagine making an amp bigger than that. I couldn't imagine anything being cooler or whatever. I was very impressed. That was probably the start of it all. That was before running into Chet Atkins and whatever forms of surreality. That really went, "wahoo" you know, and I remember those tags! I remember the white ones said "Sherman & Clay" on it. So acute, isn't it? (laughs) Anyway...

My mother was going into Sherman & Clay to get some sheet music. Back then in '59, they had a big sheet-music section, so my mother went to the sheet-music floor. I said, "I'll meet you in the musical instrument department, Ma." So I went to the musical instrument department and started to look around. I can remember what was there because I was aghast. There was a sunburst Gibson ES-175 with one pickup with that funny, weird tailpiece. It's stuck in my brain instantly to this day. And there were some acoustic guitars and they didn't register at all. I never associated that Gibson ES-175 with the Les Paul. It had nothing to do with it. I could remember the first guitar I saw was so radical with the double-cutaway. To me it had two horns on it. And it looked really bent. Plus, on top of it all, I saw Link Wray on TV with a longhorn bass and I had completely misconceptualized it. To me it looked like a longhorn, the horns of an antelope.

So I looked around and I didn't see one. All of a sudden I panicked. Here I was at Sherman & Clay... and I'm looking but it's not there. I don't see the racks of rows of double-cutaways. I see a few weird acoustic guitars. I wanted this Gibson. It looked so bad. It was a Les Paul Junior. I think the pickguard had something to do with it, too. It just disappeared.

And he handed me a Musicmaster and he said, "Here, try it out!" And I said, "God, I don't know how to play it. I just want to see it." So he plugged me into something like an old tweed Pro. And like I'm thinking, "Oh God!" About then, my mother came in and said, "Put that thing down. You don't know what you are doing… it might be loaded or something." Anyway, I was saved. So finally he gives me a catalog and that started me off with the "hot" catalog. Then I started going into stores and asking for catalogs.

RL: *When did you start playing?*

JC: *Then I started going through the painful part. Paying the dues. The reality. "Well, you're going to have to learn something." In the store my mother would say something like, "We'll get him lessons." Oh God, this is what I want to do. Freak out! My father got me a guitar so I related to it somewhat. I could put my thumb over part of it and run it around like this. I banged on it enough to break some strings on it. So I just had the three bass strings, you know? That made more sense to me. When I heard it I said, "Wow, I better put a couple more strings on there." I couldn't imagine playing more than four 'cause I only had four fingers. (laughs) What do you need more than four strings for? That just blew me out! (laughs) I really attacked the guitar barbarically. I had no interest until I had heard that lick, until I started picking out all that weird stuff.*

The multi-talented Todd Rundgren with his Les Paul SG Standard performing with Utopia in San Diego, circa 1974.

John Cipollina with his Fender/Standel amp rig and favorite Les Paul SG Standard used for so many albums and live concerts with Quicksilver Messinger Service. Note the horns hooked up to the Showman amp for the treble pickup. *Courtesy Roberto Rabonne*

Intermission

This chapter on the sculptured, double-cutaway models brings to a close the first era of the famed Les Paul guitars and amps. They soon became known as vintage Gibsons by early-seventies collectors.

In 1952, Gibson had unveiled their solid-body guitar to world acclaim, fueled by the artistry of Les Paul. That, in essence, launched over fifty-thousand guitars, destined to be played, collected, and cherished worldwide. By 1964, however, Les was no longer under contract with Gibson and, amazingly, the single cutaway solid-body was discontinued. The sculptured Gibson continued as the SG, and the new Firebird series made its debut. The popular semi-solid series endured, crowned by the revolutionary stereo ES-355.

Our companion book, *The Modern Era of the Les Paul Legacy, 1968-2007*, starts with the late-sixties Custom, Standard, and Deluxe, soon followed by the Low-Z hi-fi instruments. The seventies and eighties produced numerous special-themed models and various store-ordered re-creations of the classic sunburst Standard. All the popular artist models are portrayed. The holy grail '59 Sunburst and other jaw-dropping Custom Shop creations were achieved starting in the nineties; they remain the pinnacle of achievement in the opinion of collectors.

The book wraps up with the non-stop cavalcade of Les Paul's continuing career—with his resurgence on a Grammy Award-winning album with Chet Atkins, setting up a weekly gig in a New York jazz club, and reconnecting with the new Gibson family. His lifetime achievement awards keep piling up, and an all-star guitar party seems to emerge every time he hits another birthday milestone.

Nineteen sixty-three is the intermission to the Les Paul Legacy. More great guitars are yet to come.